ATTENTION

**BEYOND THIS SIGN
YOU MAY ENCOUNTER
NUDE SUNBATHERS**

As an aid to establishing your own informal clothes-optional recreation zones in remote areas with a proper warning to the unwary who might approach, we provide this sign, which you may tear out and have quickprinted, for fastening to trees in the direct line of access to your favorite skinny-dipping and sunning spot.

Much of the continued limited prosecution of nudity is based on evidence that an unsuspecting citizen has been subjected to nudity against his or her wishes. When the sign has been posted and is ignored by a citizen who proceeds and then complains, the legal basis for objection should disappear.

The text of this sign is identical with that used by Oregon's state parks system to forewarn citizens who might be offended should they proceed.

Partners with our environment

Lee Baxandall's WORLD GUIDE To Nude Beaches & Recreation

New For The '90s

N

N Editions / P.O. Box 132 Oshkosh, WI 54902

Thomas Eakins, Students at Swimming Hole, ca. 1883.

SITES COMPILER: RUTH PERCEY
PHOTO & SITES EDITOR: LEE BAXANDALL
DESIGNER: LARRY BILOTTA
PRODUCTION ARTIST: GLORIA DALMAN

Published by N Editions, a division of The Naturists, Inc.,
P.O. Box 132, Oshkosh, Wisconsin 54902

N EDITIONS and colophon are trademarks of The Naturists, Inc.

Library of Congress Catalog Card Number 80-50931
ISBN: 0-934106-16-9

10 9 8 7 6 5 4 3 2 1

First 1991 Edition

Printed by Castle-Pierce Printing Co., Oshkosh, Wisconsin

Preceding: Leif Heilberg, Catalonians Frolicking, Barcelona.

IMPORTANT NOTICE

Much care is taken to verify the information presented here. Reports from readers, however, are necessarily a basic resource, and the editorial team and publisher cannot and will not take responsibility for errors, let alone altered legal status of nude use.

Before you take off all of your clothing in a public place, be certain to check with persons knowledgeable about clothes-optionality in the specific circumstances. To deliberately give offense with your nakedness to those who are unwilling to share it, is indefensible and may lead to a charge of disorderly conduct.

The Guide should not be construed to justify private-property trespass if both owner acquiescence and a public, common-law, right-of-way are absent. We will correct any such inadvertent listing.

To describe and give access information to the world's most desirable, well-established, clothing-optional recreation sites, private and public, is our aim. Note that an established public nude site doesn't always have governmental designation. The most popular, enjoyable, clothes-optional zones often lack official nude status; they thrive on community acceptance and a permissive law enforcement policy. Official designation is only one way nudity as norm is claimed. So again, ask knowledgeable locals before you remove all clothing.

ACKNOWLEDGMENTS

Many people contributed to compilation and illustration of this Guide. It's impossible to thank or even remember all these generous and creative individuals, so let me say quite simply that this is a book from, as well as for those people who have put "creation" into nude recreation. - LB

PHOTOGRAPHY

Front cover, Jerry Derbyshire. Back cover, Leif Heilberg.

Photographers represented in the Guide: M. Alexander, Doug Ball, Lee Baxandall, Michel Bellanger, Vic Blandburg, Terry Blum, Marty Brittan, Eugene Brousseau, Craig Busch, Sheryl Campbell, Michael Cooney, Dave Cowling, Mike Craig, Yang Dan, Dave Davis, Jerry Derbyshire, Thomas Eakins, Giuseppe Feroldi, Charles FInley, Janis Foore, Trevor Frank, Gaby/Impact Visuals, Illiana Gencheva, Fred Gerty, Bud Godsol, Greg Griffith, Leif Heilberg, Les Hotchkin, B. Hymer, Jess Jessen, Tom Kelley, Robert Kelty, Ingrid Kemperman, Rob Coykendall, John Kramer, Bill Larson, J. C. Lavoix, Gerry Leewes, Dana Levi, Jayson Loam, Bern Loibl, Joseph Luczymski, Charles MacFarland, Ron Marsh, Eduardo Masferre, Steve Mattis, Michael Meyer, Jim Moyers, Nick Novick, Mark Orpen, Richard Pasco, Dave Patrick, Tom Phillips, Greg Price, Karl H. Reddies, Gerhard Riebicke, J. Riera Rovira, Peter Simon, Alex Siodmak, Gary Sohler, Dennis Craig Smith, Durand Stieger, Walter Sullivan, Frank Sutcliffe, Tahanga, Chant Thomas, D.W. Thorne, Doug Triggs, Bud Upmal, E. Velez, Herwarth Voigtmann, Mary Wells, John Wull, Richard Zachman.

LISTINGS

These individuals with others have assisted with site listings: Bob Adams, Richard Bangs, Frank Beach, Pru Beck, Peter Bentley, Dave Bitters, Peter Borisow, Geert Bovenhuis, T.V. Capek, Gene Caywood, Michael Cooney, Michael Corbin, Emile de Cuba, Jim Cunningham, Kevin Dart, Jerry Dixon, Karl Dressen, Jack Filak, Charles Finley, Carl Flick, Hans Frillman, Fred Gerty, Herbert Golub, Paul Govekar, Fernando Grieco, Allan Groves, Emile Guay, Judit Halasz, Bill Hamilton, Gary Hanauer, Ole Hanson, Leif Heilberg, Richard Higby, Dennis Higgins, Hot Springs Gazette, Les Hotchkin, Ralph Jacobson, Penny Johnson, Tom Kelley, Francine Nenon Kerenfort, Dennis Kirkpatrick, Bernhard Klein, Ed Lachmann, Jayson Loam, Samantha Manthe, I. Marriott, Alan McCombe, George McCormick, Angelos Mimikopoulos, Ulf Mossberg, Pat O'Brien, Mike O'Toole, Lloyd Olson, Rod Parkes, Rich Pasco, Dave Patrick, Bill Pennington, Charles Perkins, Barry Plaxen, Karl Reddies, Diane Reese, Jos van Resnwoude, Ed Rochford, Jean Rocquemont, Censo Rossi, J. Riera Rovira, Fabrizio Salvati, Brad Schewe, Morley Schloss, Irene Shannon, Dave Smith, Jan Smith, Werner Steinbrecher, Durand Stieger, Ed Stimpson, Peter Street, Sudhir Surti, Ben Symmer, Tahanga (Jefferson Poland), Douglas Triggs, Donald Tumasonis, Michel Vaís, Phil Vallack, Christian Vogt, Doug Wall, Irmtraude Wiesner, Bart Wijnberg, John Wikoff Jr., Judy Williams, Bob Wright.

CONTENTS

NORTH AMERICA

CENTRAL & SOUTH AMERICA

CARIBBEAN

EUROPE

AFRICA & THE MIDDLE EAST

THE FAR EAST & SOUTH PACIFIC

Jerry Derbyshire, Kalalau Falls on NaPali Coast of Kauai, Hawaii.

FOREWORD TO THE 1991 EDITION

This is a renewed book. The 1980-83 editions printed in some 200,000 copies were best-sellers. Clothes-free recreation has gained in approval and participation in a number of countries. You now hold a fully updated, rewritten Guide, expanded by 24 pages to reflect additional locations for the 1990s.

This edition has largely excluded sites that are marginal—either small and eco-fragile, or questionable in terms of a good experience.

We offer more clubs, resorts, contacts, guide and travel agency references with the aim of increasing your opportunities.

Naturists believe that clothes-optional lifestyles can resolve the 'eternal' Puritanism vs. Pornography confrontation. Body acceptance is the rational and healthy but suppressed answer which should be—but is denied the possibility of becoming, in today's North America—the mainstream resolution.

The more the body is censored, the more obsessively fetishizing and degrading pornography we're going to see, and the more puritanical reactions will occur. We reject both the exploitation and the censorship. However, there remain public servants who confuse "nude" with "lewd." We'd like to hear from you about them. We'd like to educate them as to the trends in law and social values.

After the first edition of the Guide appeared, the Free Beaches Documentation Center became part of The Naturist Society, an organization providing both information and advocacy of wholesome nude recreation.

You can take part in this educational venture as well as be updated by the membership magazine, Nude & Natural. Contact The Naturists at P.O. Box 132-W, Oshkosh, WI 54902 USA. Phone (414) 426-5009, fax (414) 231-9977.

Enjoy! And let us hear from you—with corrections, new sites, photographs, or experiences.

DEDICATIONS

To the great photographer Jerry Derbyshire (1948-89). His vision has informed the contemporary Naturist idea.

To Johanna Moore. Her loving support has made this book possible.

To the entire staff of The Naturist Society. For dedication, resourcefulness and good humor.

Michel Bellanger, A masquerade at Le Sapey, Haute-Savoie, France.

Following: Peter Simon, A New England Beach.

INTRODUCTION

RECREATION WITH NO GARMENTS AND WITH NO SHAME in much of the world is not the exotic or controversial choice that it once was. Indeed, one mark of a civilized host city, state or country has emerged as its nude and topfree beaches!

Nude recreation was brought forward irresistibly as popular taste in the last generation. By 1980 it became inconceivable to many that, early in the century, the foolhardy beach-goer who thrust no more than a bare knee or shoulder out of a cumbersome bathing costume was inviting arrest.

Even the Roman Catholic Church came to see nudity in a new light. Through the centuries popes and bishops consigned millions to hell for insufficient bodily fear and shame. Yet John Paul II has stated that the human nakedness that was so central to the Garden of Eden was a "universal" and "luminal" event, aiding the male and female alike to perceive and understand their humanity beyond cultural fashions.

Indeed social nudity permits us to enhance our awareness of the reality, not merely idea, of how much we are alike and, similarly, how vulnerable we are.

Discovering this, we may learn to control our fear of the gaze of another. Arbitrary and alienating barriers of social role and economic class, sex role and gender preference are reduced as we dispense with the trappings of difference, privilege and fear. Individuality can be strengthened without arrogance—our lost integrity recovered and revitalized.

The formerly taboo, now advocated presence of our bodies—of breast and genital vulnerability in a natural context, "Naturism"—contributes to perspective and health. It is foolish to equate natural processes with human welfare as such. Yet nature nourishes, conditions, and finally, restores us, insofar as this can be. When the culture into which we are born strays too far from nature's laws, we suffer; a "naturalization" is in order. The restoration of nature's balances will, conversely, make it possible to more completely "humanize" our culture.

This book is primarily a guide to opportunities for you and your family and friends to locate and enjoy recreation in the nude. And why should you and they not, at least once, try this lifestyle?

You could not imagine the taste of an apple if you hadn't directly tasted one; it is no different with a nude beach.

With the shock of recognition you may come to agree that Body Acceptance is a neglected cultural priority.

TAKING THE PLUNGE

Have you spent all your adult years without once going naked in an outdoor, sociable, recreational setting? Going through life as a clothes-compulsive personality can be hard on a person. Harder than you will ever realize if you do not try the clothes-optional alternative. And trying it is easy. You won't think twice about it once you've broken through the anxiety barrier.

Thinking it through in private is one way to get ready to go public. There's an "etiquette" to clothes-optional beaches as to all public situations. Once you get the hang of how people make themselves comfortable while naked among others, you are "home free."

You'll find it easier if you first visit a nonproblematic and well-established nude recreation site in the company of friends who are versed in the etiquette of the place.

Remember, you will be with men and women who, after growing up in a clothes-compulsive society, also had to "get the hang of it." In many ways they are not unlike yourself, except that they have already broken one of patriarchal society's most fierce, if recent, taboos: Thou shalt not be vulnerable, even among those whom you might be able to trust.

Indeed, the fear of going naked reflects the era of indiscriminate assertiveness and armoring that the English author Thomas Hobbes described as a time of "the war of all against all." Not all times have militated against trust and vulnerability. Surely the era of ruthless careerism, industrialization, exploitation of nature, and national expansion has. Only now are we finding ways to transcend the ethos of personal armoring wedded to aggression. Before Western civilization, nakedness was a normal element of life and considered acceptable in many circumstances.

Freud, in *Civilization and Its Discontents*, describes how psychological repression of the awareness of our natural being was a necessary step in building civilization. Only people motivated by abstractions rather than spontaneous perception and need, could build the cities and staff the factories, serve in the armies, and otherwise discipline themselves into taking part in vast and self-abdicating social projects.

Armoring of the natural individual has devastating effects, many have come to believe, although nothing else might have served to accomplish the purposes of Western civilization. But the post-industrial, newly greening era offers fresh options, a new ethos, a chance to integrate the natural human being with post-industrial values, technology and knowledge.

Sociobiology tries to discover what genetic codings and drives may underlie our social conduct. Sociobiology tries to scrutinize the natural species by penetrating the eons of veils overlaid by civilization and social life. Think about these questions of social adaptation as you experience the clothes-optional life-style. It may help to explain the quiet exhilaration of your new, decidedly vulnerable companions. And show yourself—by the body language that you display—to be a nonhostile, thinking person. Share in the common humanity.

You need not immediately undress if you feel too vulnerable (for vulnerable you may read self-conscious, awkward, embarrassed). That will be understood. In your nervousness, however, do not place needless "armor" between yourself and those you encounter—leave camera, sunglasses, and radio without earphone at home.

At least seem at ease. Practice will make appearance reality. Sit quietly at the edge of activity. Look around. Groom, lay back. Be open to a smile, a word, a shared refreshment. Bring something to share. Don't force the situation. Be receptive. Your open demeanor will best say that you are "getting it," that you are glad to be vulnerable, happy to be free of unneeded defensiveness.

After 20 or 30 minutes, you may find yourself no longer acutely aware of being naked. A single visit may lead you to decide that the "almost"-nude beaches, where bikinis and thongs are paraded, are more sexually titillating than a clothes-optional beach. That is certainly the case! Titillation sells the product. When the withheld is delivered, tensions and fears are erased. What is natural is more fulfilling, though it might not fit the tantalize-and-deliver sensationalism of our jaded consumer culture. A new age is slowly being born.

What about erections? Will you get one on the first visit? Possibly, but just put it in the sand, the towel, or the water until your steamy imagination adjusts to the reality that sex, as you know it, is not the reason these people are unclothed.

Will people aim cameras, come-ons, or comments at you? Possibly. But the repression of a healthy nudity, especially for females, has been one of the chief means of mind and destiny control by the patriarchy. The women who take down their straps and lie on their tummies, then roll over, get up and walk about topfree or fully naked, are shattering the invisible bonds of an inherited sex role. It may feel somewhat heroic to put up with the lascivious attentions of a beach gawker in Bermuda shorts and camera, but it is qualitatively no worse than many street experiences a free woman must endure, and the payoff—outgrowing sexist stereotypes—is of far greater benefit.

You will easily adapt to this new experience. Just ease yourself into a clothes-optional setting without putting up any more defenses than necessary. The scary questions and hovering doubts you first had—Will I be accepted? Will I find friends?—will begin to answer themselves. You'll find that you are putting behind you the obstacles to personal growth, in ways that you could not have imagined before you went clothes-optional.

THE LAW

The "law" is a possibly hostile element of your new environment. But it will not be a problem if you first visit a private beach, resort, or club. And remember that the law as administered at many public recreational areas is on your side.

There isn't any countrywide law to ban nudity on federal land. Please check for possible assimilation of a state or county law to a federal jurisdiction and for special federal regulations. However, in general, National Park Service, Bureau of Land Management, Forest Service, etc. view nude recreation—conducted with discretion and sensitivity to the varying values of others—as "legitimate activity."

In many if not most state, county, and city jurisdictions, the Victorian Age confusion of nude with lascivious is rejected in the courts. Accordingly, law-enforcement personnel generally try to avoid citation or arrest actions that could lead to court tests and waste of taxpayer funds. "Nude is not lewd" is the rule of thumb in these responsible jurisdictions.

None the less, painful and ridiculous incidents still occur. Individuals are misjudged—by elected or appointed government employees—as social deviates for enjoying the victimless "crime" or, more recently, the "misdemeanor," of innocent nudity. Archaic social codes and repressive values die hard.

Since 1975 an administrative trend has appeared to ban nudity as such—much as pets, glass containers, or bare feet may be banished—as a nuisance or nonconforming use, with no further reason required. The effective answer to such "mere nudity" curbs will be to demonstrate the community tolerance and support of naturist values. Certainly, the trend in most of the nation and the world is to decriminalization and de facto recognition of clothes-optional zones.

An enlightened culture—one providing for individual and minority liberties—lets the clad and the unclad equally share in private and public resources. No good comes from forcing a clothing-compulsive

dress code upon all so long as a dwindling majority possibly clings to it.That is not democracy. It is domestic tyranny.

Provision not only for the diversity of recreational choice but also for the security, access, convenience and site maintenance is the right of every citizen.

The law is not an inherent adversary. In fact the contrary is the case. Increasingly, law-enforcement personnel and recreation managers are overcoming their timidity before the small minority of zealots who still consider social nudity evil. They should actively promote the principle of diversity of dress codes in recreation—very much as social resources are extended to accommodate both sexes, all races, the handicapped, and the well, where tax-obtained funds are involved.

THE SUN

Long vanished is a time when you could claim a health belief as "a sunbather" for a good excuse to go naked. Excessive, irregular sunning is not the best thing for healthy skin. Not only can it possibly lead to skin cancer. It can prematurely dry, wrinkle, and age the skin. Still, the desire to enjoy the out-of-doors is natural. You must balance the desire for the sunshine with an informed understanding of what is good for your skin.

Don't confuse lying in the sun with nude recreation. The health hazard is in excessive exposure to the sun between the hours of 10 and 2. Nude recreation doesn't require much or even any sun exposure. Haven't you enjoyed running naked in the warm spring rain? Haven't you enjoyed late afternoon sports on a clothing-optional beach under stormy skies? And haven't you skinny-dipped by the moonlight? Take nude recreation and not necessarily the sun. Start out early or late. Go out in the midday sun but in moderation. And then, be active, turn your body this way and that as you run, play ball, throw a Frisbee, leap the waves. And when you are not active or at midday, put an umbrella, a tree, a tent, a sunscreen between you and the sun. A sunscreen that you squeeze from a tube can be as good as a shirt or robe, and it won't interfere with your freedom to move and be totally one with your environment.

May you enjoy your fullest freedom of body and spirit without injury!

NATURISM

"Naturism is a way of life in harmony with nature characterized by the practice of communal nudity, with the intention of encouraging self-respect, respect for others and for the environment."

– *International Naturist Federation, 1974*

Dave Patrick, More Mesa at Santa Barbara.

POINTERS FOR GRACIOUS NUDE BEACH RECREATION

- ☞ **Stay Out of the Dunes** and other environmentally sensitive areas.
- ☞ **Obey Parking Regulations** and other posted rules.
- ☞ **Help With Litter**—bring along a trash bag. Carry out more litter than you create.
- ☞ **Don't Go Out of Established Nude Areas.** To wander nude into a clothed beach or parking area will offend many.
- ☞ **No Overt Sexual Activity.** Leave exhibitionism to those attending clothed beaches.
- ☞ **Respect the Property of Others.**
- ☞ **Ask Prior Consent For Photography.**
- ☞ **Privacy Is Fundamental.** Many are at club or beach for quiet time. Body language should tell you they don't want to be disturbed. It's not wrong to look for new friends—but it is rude to intrude when you're unwelcome.
- ☞ **Come Prepared.** Bring beach supplies: beverage, food, sunscreen, towel. Mooching is not a cool way to make friends.
- ☞ **Speak Up for Standards.** Don't let some newcomer who doesn't understand the situation or our values cause trouble. Instead of doing a slow burn, go talk, politely but firmly, to the couple starting sexual activity, the can-tosser, the wanderer into the dunes.

Following: Jerry Derbyshire, The Grand Canyon.

NORTH AMERICA

UNITED STATES

NUDE RECREATION in North America is not in need of an apology or a sanction. It is at the source of our national innocence and childhood—as skinny-dipping. The frontier saw plenty of it.

Rural Americans today from Vermont to Arizona, from Georgia to Oregon, quietly believe in skinny-dipping as one of the great natural experiences of growing up. It is our equivalent of the Greek civilization's passion for Olympic games in the nude as a means of character building in a natural state of being.

Of course, our heritage absorbed the puritan lineage as well. The puritan shuns the naked and potentially sexual flesh as perhaps the chief cause of evildoing. When a child grows up in America, the stalwart heart that has been nourished naked at the quarry or the pond has to put aside innocence and assume the fig leaf of body fear. For this reason, only the boldest of American mainstream writers and artists—one thinks of Thoreau, Whitman, Eakins—dare espouse the beauty and necessity of the naked body in social intercourse.

Around 1900 the puritan heritage finally found opponents angry and convinced enough of the importance of overcoming body fear to make an issue of it. "Bohemians" first began to undermine the previous century's armored patriarchal despotism. Free spirits like Floyd Dell, John Reed, Eugene O'Neill, and Max Eastman talked of naked joy in New York City's Greenwich Village in the winters and lived it summers in the country.

Setting aside nudity from conviction among a few religious sects, the first secular community in North America to treat nude recreation as a social right may have been Home, Joe's Bay, Puget Sound, Washington, founded in 1896 by George H. Allen. A University of Toronto graduate, Allen, with his friends, wrote in an article "The Nudes and the Prudes": "Home is a community of free spirits who came out into the woods to escape the priest-ridden atmosphere of the conventional society. One of the liberties enjoyed by Homeites was the privilege to bathe in evening dress or with only the clothes nature gave them, just as they pleased."

By 1915, several farms of New England were quietly practicing nudity and other wholesome ways as a matter of natural principle. And the 1920s saw a widening rebellion against genteel society. Among other signs, the size of bathing suits began to diminish, a token that the psychological onslaught of a burgeoning managerial class on the sexuality and sensibilities of its industrial subjects and consumers would not go unchallenged. As quickly as the vitality of human nature resurfaced, however, it came to be hitched to new social controls, masked by the era of advertising as gratifications. The cult of the sleek Fischer auto body was promoted, while the beauty of the human form lacked organized champions.

Labor Day Weekend 1929 marked what is now regarded as the founding event for organizationally supported clothes freedom in North America. Drawing on experience in his native Germany, Kurt Barthel, an immigrant with an import-export business to Latin America, took his wife and two other couples to Bear Mountain not far out of New York City for the public-land camping that launched private-landed free body culture. Shortly after, permanent grounds were secured.

The first successes incited a prudish hostility. Vigilantes attacked some nudist enclaves, but sheriffs' deputies could be just as lawless. The "nudists"—as they were stereotyped, until they accepted the superficial but blunt term themselves—were forced to retrench, and created ghettos of free flesh within the armoring of high fences and eminently respectable "nudist colony" rules.

Decades passed before nudists marshaled legal forces and editorial talents to make new advances in a liberalizing America. Even then, the tactically necessary retreat into privately-operated enclaves was confusedly regarded as an unalloyed good. Nudist park proprietary interests tended to subsume the objectives of a free body culture or Naturism as a whole.

Still, the vision had been set out vividly by a manifesto published in *The Nudist* magazine of November 1933:

THE MAGNA CARTA OF NUDISM

Three Things we demand. Under proper safeguards and for the public weal we demand:

1. The elimination from our statute books of all legislation that makes social nudism per se an illegal thing.

2. The setting aside of at least some part of our public beaches, parks, picnic grounds, and recreation centers where nudists may freely live the natural life in the open.

3. The constitutional right of a free press to print text and unaltered pictures which decently and naturally represent nudism as it actually is being lived and practiced.

Today these demands represent the rightful desire of a minority; tomorrow they may represent the priceless heritage of the majority.

• Nudist publications of the 1950s, notably *Sunshine and Health*, at last won on behalf of all Americans the battle against airbrushing of genitals and pubic hair—only to see commercial exploitation magazines like *Playboy* put them out of business.

Point Two of the "Magna Carta," basing the future on increased access to public lands, was long downgraded in priority. Then in 1958, an omen. A California cohort of Stan Sohler (Jayson Loam), Ed Lange and Sol Stern rented an ocean beach for a weekend of nude play and photography. The gesture recalled the early days and spirit.

The youth culture of the 1960s turned the omen into a pattern. Obscenity law was under siege in the courts. Few shibboleths went unchallenged. Nude-ins began to occur in California. A new breed of proprietor, south of San Francisco, began to lease ocean beach and allow visitors to dress or undress as they chose. By 1967, San Gregorio was described by *Time* as the country's first nude beach. The clothes-optional use of public shorelines was underway. Something similar happened on Cape Cod and Martha's Vineyard, at Vermont quarries and Lake Michigan dunes, Georgia's rivers and the waters of Florida.

A German-born, Los Angeles nude beach user, Eugene Callen, saw progress. First bikinis, then clothes-optionality: it fulfilled the free body culture ideals of his youth. Then police began crushing the new beach culture, at times brutally—Callen watched one such "bust" at Pirate's Cove and, shocked, launched the first organization of nude beachgoers, Beachfront USA, in 1972. It evolved a state-recognized board of directors, legal challenges, the "Beachhead" monthly. Callen died in early 1978.

Los Angeles—city and county—responded to Beachfront USA's public-lands initiative by legislating tandem bans on mere nudity. These circumvented the need to prove lewd conduct or intention to a jury. Thus was the realization of Point One of the Magna Carta of Nudism delayed. This precedent was copycatted.

The only good news was that an abundance of innocuous nude recreationists on public lands was noted by the California Department of Recreation and Parks, which decided to cease warning or citing nude bathers on state lands except on citizen complaint. This major revision of public policy was recently reaffirmed.

Important to notice, the accessing of the "public sphere" for nude recreation came about with little broad organization or fanfare—largely achieved by the uncontrolled voting of millions of the young and literally with their bodies.

Official resistance on the federal, state, county and local levels slackened as the novelty proved harmless and—to tell the truth—a great way to experience one's own and external nature. The apple-pie nature of skinny-dipping was recalled. Many young rangers themselves attended the nude beaches. From 1975 a network of free beaches existed. Landed-club nudists were observing; and some were trying the nude beaches.

In 1980—organizationally a fruitful year—The Naturist Society was established. The national free beaches movement was working out dissonances and defining itself even as it lost incandescence. Release of this *World Guide* resulted in 200,000 copies purchased between 1980 and 1987, nude recreation's first best-seller.

A new president of the American Sunbathing Association, James Hadley, led a delegation to The Naturist Society first gathering, held at Ed Lange's personal-growth-oriented Elysium at Los Angeles. The Hadley leadership marked an opening away from the proprieties-oriented restriction of nudists from drinking, touching, etc., as well as towards seeking legal nude use of appropriate public lands.

During the 1980s, the paradigm of landed nudism has altered. No longer is it a smallish club, recruiting families from a hundred-mile radius, with weekend camping, volunteer workers and member-driven, family priorities. These exist in the dozens, especially in the northern tier of states. However, the trend and considerable financial success has shifted to entrepreneur-driven, clothes-optional resorts. They amortize costs from more or less year-round income as vacation destinations. A Trade Association for Nude Recreation (TANR) was formed in 1987 to enhance marketing.

The fading paradigm is the small trailer park where mom and dad relax and play volleyball and the kids skinny-dip with a safe pack of little friends. The trend is to exciting, even glitzy getaways from the kids serviced by a restaurant, poolside bar and night life. In this Guide you will find both the down-home club-in-a-woods with its above-ground pool or dammed-up stream, and the sophisticated and international nudist resort. Clothed society sets most expectations that people want to experience.

"I'll Rub Your Back." Top: Jayson Loam, Strawberry Hot Springs. Bottom: Dave Davis, Glen Eden.

During the 1980s, free beaches changed too. Thinly organized to begin with, most didn't hold their leadership, as short-term crisis and euphoria yielded to long-term hard work of organizing, lobbying and fund-raising. Those that continued, coalesced around leading personalities. Interaction of nudists and naturists, club goers and beach goers, grew.

Sadly, neither club and resort nudism nor public-beach nudity has burgeoned as expected. The 1980s became a period of cautious opportunism exploited by those known disrespectfully as "the suits," after a generation of cultural experiment. Yuppies, who may have enjoyed a nude beach when in college, but who avoided nudist or naturist ways, now colonized California hilltops overlooking the Pacific Coast—where they complained of nude beaches below their windows as "attractive nuisances," requiring elimination.

Moreover, body-distanced church fundamentalists took up positions of authority in politics and administration which grew increasingly aggressive during the 1980s. They didn't hesitate to act against nude beaches, even in defiance of community acceptance surveys, such as a 1983 Gallup Poll (commissioned by The Naturist Society), which found that 3 in every 20 Americans said they'd tried co-ed nude recreation—and nearly three-quarters said that nude recreation is acceptable in appropriate places recognized for nude use.

Nearly three-quarters approval should gain official acceptance; but not if a conspiracy of the righteous think otherwise. So Naturists became active against church-seated intolerance. Florida was—and still is—the classic instance where a high official, without a public review or recognition of his decision, orchestrated the closing of most nude beaches in 1983.

During the 1980s, the American Sunbathing Association set ambitious public relations and membership growth goals and moved with modern business methods to realize them. The Naturist Society explored emerging avenues of free body culture in a publication—*Clothed With the Sun* (1981-88), redesigned as *N (Nude & Natural*, 1989-) which, alongside the *World Guide*, drew mainstream and international respect and affiliation.

1990 saw The Naturist Action Committee emerge to share, with the publishing arm, The Naturists, Inc., the public-lands objectives and work of The Naturist Society. The maturing of durable free beach groups, and the loss of others, gave rise to this strengthening and democratization of the Naturist movement.

While the 1980s did not see the steady advance that was hoped, our free beaches were not permanently set back. Indeed, in many respects there was growth in the body acceptance movement and in the nude recreation sector.

And of course worldwide, a free body culture is on the ascendant.

ADDITIONAL INFORMATION

Many nudist resorts, parks and clubs are described by the illustrated *North American Guide to Nude Recreation*, published by the American Sunbathing Society, 1703-WG N. Main St., Kissimmee, FL 34744-9988. Phone (407) 933-2064.

Updates on the sites in this *World Guide*, with current addresses and phones of Naturist Network-affiliated clubs, groups, SIGs and businesses, appear in *N (Nude & Natural)*, published by The Naturist Society. A sample issue is $8.00. P.O. Box 132-WG, Oshkosh, WI 54902. Phone (414) 426-5009.

ALABAMA

GULF COAST

BON SECOUR NATIONAL WILDLIFE REFUGE

A fine refuge in a protected environment, Bon Secour is little visited or patrolled. Nudity is legal on most remote federal lands where it does not offend others. The compacted sand makes hiking easy as you put a mile between your party and possible beach prudes.

☞ Route 59 to Gulf Shores. Right on Highway 180 West (Fort Morgan Road) for 8.7 miles to past the 12-mile marker, and left on unmarked dirt road. (Turn is at real estate billboard, "Dune Lakes East Boundary," with a power substation on your right after you turn in.) Parking is very limited so arrive early. Walk down the beach to the east for perhaps a mile.

SANDSTONE LODGE

Seven miles from Mobile with 10 wooded acres, 5 tent and 3 RV sites, rental trailer, showers, use of kitchen, pool, volleyball, table tennis and exercise equipment. Phone (205) 645-0536.

CENTRAL

GYMNO-VITA PARK

A clothing-optional, rustic recreation park owned and managed on-site by the former director of the Birmingham Zoo. Fish-filled creek, lake swimming, some sports facilities, children are free. Campfire programs and nature walks available any time. Couples and families only. April 1 to Oct. 31. P.O. Box 121, Vandiver, AL 35176. Phone (205) 672-7105.

☞ From Birmingham, US 280 east to Shelby County Road 43. Left, 12 miles to Vandiver and 3.7 more miles on 43 to County Road 55; continue ahead on 55 for 1.3 miles and turn left following club signs.

Mike Craig, Chamber of Commerce, North Pole, Alaska.

ALASKA

NUDE RECREATION, in appropriate locations on federal land, is a "legitimate activity" according to the National Park Service—unless it is thrust upon citizens unwilling to view nudity. In that case it is punishable as disorderly conduct. U.S. Secretary of the Interior Manuel Lujan in 1991 termed nude beaches "no problem."

Moreover, the United States government owns 96 percent of Alaska, which makes the largest state potentially one huge zone for nude recreation. Temperatures are commonly in the 70s and sometimes 80s from late May into early August in much of Alaska south of the Brooks Range and away from the ocean. The possibilities are restrained, however, by more than the brevity of summer. Alaska is a wilderness, with terrain and wildlife that can overwhelm the reckless adventurer. The National Park Service here does not pamper the visitor as it does in some other park areas.

Alaska offers fine experiences, both clothed and unclad, and these tips, offered by natives, will lead you to tested sites. You will surely go nude in other places, as you hike or boat or simply bask, and no one who might object is about. It's only natural in this great outdoors state. In private saunas and the rare hot tub, too, hosts seldom expect their guests to wear anything.

ALEUTIAN ISLANDS

UNALASKA ISLAND

Remote Unalaska Island has a beautiful and popular skinny-dipping lake nestled in a hidden valley. Drive to the top of "General's Hill" and park. Hike 1/4 mile to the first lake and another 1/8 mile to the second lake. Warm in July and August, with a fine sandy bottom.

SOUTHWEST

ALASKA PENINSULA

Katmai National Park is one of the most geologically active areas in North America and on a cold and windy day the steam vents of Novarupta Volcano can be rather pleasant. Volcanoes and associated steam vents and hot springs occur up and down the Alaska Peninsula and the Aleutians.

STORMY LAKE

Stormy Lake's 50 campsites in the Captain Cook State Recreation Area are little used. Many sandy beaches for stripping down near the camping area, or canude to the far beaches.

☞ From Anchorage, Route 1 south to Kenai and take the spur road north for 26 miles to the Recreation Area and Stormy Lake.

NANCY LAKE RECREATION AREA

A state tract of about 35 square miles with some 24 small lakes, campgrounds, hiking and a canoe trail which traverses 16 lakes with 11 campgrounds; no motors allowed. Be prepared to portage. Fair fishing. Canude during the week and you may have the trail all to yourselves.

☞ North on Route 1 from Anchorage to Parks Highway (#3). Past the town of Houston, at mile 67 on the left is the Nancy Lake Parkway. The canoe trailhead is clearly posted about 4.5 miles into the Recreation Area.

CENTRAL

FAIRBANKS WATERWAYS

Several rivers offer one- to several-day canoe trips around Fairbanks. The Chena, Tanana, and Chatanika are relatively easy, accessible at both ends by road, and have nice gravel bars and often sunny banks. In the Alaska Range the Tangle Lakes are a network of such waterways off the Denali Highway, about 150 miles south of Fairbanks.

ALCAN HIGHWAY

LIARD RIVER HOT SPRINGS

Actually the Liard River hot springs are in Canada, at the B.C.-Yukon boundary, well-marked on maps. Nobody would look it up except while floorboarding towards Alaska! Enjoy!

Jerry Derbyshire, Thunder River Cave, Grand Canyon, Arizona.

Bud Upmal, On Top Of Sable Mountain, Denali National Park, Alaska.

ARIZONA

TUCSON AREA

TANQUE VERDE FALLS

Near Redington Pass between the Catalina and Rincon mountains, Tanque Verde Falls is the popular and rugged skinny-dipping spot for Tucson. Great solitude among granite boulders and giant saguaro, barrel and fishhook cacti. Nudity begins around the Falls and continues beyond. Regulars hike in the nude for miles above the Falls, but take note—in 1981 eight people died when swept over the Falls during a flash flood under sunny skies. The rainstorm was hidden behind mountains; it's crucial to hear weather reports for entire watershed. Some rocky shade. Often bone dry; running river and falls, July-August; some pools, April-November.

☞ From I-10 in Tucson, go east on Speedway. Turn north at Wilmot, which becomes Tanque Verde, which becomes Redington Road. When pavement ends, follow rough gravel road for 2 miles. Park on left side of road, and trek down the Upper Tanque Verde Forest Trail on your right about 20 minutes to the stream. Clamber upstream to the Falls, about a mile away.

SABINO CANYON

Sabino Canyon Recreation Area has been posted clothed. Our directions take you beyond, into the Coronado National Forest where folks still skinny-dip.

☞ Access is by foot, bicycle or the Forest Service tram which runs at least every hour, 9 a.m. to 4 p.m, from the Visitors Center at Sabino Canyon entrance. Weekends it runs every half hour. Check for time of the last tram out. Take tram to Stop 9, the end of the road, hike down the quite good trail to the canyon floor, then upstream (north). Five to ten minutes should take you far enough to avoid offending anybody.

JARDIN DEL SOL

A family-oriented nudist park in the Sonora desert 35 miles northwest of Tucson. Pool, hot spa, tennis and volleyball, community kitchen, cacti garden, desert trees. Tent and trailer sites. P.O. Box 581, Marana, AZ 85238.

PHOENIX AREA

SHANGRI LA FAMILY NUDIST RESORT

Phoenix's only landed nudist park offers tent and RV sites and some motel rental, heated pool, sauna, whirlpool, tennis, shuffleboard, horseshoes, volleyball, nude hiking in surrounding hills and nearby clothed horseriding. HC2 Box 4343, New River Road, Phoenix, AZ 85027-9355. Phone (602) 465-9416.

BUCKHORN MINERAL WELLS

Just east of Mesa on Route 60 is this older 12-room spa hotel. Each room has a tub equipped with whirlpool pump. Great view of red rocks. Massage, lodging and meals available. P.O. Box 3270, Mesa, AZ 85205. Phone (602) 832-1111.

HOMELODGING

B&B offers pool, spa, meals, bedrooms w/TV/VCR, exercise equipment and laundry. Nearby sports. If in Phoenix on business, Homelodging has a fax, copier, PC and printer. P.O. Box 40246, Mesa, AZ 85274. Phone (602) 831-5758.

CANYON STATE NATURISTS

Numerous outings on public lands and to clothing-optional hot springs. Mail SASE to P.O. Box 33431, Phoenix, AZ 85067.

ARIZONA WILDFLOWERS

Arizona's oldest ASA family-oriented club hosts member pool parties, potluck suppers, some campouts. Mail SASE to P.O. Box 26465, Phoenix, AZ 85068.

CENTRAL

VERDE HOT SPRINGS

Clothing-optional is traditional at this Verde River site where the Tonto and Coconino National Forests meet. The hot springs in this high desert canyon are all that remain of a former resort, one of many built in Arizona in the '20s and '30s. Regulars have made many improvements to the camping area and the bathhouse—including the excavation of caves—which render wintertime soaking the more enjoyable. The heavily-mineralized water is rated at 104°F and additional hot springs along the river provide a usually mellow, rarely crowded setting.

☞ Follow I-17 about 100 miles north of Phoenix to the Camp Verde turnoff. Forest Service station here can advise on road and river conditions. Last source of supplies. Follow turnoff east 3 or 4 miles to Camp Verde and a fork. Turn right on the road to Payson. About 6 or 7 miles down this road is a small sign and dirt turnoff to Childs. Turn right (it is Fossil Creek Road, also marked as Coconino Forest Road #708) and follow it about 17 miles to a fork, and turn right toward Childs, another 5 miles. This road dead-ends before Childs. Take gravel road on left down to Verde River where you'll find a primitive USFS camping area. Park or camp here and hike one mile-plus upstream, crossing river to the old bathhouse. You will know you are close when you see "get nude" signs painted on the rocks.

NORTHERN

LAKE POWELL

Jim and Yvonne Coffman offer nude houseboat outings on Lake Powell. See Lake Powell listing under Utah.

Leif Heilberg, Shangri La Resort.

ARKANSAS

NORTHWEST

FAYETTEVILLE

Nude recreation in this Ozark frontier developed a special complexion from the late 1960s as University of Arkansas-Fayetteville students started coed skinny-dipping. It spread to the Buffalo National River and Ozark National Forest. Couples and groups could be seen nude in remote places along the Mulberry, White, Buffalo, Savoy, Spavinaw, and Illinois Rivers. There are literally hundreds, if not thousands, of remote swimming holes in the Ozarks that one may enjoy nude. Here are a few. For a list, send an envelope and donation to Arkansas Naturists, P.O. Box 821, Fayetteville, AR 72702.

WHITE RIVER (Greenland)

Fayetteville's favorite spot, primarily because it is close to the university yet isolated from traffic. The rocks are rugged and can get really hot in the summer sun, so it's wise to bring a thick blanket to lie on or bring an air mattress float.

☞ From downtown Fayetteville, US 71 south past the airport and the small town of Greenland. After crossing the White River (West Fork) Bridge, go 1/4 mile to the first road to the left. Make a sharp left back toward the river, following the paved then gravel road 1 mile, bearing to the left at all times. Past the red barns and white house on the left, follow the road downhill a few feet to the tree-shaded area and park. Be sure not to block the wire-strand gate—offending cars have been towed. Walk through that gate to the river, cross it (it's shallow here), and follow the trail upstream 1/4 mile to the swimming and sunning area.

TEN MILE ROCK

Named for being exactly 10 miles from Fayetteville. Though right off US 71, authorities do not bother anyone; in fact, one correspondent has reported two deputy sheriffs skinny-dipping off duty. Some disapproving families do show up; do not offend them. On opposite side of highway and 1/4 mile north is a sheer cliff where university students do free-handed climbing, with a superb view at the top.

☞ Follow US 71 south of West Fork for 2 miles until you see a large rock on the right between the highway and the river. Park near the rock turning right, walk to the north side of it and down the short trail to the river. A small but popular area.

BLUE HOLE

South of Prairie Grove, a beautiful, restored piece of America where "The Blue and the Gray" was filmed. 'Free people' settled in this area in the 1960s and often skinny-dipped, a tradition they and local farmers carry on today; but avoid offending the families that may appear on weekends. Sun on the great boulder; dive from it, or the bluff, into the deep-hued waters, and drink freely—the water comes from springs in the mountain. Good camping is available on site.

☞ US 62 southwest from Fayetteville to historic Prairie Grove. From the four-way stop signal at the center, drive south on paved County Road 28, forking right on Route 21 about 2.5 miles out, until you've gone 9.3 miles to the end of the pavement. Keeping left, take the gravel road for 5.5 miles, across the little bridge and passing a waterfall and spring. Notice Flyaway Game Farm; it's 1 mile before Blue Hole. After the 5.5 miles of gravel turn left onto a narrow dirt road through the woods (if you reach a wooden bridge on the gravel road, you've gone too far). 300 yards in is Blue Hole. Park off road, take out all trash.

HOGSCALD HOLLOW

Also called "Big Clifty" for the high limestone cliffs around the lake, the general area was named after the natural pools in rocks where farmers many years ago built fires and scalded their hogs at slaughter. Skinny-dipping is now downstream from the "Hollow," on a cove of Beaver Lake. "Big Clifty" is the waterfall

Nick Novick, A Swim After the Sweat Lodge, Rainbow Gathering, 1986.

that marks the start of skinny-dipping above the cove. Weekends, locals in speedboats come over to jeer and gawk, so skinny-dippers now come out only on weekdays. Spectacular scenery, although a German neo-baron built an ill-fitting manor overlooking one of the finest waterfalls.

☞ From Eureka Springs drive Route 23 south a few miles to sign for "Hidden Cove Campground." Turn right onto paved road (Route 127), go 3 miles west to the end of pavement, then follow gravel road. You'll spot a huge bluff above Beaver Lake; follow the road down to the boat ramp. Park. Take trail leading back eastward. Weekday skinny-dipping on rocks along here.

TISDALE FORD

Skinny-dipping with a sandy bottom and a bluff for diving. Take Route 45 east from Fayetteville to Goshen; then turn south on Turtle Road for 3 miles, passing the Barrow Farm, to bottom of the hill. An almost impassible sandy road to the right leads to Richland Creek. Park, off the paved road, if you lack a 4WD, and walk in! Follow road to creek and bear downstream (right) to the baring area; it's not far. Don't bare if a disapproving local family is there first.

BIG HOLE

Big Hole has been a skinny-dipper's delight at least since 'free people' from far corners of America came to the Ozarks in the late 1960s to settle on farms and communes. These same folks started the Electric Moo Festival; clothes-optional was the music festival's dress code. Big Hole remains their favored swimming hole. A waterfall spills into the pool. It's hard to reach—4WD is advisable. Those who come usually camp for a weekend. Do check the water depth before diving, and take your trash out. Ozark National Forest posts against nudity; use discretion.

☞ It's 48 miles from Fayetteville on State Route 16, southeast through Brashears, St. Paul and Pettigrew. A mile beyond the community of Boston, look for the first gravel road to the right. You'll see a microwave tower ahead as you turn before reaching it. This rough road leads down the mountain after 3 or 4 miles to Big Hole.

Jerry Derbyshire, In the Flow.

DEVIL'S DEN STATE PARK

Lee Creek is a terrific secluded swimming hole surrounded by boulders for sunning and diving.

☞ Take Route 71 south from Fayetteville and at West Fork go west and then south onto Route 170 to Devil's Den State Park. Pass the saddle camp, following a gravel road (Route 220) 6 miles to Lee Creek, near where the road again becomes paved. Find the swimming area secluded from traffic, and enjoy.

SPAVINAW CREEK

Spavinaw Creek has tall shade trees, bracingly cold spring water, bluffs, fish-filled, crystal-clear water. People skinny-dip downstream from the parking area, then lay out on the bluff above. It's the norm, but be cautious.

☞ Take Route 68 west from Fayetteville to Siloam Springs, then Route 43 for 7.6 miles north to Route 12. Continue on Route 43 another 5.9 miles past the community of Cherokee City and two Spavinaw Creek bridges. Continue a half mile after the second bridge to the cut in the hill; turn right on the narrow gravel road, follow it 0.9 miles, bearing right, to the creek; park under the tall trees and follow the trail downstream. The "No Trespassing" sign is a ruse. The farmer attempted to exclude the public but lost in court—the creek is public property.

OZARK NATIONAL FOREST

The Russellville region of this large national forest affords numerous opportunities for good nude fun. Rock faces of limestone and granite create wonderful waterfalls, while artesian springs and creeks are common. Some sites of particular interest are Devil's Canyon, Richland Creek, and Mulberry Creek. Long Pool Recreation Area, with a wealth of caves, woods, creeks, and coves, offers a day-long joyous adventure; local couples enjoy converging on Long Pool or the creek above it around dusk for a culminating skinny-dip. Forest Supervisor J. R. Crouch in 1981 told a USFS survey: "We do not attempt to control nudity outside of developed recreation sites. There are no reports of other forest visitors being offended by the activity."

☞ To Long Pool: From Russellville drive 12.5 miles north on Route 7, and follow Long Pool signs for 10 miles. Skinny-dippers camp at the right (east) and work their way down the hill to the water. People in costumes get to enjoy swimming the rapids at west end. Write to the Ozark National Forest, Russellville, AR 72801 for maps covering all sites.

Dave Patrick, Black's Beach Celebration, 1977.

THANK·YOU
SAN DIEG
FOR ED
TOTAL TAN
IS
WE LOVE
MOTHER
NATURE
FREEDOM

CALIFORNIA

California—the Nude Beach Mecca! So it seemed in the '60s and '70s as the American youth culture was establishing its highly attractive but vulnerable freedom zones. Unsurprisingly, greed culture recaptured hegemony by the '80s as even the conviviality of the hot tub, influential in all the world, shriveled.

Free beachers struggled to retain the major coastal enclaves, such as Black's Beach in San Diego County, and remote clothes-optional zones such as Deep Creek Hot Springs in San Bernardino County.

On pristine headlands above nude beaches including San Gregorio, Pirate's Cove at San Luis Obispo, Santa Barbara's Summerland Beach, Yuppies placed lavish homes then complained of nude persons on public beaches within the sightlines they'd purchased.

Some nude beaches—including More Mesa in Santa Barbara—were saved only by defeating development plans on environmental or water supply grounds.

The Chad Merrill Smith decision of the California Supreme Court (1972) both recognized and altered social attitudes, declaring that public nudity not intended to be lascivious was not, in fact, a sex crime. Los Angeles ecclesiastical authorities then organized the faithful and called in city and county political debts to establish a new national pattern of "mere nudity" (as distinguished from lewdness or indecency) ordinances. A few intolerant, 'religiously' inspired recreation officials went along and sought to ban or cite for nudity, but federal law lent them no vehicle.

Charles Finley, Protesting Los Angeles Beach Nudity Ban, Malibu, 1976.

Lack of self-confidence and excessive greed conspired to produce a dispiriting loss of public space for individuality. Obviously, nude bodies didn't go away—but disappeared under designer threads and to the ends of intimidating trails.

A Mexican worker influx has accumulated to almost a quarter of the California population—more in southern counties. Catholicism deeply troubles a Mexican man who buys a six-pack and goes with buddies to a coastal cliff to sip some cold ones and gawk at the non-Mexican women brazenly getting all-over tans below.

Understandably the body anxiety and denial which gives rise as well to a pornographic exploitation of the repressed may inhibit shy women from visiting California nude beaches.

For a secure experience in conservative times, California has nudist parks and resorts—but not many. There's a threshold of acceptance and financing that is still to be crossed for clothes-optional enterprises to become a major economic fact.

For additional information, check these established in-state resources: David Patrick, *California's Nude Beaches* (Bold Type, Berkeley, current edition), and the annual *San Francisco Bay Guardian* nude beaches update by Gary Hanauer (usually late June).

Southern California

SAN DIEGO COUNTY

BLACK'S BEACH

Secluded below a 300-foot cliff, north of University of California–San Diego at La Jolla, the shifting legal status and demographics of Black's Beach and its off-again-on-again turmoil with the city, the county and state parks reflect the advances and setbacks of nude recreation in all California. Nude use was condoned by San Diego City Council in 1974. Attendance happily shot up, with small children brought and altogether a good people mix. Declared illegal after intense ecclesiastical pressure and a bitterly fought, narrowly lost city-wide referendum in 1977, Black's Beach became mostly avoided except by bolder regulars and visitors, those adults who—unlike most Americans—will 'act outside the law' when a controversial freedom is at stake. A lively beach culture continues and, as before, breezes soothe, surf rolls, hang gliders soar. You will be rewarded by almost daily horseshoes, volleyball, frisbee, sandcastling, kiteflying and bodypainting. Contact: Black's Beach Bares, P.O. Box 12255, La Jolla, CA 92019.

Include in your visit to Black's Beach a side trip to Scripps Aquarium located between downtown La Jolla and the turnoff to Black's Beach from the Torrey Pines Road at the Sauk Institute. Adjacent to Black's parking is the Torrey Pines Glider Strip where updrafts sustain hang gliders and remote control model planes.

☞ Driving from San Diego, exit I-5 on Genessee Avenue West. Go up the hill to the first light where Genessee becomes North Torrey Pines Road and curves left. Drive 1/2 mile to the entrance to the Salk Institute on your right, turn right onto Torrey Pines Scenic Drive. This will take you to the clifftop gliderport launch and lot. To the left (south) of the gliderport is a steep set of stairs, built over five years by selfless volunteer Steve Simms, leading down to the beach.

Alternative: continue on North Torrey Pines Road past the gliderport turnoff, and at the next light turn right onto La Jolla Shores Road and immediately right again onto La Jolla Farms Road. Go 1/2 mile and you'll see Blackgold Road on the right. A paved trail can be identified by a large black gate with a U.C.S.D. sign inside. You may be lucky and park on the street nearby—observe posted regulations or be towed.

Another approach but a very long walk: Park at Torrey Pines State Beach and head south.

SWALLOWS SUN ISLAND

Many residents, room rentals, campsites, restaurant, tennis, volleyball, pool, spa, rec hall. San Diego's nudist park. 1631 Harbison Canyon Road, El Cajon, CA 92021. Phone (619) 445-3754.

CAMPING BARES OF SAN DIEGO

Camping Bares enjoy house parties nude and operas clothed, but most of all, they hyperactively hike and camp au naturel where others do not go. SASE to P.O. Box 81589, San Diego, CA 92138.

IMPERIAL COUNTY

OH, MY GOD! HOT WELL

These hot pools in the desert draw a variety of individualists. No facilities, but overnight parking is permitted.

☞ From Salton City, take the Salton Seaway (S22) west for 2.8 miles. Turn left on a graded dirt road and continue for less than a mile. This road passes a few yards from the pools and you should see parked vehicles.

PALM OASIS HOT SPRINGS

Surrounded by a wood platform, head-high bushes and bullrushes and two palm trees, Palm Oasis is neat, clean, and more convenient than Oh My God! Hot Well for San Diegans. Water is 90°F, plenty of camping room, nude is the norm.

☞ From Brawley, take Route 78 east for 15 miles until you cross the Highline Canal, marking the end of farmland. Take second dirt road to the right, follow it 3/4 mile until you cross under the powerline. Stop here and look straight ahead to spot the only two palm trees (oasis) in view. That's it.

RIVERSIDE COUNTY

LE PETIT CHATEAU

Le Petit Chateau, a charming B&B on a south end side street only a 10 minute walk from Tahquitz Canyon. Ten rooms with king beds, most with brick patios and kitchen. Brunch, afternoon wine are included. Tree-bordered pool, jacuzzi. Appeals both to seasoned naturists and first-timers. 1491 Via Soledad, Palm Springs, CA 92262. Phone (619) 325-2686.

RAFFLES PALM SPRING HOTEL

Nine of 11 air-conditioned rooms on the patio have kitchenettes; all with fridges. Heated pool with mountain view, spa, exercise bike, shady nooks, Australian breakfasts, afternoon snacks. 280 Mel Avenue, Palm Springs, CA 92262. Phone (619) 320-3949.

TREEHOUSE TOO

Treehouse Too has 29 large rooms with TV, phone, fridge, plus heated pool, jacuzzi, sunning lawn, flowers, palms, playground, with breakfast, snacks and beverages during social hour. Rates competitive with other hotels in Palm Springs. 1466 N. Palm Canyon Drive, Palm Springs, CA 92262. Phone (619) 322-9431 or 327-9880.

GLEN EDEN SUN CLUB

The largest family nudist resort of the West, Glen Eden Sun Club schedules many sports and social events. Volleyball, tennis, indoor and outdoor pools, sauna, tent and trailer sites. 25999 Glen Eden Road, Corona, CA 91719. Phone (714) 277-4650.

ORANGE COUNTY

SAN ONOFRE STATE BEACH

To the north you will see twin globes—"Les Boobs"—of the San Onofre nuclear energy plant. On a clear day to the south you may view the headland of Torrey Pines State Beach just beyond which lies Black's Beach. San Onofre's own sandstone cliffs are more sculptured (if not as high or dangerous) as those of Black's Beach, and the broad beach is a delight. San Onofre has lifeguards, toilets, trash cans, lizards, swallows and squirrels. In the past, north district San Diego sheriff's deputies issued citations and Camp Pendleton M.P.s evicted sunbathers. No current problems.

☞ At the meeting of Orange and San Diego counties on I-5, turn off on Basilone Road and take the crossover to the nuclear plant; continue south to the

Following: Marty Brittan, Santa Cruz, North Coast.

park entrance ($6/car), and on to park at trailhead No. 6. Take trail to the beach. From the beach walk south toward Camp Pendleton fence.

SAN JUAN CAPISTRANO HOT SPRINGS

Hot springs feed into 25 redwood tubs beneath sycamore, live oak and alders. Campground, swimming pool, picnic area. 35501 Ortega Highway, P.O. Box 58, San Juan Capistrano, CA 92693. Phone (714) 728-0400.

☞ About 13 miles east of the Mission. Take Ortega Highway (Route 74) from Route 5 in the direction of Elsinore, and turn left on Hot Springs Canyon Road.

CAMP McCONVILLE

The oldest nudist park in California (1934) and set above the smog, McConville is a 'ghost ranch' that sprawls up a wooded gulley and hillside within Cleveland National Forest. Cabins, tent and RV sites. Volleyball, large unheated pool, hot tub, tennis, horseshoes, hiking, children's play area. Look for McConville on the first road to the right after turning onto Los Pinos Road. P.O. Box 477, Lake Elsinore, CA 92330. Phone (714) 678-2333.

While in the area, explore the back-country of the Cleveland National Forest. Skinny-scouters have staked out the Caspers Wilderness, Los Pinos Recreation Area and the San Juan Upper and Lower Campgrounds (especially the southernmost pools) as likely naturist spots.

LOS ANGELES COUNTY

SACRED BEACH

Known as Pirates, Smugglers, Abalone or Sacred Cove, it offers the sole tolerated nude beach of Los Angeles County—a status secured when Rancho Palos Verdes, whose residents are core users, prudently leased the cove and its control from the county in 1982. It is a very large bay of shale more than sand, quite comfortable and secluded.

☞ RTD bus route 255 from Los Angeles (except Sunday) and see below. Or drive Palos Verdes Drive South, westerly from Long Beach by auto or bus, to where residential Peppertree Drive intersects it on the Portuguese Bend (there's a bus stop there). Walk 100 yards west from the Peppertree Drive bus stop to the large tree on the bayside of the road, where you'll find a hole under a cyclone fence and a path that scrambles down to the beach.

If you drive you can park 1 mile west of the path at the new Abalone Cove beach lot, and then walk back either along the road or (in good sneakers) along the shore to the cove, over sand and rocks. Portuguese Bend is just below the hill on which Wayfarer's Chapel and its parking lot occupy the hillside.

ELYSIUM FIELDS

Breath of innocence, gleam of sunlight in a smoggy county. Elysium Fields offers personal growth opportunities (open to nonmembers) through its Journal of the Senses. Sun lawn, jacuzzi, pool, sauna, tennis and volleyball courts, picnic areas, community kitchen. Families and children welcome; guest passes for nonmembers available at a nominal charge. 814 Robinson Road, Topanga, CA 90290. Phone (213) 455-1000.

SAN BERNARDINO COUNTY

DEEP CREEK HOT SPRINGS

These marvelous springs can only be enjoyed properly in the nude—and that is how US Forest Service rangers supervise it, asking only that you take your litter out and do not camp at the springs. Many hike au naturel. The chilly creek flows past a selection of large and small, naturally hot pools. People are evicted in time to make the climb out before nightfall. If you do want to camp, you may do so at the nearby Bowen Ranch but you'll have to bring everything, since the ranch supplies nothing—not even water.

☞ Go north on I-15 through Cajon Pass into the Mojave Desert. About 6 miles beyond the Pass, take the Hesperia/Phelan exit. Turn right at the off-ramp stop sign onto Main Street and go 7.4 miles through Hesperia. Turn left onto Rock Springs Road; this turn occurs just after the road bears to the right past a Silverwood Lake sign with a small wooden water tank on the left. Go 2.5 miles to a T-intersection; turn left onto Kiowa. Go 0.5 miles and turn right onto Roundup Way. There is a Mariana Rancho sign here. Follow Roundup Way to the end of the paved section and go exactly 1.4 miles on the dirt section of Roundup Way and turn right onto Bowen Ranch (no road sign here). Go 5.8 miles on Bowen Ranch Road, bearing right at the only major intersection, to the ranch house where there is a chain across the road. Honk your horn, even if late at night, to get someone to come to the door. Pay the $2 fee and continue another 0.3 miles to a large flat area for camping. Hike 0.5 miles to the end of the road, go down the trail between the large rock pile and the Joshua tree and bear left through the fence, where there is a large iron sign which says Area Closed To Vehicles. Continue about 50 yards and bear right into the first canyon. Follow the Forest Service Trail about 1.5 miles (800 foot elevation drop) to the creek. The last part is a steep hill with a surface of decomposed granite—good track shoes are recommended. You can take an easier but longer trail by turning sharp right at the top of the steep hill. Both ways will take you to the bottom of the hill. Ford the creek to the hot springs.

OLIVE DELL RANCH

A small well-equipped nudist park with rentals, restaurant, guest passes, an hour's drive from Los Angeles. Route 1, Box 393, Colton, CA 92324. Phone (714) 825-6619.

SILVER VALLEY SUN CLUB

In the smog-free Mojave Desert on the way to Las Vegas, an oasis with small lake, islets and boats, cottonwoods shading tent/RV sites, shuffleboard, volleyball, clubhouse-restaurant noted for hospitality. Information and list of area attractions: 48382 Silver Valley Road, Newberry Springs, CA 92365. Phone: (618) 257-4239.

☞ About 2 1/2 hours from Los Angeles; from Barstow take I-40 east for 18 miles. Turn off at the first exit for Newberry Springs and drive parallel to I-40 for 1.8 miles then turn left (north) on Newberry Road crossing I-40. Continue for 2.9 miles, until you reach Silver Valley Road; turn right, drive 3.3 miles.

About 2 1/2 hours coming from Las Vegas, take the Harvard Road Exit from I-15 about 20 miles before reaching Barstow. Turn right onto Newberry Road for about 8 miles. Turn left onto Silver Valley Road.

TREEHOUSE FUN RANCH

Noted for PR events—Mr. and Ms. Nude, skydiving, chili cook-offs. Lobbied for and won first 'nudist liquor license,' service permitted to nude patrons (still no nude dancers at same time however!). Treehouse has many residents, large pool, spa, tennis, volleyball, rec hall. 17809 Glen Helen Road, Devore, CA 92407. Phone (714) 887-7056.

SANTA BARBARA COUNTY

BIG & LITTLE CALIENTE SPRINGS

Caliente Hot Springs receive a lot of use, both nude and clothed. There is a specific rule against nudity here, so caution is a necessity.

☞ Take the Gibraltar Road, which climbs 7 miles up the Santa Ynez mountain range behind Santa Barbara. It mounts steeply to the crest, where one gains almost breathtaking views of Santa Barbara and the Channel Islands. At the crest, turn right on Camino Cielo. The asphalt road turns to dirt after 7 miles and at Romero Saddle it becomes narrow, winding and rough. At Juncal Campground, the road doubles back to the left just past the concrete creek ford and goes 3 miles to the Pendola Ranger Station.

To reach Big Caliente, take the right fork from Pendola. The road goes another 3 miles to end at the spring. Nude use is not recommended here.

To reach Little Caliente, continue straight ahead on the road at Pendola Station for 5 miles to Mono Campground. There is no longer a locked gate on the road just past the campground, so drive the last mile to the spring, taking the right fork. Follow the road to a point where it starts to climb and makes a horseshoe bend back to the left to cross a low ridge. Take the trail from the parking area marked by wood-retained steps to the right of the spring. Smaller and colder than Big Caliente, Little Caliente is more isolated and freer of hassles. Not accessible during fire or rainy seasons, so check with Los Padres National Forest Ranger Station before setting out.

MORE MESA

Many Santa Barbarans swear by More Mesa's white sand, sheltered location, and broad prospects. Sheriff's plainclothes deputies did "riot" against beachgoers one infamous day in 1978, but this has long been a very mellow spot where troubles are forgotten. Sheriff's office now says it would issue citations "on complaint" only. Complainers are nonexistent; horseback riders, surfers, volleyball zealots, Frisbee hurlers, elderly and infants share the beach.

On the mesa top the sandy soil supports one of the few remaining natural ecologies in greater Santa Barbara. That, plus the view, inspired environmentalists to preserve the large tract.

☞ From Route 101, exit on Turnpike Road to the south, then left on Hollister, going 2 blocks and turning right on Puente Drive. Follow Puente about 3/4 mile (road turns into Vieja Drive) and park near the entrance to Mockingbird Lane. Mockingbird Lane is an access road that is no longer open to vehicles of any kind, so walk to the end and take the established descent at the terminus of the ruts in a stand of eucalyptus trees. Any other route is dangerous. Considering the parking problem, the best solution is to take the Hollister/State Street bus. It stops at the end of Puente Road—a 20 minute walk from the beach.

CEMETERY BEACH

Known also as Butterfly or Graveyard Beach. Very convenient for free beachers who are employed or live in downtown

Dave Patrick, Bonny Doon Beach.

Lee Baxandall, Deep Creek Hot Springs.

Santa Barbara. Sheltered beneath the bluff, it's a very pleasant spot, especially during the week. Restrooms, showers and refreshments are available at the Cabrillo Recreation Center.

☞ Take Route 101 to the Harbor Exit. Go to the ocean, then left on Ocean Drive about a mile to the numerous volleyball courts on East Beach. Park and walk along the ocean side of the high hill on which the cemetery perches. Or circle the hill on Ocean Drive, and as the road turns to the ocean side look for Butterfly Court on your left and park nearby. The Biltmore Hotel is ahead, but walk back again beneath the high hill.

RINCON BEACH

Rincon is Santa Barbara's southernmost nude beach. Amenities: paved parking, restrooms, picnic area, paved footpath to beach. Marine life in tidal pools and seals frolic offshore. Around the point to the east (where you must be clothed) find radical surfers. Popular for nudity but raided too often by sheriff deputies to be used without checking the current status.

☞ Access is from Highway 101 at the Ventura County line, 15 miles west of Ventura and 10 miles east of Santa Barbara. Look for the Bates Road exit 12 miles past Ventura. Take the exit and turn left, going under the bridge and toward the ocean. Signs for the beach will appear on your right, as will the beach gate. Enter the gate and go up a rise to the day-use lot. Take either the staircase at the end of the lot or the ramp near the picnic area down to the nude zone—north of the drainage pipe and near the volleyball nets.

GAVIOTA BEACH

Actually a stretch of lonely beaches north of Santa Barbara. Park along highway; frequently, access is at mile 341. Auto break-ins have increased so lock what you don't take with you.

SHARK'S COVE

The foot of Eucalyptus Lane (the south end of San Ysidro Road) gives onto Miramare Beach, which is often rocky and always private. Keep hiking east and you will finally reach Shark's Cove, an extremely narrow stretch of sand below the railroad tracks that attracts nude bathers.

GUADALUPE: NIPOMO DUNES

Little known are the fabulous 19-mile coastal Guadalupe Dunes—preserved by many miles of federal land including Vandenberg Air Force Base at the northern line of Santa Barbara County. It's not a simple trip in. You won't find much of a social nude beach; rather, an environment for free spirited gamboling in the sun and waves and dozing in the dunes, an unsurpassed encounter with nature.

☞ From Route 101 in Santa Maria, take Route 166 west to the town of Guadalupe, then further west on Oso Flaco Lake Road to a parking area 40 minutes walking distance from the ocean; 4WD vehicles can and do proceed onto the trackless sands. Ocean at the northern end.

You may also go south on old Route 1 at Guadalupe town, for 4 miles, where it turns west for 2 miles, into horse-pasture Carralillo Canyon. Stay with the road as it becomes dirt, nearly doubles back at the far side of the canyon, then loops left and sharply up a 2-to-3 mile incline, becoming paved again, to drop about 3 steep miles to a gravel parking lot just above Point Sal Beach. A small cove across the rocks at the north end of the fine sand beach is usually nude; try to arrive at approaching low tide. Avoid this route in poor weather and watch for riptides.

SUMMERLAND BEACH

Summerland's clothes-optional area is just east of Lookout Park. Easy descent to the beach makes this a popular spot with kiddies and oldsters alike. Lots of bodysurfing, volleyball, and swimming, and many users have come for a decade. It is wise to check out current conditions before disrobing.

☞ Go 6 miles east of Santa Barbara on Route 101. The Summerland exit from the southbound lane takes you onto a frontage road. Follow it (Wallace Avenue) south, parallel to 101, until just before it merges back onto Route 101, where you instead take a right onto Finney Street and park. Descend the embankment and walk south to the nude area. Or for an alternate access, you may take the Padero Lane exit from 101, 1 mile south of Summerland exit, and go right. Park alongside the road just past the curve. Look for the path north along the railroad tracks, which will lead you back under the overpass; 50 yards beyond is your path to the beach in the middle of the nude area.

SAN LUIS OBISPO COUNTY

PIRATE'S COVE

A beautiful, no-hassle beach. The county supervisors decided years ago they had more relevant things to do than bother nudies. Indeed, the county provided an officer to assure the peace and order of the recreation site, setting the precedent for other California jurisdictions. Pelicans dive and seals frolic.

While in the area, visit nearby Sycamore Hot Springs in Avila where you can choose from clothing-optional secluded redwood hot tubs on grounds or private hot tub on balcony of each motel room. Swimming pool, massage. 1215 Avila Beach Drive, San Luis Obispo, CA 93401; phone (805) 595-7302.

☞ Take the Avila Beach exit from Route 101. Drive west 2 miles on Avila Road. On your left as you approach Avila Beach you'll see a bluff, and on your right a golf course. Beyond these are 10 huge oil-storage cylinders atop a hill. Take the first blacktop spur cutting off to the left; it's marked "Not a Through Road—No Overnight Camping." Follow this blacktop up and over the top of the sea ridge, to the left of the oil tanks, about 1/4 mile to the parking area. After a rather steep descent, you'll be on the beach.

MONTANA DE ORO STATE PARK

The shore offers a series of reefs jutting out, many semiprivate coves and tidal pools. Above the long, narrow canyon are green pines; on the rolling terrain, buttery-yellow flowers ("mountain of gold"). Camping, natural history museum, abalone collecting, horse rental, acres of eucalyptus trees crowned with butterflies from October to April.

☞ From Route 101 turn off on Los Osos Valley Road just north of the Nuclear Information Center west of the highway. Follow it to Los Osos. Turn onto Pecho Road for 5 miles to the park entrance. At Montana de Oro beach on Morrow Bay, walk 1 mile south to Hazard Canyon Beach, your goal.

HEARST STATE PARK

Hearst State Park at San Simeon has a parking lot (fee charged) from which you can walk to "the cove," a strip of beach beyond a row of state park pilings that serve as boundary markers. Nude sunbathing in the cove has annoyed Hearst Corp. managers but it's public land to the high tide mark.

KERN COUNTY

DELONEGHA HOT SPRING

On Kern River between Bakersfield and Lake Isabella, Delonegha is a popular nude soak. Recently three new pools were built and there is a small 2-person pool on the downstream side of the cliff.

☞ Take Route 178 (old highway) up the river from Bakersfield. After miles of a winding two-lane highway, it crosses the Kern River and becomes a

Gary Schiller, How Deep Is Deep Creek?

Tom Kelley, Los Angeles Police At Venice Beach August 31, 1986. Dave and Suzy Davis Thrown Down To End A Peaceful Nudity Celebration.

four-lane highway. The springs are located between mile markers 32 and 32.5. Pull off at the first curve after the start of the four-lane section, and park. The springs are down the river a hundred yards below the road.

REMINGTON HOT SPRINGS

Two miles from a Forest Service campground; two small volunteer-built cement tubs; water temperature 104°F; the site is kept extremely clean. If spring is closed by high water, visit Delonegha Hot Springs.

☞ From the town of Lake Isabella, drive west on old Highway 178, through Bodfish and to Miracle Hot Springs. Continue west 1 1/2 miles to a large turnout with a telephone pole in the middle. A trail leads to the springs. The descent is steep so wear appropriate footgear.

MONTEREY COUNTY

GARRAPATA BEACH

Now entering the State Park system, this half mile of beautiful beach with many caves and coves for wind protection is treasured by the locals. Equally warm in winter and summer. High cliffs with a variety of wild flowers give privacy; excellent sunbathing—but swim with caution. Unimproved and unhassled, The Friends of Garrapata Beach hope to keep it that way.

☞ The Garrapata River runs beneath Garrapata Bridge into the south end of Garrapata Beach. It is the 6th bridge on Highway 1, going from Rio Road in Carmel (i.e, about 9 miles south from Rio Road). Driving north from Big Sur it's the second bridge on Highway 1 in Carmel after the Rocky Point Restaurant, about 1/2 mile beyond it. A landmark stone house is sited on the cliff near the bridge, where you park and descend the 20' cliff on dirt steps to the riverside. From there it's an easy walk to the beach. Nudity occurs on the north and south ends of the beach; the middle area is clothed.

PFEIFFER BEACH

The wild and rugged Big Sur coast offers many opportunities for solitary clothes-optional activities. Pfeiffer Beach provides, quite simply, a social occasion with a fine breeze and a view of offshore rock formations and huge floating kelp.

☞ Go 12 miles north of Esalen Institute on Highway 1. Pfeiffer Beach is in Los Padres National Forest. When you pass the Shell and Arco gas stations, begin measuring a mile. Just over the Pfeiffer Canyon bridge, turn off toward the ocean on poorly-marked Sycamore Canyon Road—itself a delight for its 3-mile length. At the end of the road is the state beach parking lot; park and take the path to the beach. Walk north along the sand about 1/4 mile to the nude haven, well out of the view of the casual beach tourists.

ARROYO SECO CANYON

Arroyo Seco Canyon in Los Padres National Forest has a lovely uncrowded river for sunbathing, if you'll hike a mile or so from the US Forest Service campground. Find it between Soledad and Greenfield, west of US 101 on Arroyo Seco Road.

SAND DOLLAR BEACH

Sand Dollar is a lovely beach in the Los Padres National Forest. Protected from the wind, it is often much warmer than Pfeiffer.

☞ Follow Highway 1 for 10 miles south of Lucia. Look for the signs for Sand Dollar State Picnic Area, park, and walk north along the beach until you reach the clothes-optional section.

Central California

EIGHT MILE BEACH

Clean white sand with a small lagoon at the end of the beach.

☞ From the southernmost stoplight in Carmel (Carmel Valley Road, with a shopping center), it's precisely 8 miles south on Highway 1, between Rio Road in Carmel and Hurricane Point on Highway 1. Cars parked by the road are a giveaway. Park at the south end, walk down the slope, and then walk back north about one-half mile.

ANDREW MOLERA STATE PARK

Rangers haven't been tolerant of people who strip naked on the first beach reached. Go south, crossing the footbridge over the lagoon, and continue south, and chances are you'll find one of many secluded coves to enjoy au naturel. Offshore barking seals are a big attraction; water is cold, bring windbreaker.

☞ Located off Highway 1, north from the town of Big Sur, at the south end of Old Coast Road. Do not go nude along the Little Sur River.

ESALEN INSTITUTE

Esalen Institute is a world-renowned center offering workshops in a wide variety of human potential development areas. The clothing-optional, naturally hot sulphurous baths are open to non-registered guests by reservation only, from 1 a.m. to 3:30 a.m. only, Monday through Friday. Reservations may be made only on the morning before your intended visit by calling (408) 667-3047 between 9 a.m. and 10 a.m. only. A maximum of 30 reservations will be taken. The hours may seem outlandish but interface appropriately with the purpose of the Institute and lend themselves to wonderous meditation on nights when the moon plays on the kelp beds offshore, while candles illuminate the soaking souls within the tubs.

☞ By itself on the coastal slope of Route 1, 45 miles south of Monterey, 50 miles north of Hearst Castle. Ask for a catalog, you may want to go for a two or five day program.

TASSAJARA MOUNTAIN CENTER

A Zen monastic center in the Los Padres National Forest at 5,000 feet. Established 1967 by the Japanese priest Shunryu Suzukiroshi, the center accepts some day, overnight, weekend, or week-long visitors—but not without a prior reservation. The bathhouse, across a wooden bridge on the creek, has a Buddha alter and statue at the entry. The sulphurous hot springs, 110°F, feed a plunge bath, and a mossy rock contemplation area downstream. One side of the bathhouse and creek is for women only, the other is coed. Nudity is the norm on both sides. Beautiful redwood cabins, Japanese-style guest houses and lodge suites are available. The atmosphere is one of peace and relaxation; guests are invited to join in the Zen activities. The drive is difficult and should not be attempted after dark. Carmel Valley, CA 93924. Phone (408) 659-2229.

VENTANA INN

Japanese hot spa, nude sunbathing, ocean-view rooms, restaurant. Known for its tranquil environment. Big Sur near Esalen. Phone (408) 667-2331.

SANTA CRUZ COUNTY

BONNY DOON BEACH

A showplace of California naturism. The community spirit of the regular users added to the natural beauty should put Bonny Doon on any itinerary. Bonny Doon can be windy. The cliffs offer protection—but note, unstable rock makes it dangerous to stand or lie directly below the cliffs! There are caves on the north side and hang gliders sometimes launch from the south.

☞ Highway 1 to the intersection with Bonny Doon Road, 11 miles north of Santa Cruz or 2 miles south of Davenport. Park in the lot on the west side of Highway 1 and walk up behind the highway 27.6 mile-marker sign, over the railroad tracks, and down the steep trail to the beach.

FOUR MILE BEACH

A young crowd gathers here to surf, sun, and party—unfortunately leaving trash as a sort of trophy of their festivities. Now part of Wilder Ranch Estates State Park; portable toilets have been added and rangers have, on occasion, admonished nude users on the south end of the beach.

☞ Starting from Santa Cruz, Four Mile Beach is 4 miles north of the junction of Mission Boulevard with Highway 1. It is at the Baldwin Creek crossing of Highway 1. Park on the unpaved turnout, walk 1/4 mile down the dirt road to cross the railroad and wind to the left of a marsh and standing water to the beach.

PANTHER BEACH

Panther has a truly spectacular setting—high rock tower, natural bridges and caves. Not a well-known nude beach, on a good day no more than 100 visitors.

☞ The beach is 10.6 miles north of Santa Cruz on Highway 1 between mile-markers 95 and 96. Park on the small dirt road on the west side off the highway and climb down to the beach from the north end of the lot.

RED, WHITE, AND BLUE BEACH

A benevolent proprietary utopia run by Ralph Edward for many years, this fine beach has the amenities of a state park plus clothes-optional everywhere. What more could you ask? Edward keeps out the gawkers, forbids photography, and encourages sociability and trust. The 600 yards of deep, sandy beach are bounded by beautiful cliffs—and those on the south can be passed at low tide, opening up yet another mile of unspoiled beach. Though Edward claims to be only in it for the money, don't you believe him; he's one of the pioneers of new life-styles. There is a nominal entrance fee and overnight camping is allowed. Day-use hours are from 10 a.m. till 10 p.m. Phone (408) 423-6332 for weather information.

☞ Access is by Highway 1, 7 miles north of Santa Cruz or 4 miles south of Davenport. Look for a large red, white, and blue mailbox with the number 5021 on the west side of the road. Turn onto Scaroni Road, a crescent—the first entrance, 100 feet past mile-marker 24.67, coming from Santa Cruz; the second, larger entrance, 30 feet before marker 25, go in through the gate.

2222 BEACH

A 100 foot cliff is all that segregates this tranquil clothing-optional cove from the very expensive homes of West Cliff Drive. Named for the facing house number, 2222 Beach establishes a model of viability for urban nude beaches with its durable acceptance in a residential neighborhood.

☞ In Santa Cruz turn off Highway 1 on Swift Street to the Pacific, then right (north) on West Cliff Drive for five blocks. 2222 Beach is between Auburn and Chico avenues—do not park on West Cliff Drive, look for the lot on the sea side of the Drive near the beach.

Central California

SHARK'S TOOTH BEACH

Named after a massive rock formation 50 yards from shore, Shark's Tooth is a deep sandy beach in a cove with cliffs to the north.

☞ Access from a pulloff (blocked by a long barred gate) a half mile south of Davenport. Or you can walk south along the railroad bed a half mile from Davenport Beach or north a half mile from Bonny Doon Beach.

LAGUNA BEACH (SANDHILL BLUFF)

Laguna Beach is next south from Bonny Doon at a horseshoe-like curve of coastal Highway 1. It is a long beach in a cove, so wind can be avoided. Shells and Indian scraper relics can be found.

☞ From its dirt parking beside Highway 1 less than a mile north of Red, White, and Blue Beach, cross railroad tracks and a field before slowly descending a crumbly path to the shore.

SUNSET STATE BEACH

Sunset State Beach west of Watsonville has a growing nude contingent. Heavy surf, dunes, firepits, restrooms, showers, 90 campsites. Famous for Pismo clams, September to April.

☞ About 17 miles south of Santa Cruz via Mar Monte exit, then the San Andreas Road directly to the 7-mile beach, just north of Zmudowski Beach.

KIVA RETREAT HOUSE

Hot tubs community and individual, cold plunge, showers, sauna, social room, sunning lawns, library/reading room with fireplace, at this entirely clothes-optional retreat located near downtown Santa Cruz. $8 per day; massage extra. 702 Water Street, Santa Cruz, CA 95060. Phone (408) 429-1142.

HEARTWOOD SPA

Friendly establishment with clothes-optional in community hot tub garden area; massage, other bodywork available. Noon to 11 p.m. daily. 3150-A Mission Drive, Santa Cruz, CA 95065. Phone (408) 462-2192.

HENRY COWELL REDWOODS STATE PARK

Nearly a mile of secluded creek in a lushly wooded steep canyon; several small swimming holes, some with sand beaches. Main problem is summer fog, which usually but not always burns off by noon.

Cowell Park has a campground which fills rapidly in summer so reserve ahead. For reservations or trail map, write Henry Cowell Redwood State Park, P.O. Box 53, Felton, CA 95018; phone (408) 335-4598.

You could finish a memorable day by riding through the big trees on the authentic, 1890s steam-driven, Roaring Camp & Big Trees Narrow Gauge Railroad—phone (408) 335-4484—with a stop at Cowell Park headquarters on Graham Hill Road.

☞ From San Jose, Highway 17 south to Scotts Valley, take the Mt.

Leif Heilberg, Hot Spa At Glen Eden: The Western Naturist Gathering, 1982.

Hermon Road turnoff, continue to Felton. Take Highway 9 south past the main entrance of Cowell Park, 1.3 miles to roadside parking at the park maintenance road gate (Ox Road Trail). Walk 1/4 mile east to the railroad tracks, turn right, and follow the railroad. The best swimming holes are 1/4 mile down the tracks; take the path just before the tunnel down to the river, then upstream a bit. Other, steeper paths to the river are south along the tracks. Or check the big stationary map at the parking area for Garden of Eden and Big Rock Hole.

Lee Baxandall, 2222 Beach in Santa Cruz.

SANTA CLARA COUNTY

LUPIN NATURIST CLUB

Two pools and hot spas, tennis, volleyball, massage, children's playground, hiking and camping on 110 wooded acres in the scenic Santa Cruz Mountains. Open year-round in sunny, temperate climate. Near San Francisco Bay Area tourist attractions and nude beaches. Restaurant, clubhouse and lodging are being rebuilt following the '89 earthquake. Call for directions, current information and activities schedule. P.O. Box 1274, Los Gatos, CA 95030. Phone (408) 353-2250.

ALAMEDA COUNTY

SEQUOIANS

More than 40 years tradition, Sequoians has 80 acres and over 150 members. Volleyball, pool, hot tub, tent and trailer sites. P.O. Box 2095, Castro Valley, CA 94546. Phone (415) 582-0194.

SAN MATEO COUNTY

SAN GREGORIO NUDE BEACH

The historic "first" among recognized nude beaches in America. The 120 leased acres include caves, cliffs and 2 miles of beach with a relaxing atmosphere. Attendance is 800 maximum on a weekend. Jogging, volleyball, driftwood shelters in the sand, nature walk to lagoon behind the beach. No camping, fires, food or water but there are now chemical toilets near the parking area. Fee is $2 per person with a $3/car minimum. Fog is a big problem here.

☞ From San Francisco, go south on Highway 1. Pass Half Moon Bay and after about 11 miles, look for the intersection of highways 1 and 84. Just opposite and 100 yards north of this intersection, turn in and go through the large white gate bearing the sign "Toll Road"; pay the fee and park. A trail from the lot leads to the beach, which closes at about 7 p.m. daily.

POMPONIA STATE BEACH

Clean, quiet, sandy beach extends for over a mile. State officials indicate there will be no problems unless complaints are made. Nude area is at south end of beach. Restrooms located at main beach.

☞ Go 4 miles south of San Gregorio Nude Beach on Highway 1. Enter the park and turn south. Park in the lot past the circular parking lot and do not leave valuables in your car. Walk to the circular lot, take the trail down to the beach, the southern end is the nude area. Note: The last part of the trail is steep and narrow so wear appropriate shoes.

GRAY WHALE COVE

Previously named Edun (nude spelled backwards) Cove, privately-leased Gray Whale Cove features 300 yards of clean beach with restroom facilities, a hot dog stand and soda machine. The water is cold for swimming and the undertow is strong but one can join in a game of frisbee, volleyball or paddleball and there is plenty to do for those who like to explore tidal pools and the nearby rocks. Admission is $5; beach closes at 7 p.m. and is not open on rainy days. For road and weather conditions, phone (415) 728-5336. No fires, camping, cameras or binoculars allowed.

☞ Highway 1, 5 miles south of the San Francisco suburb of Pacifica, and 1 mile north of the town of Montara. Look for Devil's Slide—a cliff that drops dramatically to the sea—then spot the sign "Beach Parking" on the left. There is a huge asphalt parking lot; cars parked along the road are often towed. Transportation to the beach is provided for the handicapped, pregnant or elderly; all others must take the stairs that lead down to the beach.

SAN FRANCISCO COUNTY

GOLDEN GATE: BAKER BEACH

Seaward from the Golden Gate lies Baker Beach, with its secluded sands offering the view on the back cover of this *Guide*. One way to get there is starting at the southwest corner of the Presidio, by way of Fort Point (off Lincoln Boulevard), west onto Bowley Street; on to Gibson Road and at Gibson's west end, walk north. Take a path down to the beach and walk further north to Baker Beach. Golden Gate National Recreation Area ably manages Baker for clad and unclad.

Staying in San Francisco? It needn't be prohibitive—try the American Youth Hostel at 3 miles from Golden Gate and 5 minutes from Fisherman's Wharf. Families, singles of any age welcome. AYH Hostel, Building 240, Fort Mason, San Francisco, CA 94123. Phone (415) 771-7277.

ANGEL ISLAND

This island in San Francisco Bay is a popular day-off treat—hike/bike trails, unafraid wildlife, secluded beaches where the day's Bay fog comes late. State Park ferries run, inquire for current times. A 45 minute walk from the dock is clothes-optional Perries Beach.

AFLOAT

One of the best bets for good weather and safe sunning in the Bay Area is to join the fleet that regularly turns up in the sunnier delta area at the northeast end of Frisco Bay.

Dave Patrick, Nude Wave, Marin County.

LAKE TAHOE

EMERALD BAY

If much of Lake Tahoe's California side is private, naturists have hunkered on the southwest shore between Emerald Bay and Bliss State Park, and south from Eagle Point at the south side of the Emerald Bay inlet. Access involves some walking. Obtain a map of the Tahoe Basin from the U.S. Forest Service Visitors Center several miles south of Emerald Bay.

MONO COUNTY

MAMMOTH LAKES

East of Mammoth Lakes are several au naturel hot springs. Crab Cooker (112°F) has a beautiful view. Shepard Hot Spring has adjustable temperature. Dave's Warm Tub can hold one person in its porcelain tub. Red's Pond is within walking distance from Mammoth Lakes; up to fifty percent of the bathers may be nude and others are topfree. Pulky's Pool, off Benton Crossing Road, is recommended as are Crowley Hot Spring, Hot Tub, and Wild Willy's. To locate, ask locals for directions and check J. Loam, *Hot Springs and Pools of the U.S.*, 1990, pp. 189-191.

TRAVERTINE HOT SPRINGS

The famous hot springs are flowing again! View the Sierra from one of two pools where locals have built a concrete tub and a smaller shallow tub. Sunning area, camping space. Afterwards visit the ghost town, Bodie, or explore an abandoned mine.

☞ From Bridgeport, take US 395 south for 1/2 mile and turn left onto Jack Sawyer Road. At the second fork, take the dirt road straight and continue to the right on the road up the hill. Continue straight a half mile and park in the lot near the hot spring. Walk down slope to reach the pools.

"BIG HOT" WARM SPRINGS

Geothermal pools; some quite deep. Water temperature 80-85°F. Located less than two miles east of Route 395, south of Bridgeport in Mono County. Walking or FWD is recommended for the last part of the road. Close any gates you open.

TUOLUMNE COUNTY

TUOLUMNE RIVER

From Groveland east of Stockton, near the west side of Yosemite National Park, drive about 15 miles east on Route 120 to the South Fork of the Tuolumne River. Just after crossing the bridge, turn left. Another immediate left leads to the Rainbow Pool (on the upstream side of the bridge). Skinny-dipping is common above and below the main swimming hole, and occasionally in the Rainbow Pool itself. The most attractive sites are to be found by parking near the blocked dirt road, descending from the road down to Rainbow Pool, and hiking down the steep dirt road about 3/4 mile to the confluence of the South and Middle Forks.

For Preston Flats, follow the above instructions as far as crossing the bridge and turning immediately left. But then, having turned left, immediately turn right instead of another left; this puts you onto the road towards Cherry Lake. Follow 8 miles to the Tuolumne River at Early Intake. Cross the bridge, turn right, and continue past residences and Kirkwood Powerhouse to the end of the road. Park and follow the trail 1/4 mile to 4 miles upstream. The trail is easy, with gentle slopes and good camping. Best spot, 3 miles up.

YOSEMITE NATIONAL PARK

To complement its breathtaking escarpments and waterfalls, Yosemite has a treat for naturist visitors—the Devil's Bathtub. Uptrail behind the Awanee Hotel, ask any employee for directions, it is a 20-by-50 foot ledge and pool at the foot of the falls, a secluded sunning spot in a busy park.

DON PEDRO RECREATION AREA

This private lake with a 160-mile perimeter doesn't sponsor nude camping and swimming but doesn't discourage them either—as long as it's done discreetly. You'll only have a problem if you don't stay away from developed areas when unclad.

☞ Take Route 132 west from Modesto to the reservoir and follow signs to Don Pedro Recreation Area.

CALAVERAS COUNTY

ANGELS CAMP RIVER CAVE

A gorgeous natural cave several hundred yards long, with stalactites, that you can swim through. Clothing-optional in usage.

☞ Go 5 miles east of Angels Camp immediately beyond the eastern city limits of Vallecito. Then south on Parrots Ferry Road for exactly 3 miles. Park on the right side in the designated parking area near the horse corral. Walk down a steep grade to the cave.

You may also drive another 0.3 miles on same road, park on the tributary road, and hike an easy 1 mile path that leads from there to the cave.

AMADOR COUNTY

COMANCHE RESERVOIR

A manmade lake near Lodi, filled by the Mokelumne River. The 52 mile shoreline has access gates at north and south. Sunbathing, fishing, boating, waterskiing, camping, horseback riding are popular year-round. Skinny-dippers mostly use small coves reached with the boats that may be rented from concessioners located at the access gates. For sunning without a boat, try the north shore camping area. Skinny-dippers have coexisted with the clad without hassle, and if you are considerate of others' rights, this situation should continue.

RANCHO CICADA RETREAT

In the Sierra foothills 45 miles east of Sacramento. Fifty wooded private acres of prime river frontage for swimming and rafting, hiking, games. Accommodates groups up to 40 with modern tent platforms with mattresses, community kitchen, hot showers. Catering available for groups. Reservations necessary. P.O. Box 225, Plymouth, CA 95669. Phone (209) 245-4841.

MARIN COUNTY

BONITA COVE

In the Marin County headlands, this cove offers two separate beaches. One is about 1/4 mile in length, with dark sand. The other lies to the west of this and is separated from it by a large pyramid-shaped rock. The water is cold and a strong ocean current makes it dangerous for swimming. But the cove is indeed a paradise, with an excellent view of the San Francisco skyline, the bridge, some interesting rock formations, a cave in the distance, and an abundance of wildlife.

☞ The access is somewhat tricky. After crossing the Golden Gate Bridge from San Francisco, take Alexander Avenue (the first major turnoff to the right) toward Sausalito. Cross the highway to the left after a couple hundred yards and turn left on Conzelman Road. Follow Conzelman and traverse McCullough until it becomes a one-way road. Look for the small parking pull-off on the oceanside and park. Take the broad path down and look for the second intersecting path, follow this to the beach. If you get lost, go to the Rodeo Beach Ranger Station and ask for a copy of a map outlining the trails through the entire Golden Gate National Recreation Area. The mile hike down to these spots is well worth it, but contracting poison oak is not. Be sure to wear long pants, socks and shoes.

MUIR BEACH

The beach is very popular and relatively hassle-free. The unclad part is, in fact, located in front of private property. To reach it, you must either climb over the rocks that divide it from the public Muir Beach, or wade around at low tide. An excellent site for swimming, since the waves are small and it has a sandy bottom. Arrive before 11:30 a.m. on weekends to get a parking spot.

☞ North from San Francisco on Highway 1. Muir is just south of Stinson Beach; turn left from Highway 1 onto Pacific Way, and park in the public lot for Muir Beach (cars parked on Pacific Way will be ticketed).

LITTLE STINSON BEACH

Take Route 101 north over the Golden Gate and along the coast to the public Stinson Beach. Park at Big Stinson Beach and walk along the shore to the south. If accessing from Red Rock, walk north. Once you've found Little Stinson, and if you're a morning beachgoer, you may become one of the few who manage to park at the road turnoff directly above the beach.

RED ROCK BEACH

With merely a hundred yards of sand between two points, Red Rock has a lot going for it—frisbee, hot pool and ocean swim, sun and conversation, rock climbs, even a newsletter.

At low tide visit the hot spring. About 50 yards up the trail to the parking lot is a saddle. Go down to the beach from this saddle and along the shore to the hot spring; you'll have to wade even at low tide. Clambering over the rocks is not recommended.

☞ A half mile south of Stinson Beach on Highway 1 find a large red rock that looks like it belongs in Utah, and join the cars parked in a turnout on west side. Trail begins near the trash bin. Some folks overnight at the Steep Ravine Environmental Cabins: take the trail from the cabins to the beach and walk 400 yards to the hot spring.

BOLINAS BEACH

Bolinas is a favorite with affluent Marin County residents, who, if generally mellow, are uptight about visitors drawn to the nude beach who are occasionally cited. Bathing is on Bolinas Bay, not the lagoon, which is a receptacle for raw sewage. Swimmers should be cautioned to approach the sea with full respect for a strong undertow.

☞ About 30 miles north of the Golden Gate on Highway 1. You'll drive past the inner rim of Bolinas Lagoon, then turn left onto Olema-Bolinas Road and follow it through Bolinas to the beach.

POINT REYES NATIONAL SEASHORE

San Franciscans seem scarcely aware of the natural resource they might enjoy in less than an hour's drive up coast on Route 1. Point Reyes National Seashore stretches from Bolinas at the south to Tomales Bay State Park at the north. Together they comprise a refuge peninsula 30 miles long, and 12 miles from Tomales Bay inlet on the east to the outermost point of Point Reyes Lighthouse on the wild Pacific.

Clothing-optional use: little-used Limantour Beach has 7 miles of rolling sand dunes. The sole tree in sight marks a campground 2 miles distant. Then, Sculptured Beach adds high cliffs to sand dunes, tidal pools, sea lions and no civilization for miles. From Limantour Beach, hike south 3 miles, passing Coast Camp, for Sculptured Beach and time your visit to low tide.

Bass Lake lies on the Palomarin Trail about 2.8 miles from the Palomarin trailhead at the end of Mesa Road. Take Route 2 from Stinson Beach and just north of Bolinas Lagoon, turn right on the exit to Bolinas. Follow the road back on the west side of the Lagoon. The road will dead-end at Olema-Bolinas Road. Take a left and continue 0.5 miles to a stop sign at Mesa Road. Turn right and follow road to the end (it becomes a dirt road) to a parking lot and trailhead. A sign at the trailhead directs you the rest of the way to Bass Lake.

All food must be brought and don't forget binoculars for bird, whale and seal watching. Warm days of spring and autumn are the best and most fog-free. Phone 663-1092 for weather and tide.

☞ Point Reyes National Seashore is 40 miles north of San Francisco. Exit Highway 1 at Olema, parking at Seashore headquarters to pick up trail map and follow Limantour Road to the end.

Not far from Sculptured and Limantour beaches is an American Youth Hostel which offers accommodations to all for $7/person. Box 247, Point Reyes Station, CA 94956, phone (415) 663-8811. Point Reyes also provides four nights of free camping; four backpack camp sites (no car camping) available. Permit required; wood fires not allowed. Contact Bear Valley Visitor Center (415) 663-1092 Monday through Friday for reservations.

HAGMAIER POND

Hagmaier Pond turns weedy then dries up starting early July, so enjoy in late Spring.

☞ From San Francisco, drive Highway 101 north to Greenbrea, then Sir Francis Drake Boulevard exit west. Or from East Bay, take the Richmond/San Rafael Bridge and about 1 mile beyond the bridge take San Anselmo exit; this becomes Sir Francis Drake Boulevard when it passes under Highway 101. Either way, go westerly on Drake Boulevard, following signs to Olema, where you turn south on Highway 1 and go 4 1/2 miles to find the turnstile entrance on east side (if you reach Dogtown Pottery you've gone too far).

Marty Brittan, Over Second Slide, University Falls, Near Sacramento.

SACRAMENTO COUNTY

LAGUNA DEL SOL

Rawhide Ranch was the name until 1991; 20 miles southeast of Sacramento. A 120-acre nudist park with grassy camping areas, motel and RV rental, gleaming entertainment center, lake with fishing and boating, spa, tennis, volleyball, 2 pools and restaurant. 8683 Rawhide Lane, Wilton, CA 95693. Phone (916) 687-6550.

RIVER DIPPERS

Excellent, informative newsletter, family events. Send SASE: P.O. Box 2693, Sacramento, CA 95812.

HOUSEBOAT HOTLINE

For houseboating on the Delta, give the Houseboat Hotline a call. You'll receive an hour of training before you shove off on a rented houseboat that can accommodate up to 10 people and comes equipped with everything except bedding and linen. 6333 Pacific Avenue, Suite 152, Stockton, CA 95207. Phone (209) 477-1840.

PLACER COUNTY

FOLSOM LAKE

Folsom Lake offers many skinny-dipping coves and beaches, but perhaps the best, especially for those without a boat, is just upstream from Beeks Bight. The Folsom Lake State Recreation Area maintains toilets at the parking lot, among other amenities, and the town of Folsom is quaint and fun to visit.

☞ Enter the park at the Granite Bay access off Douglas Boulevard (admission is charged). Drive north from Granite Bay, past Dotons Point to the Beeks Bight parking. Take the footpaths near the shore for 15 minutes to the north shore of Beeks Bight and a number of beaches and coves that are separated by rocks (difference in water level makes a difference in how much beach is exposed). Proceed far enough north along the point so you are not in view of the clothed folk on the south shore of Beeks Bight.

One can also go by Sacramento's bus line which runs to the Placer County line and requires a short walk from Oak and Main Street. The bus fare is 60¢ per bus (no transfers; one-way trip requires 2 buses) and only 1 bus runs on Saturday; neither bus runs on Sunday.

AMERICAN RIVER

The north fork of the American River has a sandbar in the undeveloped Auburn Ravine that is well-known to skinny-dippers. The area has some sand beaches and many sunning rocks.

☞ Drive I-80 northeast from Sacramento to the Elm Avenue exit at Auburn. Follow Elm east to the first traffic light (High Street), turn left on High Street, which becomes Route 49. Continue on 49 for 2 miles, to a wider stretch of road with parking space on both sides. This is 1/2 mile before the Route 49 bridge over the North Fork American River. From the parked cars, take the path down to a wider dirt road, formerly a railroad grade; cross over this dirt road and, somewhere nearby, you'll find the footpath leading directly down to the nude beach.

NEVADA COUNTY

YUBA RIVER, SOUTH FORK

The South Fork of the Yuba River near Grass Valley is popular skinny-dipping for locals who keep the area free of litter; do likewise. Route 49 northwest out of Auburn; at Grass Valley take Route 20 west for 8 miles to Pleasant Valley Road; turn left (north) on it, past Lake Wildwood, to South Yuba River. Cross the new bridge, park on either side of the road. Walk on the dirt road toward the river and then upstream until you notice a dip in the road. After walking another 3 minutes, you'll see a second dip. From here, take a footpath on the left, go up a hill and walk for 7 minutes until you reach a nearly-level former flume grade. Follow the footpath upstream along the grade, walking by the downhill paths at the 11 and 14 minute points. After about 15 minutes, look for a footpath to the right. Take it down to the water; this and other areas further upstream are best for skinny-dipping. The entire walk should take about an hour. Downstream areas are clothed; avoid. No overnight camping.

Another site for family skinny-dipping is at Edwards Crossing Bridge. Where Spring Creek enters the Yuba River and acts like a natural jacuzzi is the most popular (be sure to arrive early). From Nevada City follow North Bloomfield Road over the Edwards Crossing Bridge. Facing downstream, take the trail on the right bank for 10 minutes until you come to Spring Creek. Cross it and look for a trail roughly parallel to the creek leading down to the river. BLM's South Yuba Campground is near the bridge with other campgrounds at Malakoff State Park and Grizzly Creek.

Durand Sieger, At the Yuba River.

OREGON CREEK

Oregon Creek widens into a pleasant little pool with several waterfalls. Warm spring water. Flat granite ledges for sunning surround the pool. Mostly nude use by local families.

☞ From Sacramento area, take I-80 to Auburn, then Highway 49 north past Grass Valley and Nevada City. Continue on Highway 49 about 3 miles past North San Juan, where you will cross the Yuba River and the Oregon Creek Campground. Immediately after the second white guard rail (or 1/2 mile past campground), take the dirt road that leads to the large dirt parking lot, then hike the short and easy trail to the pool.

COLUSA COUNTY

WILBUR HOT SPRINGS

A spacious former stagecoach hotel in the boonies with a San Francisco clientele who return for the relaxation, yoga, massage, Japanese-quality soaking pools, swimpool, sundeck, community kitchen. 240 acres in an open hilly terrain great for hiking, biking. Williams, CA 95987. Phone (916) 473-2326 for reservations.

LAKE COUNTY

HARBIN HOT SPRING

Formerly a major society spa, now Harbin's unceasing waters, clear air and skein of hillside trails lead to a new age. Cold, hot and hotter pools, sundeck, massage, vegetarian restaurant. Clothes-optional everywhere except restaurant. Day visits, camping, cabin rental, conferences. P.O. Box 782, Middletown, CA 95461. Phone: (707) 987-2477 for reservation.

MENDOCINO COUNTY

LILIES BEACH

On a bend of the Big River on the grounds of the Mendocino Woodlands summer camp, Lilies Beach enjoys sunbaked days while the oceanside beaches shiver in fog; but the bottom is stony, and the water is cool. Wading downstream from Lilies Beach (shoes recommended) will bring you to other sandbars and swimming areas. Look for such sites after the third, fifth and sixth bends.

☞ North of Mendocino, turn right from Highway 1 onto Little Lake Road; the first available right-hand turn past the main Mendocino turnoff sign. Go out Little Lake Road eastward 4 miles and spot the Mendocino Woodlands sign. About 200 yards further, turn right on an unmarked paved road that begins near a "Weight Limit–9 Tons" sign. (The road is paved the first 20 yards, then is unpaved.) Follow road 3 miles, turn right at bottom of the hill where it forks, park at road's end and follow trail 10 minutes rightward to the beach on the river.

ORR HOT SPRINGS

A small clothing-optional community bought historic glen from Orr family in 1975. Up to 40 adults (kids okay) reserve cabins or campsites for visits Friday to Monday. Splendid individual and group hot tubs, warm creek-flow pool, sauna, flower and vegetable gardens, lodge and community kitchen; massage available. No visit is complete without a half day, perhaps picnicking, two miles west by a stream in primieval Montgomery Redwoods—many trees 300 feet tall and 1,000 years old. 13201 Orr Springs Road, Ukiah, CA 95482. Phone (707) 462-6277.

SIERRA COUNTY

SIERRA HOT SPRINGS

Rustic spiritual retreat renovating century-old hotel offers hot tubs, soaking pools, campsites on wooded 670 acres. Massage available. Go 25 miles north of Truckee on Route 89; right on Route 49 in Sierraville at T intersection; go 3/4 mile and turn right on Lemon Canyon Road; go 1/2 mile and turn right on Campbell Hot Springs Road; 1/2 mile to parking lot at second trailer; 5 minute walk. Deerwater Airfield, county maintained, is adjacent. P.O. Box 366, Sierraville, CA 96126, Phone (916) 994-3773.

BUTTE COUNTY

BUTTE CREEK

A popular area with Chico College students. Spring and summer offer ample water.

☞ From Chico, take Skyway Road east to Humbug Road. Follow Humbug Road east and northeast along Butte Creek. Look for parked cars a few hundred yards before and after the intersection with Honey Run Road; skinny-dipping in both areas.

Or continue along Humbug Road, turn left on Helltown Road and follow it to the dead-end. Park, walk down the road and across the bridge, and follow trail to the right upstream along Butte Creek about 1/4 mile.

BIDWELL PARK

A number of families as well as Chico College students play here. Lower Bidwell Park goes right into downtown Chico; use only Upper Bidwell Park for skinny-dipping.

☞ Best from Highway 99 by the East Avenue ramp into the Wildwood Avenue entrance: right turn on Golf Course Road, left on Upper Park Road which leads into the gravel road. Take it to parking lot 'M' in Upper Bidwell Park; park and lock. A trail leads to a small canyon between 100' basalt sides to the creek, a 5 minute walk. You'll find 2 small beaches of fine gravel, small rapids for sliding in, lots of fish for chasing.

Jim Moyers, Country Band Celebrates National Nude Weekend, More Mesa Beach, Santa Barbara.

LAKE OROVILLE STATE RECREATION AREA

No declared 'free' beaches, but bare-boating is common. Boat-in camping is allowed on 100 miles of shoreline. For camping, weather and park information, call (916) 538-2200.

☞ Take Route 70 to Oroville, then east on Route 162 (Oroville Dam Boulevard). Turn right onto Olive Highway (still Route 162). Go about 5 miles to Kelly Ridge Road, turn left, and continue for 1.5 miles. Turn right onto Arroyo Drive. Left at "T" to the park kiosk.

PLUMAS COUNTY

WOODY'S FEATHER RIVER HOT SPRINGS

Offers hunting, fishing and swimming on the Feather River; two soaking pools, restaurant, motel. P.O. Box 7, Twain, CA 95984. Phone (916) 283-4115.

SHASTA COUNTY

CLEAR CREEK

Local families and couples skinny-dip in peace in the beautiful pools and small beaches. Stream flow is low but steady throughout summer. Located near Redding.

☞ From Redding head west-southwest on county road I-16 (Place Street becomes Placer Road) for 12 miles toward Igo. Before crossing the new bridge high above Clear Creek, park and hike down the trail on the left side of the creek. Follow the footpath downstream around the bend.

TRINITY COUNTY

CAMP PREVENTORIUM HOT SPRINGS

A clothing-optional commercial spa with a big outdoor soak tub, pools along the river, and rental cabins available. No smoking, alcohol or drugs. 196 Hot Springs Row, Big Bend, CA 96001. Phone (916) 337-6680.

HELLS GATE CAMPGROUND

The South Fork of the Trinity River and its hiking trails are a skinny-dipper's delight. Recommended is the Hells Gate Forest Service Campground 2 miles from Forest Glen. Good camping facilities and a mellow crowd of young people from May to October, with nudity the norm along the riverbank. This remote and little used area is about 50 yards long and 25 yards wide. Backed by thick woods with sheer cliffs in the front, the beach is hassle-free.

☞ From I-5 at Red Bluff, drive Highway 36 west for 70 miles. Upon reaching Hells Gate Campground, follow the campground road for about a mile to its end. Park here or at any campground area. Walk upriver for 500 yards; the small beach is to the right.

HUMBOLDT COUNTY

COLLEGE COVE

Part of Trinidad State Beach, College Cove is popular on the relatively few sunny days that the region enjoys. Nude use is south of the big rock; water is icy.

☞ From Eureka, drive north on Highway 101 about 25 miles to Trinidad. Follow signs to Trinidad State Beach parking area, but continue on the old highway about 3/4 mile more (crossing a lovely fern-shrouded ravine) and look for the dirt parking lot on the left (if you reach Abalone Beach, you've gone too far). Park and follow trails to the beach.

If College Cove is too crowded, turn around and head for Baker's Beach, which is 12 miles north of Arcata on Highway 101. Take Westhaven exit to Scenic Drive north. Stop at parked cars and large, vine-covered residence sign and its rusted metal "Private Property" sign on right. Parking on Scenic Drive has caused some problems for residents; be sure to leave enough road clearance for passing traffic.

TRINITY RIVER

Both Trinity River and Willow Creek (west of the town with the same name) offer a number of skinny-dipping areas. The Elbow, a favorite, lies about 7 miles southwest of Willow Creek and 1.7 miles northwest of Hawkins Bar/Trinity Village, at a small horseshoe bend in the Trinity River. A narrow dirt road runs inconspicuously off Route 299 to the northeast for a 1/4 mile along a narrowing ridge. Park among the oaks and hike 200 yards down a steep trail to the river, where it makes a sharp bend. This Forest Service land includes cliffs and wooded hillsides, and at the river beach you can tan, raft, fish and swim.

Or try Boogie Bar, 3 miles west of Willow Creek on Route 299. Cross the Trinity River Bridge, turn right onto South Fork Road and look for the parked cars 5 minutes further.

MAD RIVER FISH HATCHERY

Upstream from the Mad River Fish Hatchery is the clothes-optional Mad River fun spot; used mid–April to late September.

☞ From Coastal Route 101 just north of Arcata take Route 299 east, through Blue Lake by the off-ramp, and then following Hatchery Road. At the hatchery, cross the Mad River and hike upstream about 3/4 mile to the sandbars and swimming holes. You could also check out the Mad River at Maple Creek and at Swinging Bridge (ask locals for directions).

Dave Patrick, In the Surf, South of Devil's Slide.

COLORADO

DENVER AREA

ROCKY MOUNTAIN BARES

This Denver naturist group offers a lively program of health club events that include swims, and frequent backcountry excursions. Send SASE to P.O. Box 740159, Arvada, CO 80006.

An umbrella for naked Colorado is Colorado Naturists, P.O. Box 88, Denver, CO 80201.

MOUNTAIN AIR RANCH

A 150-acre modern resort with cabins, tent and RV sites, pool and spa, rec and dance hall, restaurant, playground, and mountain view. Convenient to Denver; phone (303) 697-4083.

BOULDER CANYON

A dramatic if difficult clothes-optional getaway at the end of a rough road. Beware of high waters during rain runoffs.

☞ From Boulder, drive west toward Boulder Falls 7 miles to a switchback road called Sugarloaf. It's about 1.5 miles before Boulder Falls. Take Sugarloaf about 7 winding miles to the unpaved left turn on Lost Angel Mine Road. Take it, and watch for the red caboose (it's someone's home), and stay to the right at the fork immediately beyond. Go all the way to the parking at the end of the road. Walk on the jeep trail 20 feet to the foot path, going to the left for about 50 feet, to a path descending on your right. As you wind your way downstream there are many nice areas used by the Boulder College students to get that all-over tan.

SOUTH CENTRAL

DESERT REEF BEACH CLUB

Artesian well water cools from 130°F flowing into two pools and a spa to create a nude recreation oasis. This family-oriented day resort offers weekend live music at its Lost Bikini Bar. Picnicking lawn. Entirely clothing-optional; about half the visitors choose nudity. Open 10 to 10, Wednesday through Sunday year-round. P.O. Box 503, Penrose, CO 81240. Phone (719) 784-6134.

☞ Take Route 115 from Colorado Springs to the outskirts of Florence, where you will find the sign for a road to Portland; take that road and after 1.1 miles find the small sign for DRBC; turn right, drive over the cattle guard and bear to the right for a couple of miles.

VALLEY VIEW HOT SPRINGS

Southwest from Colorado Springs, an hour from the Monarch and Wolf Creek ski areas, located on the west slope of the Sangre de Cristo mountains at 8700 feet, Valley View offers unobstructed views of San Luis Valley. Entirely clothes-optional. Hiking and music-making, four natural pools for soaking and an 80-foot swimming pool. Rustic cabins and rooms are available (bring your own bedding; reservations recommended!) or camp out. Nearest food service and purchase is 13 miles away. Kitchen facilities and sauna, firewood provided. Children free. Weekdays open to the public. Weekend and holiday use reserved for members and their guests. P.O. Box 175, Villa Grove, CO 81155. Phone (719) 256-4315.

☞ From junction of US 285 and State 17 near Mineral Hot Springs, take the gravel County Road GG due east for 7 miles.

TELLURIDE AREA

DUNTON HOT SPRING

Telluriders find this a good place to meet new folks and old friends. A hot spring in a barn at a privately-owned town in the middle of wilderness.

☞ Find the Dunton town access road about 17 miles southwest of Telluride—it's a loop dirt road off Route 145, maintained by the US Forest Service, with Dunton named on signs at each end. You can go in about 4 miles west of Stoner, winding some 25 miles in great scenery. The other entry, offering a shorter but steeper route, is about 7 miles east of Rico. The road is open after the April snow melt through mid-October. Stay at the USFS campground nearby or rent a cottage from Dunton's proprietors.

WESTERN SLOPE: ORVIS HOT SPRINGS

Go 1.3 miles south of Ridgeway from Route 550 in the direction of Ouray. This rustic lodge with a scenic view of the Mt. Sneffels Range rents tentsites and six guest rooms, bicycles, cross-country skiis, and access to four indoor tiled soaking pools and several outdoor hot pools. Day or overnight rates. Less than an hour from Telluride. 1585 County Road 3, Ridgeway, CO 81432. Phone (303) 636-5324.

WESTERN

ESCALANTE CANYON

The Escalante Canyon is now an accepted nuding refuge. Large rocks lend themselves to sunning and July warms the pools. Go upstream, leaving lower pools to sedentary/hostile types. Take out trash. Camping permitted. Grand Junction has a youth hostel for all ages, phone (303) 242-9636.

☞ Drive Route 50 southeast from Grand Junction. Halfway to Montrose look for a sign, "Historical Marker Ahead," and then the gravel road leading south along the canyon. From the highway exit, you first travel three miles down to a one-way bridge, then another 8 miles to a stone house with "Captain Smith's Cabin" engraved on its wall, and a mile further look for the turnoff marked "Potholes" on your left. Park in the parking area and follow the signs to the creek, then hike upstream 10–15 minutes.

ASPEN AREA

CONUNDRUM HOT SPRINGS

Conundrum: how do you get a hot springs that holds up to 25 persons at 11,200 feet? Answer: you hike, from June to September, up a spectacular 8-mile trail. The US Forest Service supplies maps and advises that you stay overnight, but don't camp closer than a mile to the thermal pool and do bring a primus stove—firewood is nearly nonexistent. Don't forget your sunblock.

☞ The Conundrum Creek trailhead is reached by driving about 5 miles southwest from Aspen on Castle Creek Road, where you'll find a dirt track on the right (Forest Service Road 128) that descends and crosses Castle Creek. Take this road 1 1/2 miles to the trailhead; it is narrow, rocky and steep, unfit for large or ailing vehicles. Park and follow the well-marked trail along Conundrum Creek for 8 steep miles.

Jerry Derbyshire, Rocky Mountain High.

Another nice route is to park at the East Maroon Creek trailhead, almost to Maroon Creek on the Maroon Creek road. Follow east Maroon Creek to the end, bearing left, and cross both Triangle and Copper Passes, then drop one mile down to the springs. This provides a loop trip that lets you see twice as much of the Maroon-Snowmass Wilderness, with your soak as serendipity reward.

CENTRAL

ROARING FORK RIVER GROTTOES

On hot summer days Aspeners head for the 'grottoes'—pools carved in a rock streambed by the icy runoff waters of the legendary Roaring Fork River. The area becomes a sort of 'cold springs' retreat, the contrary of Conundrum's function.

☞ Take Route 82 east from Aspen. After several miles, find the wooden sign with inlaid white lettering, "Grottoes," and an arrow pointing to the right (visable from the eastbound lane only). Park and hike in.

COTTONWOOD HOT SPRINGS INN

Several small pools, cabins, restaurant and meeting rooms available at this rustic lodge near the San Isabel National Forest that permits nudity within fenced areas. 18999 Highway 306, Buena Vista, CO 81211. Phone (719) 395-6434.

NORTHERN

STRAWBERRY PARK HOT SPRINGS

"Woodstock never ended at this outdoor recreation area seven miles north of town on Park Road," says Colorado Springs' Gazette Telegraph. Delightfully primitive and increasingly popular. Geothermal fissure flow collects in several pools. Sauna. Massage, cross-country skiing, and saddle-horse trips by appointment. Rental cabins and camp-sites. Nudity only on specified days (Monday and Wednesday) in summer, every day in winter, and always after nightfall. P.O. Box 773332, Steamboat Springs, CO 80477. Phone (303) 879-0342.

☞ From US 40 in Steamboat Springs, turn north on 7th Street. Follow signs 7 miles to area.

SILO COUNTRY CLUB

Silo Country Club, 25 miles south of Cheyenne, is a clothing-optional campground with in-ground pool, hot tub, game room, and lawn sports. Open weekends. Write P.O. Box 455, Wellington, CO 80549.

CONNECTICUT

Connecticut residents deserve better than to be required to cross state lines for skinny-dipping. Yet for hassle-free good times, with few exceptions, they have two choices—either drive east to Rhode Island's NENA Beach or take the Bridgeport ferry to Port Jefferson on New York's Long Island. This summertime special departs from Bridgeport Harbor Terminal at the Union Square Dock (exit 27 on the Connecticut Turnpike). A charter bus transfers passengers from Port Jefferson to Smith Point Park on Fire Island. Not costly. Phone (203) 367-3043 for schedules.

NEW LONDON AREA

NEHANTIC STATE FOREST

Nehantic State Forest has long had both clothed and nude users. Some recent policing for nudity; avoid weekends.

☞ Twenty-five miles west of New London. From Lyme, go 4.5 miles north of Route 95 on Route 156. Look for the well-marked entrance of Nehantic State Forest on your right. Proceed for 2 miles on the narrow paved road, and pass the boat launch to the right (stay left). The first skinny-dipping spot is 0.5 miles after the boat launch and is reached by taking the turnoff to the right. Continue up the hill and park near the path to the right that leads to the lake. The second spot is 500 yards (0.3 miles) beyond. Take the right-hand turn, turn right again almost immediately and park in the "developed" and therefore non-nude area. Approach the water bearing left after you park. You'll pass the outhouses. Follow the path as it descends the hill to the lake. Though not the best place to sun, the water is clean and clear.

MIDDLETOWN AREA

MILLER'S POND

Higganum Reservoir State Park shelters a "pond the officials forgot"—but rangers have appeared recently in this small and quiet retreat with clean water, an adequate beach, good hiking trails, and a skinny-dipping tradition.

☞ Take Route 17 south from Middletown to downtown Durham. Where Route 68 goes west, and Tigner Insurance and Durham Family Practice occupy kitty-corners, get onto (unmarked) Maiden Lane going eastward. Follow it 11.3 miles to just past an old rusted windmill and turn south (right) at a diagonal intersection, for 1.6 miles to a stop sign. Here turn right up a hill, going 1.3 miles to a small dirt parking lot opposite a sign for Horselover's Shop. Find the rocky path on the east side into the park, to the beach, and continue beyond the beach out to where you can see the dam at the western end of the pond—this is the nude area.

NORTHEAST

SOLAIR RECREATION LEAGUE

Founded 1933. The 350-acre member-owned Solair is 5 miles south of Southbridge, MA and 10 miles from historic Old Sturbridge. Features a private lake and wooded hiking trails. Rental units, tent and RV sites, snack bar, tennis, volleyball, boating and fishing, hot tub, sauna, dances, playground. Guests admitted with prior contact April to November. P.O. Box 187, Southbridge, MA 01550. (203) 928-9174.

DELAWARE

SOUTHEASTERN

DELAWARE SEASHORE STATE PARK

Extending from two to nine miles south of Rehoboth Beach on Route 1, the Delaware Seashore State Park offers "shorelovers...whatever it is about the shore" they might "love," including unofficial nudity. Surfcasters and 4WD racers also are users. It's a huge shore with space for all.

☞ North or south from Conquest Road you may find beaches with unclad users. Keybox Road offers another access from the north. Pay fee to park. Walk well away from clothed users.

CAPE HENLOPEN STATE PARK

You can drive into southeastern Delaware from Annapolis using Routes 50 and 404 to Lewes. Drive from the north via Wilmington—or cross from Cape May directly to Lewes by ferry, a relaxing, 90 minute trip. Ferry schedule: (302) 645-6316.

As the southern lip of Delaware Bay opposite Higbee Beach in New Jersey, Cape Henlopen gets a crashing surf on its sandy outer beach. Amid its bogs and dunes are nature trails and church camps—and a mile or so of the northern-most Cape sees pockets of discreet nude use. Hike northeast from the Cape May–Lewes ferry dock onto the Cape. Or drive east from Lewes on Cape Henlopen Road which becomes Post Lane, turn left on Point Road and park at its terminus. To request a map, phone (302) 645-8983.

Also in Cape Henlopen State Park is Gordon Pond Wildlife Area southeast of Lewes. Bun-sunners locate themselves midway between north and south Gordon Pond parking lots amid hilly dunes and pines about 200 yards back from the berm.

FOWLERS BEACH

Prime Hook National Wildlife Refuge includes a 50-foot-wide, seldom-trod long beach with grungy bayside. Before stripping down check the ranger attitude toward skinny-dipping.

☞ From Route 1, take the Fowlers Beach access road (7.5 miles south of Milford), park at the public boat landing and walk a mile north along the beach. Plenty of privacy since the clothes-compulsive stay near the landing. Parking is maximum of 40-60 cars so come early.

DISTRICT OF COLUMBIA

CAPITOL HILL

They call it life inside the beltline. Members of that exclusive club the U.S. Senate may frolic in the Russell Senate Office Building Pool without a belt or a stitch; your public servant has a clothing-optional health club key. The few female Senators make appointments to assure there won't be males on hand. Men in the House of Representatives, less privileged, get only a clothing-optional steam room—where President Bush is said by *Newsweek* to hang out sans towel with his buddies.

☞ Contact National Capital Naturists for convenient skinny-dipping for the rest of us. P.O. Box 3122, Fairfax, VA 22038. Phone (703) 241-BARE.

Peter Simon, Mowing.

FLORIDA

We wrote in the 1983 edition: the best-established nude beaches were all subjected to repression in the summer 1982, evidently as a concerted response to their growing popularity and acceptance by the public. The county sheriffs and state attorney general, who are responsible for the violations of civil rights, are in defiance of recent court decisions that have disabled Florida statute 800.03, the archaic law that traditionally confused lewd with nude. This is a time that tests the commitment of the state of Florida to civil liberties, not least in the area of nude recreation rights.

Sadly, little improvement at the state level is in evidence since 1983. Gov. Martinez stiffened the Florida Parks rules against nudity. Topfree and thongs were specifically banned. Locally, there is change. Jury expression of community values led to dumping State statute 800.03 from the county interpretation applied to Cape Canaveral. Miami Beach ignores an aging State Supreme Court finding which cited the Old Testament as sole authority for charging lasciviousness against topfree sunbathers.

The outcry grows to apply true and determinable community standards, not Biblical edicts. A mellowing is evident in newspaper and media coverage and in county and local enforcement. Nonetheless, make inquiries before you undress at any site on public land. All may be well—but you should inform yourself before risking arrest.

More information with SASE from Florida Beach Coalition, 14125 North Road, Loxahatchee, FL 33470.

Alex Siodmak, Strutting the Thong, Daytona Beach.

Alex Siodmak, Topfree German Couple, Miami Beach.

FLORIDA KEYS

KEY WEST GUEST HOUSES

Key West—behavioral outpost. Unisexed thongs thronging the carnival-like streets. Topfree as the house dress code for both sexes at the posh Pier House pool and beach.

Gay-owned guest houses feature sophistication, patios with pools, and nude sunning decks. Most accept guests without concern for gender or gender preference. Inquire at Lime House, La Di Da, The Sea Isle, The Palms, Island House, Garden House, Southwind, Colours, Newton Street Station and Normandy South Miami Beach for lodgings with dress optional in part.

Atlantic Shores Motel is a perfect choice for first timers with nude swimming and rafting on the beach and a topfree pool with outdoor bar and grill.

The Watson Compound consists of 5 rental houses with a common area including heated pool, hot tub and grill area that is clothing-optional. Watson Compound, 1111 Watson St., Key West, FL 33040.

OFFSHORE

Americans go to sea from Key West to shake the dust of archaic dress codes from their flesh. Examples—

Reef Raiders say that all cruises are clothes-optional—the chartering party sets the dress code. Visit coral reefs on sociable, scuba/snorkel, half or full day voyages. 12-person capacity. Phone (305) 294-3635.

Windjammer Appledore has a Sunday brunch cruise with "suntan lotion being your only cover, if you so desire." 3 hour cruise begins 11 a.m.; $35 buys brunch, mimosas, beer, wine, soft drinks. Reserve (305) 296-9992.

KEY LARGO

Key Largo Sheraton has topfree and thong at the bayside hotel adult pool and jacuzzi. Children not permitted in this area; open to the public.

SOUTHEAST

MIAMI BEACH

20th Street Beach offers a wide sunning arena backed by public metered parking, with lifeguard station, refreshment truck, lounge chair rentals. This 'European style' zone is from 20th to 23rd Streets. Miami Beach policy, on the evidence, is that even full nudity is okay as long as the genitalia are pressed to the public sand. Topfree sunning has been accepted since 1986.

Miami beach hotels as of early 1991: Shawnee Hotel on 39th and Collins, topfree on the hotel beach. Sasson Hotel, around 20th and Collins, topfree and thong hotel pool, sundeck and beach. Shellbourn Hotel, 17th and Collins, topfree pool, sunning area and beach. Sea Breeze Motel, 16th and Collins, topfree and thong beach. Deauville Hotel, in-season topfree beach. The back pool of the Rodney Hotel is topfree, as is the beach.

SOUTH FLORIDA FREE BEACHES

Information, activities resource for Miami and southeast Florida. SASE to P.O. Box 330902-WG, Coconut Grove, FL 33133. Phone (305) 721-2030.

SUNSPORT GARDENS

Our southernmost-listed, most tropical nudist park gets a loyal following from Miami and points north. Social club, volleyball, pool, spa, sauna, fishing, tennis; restaurant, laundromat on premises. Tent and RV spaces available. Twenty miles to North Palm Beach. 14125 North Road, Loxahatchee, FL 334370. Phone (305) 793-0423.

MacARTHUR STATE PARK

Word has it that in the late '60s when the late billionaire John D. MacArthur was courting Walt Disney to build his East Coast Disneyland in Palm Beach County, the pair went skinny-dipping off Air Force Beach, an area now integrated as state park land and renamed MacArthur Beach.

MacArthur owned the secluded beach off State Road A1A in North Palm Beach and two years after his death, MacArthur's foundation donated and sold the land to the state. His son Roderick later wrote to remind the governor that MacArthur intended a portion of the beach to be designated clothing-optional. MacArthur's wish was spurned. Park rangers arrest nude users when their numbers grow.

Similarly naturists who seek to advocate the nude use—T.A. Wyner most prominently—are arrested. We list

MacArthur State Beach because of marginal nude use and, more importantly, because the State of Florida has an unmet moral and community obligation.

SOUTHWEST

EVERGLADES NATIONAL PARK

On Cape Sable Island in Everglades National Park you may enjoy 10 miles of fabulous beaches. Assemble a boat, tent, camping gear, and enjoy a unique natural experience. Walk the beach naked as a Seminole without seeing anybody. Bring repellent for the no-see-ums and possible mosquitoes. Lodge and restaurant available at the marina. January to March is the ideal time.

☞ Drive south from Miami to Homestead and down Route 27 all the way to Flamingo. Stop at Park headquarters to get a permit and launch or rent your boat. Steer west on Florida Bay, following the well-marked channel around the East Cape point and north to Middle Cape Beach. Establish your camp on a white sand stretch backed by coconut palms, enjoy the sun and sunset.

10,000 ISLANDS

Access by boat. Lovely, secluded islands dot the coast along the length of the Everglades, suited to nude boating, canoeing, camping and hiking. Backcountry permits required.

☞ From Naples, take Route 41 south. Then Route 92 to Goodland on the southern tip of Marco Island and launch from there. Follow the inland waterway south to the Gulf. Pick an island away from other boaters and you can enjoy the day in the nude. There have been no problems with police patrols that occasionally pass. Camping is possible on remote islands.

SANIBEL NATURISTS

A dynamic beach group for member events with lots of adventures. SASE to P.O. Box 6789-WG, Ft. Myers, FL 33911. Phone (813) 939-1784.

EAST CENTRAL

CAPE CANAVERAL NATIONAL SEASHORE

Cape Canaveral offers Atlantic Coast refuge for such now rare creatures of nature as sea turtles, bald eagles, skinny-dippers, manatees, pelicans and ibises. Skinny-dippers are restricted in enforcement practice to upper Playalinda Beach. And Playalinda closes for NASA space launches—phone (407) 867-2805 before going to avoid disappointment. If closed, try the beach at South Apollo. Camping is permitted at Playalinda from October to May 15, and campgrounds may be found nearby. Exit the Seashore by way of the Merritt Island N.W. Refuge dirt road for a direct encounter of endangered species. A stiff ocean breeze will hold down insects, rare or not, but bring insect repellent just in case. Consider touring the NASA facility reached by another road from Titusville.

☞ From Highway 1 or 95, Route 406 east through Titusville. Cut onto Route 402, pass the Seashore headquarters, and continue on to the beach. Turn left (north) through the gates and for 5 miles follow the paved road behind the heavily used Playalinda Beach. Get as close to the dead-end as possible and park. Parking is limited; arrive early! Continue on foot to at least 1/2 mile north of the last parking area before getting natural. Even then, be tactful, as prudes are occasionally great walkers. Stay out of the dunes no matter what.

SOUTH APOLLO (KLONDIKE) BEACH

The northern access to Cape Canaveral National Seashore is South Apollo Beach. South from it is Klondike Beach, the wild shore colonized by naturists which, 10 miles south, gives way in turn to clothed Playalinda Beach. It is not affected by space shot closings, but arrive by 8:30 a.m. due to very curtailed parking. Route I-95 or Highway 1 to exit at New Smyrna Beach. East on Route 44 to the Cape and A1A south to Apollo Beach, about 8 miles from town. Park at the southernmost available area and walk further south to marker #29 or so. Leave nothing but footprints. Camping is permitted but you must apply on arrival for a wilderness permit. No glass allowed.

CENTRAL

CYPRESS COVE

Convenient to Disney World, Cypress Cove is a showplace among clothes-free resorts with manicured lawns, paved streets for the many residents, pool, lake, waterskiing, tennis, volleyball, basketball, whirlpool spa, restaurant. Villa apartments, motel rooms, tent and trailer sites available. 4425 S. Pleasant Hill Road, Kissimmee, FL 34746. Phone (407) 933-5870.

TARA OAKS

Renovated colonial home and garden, converted for bed and breakfast. Library, billiards, and toddler playrooms, pool, spa, volleyball, and lawn games. Gourmet meals, picnicking area and camping. One and one half hours from Disney World. Reservations suggested—day visitors welcome. P.O. Box 836-WG, Sparr, FL 32192. Phone (904) 622-8990.

WEST CENTRAL

PARADISE LAKES

Seventeen miles north of Tampa Airport via Dale Mabry Boulevard; an upscale, partying, vacation resort with hotel rooms, RV spaces, mobile homes, rental or time-sharing condos—Paradise Lakes has 75,000 annual visitors and 2,300 members. Retail stores, restaurant, nightclub, poolside bar and grill, spas, sports courts and, oh yes, a cypress-bordered lake where ospreys fish. P.O. Box 750-WG, Land O'Lakes, FL 33539. Phone (813) 949-1313.

LAKE COMO CLUB

This pioneer Florida nudist park has 250 acres, much of it in orchards, on its own lake, 20 miles north of Tampa Airport. Pool, whirlpool, sauna, tennis, volleyball, nature trail, fishing, rec hall, shuffleboard. Trailer hookups, tent sites and rental rooms, restaurant. Clean, reasonable; many snowbirds and retirees. Inquire P.O. Box 898-WG, Lutz, FL 33549. Phone (813) 949-1810.

'Cot of Como,' manager in the early years, chose to go to jail rather than conform to discriminatory law and close Como. His civil disobedience opened Pasco County to community acceptance and nudist prosperity.

CITY RETREAT NUDIST RESORT

This laid-back alternative to urban crowding offers pool, restaurant, store, laundry, rec room, volleyball, tent and trailer sites in spacious wooded park. 13220 Houston Avenue, Hudson, FL 34667. Phone (813) 868-1061.

RIVERBOAT CLUB

Volleyball and basketball courts, hiking trails, horseshoes, hot tub, library, snack machines, gift shop and visitor room. Tent, RV sites and rental cabin available. P.O. Box 1156-WG, Land O'Lakes, FL 34639. Phone (813) 996-6008.

ENGLEWOOD BEACH

Englewood, in Sarasota County, is reached from Venice by Route 775. Route 776 goes over the causeway to Englewood Beach.

Florida

Middle Beach, a.k.a. Blind Pass Beach: turn right on North Beach Road and drive 3 miles to public beach. Walk left (south) on this beach 1/4 mile, past signs indicating end of public beach. In front of the homes and shielded by the dunes, well back from the water, sunbathers quietly have a nice day. Avoid weekends to avert complaints.

Stump Pass Beach: turn left on Gulf Boulevard and follow it to end. Avoid parking in front of motels; bicycling from public beach parking may be best. Walk nearly 1 mile south of road end for best spot. As Manasota Key nears its end it widens, with many secluded gullies for privacy. County property, no houses or road access.

ANCLOTE KEY

A wildlife preserve in Pasco County. Three miles of unspoiled beach on its western side, virtually deserted weekdays. Weekends, first to arrive set dress code. North from Honeymoon Island; about 3 nautical miles west from the mouth of the Anclote River at Tarpon Springs where there is a boat ramp.

LITTLE HONEYMOON ISLAND

Little Honeymoon, a.k.a. Dog Island, is at north of Honeymoon Island, an attraction of the Clearwater coast. It's a popular if not hassle-free nude beach; vehicles can be heard approaching. Road access is lacking to the narrow beach on the east side of the lagoon. Causeway from Alternate 19 between Dunedin and Tarpon Springs.

THIRD ISLAND

'Three Rooker Bar,' a.k.a. Third Island, is a sandbar evolving into an island about 2 miles north of Honeymoon Island. Hard to see with naked eye. Access by boat only. Caution, shallows on east side! A Pinellas County sheriff's boat comes by occasionally.

NORTHEAST

LITTLE TALBOT ISLAND STATE PARK

Unharassed is this lovely park with salt marshes and dunes just north of Jacksonville on the Atlantic. Route A1A runs right through Talbot Island. Pick up a map at the entrance station, park in the first lot and walk north into the roadless upper part.

PONTE VEDRA BEACH

Undeveloped and several miles long, Ponte Vedra Beach is out of sight of the parallel highway owing to dunes. Drive Route 90-E from Jacksonville to Jacksonville Beach; turn south on Route A1A to Ponte Vedra Beach. Several miles further south, beyond the developed resort area, is the undeveloped beach and a large parking area. Better, go a mile further to the boat landing where trails lead directly across the road to the sand dunes and beach.

PANHANDLE

TALLAHASSEE BARE-DEVILS

The Tallahassee Bare-Devils know of some wonderful spots—springfed wilderness rivers for canuding, gin-clear springs for skinny-dipping, and forest trails for nude hiking—but all are difficult to locate without a guide. For detailed directions, send SASE to the Bare-Devils, P.O. Box 20656, Tallahassee FL 32316.

SUNBURST RESORT

Two hundred members, 20 wooded acres, pool, lighted volleyball court, jogging track, fishing pond, gift shop, restaurant, rec hall with fireplace, TV and sofas. Rooms, tent and RV sites. Route 3 Box 120-WG, Milton FL 32570. Phone (904) 675-6807.

ETHOS TRACE

Recently-founded nudist park with pool, hot tub, volleyball, sundeck, horseshoes. RV, tent and trailer sites. Close to Pensacola and the Gulf of Mexico. P.O. Box 2255, Pace, FL 32571. Phone (904) 994-9160.

PANAMA CITY

From boatslip at the north end of the state park, cruise over to Shell Island. The long, Gulf-side beach is gorgeous with sugary-white sand and pellucid blue water. Go well away from landing area: best to use on weekdays to avoid clothed beachcombers.

West of Panama City, you may drive to a fine white sand beach with clear, warm waters and regular nude users. Caution: stay out of the dunes.

GRAYTON BEACH STATE PARK

The eastern edge of Grayton Beach State Park has discreet nude use in the winter months. Find it east from Fort Walton Beach, at the west end of Seaside. Where Route 30A turns inland, park along an old spur of road (150 yards long) which follows just behind the dune line. Cross the dunes and walk west (right) to the edge of Grayton Beach State Park.

GULF ISLANDS NATIONAL SEASHORE

This federal recreation area extends across the state lines of Mississippi and Florida. Here, clear blue water, mild surf and gently sloping beaches abound. Add to that a rich history dating back to the 16th-century Spanish explorations and you can see why this is a popular spot for tourists. The Florida portion consists of the islands and peninsulas surrounding Pensacola Bay.

Perdido Key. A fairly secluded place used by local sunlovers. Federal rangers issue warnings for reckless nudity, be discreet! Drive onto Perdido Key (reached by Route 292 from Pensacola), by taking Perdido Key Drive to the Gulf. Cross the bridge and 1 mile further, turn left onto Johnson Beach Drive. When road ends, you may park on sides of the road, then walk 15 minutes east to a beautiful beach. Lodgings at Perdido Key or at Gulf Shores, Alabama, only 10 minutes away.

Navarre Beach. On Santa Rosa Island, 13 miles of superb white sand and lightly visited; the sunsets are terrific! County officials from time to time 'crack down,' even making a hot pursuit of nude bathers who go onto adjacent Eglin Air Force Base beach. Concession stand, toilets, where tollroad makes right turn.

☞ Take I-10 or US 98 for 12 miles west from Fort Walton Beach, or 25 miles east from Pensacola. Take Route 87 over Navarre tollbridge. Notice the large domed building on the left, part of the Eglin Air Force Base where you're headed. Turn left where the main road angles right onto Santa Rosa Island. Drive through picnic site, down a shell road about 1/4 mile and park. Walk to Gulf beach and along it to military area. All bathing on the far side of the fence marking the boundary of a military reservation is clothes-optional.

FT. PICKENS

Ft. Pickens is a civil war fort, now a federal recreation area with campground, dune trails, and museum. Scuba rental at western tip. A good remote dune area on the Gulf for sunbathing. Advice is to avoid weekend boaters. Federal rangers may warn, or even cite, nude sunbathers on the basis of a citizen complaint so be cautious. April through October are the best months to visit.

☞ Take Pensacola Bay Bridge to Gulf Breeze and then the toll-bridge over Santa Rosa Sound. After bridge drive a half mile, turn right at a light onto Ft. Pickens Road, and west to National Seashore entrance. Pay fee, proceed west past campground and store, and find entry to one-way loop on left to Battery 234 and Battery Cooper. Take it and park at first of two small lots and walk to water and then to right for about 1/2 mile.

Another access to the favored dune area is to drive beyond the loop to near the western point, find the parking lot for Battery Payne, walk to the Gulf and then to the left to avoid the strong currents at the tip.

Dave Cowling, Tallahassee Bare-Devils, Paradise Spring.

GEORGIA

A universal struggle between the body and clothing is etched with a harsh light in Georgia—where frenetic Baptists and the robed and hooded Ku Klux Klan allied to close a nudist park in 1989 (unsuccessfully), and deputies will jail skinny-dippers in waters as clearly natural for nakedness as the legendary Chattahoochee River, where arrests continue.

By no coincidence, Georgia is noted for producing founders of nudist parks and, especially, for campus streakers. On March 7, 1974, more than 1,500 students went naked on their Athens campus to set a world record. It took tear gas to get the students into their jeans—a kind of Kent State for free body culture.

Today, of course, Atlanta leavens the mixture. Yuppies inject a laid-back body acceptance that begins in nudist parks, spreading through the professional and business ranks.

SOUTHEAST COAST

CUMBERLAND ISLAND NATIONAL SEASHORE

Eighteen miles of white sand ocean beach with gentle dunes, marshes, freshwater ponds and the appropriate birds. Limit of 300 persons per day. The NPS-run ferry is the only general access with no visitor's cars, bicycles or pets admitted; bring everything you will need as the island has no shops. Or reserve at the posh Greyfield Inn (904 261-6408) which runs a guest ferry from Fernandina Beach, FL.

☞ Take Georgia Route 40 east from I-95 near Kingsland to coastal St. Marys. Round trip NPS ferry $7.95. Four primitive camp-sites. Reservations at 16-place developed camp-site (seven day limit) and on ferry is mandatory: P.O. Box 806, St. Marys, GA 31558. Phone (912) 882-4335. Daily ferry in June, July and August—Thursday through Monday off-season.

SAVANNAH AREA

WASSAW STATE WILDLIFE REFUGE

The two islands of the Wassaw refuge are reached only by boat. Avoid weekends and anchorages, try beaches with south/eastern exposure. Consult Ocean Survey chart 11509 (large scale) or charts 11511 and 11512 (detail). Day charters available. Remember bug repellent.

ATLANTA AREA

LAKE LANIER

This lovely lake 40 miles northeast of Atlanta has many coves for sunbathers with access to a boat. Those landlocked can drive I-85 from Atlanta to the Buford exit, follow Buford Dam Road to the Buford end of the dam, explore for small roads that lead to the coves on federal land. Weekdays best; discretion called for on weekends.

HIDDEN VALLEY

This 110-acre family-oriented nudist resort in the foothills near Lake Lanier offers pool and spa, volleyball, tennis, horseshoes, tent and trailer sites and motel. Route 3 Box 3452, Dawsonville, GA 30534. Phone (404) 265-6110.

BELL ACRES

Ku Klux Klan notwithstanding, Bell Acres Recreation Enterprise (BARE) opened in 1989 on 42 wooded, hilly acres with hiking trails, hot tub, pool, clubhouse. Seventy miles northeast of Atlanta. P.O. Box 302, Maysville, GA 30558. Phone (404) 677-2931.

AUGUSTA AREA

CLARKS HILL LAKE

One thousand miles of shoreline, secluded coves and small islands—the Sumter National Forest borders most of Clarks Hill Lake, guaranteeing little development. Located near the intersection of routes 150 and 221 northwest of Augusta.

Leif Heilberg, Volleyball, The National Sport.

HAWAII

A chief appeal of the Hawaiian Islands, if you drive beyond the customary tourist stops, is the opportunity to be integrated into a world-class if obscured Eden where clothes are insignificant.

Eden should not be banned by law, and yet the return of body acceptance from the mainland causes some island elements to call for enforcement of state bans on nudity. Other Hawaiians are happy for the Naturist havens at secluded beaches.

Indeed, the Polynesians wore little clothing, and then not compulsively, until the missionaries arrived with Captain Cook in 1776 to order changes.

SELLING THE HAWAIIANS ON CLOTHING. A 19th century engraving based on a sketch by J. Webber, shows cloth merchants unpacking wares at Wimea on Kauai. Natives still wore little or nothing. – Courtesy Bishop Museum, Honolulu.

THE NATURIST'S HAWAII

Hawaii can be a tourist trap of huge, impersonal hotels and camera-draped, bus-touring sightseers in leis. Or it can be experienced in a manner befitting a naturist.

Visitors to Maui, Kauai and Hawaii Islands can reserve cabins in the state parks. Though the amenities vary in accordance with price, the most expensive rent for a fifth of what a hotel would cost—and the wild landscape gardening is terrific. For information and reservations, send SASE to State Parks Division, Department of Land & Natural Resources, at the following addresses: Hawaii, P.O. Box 621, Honolulu, HI 96809, phone: (808) 548-7455. Maui, P.O. Box 1049, Wailuka, Maui, HI 96793, phone: (808) 244-4354. Kauai, P.O. Box 518, Kekaha, Kauai, HI 96752, phone: (808) 335-6061. (The Hawaii Island office can also supply a complete list of Hawaii state parks.) Recommended are the Waianapanapa cabins on Maui, and the Kokee area on Kauai, convenient to NaPali Coast and Waimea Canyon.

Many naturists like to travel with a camper—it cuts costs and adds flexibility. Two sources: Beach Bay Enterprises, 1720 Ala Noana Blvd., Honolulu, HI 96815, specializes in cab-over campers suitable for two; and Holo-Holo U-Drive, Box 11, Hilo, HI 96720 has a broader range.

For cheaper air fare, go with super-savers or a consolidator rather than full-fare coach.

Recommended reading on a natural Hawaiian experience: John Clark, *Hawaii's Secret Beaches* and his county *Beaches* books (University of Hawaii); *Hawaii* and *Maui* handbooks, J.D. Bisignani (Moon); *Hidden Hawaii*, Ray Riegert.

OAHU

DIAMOND HEAD

Diamond Head, the volcanic promontory a bus ride from crowded Waikiki Beach, is still visited for (illegal) nude sunbathing beneath the lighthouse which is on the coast side of the road.

☞ The #14 Marnalani Heights bus goes to Diamond Head from in front of the Park Shore Hotel on Kapahula St., Waikiki. Driving? Take Kalakaua Avenue south through the Kapiolani Regional Park, continuing along Diamond Head Road. A half mile before Kuilei Cliffs and just at the lighthouse, find Beach Road on the right. Turn in and park along Beach Road. Walk east past the few rocks of Kuilei Cliffs to the steep walkway down just beyond. The trail on the beach, skirting the eastern edge of Diamond Head, is narrow and rough. The actual beach is dirty and unswimmable, but offers great surfing and windsurfing to watch. Those observing may also watch you; this is a tourist city, after all.

MALAEKAHANA STATE PARK

This bird sanctuary includes offshore Goat Island—Mokuauia in Hawaiian—which may be visited midweek for sunbathing. Malaekahana proper is a narrow coastal strip with a wide sandy beach, without facilities or fresh water. Avoid in the rainy season.

You wade up to your waist to reach the island and you need to wear tennis shoes to avoid cutting your feet. Because of these deterrents, you'll probably be in secluded skinny-dipping heaven when you do reach the island. It has two fine beaches facing the mainland, and its 18 acres are covered with ironwood, sea grape and grassy cover for the sea birds that nest. Its better beach is 300 yards long and 25 yards deep with a gentle lagoon of good sand. Note: Goat Island is sometimes closed due to hatching—phone ahead.

Camping allowed without a permit. Nearby lodging is in Laie, a Mormon community, at the Laniloa Lodge, or in the Kuilima Hotel at Kahuku a few miles north.

☞ Malaekahana State Recreation Area is in the northeast of Oahu—only two miles north of the Polynesian Cultural Center. The #52 bus, Kaneohe-Wahiawa, runs from the Ala Moana shopping center near Waikiki to Malaekahana. From the parking lot, walk south on the beach 1/4 mile to Kalanai Point. It's only 250 yards to ford here. Be sure to walk straight out!

KANEANE BEACH

Kaneane Beach, at Makaha, has become the unofficial clothes-optional beach on the western coast of Oahu. With few users on weekdays, even Makaha Beach itself gets some nude use. Although Kaneane Beach is not too good for swimming it is secluded, nearly deserted, and great for sunbathing and shelling.

☞ Park across from Kaneane Cave, where "car thieves" is written on a rock. Walk down a small path that starts next to the rock for 20 yards to the ocean and then 20 yards to the left.

An alternative nearby site for discreet isolated nudity is Kaena Point. From Yokahama Bay, take the rugged 2 mile road leading up to a satellite station above the point. Park at the 'Y' and walk 50 minutes to sand dunes and wading pools. Road access is difficult; 4WD is suggested.

HAWAII (BIG ISLAND)

HONOKOHAU BEACH

A popular unclad bathing site, beginning from the ancient Hawaiians—now the only public beach in the area, and soon to

Leif Heilberg, Waterfall at Kapaa, Kauai Island.

Leif Heilberg, The Next Generation, Hawaii.

be a major National Park Service center for culture and recreation. With its pond and lush grasses behind the beach, the sloping sands to the water along a half-mile crescent, and nearby Queen's Baths, Honokohau Beach is a pleaser and often appears in photography. Easy access, nude users outnumber clothed. Worth a swim too.

☞ North from Kailua on the "airport" road. Or south from Keahole Kailua-Kona Airport. Turn to the sea on the Honokohau Harbor Road. Now keep bearing right until you dead-end, more or less, on a bumpy dirt road just past Kona Marina. Follow the main road circumventing the marina. A sign points to the beach as well as "NB" painted on rocks along the road. Park, lock, and take the grassy trail that leads north to the beach.

AINALANI GARDENS

Two guest cottages on the secluded property of a small coffee plantation where nude living is possible. Fine sea view, sauna, hot tub, sundeck, lush foliage, and a short trip to Honokohau. Contact Jim and Carolyn Wallace, P.O. Box 419, Honaunau, HI 96726.

SOUTH LYDGATE BEACH

South end is best for nudity as the showers and restrooms are at the north end. Five minutes from South Kapaa hotels; restaurants you can walk to.

☞ Turn off Route 56 onto Leho Road, then take the first right off (if traveling north) or first left (if traveling south on Route 56) to get onto Nehe Road. Follow Nehe Road beyond the end of the paving and to the beach; there turn right (south) on the last track before the sands, and park at the beach, without getting stuck.

GREEN SAND BEACH

Take a day to drive and explore—or skip this 100 yards of olive-green sand below towering volcanic cliffs near the southernmost point of the U.S. The undertow is rough, with strong waves.

☞ It's 61 miles south from the Kona airport to the South Point sign where you turn and go to Land's End. At 300 yards before that point, take the left fork to a boat ramp. Park, and prepare to hike an hour to the east. Only 4WDs can drive this track to the high volcanic cliff overlooking the ocean.

KEHENA BEACH

Pronounced keh-HEH-nuh (if you get lost and need to ask), Kehena Beach has sunning, swimming, bodysurfing, snorkeling, fishing, beach surfing, some windsurfing, and scuba activity. Frequent sightings of whales, dolphins, sea turtles. Good anytime. A lava flow from Kilauea in 1955 created its black sand, shaped by the waves and weather.

Note: the Kalani Honua Center is only 3 miles away on Route 137. Food and showers available also at Harry K. Brown Park at Kalapana, just down the road on Route 130 from the Route 137 turnoff. Kalapana with its painted church is famous Old Hawaii. Be sure to ask where the latest lava flow is, you may be astonished. Complete the day at the Steam Vents?

☞ Take Route 130 south for 30 miles from Hilo; you must do almost a U-turn into Route 137 on your left as you reach the coast. If you get to Kalapana you've gone too far, turn around and go back to Route 137. At 4 miles from Route 130, mile-marker 19, park, descend the easily negotiable footpath about 125 yards northeast to the 'Scenic View' parking atop the sea cliff. At the beach go left (northeast).

PAHOA STEAM VENTS

South of Hilo, in the Puna District. The rising steam from several small cones or hills in the woods is visible from the highway. Remember to bring some wash-off water in gallon jugs. Best time to go is dawn or evenings; daytime is much too hot.

☞ Going south from Hilo for 22 miles on Route 130, about 3 miles south of Pahoa is a "scenic point" turnoff. Three short trails lead from the roadside to the last cinder cone. Climbing it, you'll discover a bi-level natural sauna! The Natural Food Store in the center of Pahoa may provide updates on naturist sites.

KALANI HONUA

This intercultural retreat and conference center offers arts and cultural events, also opportunity, near Kehena Beach, to live more naturally with clothes-optional occasions at the Retreat. Community kitchen, bath in each lodge, 20 lush acres, sauna, 24-meter pool, jacuzzi, arts and crafts, yoga, dance, bicycling. Send for brochure.

☞ Access from Hilo is restricted due to lava. New access is from Pahoa to Pohoiki, taking a right on Route 137 southwest to Kehena.

MAUI

IAO NEEDLE

Minutes from the main Maui airport, the Iao Needle parkland offers nude relaxation if you wander off from the beaten path. Give yourself time. The 2,250 foot volcanic spire towers over streams and ferny paths.

☞ From Iao Needle parking, walk past the restrooms to where two rivers join, then take the left fork upstream a quarter mile to pools where the nude bathers gather.

LITTLE MAKENA BEACH

Located on sunny south Maui with good bodysurfing and a view of migrating

Jerry Derbyshire, Resting Place, Iao Needle, Maui.

whales in season, this is a world class nude beach—an asset for native Hawaiians which many still deprecate. Ongoing legal battle had Little Beach (Puu O Lai in Hawaiian) technically declared illegal, but current reality is tolerance.

Lodging in walking distance at the luxury Maui Prince, or perhaps through Friends of Little Beach, P.O. Box 403, Kihei, HI 96753. The Hong Kong restaurant of Kihei can provide a modestly-priced but tasty meal.

☞ Little Makena Beach is the reward at the end of Route 31. Take it south past the expansive Wailea golf resort complex, and exactly a mile beyond the Maui Prince Hotel make a right turn on a bumpy road to the parking. Walk to the beach and climb the lava formation you'll see down the beach to your right.

WATERFALLS

You'll be greatly assisted in finding waterfalls and other elusive wailele if you'll write the University of Hawaii Press for its "Reference Maps of the Islands of Hawaii" as also its Atlas of Hawaii where dozens of waterfalls are listed by height, volume, and directions. The alternative way to find waterfalls: look for the parked cars!

Nudity is at your risk at waterfalls—with luck you can have a marvelous natural experience. Maui's the island for waterfall delights. The 52-mile, extremely curvey road to Hana is the access. Twin Falls, at Hoolawa Bridge along the notorious Route 36, is the first of a dozen Hana coast waterfalls. Follow the marked paths.

HANA: RED SAND BEACH

Located on Maui's east coast on Kaihalulu Bay south of Kauiki Head, Red Sand Beach is a well-known site accepted by locals for skinny-dipping. Go before 11 a.m. as later sun is blocked by towering cliffs. A mini-reef creates a fish basin—bring snorkel gear, as well as shoes and a towel against the sharp sand.

☞ Entering Hana from the north on Route 36, take the left fork and follow signs to Hana Bay Park. At the park entrance, take Ua'Kea Road 2 blocks south to the Old Hana School, now labeled "Hana Community Center," on your left. Park. Walk down the dirt road behind the school to a Japanese cemetery. Just before you reach it, find a path descending to the shore. Then walk about 200 yards left and around a point to the coarse volcanic sands of Red Sand Beach.

SEVEN SACRED POOLS

Haleakala is an awesome 10,023 foot volcano. The Seven Sacred Pools are indeed a number of natural stone basins on the southeastern slope of Haleakala National Park. Rains cascade from one to the next from Oheo Gulch to the sea. The ascent takes 45 minutes at 25 mph on a narrow, winding, bumpy road ($3 entrance fee). Plan to spend a full day, getting there early in the morning for the best opportunity to skinny-dip. Be sure to leave while there's still light if your return trip on the Hana Highway is long—it's not wise to drive the highway after dark.

Advance reservations can guarantee lodging in one of 12 cabins at the Waianapanapa State Park. Located in Hana, the cabins rent for $12 with a five-day limit. Reservations: Division of Parks, P.O. Box 1049, Wailuku, Hawaii 96793; (808) 243-5354.

☞ Drive to Kipahula,15 miles beyond Hana. Skinny-dippers seclude themselves in the upper pools, and rangers observe the same policy as in all national parks: if the nudity is discreet, it's legitimate.

Another Hana area pool: about a mile past the Hana airport, look for a paved road on the coastal side marked Ulaino. Continue on the road until you reach a stream bed; drive through if the water is low enough. Botanical Garden should be on your right (if visitors are absent, a nude stroll through the gardens is possible). Turn right on a rough, unmarked road. Continue 3 miles, passing homes and crossing more stream beds until you reach the end of the road. Park at the top (parking at the bottom will get you stuck) of the last stream bed and walk a quarter mile across a rocky beach to the waterfall. The pools are well worth the effort. Please remove trash, even if it's not yours.

KAUAI

LIHUE: A SWIMMIN' HOLE

Go to the Old Swimmin' Hole midday for the sun. A small, gentle waterfall with a nice pond and a swing rope. Most people are skinny-dippers, the code is clothing-optional.

☞ Take Route 50 from Lihue toward Koloa. Turn left at Kipu Road, about 3 miles out of Lihue. Stay on Kipu Road's asphalt surface for 1/3 mile, to a fork and go right. Another few minutes bring you to a sign indicating "one-lane bridge." Just before that is a small dirt road going left. Take that for a very short way and park where this road forks. Walk forward about 100 yards and on your right find a path leading down to a rivulet. Hiking up into the rocks you see both the small waterfall, on your right, and to the left a pond about 25 feet below.

DONKEY BEACH

On the east coast, well-known and recommended for nude use by locals. Lovely meadow and ironwood trees lend charm to a long crescent beach with formidable bodysurfing.

☞ Take Route 56 north from Kapaa through Kealia toward Ahahola. At the 11 mile-marker the road begins to climb slowly, then descend. At the end of the descent, just before the 12 mile-marker, is a cane plantation road on the right. Take this road, bear right and watch for Donkey Beach on the left within 1/2 mile.

If the cane road is barred, leave your car on the south side of the foot highway bridge. There is a short trail to the east that starts behind the metal guardrail and climbs a moderate hill until it hits a cane field. Along the edge of the cane field is a level cane road toward the beach. At the end of the cane road you'll find several paths leading to the beach. The beach is slightly south of where you exit the cane field.

SECRET BEACH

Secret, also known as Kauapea Beach: its 300 foot protective cliff lurches from the sand. A stream cascades down its slope. Elsewhere, fresh water flows from the lava rocks, slacking thirst. High, even excessive surf—anyone less than expert at swimming should choose the south end of the beach. Most visitors are nude and you can walk a half mile. Interesting tidal pools at the western end. There's an excellent view across the waters to the NaPali cliffs. It's said the wimps who won't risk the Kalalau Trail do come here to admire it!

In winter months, the east end of the beach disappears but nude use continues on the west end, where there is plenty of beach for everyone.

☞ From Kapaa take Route 56 northwest to Kilauea. Just beyond the 23 mile-marker you turn abruptly right at the Shell station, and 100 feet forward turn left onto Kilauea Road. From the Shell station it is 1.35 miles to hardtop Kauapea Road on your left. Locals park about 1/4 mile east, before the private driveway marked #2860-G. Follow path to the beach.

Alternate access: continue past the Kilauea Shell station on Route 56. About

1 mile later, just before the road to the Kalihiwai Beach, is a dirt road on the right; take it. At the last, almost 90 degree, right turn, the road descends rapidly to the bottom of the hill. Park in the lot and follow the steep trail to the beach. Heavy rains can turn both the trail and parking lot to deep mud—best to have 4WD.

TUNNELS BEACH

The Zodiac boat to the NaPali Coast departs from Tunnels Beach, itself now a fine nude beach!

☞ Take Route 56 along the north coast, through Hanalei Bay Village. About 0.9 miles past Charo's Restaurant is a tree with a red stripe (near mile post 8—the tree is hard to find, traveling west, but can easily be seen going back east). Turn right, then left, and park. Follow the fence about 100 feet to the beach and turn right. Scuba and snorkeling along the reef. Nude use just beyond the concrete blocks, a 3 minute walk.

HANALEI BEACH

This is a small beach just beyond the Hanalei Colony Surf Resort. Swimming and snorkeling are probably the best on Kauai—unique in the area.

☞ Continue north from Hanalei on Route 56 to mile-marker 36. About 4/10 mile further, turn right into a narrow dirt road through the jungle to the beach. The nude area starts to the north (left) and continues about 150 yards.

KEE BEACH

Kee Beach is our trailhead to the NaPali Coast. It's also an in–and–out Eden, for those who cannot hike for a full day into Kalalau Valley and yet won't wear a bathing costume as now demanded by rangers at the nearer, daytrip NaPali Beach. Indeed, at Kee Beach you can swim nude out to a coral reef, explore a cave with its own clear stream, or hike east a short way to Haena Beach Park (take your sneakers).

☞ Located at the very end of Route 56. Park at the Kalalau trailhead, then walk east along the shore about 3 blocks, around a point.

NAPALI COAST: KALALAU BEACH

On the NaPali Coast, this is the Paradise of paradise. Shielded from conventional tourists by 12 very difficult miles of trekking—often along with a 1,000 foot cliff face, slippery with mud when it rains, as it frequently does—the NaPali Coast is not forgiving of the idle mind. It's located on the northwest edge of the 553 square miles of Kauai. You need a state parks permit, good shoes, water, a complete food provision and other supplies.

The reward: unbelievable green sculptured cliffs, wild goats scampering amid a rainbow of blues, violets and orange blossoms.

Camping is permitted at Hanakoa, Hanakapiai and Kalalau beaches; permit required. Discreet nudity occurs along the trail but is mainly confined to the camping area at Kalakau and the far end of the beach. Hang gliding, sea kayaking and hiking are among the activities available in the area. This hike is not an off-the-cuff decision! *Hiking Kauai* by Robert Smith is recommended.

☞ Begin hiking at Kee Beach, at the end of Route 56. But let's get serious: begin by writing for a map, regulations and permit for "Kalalau Trail." Address: Dept. of Land & Natural Resources, Division of State Parks, Box 1671, Lihue, HI 96766. Phone (808) 245-4444.

MAHALAPU BEACH

A long, beautiful beach east of Poipu on the south coast. Low midweek use; a little hard to find. Tidal pools, cliffs, shade trees. Bring drinking water, watch for strong water current. The east end of the beach is best for naturist use and a 5 minute hike eastward over a rocky promontory leads to another isolated bay with a sandy beach, very suitable for nuding. The island capital of Lihue is only 30 minutes away.

☞ Take the cane road at the end of Poipu Road. Pass the turnoff to Shipwreck Beach and follow the cane road east, passing all narrow dirt roads until you see one that looks wide and well-traveled. Take a right onto this road and proceed east until you pass a quarry on the right. At the next intersection, turn right and head toward the water. You can turn right or left at the end of the road, and go to either the east or west end of the beach. The drive covers about 2 1/2 miles and should take about 1/4 hour.

POLIHALE STATE PARK

A beautiful beach on the southwest tip of Kauai—with moderate clothed use close to the parking lot, and beach buggies to intrude on privacy. Unbelievably hot; bring water, and perhaps a beach umbrella as there is no shade. The sea is splendid. Many dunes provide secluded off-beach hideaways. The sign warning against nudity is still up, unmolested and often disregarded. The southward expanse of this beach is not established as nude—it's just so huge you won't meet anybody. Both ends have considerable use by people cruising in pickups; don't leave valuables in your car. Camping at the north end. Strong currents in winter make swimming unsafe.

☞ At the western end of Route 50 you'll find the state park. Leave the highway at the sign pointing left to Polihale. Take the 15 minute drive down the unimproved road (muddy when wet) to the huge tree with an attached sign pointing right to the state park. (This road is longer, bumpier and will lead to a clothed beach with facilities.) Instead, turn left. After a short drive you'll come to a turnoff to the right, leading to a parking area. The area is much more private, with people spaced several thousand feet apart.

KEKAHA BEACH PARK

On Kauai's southwest coast, west from Kekaha and extending miles and miles, is a beautiful, open and unshaded beach beside the highway, largely invisible to automobiles. Many turnoffs will take you in. It gets low use in midweek. Not used by the locals. As the road runs along the beach for a stretch, nude use is best by the Barking Sands Missle Range boundary.

MOLOKAI

MOLOKAI

Hawaii's "country island" is losing its virginity to a Japanese developer. Tokyo Kosan has acquired the five miles of shore fronting the Kaluakoi Hotel & Gulf Club as well as the 2 1/2 miles of Papohaku Beach, the longest white sand beach in the state. (The beach is great but swimming is dangerous due to the strong undertow.)

Most naturists have gone to the 1/2 mile of secluded coves and tidal pools along the shore of the golf course north of the Kepuli Sheraton, at the east end of the island. Best are the coves just north of the last hole of the gulf course. Or double back east on the road to the Sheraton, and take the cutoff northwesterly to a small county park, further upshore to the north.

The less expensive hotels on Molokai are rustic: Hotel Moloaki (800-367-8047, car package available); and the companion Pau Hana Inn (same phone), situated on a lagoon useless for swimming.

Top: Leif Heilberg, Little Beach, Maui. Bottom: Honokohau Beach

Top: Leif Heilberg, Yoga at Honokohau Beach, Big Island. Bottom: Beachball at Honokohau Beach.

IDAHO

Idaho shelters more "unimproved" (translation: natural, noncommercial, clothes-optional) hot springs on public lands than do the other northwest states taken together. Rafting remains the readiest way to reach many of the hot springs, as they're often hard by the wild and scenic rivers and distant from the roads. Rafting is also a tremendous rush and the Forest Service confessed that there is hardly a Salmon River raft trip that's not naked.

MISSOULA AREA

JERRY JOHNSON HOT SPRINGS

Missoula is across the Idaho border in Montana. Legendary Jerry Johnson Hot Springs flows out of a mound of minerals of its own making at the fabulous rate of 450 gallons per minute. The 115°F water runs into crudely formed boulder tubs, where it mingles with icy waters from Warm Springs Creek. Hence, part of you can be parboiled while the rest is chilled—a stimulating experience. Most seem to choose to soak seated, moving from cooler to warmer mixes, though some like to take an icy plunge for variation. You can camp nearby; evening soaking is popular; year-round use.

☞ Jerry Johnson is located off US 12, 20 miles into Idaho from the Montana border. Find the Warm Springs Park bridge trailhead a half mile west of mile-marker 152. Hike 1 mile southeast on Forest Service Road 49 to the first set of pools, which will be down an embankment to your right; shallower pools are 100 feet further up.

BOISE NATIONAL FOREST

MIDDLE FORK OF THE PAYETTE RIVER

An adventure bouncing along the back roads, then hiking and fording a river several times, will bring you to the hot springs—Moon Dipper, Pine Burl, Bull Creek—which await the deliciously weary traveler on the south bank of Dash Creek before they spill into the Middle Fork of the Payette River. Each has primitive rock and log pools which allow you to mix cold river water with the hot mineral water.

☞ Purchase a Boise National Forest map at any ranger station and follow Forest Service Road 698 north from Crouch to Trail Creek Campground and the Boiling Springs USFS guard station (20 miles of unpaved road). From here hike north for 2 miles on a clear but unmarked path along the river to where the springs appear on the map. Wear shoes that can get wet.

VULCAN HOT SPRINGS

The boiling hot creek is tamed to a mere 105°F in a soak reservoir behind a log dam on the South Fork of the Salmon River. From Cascade, take Forest Service Road 22 to FSR 474 and travel south 7 miles (a mile past Stolle Meadows) to Vulcan Hot Springs unofficial camping. Park, hike 1 mile west to the springs.

MOLLY'S TUBS & HOT SPRINGS

Same as road to Vulcan Hot Springs. From Forest Service Road 22, along South Fork of the Salmon River, turn south on gravel FSR 474 for 1.3 miles to a pullout on the right. Hike down to several tubs. For Molly's Hot Springs, go south another half mile to intersection with road heading east to Warm Lake. Park here and hike west on blocked road for 300 yards, cross bridge, take a right on unmarked path for 100 yards.

CHATANOOGA HOT SPRINGS

A large, sand-bottomed pool at the base of a thermal cascade amid spectacular scenery enjoyed by a well-established group of nude users. From Boise take Route 21 north 15 miles. Turn right onto Forest Service Road 268 and continue to Atlanta, about 35 miles. Hot springs are located 1/2 mile past Riverside Campground. Park in the area at the top of the cliff.

BONNEVILLE HOT SPRINGS

The Hot Springs Gazette (12 S. Benton, Helena, MT 59601) rates Bonneville Hot Springs five stars. Spring temperatures to 180°F mix with cold creek water. Year-round use. Twenty miles east of Lowman, off Highway 21: the 1/4 mile trail begins on the north side of the Bonneville Campground.

ILLINOIS

LAKE MICHIGAN

ILLINOIS BEACH STATE PARK

South of the nuclear plant at Zion are 3 miles of sand dunes—not high, but unusual for having survived developers—which are the reason for this state park. Sunbathing is traditional in the attractive natural setting of the Dead River mouth at the far southern end of the park. Park police generally do not hassle the sunbathers in the dunes or as they take a brisk dip in the lake—but the conservation area just south of the Dead River is strictly forbidden.

☞ Illinois Beach State Park is clearly indicated on signs along highways I-94, 41 and 173 near the Wisconsin border. Drive east to Lake Michigan and the park entrance. When you are almost at the shore, a fork to the right will take you south to the lodge. Park your car here or just south, at the Interpretive Center. Then walk south for about 20 minutes, either along the shore dunes or the Bobolink Trail that originates behind the Center lot and follows the course of Dead River to Lake Michigan.

WOODLOT NATURIST RETREAT

Eugene Gall's 20 secluded acres ("Not for profit, just for fun!") provide a wildlife refuge, waterfall and 1.5-acre spring-fed pond. Tent and RV sites, no hookups. If cooking, bring grill briquettes. The main house has a sauna and heated pool in a 20' x 30' attached greenhouse with fireplace room that accommodates up to 30 guests. Horseshoes, volleyball, spacious sunning lawn. Couples, families only. Hour from The Loop, 5 miles from Woodstock Conference Center. 14609 Nelson Road, Woodstock, IL 60098. Phone (815) 338-5949.

☞ Two miles north of Woodstock on Route 47, turn west on Charles Road (overhead stoplight), for 2 miles, then left on Nelson Road for 1/2 mile to Woodlot Retreat over a mailbox.

CHICAGO SUN CLUB

Chicago Sun Club schedules health club, social, and lakeside activities. SASE to P.O. Box 853, Chicago Heights, IL 60411.

MOLINE AREA

BLUE LAKE COUNTRY CLUB

Wooded 20 acres, Rock River Valley. Motel and tent/trailer sites, lake, volleyball, rec hall, snack bar, whirlpool. May–October. P.O. Box 13, Erie, IL 61250. Phone (309) 659-9297.

INDIANA

Some athletic events do not invite promotion by a beer or cigarette merchandiser, a university or city. The Purdue Nude Olympics is such an event. On what is estimated to be the coldest day of the year in Lafayette, undergrads—male and female—burst from their dorm rooms at Cary Quadrangle to race nude around the sidewalk of Spitzer Court. The winners of the Nude Olympics stay the course the longest. Although the Nude Olympics streak goes back to 1957, Purdue took harsh measures in the late '80s—yet failed to stop the Olympics. Hoosier engineers have thick skins.

SOUTHERN

HOOSIER NATIONAL FOREST

Blackwell Lake. From Bloomington take Route 446 southeast 12.5 miles to Tower Ridge Road. (Sign: Maumee Reservation Boy Scout Camp.) Turn left (east), drive 0.3 miles to Blackwell Lake; turn right at sign, park.

Terril Ridge Pond. Continue past Blackwell Lake another 6.3 miles and park at Hickory Ridge Lookout Tower on the left. Hike 1.7 miles through wilderness on fire trail to visit Terril Ridge Pond, the site of the 1984 regional Rainbow Tribe gathering.

Grouse Hollow Lake is new, as is the access. Cozy, surrounded by forest, a camper's paradise. No facilities. The most promising skinny-dipper site in the Hoosier National Forest. From Bloomington, take Route 446 southeast 15.3 miles, turn left on Hunter Creek Road (just over county line), immediately turn right and travel 1.2 miles to road L4E7N and turn left. Drive 3.2 miles to parking on left; hike 0.5 miles to lake.

The vast Charles C. Deam Federal Wilderness Area will be preserved unspoiled in the Hoosier National Forest. Numerous small lakes and unpolluted streams await those who venture into this wooded hill country. Excellent sites abound. Full naturist exploration of the 13,000 acres will be facilitated with Allens Creek and Elkinsville quadrangle maps ($1.50 each) from US Geological Survey Office at Indiana University, Bloomington. (By mail from Indiana Dept. of Natural Resources, Indianapolis, IN 46204.)

SAUNDERS QUARRY

A classic stone quarry with sunning rocks. Take South Walnut out of Bloomington. When Walnut branches into a 'Y,' take the left onto Country Club Road and go up the hill, merging into Old Walnut. Continue 2 miles and turn left at the 'T' intersection. You will see Bloomington Speedway on your left and you should be on Fairfax Road. Take Fairfax 2-3 miles and go up a long hill. As you head down the hill, you will see a small turnout on the right and a path that leads to the quarry. Don't park on the road shoulder (over 200 people were towed in 1990). Follow the path until you see a few deep quarries on the right. The path will 'Y.' To the right is the famous quarry in the movie "Breaking Away," which is textiled. Follow the left branch of the 'Y' and you will come to another quarry, called Ray Hole. There is a road to the left which will take you to the water. The second left is where the best sunning area is.

TRI-STATE COUNTRY CLUB

A scenic getaway for the Indiana, Ohio or Kentucky naturist happy with a tent and the great outdoors. Above-ground pool, rec hall, community kitchen, tent and trailer sites and cabins. No pets or cameras. May–Sept. R.R. 1, Box 198, Bennington, IN 47011. Phone (812) 427-3914.

FERN HILLS CLUB

About 7 miles from Bloomington with 70 acres, tent and RV sites, pool, sauna, volleyball, rec hall. May–October. 7339 S. Rockport Road, Bloomington, IN 47401. Phone (812) 824-4489.

LOTHLORIEN NATURE SOCIETY

Ninety-two acres of forest preserve, miles of winding pathways, camping, ceremonial grounds, circle fires, solar showers and no electricity, a culture refuge for nature religions—and "not for an exclusive few. We share the sanctuary with all who live the peaceful path of harmony…One may skinny-dip or sunbathe without hassle. If you wish to hold a play, play a tune, celebrate a season, or howl at the moon, it's okay with us. We're especially interested in experimenting with alternative and ecologically sound lifestyles." Best time to get acquainted is at one of several festivals at Lothlorien. Membership otherwise required. P.O. Box 1082, Bloomington, IN 47402. Phone (812) 332-0048, Mon.–Sat. 12–6 p.m.

CENTRAL

SUNSHOWER COUNTRY CLUB

Near Indianapolis. Tent and RV sites, pool, volleyball, playground, rec room. May–October. 3039 Mattie Harris Road, Centerville, IN 47330. Phone (317) 855-2785.

NORTHERN

LAKE MICHIGAN: INDIANA DUNES

Sixty miles east of Chicago are 12,000 acres of clean, sometimes dramatic dunes among wetlands, administered by the Indiana and national parks systems. US 12, I-94, Route 49 and the Indiana Toll Road bring you into the area.

Mount Baldy is the nicest, most accessible nude beach in the Chicago to South Bend area. Mobs of clothed visitors are making nude use more chancy. Weekends are a poor time to go unless in a group and well north toward the NIPSCO generating station—the only way to go. Nudity after dark is the choice of many. A lot of skinny-dipping also occurs from boats in the area. Most clothed visitors stay close to the main dune. From the NPS parking lot at US 12 and Kemil Road, walk a full mile toward the power plant. Find the small bay with rocks convenient for swimming.

Kemil Road Beach is in a wildlife refuge with few patrols or sunbathers, north of the federal Visitor Center. Little parking, so you may want to bike. Cross west over state park line to out of sight of the guarded beach, and look out for boaters and beachcombers.

Bailly Beach. Pristine dunes backed by woods; no hassle, few visit. Bordered by Cowles Bog on the south, Bailly Generating Station on the west, and the Town of Dune Acres on the east. The only access is by boat—or a long trek on the Cowles Bog Trail, starting from guard station at entrance to Dune Acres. Park at corner of US 12 and Mineral Springs Road. You can also get there by taking the South Shore Line, from Chicago or South Bend, and ask to get off at Mineral Springs Road. The Line will also pick you up. Stay well west of the nearest homes in Dune Acres. Remove your litter, bring your own water.

SUNNY HAVEN RECREATION PARK

A relaxing, family-oriented spot in the South Bend area. Heated pool, sauna, volleyball, weekly social activities, teen clubhouse, archery range and restaurant. RV, tent and trailer sites. P.O. Box 95, Granger, IN 46530. Phone (219) 277-5356.

LAKE O' THE WOODS CLUB

An hour from Chicago, 200 wooded acres with 26-acre lake, water sports, volleyball, hiking, camping, sauna, rec room. Open year-round. P.O. Box 53-WG, Valparaiso, IN 46383. Phone (219) 464-4894.

IOWA

SOUTHWEST

GLENWOOD SANDPIT

A private pond with wooded grove to block the view; used for years with minimal problems. From Council Bluffs drive south on I-29 to exit 35 (Glenwood). Take the gravel road on the west side of the Interstate south for 2 miles to the stop sign. Go left for 1/2 mile. The sandpit is on the right. Take the road around to the west and south sides, which the skinny-dippers use.

John Kramer/SOBEK. Middle Fork Boatmen, Idaho.

KANSAS

TOPEKA AREA

PRAIRIE HAVEN

Thirty wooded acres, tent and RV sites with hookups, community kitchen, gazebo hot tub, heated pool, lighted volleyball and tennis courts. April–October. Route 1, Box 169-WG, Scranton, KS 66537. Phone (913) 793-2738.

CENTRAL

LAKE MARION (Marion Reservoir and Wildlife Area)

Located east of McPherson between Hillsboro and Marion on Route 56, Marion Reservoir and Wildlife Area has miles of largely unvisited shoreline and offers all the coves you need for perfecting an all-over tan. Recommended is the northwest end of the lake; the shoreline is surrounded by dense woods. A boat is needed to reach the out-of-the-way spots, and boat rentals are available at most Lake Marion accesses. Off-road parking is illegal and you're expected to take your trash home (thus, no trash cans available).

SANDY LANE CLUB

Weekends only, 7 miles from Hutchinson. Forty acres, pool, tent and RV sites, cabin. Guests welcomed to groomed grounds in a catalpa grove. P.O. Box 1866-WG, Hutchinson, KS 67504. Phone (316) 543-2645.

Durand Stieger, Girl With Bible.

KENTUCKY

EASTERN

RED RIVER GORGE

Eastern Kentucky is graced by the large wilderness tracts of Daniel Boone National Forest. The many trails, seclusion and scenery of Red River Gorge, near Lombard, offer naturist delights to the discreet woodsperson following in the tracks of Boone, who himself never wore a stitch when enjoying a dip. Do use with caution and pick up before leaving.

☞ Entering the Gorge from the Nada Tunnel, follow the paved road to the bridge at the Powell-Menifee county line. Immediately after the bridge a gravel road turns off to the left (County Road 1067, if you have a map). Take it. Likely spots begin almost immediately, for a fallen tree 0.4 miles up the road prevents canoes from reaching the points beyond, guaranteeing you a relaxing cove.

CENTRAL

GREEN RIVER LAKE STATE PARK

Many coves where you may tie up a boat and be au naturel. Camp-sites on upper west shore. Southeast of Campbellsville; several roads off Highway 55 lead to lake.

Peter Simon, In the Vineyard.

WESTERN

LAND BETWEEN THE LAKES

Kentucky has many backcountry sites where a girl and her fellow can skinny-dip, but the best-established nude water-recreation area in the state lies along the many miles of shoreline of the Land Between the Lakes, extending nearly 50 miles along either side of Route 49 between Padacah and Fort Donelson, Tennessee. Murray State University students are the Daniel Boones of this area.

JOE FORD NATURE CENTER

Discreet nude use occurs at the Joe Ford Nature Center of Owensboro. This is not a naturist park; however, the wooded grounds include two ponds and nature trails perfect for solitary strolls or bird-watching.

LOUISIANA

SOUTHEAST

INDIAN HILLS

A pleasant, relaxed 50-acre nudist resort in Sidell, northeast of New Orleans. Pond, pool, whirlpool, volleyball, hiking trails, paddleboats, fishing, arts and crafts, playground. RV, tent and trailer sites. Families, singles welcomed. Box 2484, Covington Highway, Slidell, LA 70460. Phone (504) 641-9998 or 899-0215.

LA PINES RANCH

An hour from New Orleans across Lake Pontchartrain. Pool, whirlpool, rec hall, community kitchen, laundromat, playground, volleyball, shuffleboard. Tent and RV sites, rental trailers. P.O. Box 21-WG, Lacombe, LA 70445. Phone (504) 882-5662.

LAST ISLAND

Last Island, *L'isle derniere*, is really a series of barrier islands that stretch westward from the west end of the New Orleans beach frontage, all the way to Morgan City. Perhaps once it was a single island, but cuts made by storms have created a chain, the best of which for getting clothes-free are Coon Point, Whiskey Pass, and Coupe Coline. You can put your boat in at Cocdrie or another bayou. If you're a fisherman, or good fishing could interest you, this is the water for speckled trout and redfish. The islands are about 8 miles out. Bring everything you'll need; nothing is there but the sand, the sun and sea.

SOUTH CENTRAL

NATURAL CAJUN PLACE

Seven miles from New Iberia, Natural Cajun Place offers tent and RV sites, pool, volleyball, bayou fishing, hookups, showers, laundromat and community kitchen. Convenient to Avery Island Jungle Gardens and Bird Sanctuary, US Experimental Farm. Route 6, Box 520-WG, New Iberia, LA 70560. Phone (318) 364-0949.

SOUTHWEST

BUNDICK LAKE

Straight north from Lake Charles, Bundick Lake is 15 miles southeast from De Ridder. Camping is free; remove your trash. Ample parking. Maintain a low profile, and enjoy nature at its best.

☞ Take Route 171 south from De Ridder for 7 miles. Turn left (east) on Route 394, direction of Dry Creek, and go 13 miles past the Bundick Lake Recreation Area, to the turnoff (left) just beyond the lake. Follow this spur 1/8 mile to the spillway. Go on to the end of hard surface and the creek turns left. Continue north for 100 yards on the dirt road. The creek turns right here, with a large sandbar. Numerous coves and secluded areas to be found downstream.

SHREVEPORT AREA

HAMELS MEMORIAL PARK

The Red River divides Shreveport and Bossier City. From downtown Shreveport the Clyde Fant Parkway runs along the Red River to the southeast outskirts. Nearby this terminus is Hamels Memorial Park. From the highway you can see it on your right but you don't see the river bank. Seclusion has made the park popular with both clothed and unclothed bathers. In the summer months you have a choice of sunning spots along the riverbank and even on sandbars; most of the nude bathers go to the north end and past the hills.

Peter Simon, At the Pond.

MAINE

Maine delights the canuder or hiker with the feeling of breeze and sun on naked skin. The rocky shoreline is great for basking. We've provided a few social settings and backcountry destinations; the explorer will not be limited by these suggestions.

Information on the ever-changing possibilities of Maine: Maine Coast Solar Bares, P. O. Box 262, Thomaston, ME 04861.

PORTLAND AREA

CASCO BAY

Casco Bay is enjoyed for nude sailing and so are other waters away from Portland Harbor and the islands immediately outside the harbor.

MT. DESERT ISLAND

DUCK BROOK

Known also as Bare Ass Depot (B.A.D.). Regular users each spring rebuild a rock dam below a natural pool in Duck Brook. Pool can reach 8 feet deep when dam is well-built, but in late season the water sinks low. Small falls where water enters pool. Midday use is best for sunlight and warmth.

☞ Drive from Bar Harbor's Main Street on Route 3 towards Hulls Cove. After 0.4 miles Route 3 crosses Route 233. Stay on Route 3 (it goes right at this junction) for 0.2 miles to where grass islands split the road. Turn left between the two islands, go 0.6 miles to first right after passing the gates marking the park boundary. Turn right, go down road under the stone bridge to the first curve left. On the right you'll find a 2-car turnout. If full, continue on to stone bridge at old pumphouse and park. From the turnout, take the old logging road that starts here, to another well-used trail going left to Duck Brook. (Stay on the most-used trail. There is a cutoff trail to right leading to B.A.D. annex pool). From the stone bridge, walk along the gravel carriage road (no cars), north to just before it starts to veer slightly left (west), where you'll find a trail to the right leading down the hill to the brook. Halfway down, it forks; easiest descent is to right.

LAKE WOOD

In Acadia National Park, a sunwarmed, naked-granite beach, sloping to the warmest freshwater lake on the island. Look for blueberries in August.

☞ From Main Street and Route 3 in Bar Harbor, follow Route 3 for 3 miles to Hulls Cove. Turn east, inland, on Crooked Road. The Acadian Restaurant is 50 feet south of this intersection, with the Cove Motel on the west side. Drive 7 miles, past the gravel pit/quarry to 2 lefts just after the gravel pit, and take the second left. There's a semi-concealed park sign here indicating day use only. This road starts rough, gets better. Drive 0.3 miles to developed parking, or park on grass.

Leave no valuables in car. A maintained trail leads from the parking area to clothed swim area. For nude area, walk clockwise to left around lake, either at shore or on grassy ridge above (trail starts at grassy parking). Ledges for nude sunning and leaping are 1/2 mile easy hike halfway down east side of lake. On private property but no one complains.

Need lodging? The American Youth Hostel in Bar Harbor accepts all ages. June 16–August 31. Phone (207) 288-5587.

LONG POND

Also called Great Pond. Rowboat and canoe rental to access the coves, or skinny-dip as you hike around the pond. Easily found on maps.

NORTHERN

MOOSEHEAD LAKE

Bare backpacking, canuding. US Forest Service maps include camp-sites. We draw your attention to Spencer Bay but in general, sites which are remote and show only one or two tables ensure a low population.

Bud Godsol, Canuding On Flagstaff Lake, Maine.

MARYLAND

MARYLAND SHORE

ASSATEAGUE STATE PARK

Assateague Island appears perilously at risk from rowdy recreational sprawl at Ocean City. A more apt breed of shore visitors are the Naturists. Ecologically aware of impact and alert to stop misbehavior, Naturists have been a boon to coastal administrators.

☞ From Baltimore and Salisbury take Route 80 east. At Ocean City West turn right on Route 611 and cross bridge to Assateague Island and continue straight east to State Beach paved parking with showers and concession stand. $3 entry fee. Walk to main beach, then to the left at least 1 mile north of McCabe ranger station/guest house before taking it all off, which brings you within the northern segment of Assateague Island National Seashore. Stay near the ocean. Camping is $18 per night at state park, phone (301) 641-1441.

ANNAPOLIS AREA

CHESAPEAKE BAY

Citizens of several states congregate to skinny-skipper their craft on the relatively calm waters of this giant bathtub. Taking your values to sea may be the best solution in officially unliberated Middle Atlantic states. Bring along your friends, they'll thank you. But be aware that the saline solution grows more toxic with each year—think before you open your mouth while skinny-dipping from your boat, and join the Naturists concerned to clean up the mess. Save the clams!

PINE TREE ASSOCIATES

Among the largest, oldest East Coast nudist parks. Eighty rolling secluded acres an hour from Washington and Baltimore. Mostly wooded with private cabins. Tent and RV sites, rental rooms, trailers available. Twenty grassy acres for sunning and sports. Heated indoor pool, outdoor pool, tennis, volleyball, shuffleboard, sauna, rec hall. Snack bar in summer. Open year-round. P.O. Box 195-WG, Crownsville, MD 21032. Phone (301) 841-6033 or 261-8787.

BALTIMORE AREA

PATUXENT RIVER

Excellent area for tubing and good sunning spots. Some clothed fishing and canoeing. From Capital Beltway I-495 in MD, take New Hampshire Avenue north (Route 650) to small town of Ashton. Turn right on Sandy Spring Road (Route 108) and go about 2 miles to paved Mink Hollow Road. Turn left and continue to the bridge that crosses the Patuxent River. Park before the bridge (space enough for 2 cars), follow path right (downstream).

Lee Baxandall, Woman With Cigar.

ELK NECK STATE PARK

Crowded with boaters on weekends. Weekdays a few skinny-dippers appear at this coastal park. Low tide is best for walking to privacy down shoreline, past fallen trees.

☞ Reached by I-95 north out of Baltimore for about 50 miles to North East-Rising Sun exit (Route 272), taking 272 south through town of North East about 13 miles to the park entrance (sign on left). Drive Route 272 to 1 mile past swimming/picnic area, and choose one of the unpaved parking spots along road. The last of these is across the road from boat launch. Park, follow footpaths down hill through woods 100 yards to beach. Locate a secluded spot—be discreet!

GUNPOWDER FALLS STATE PARK

All but 300 of the 10,000 acres of Gunpowder Falls State Park remain undeveloped. Nude use is sparse but the potential for frustrated skinny-dippers is excellent. Of note is the area on the Big Gunpowder River just above Prettyboy Reservoir—great swimming and tubing, with waterfalls and rocks for sunning. Local teens stake out the most accessible sites for boozing and whatnot—you should be able to locate some less-accessible seclusion with no problem.

☞ Take I-83 north 15 miles from Baltimore to MD 137 (Hereford exit), then north 2 miles on MD 45 to the river. Or take MD 137 west 1 mile to Masemore Road (on right) and to parking area. Also of interest is Little Gunpowder Falls. Follow MD 147 10 miles northeast from Baltimore, left on Fork Road 2 miles, right on Bottom Road 2 miles to the picnic area. From this access point, scout along the trails. Little Gunpowder is too shallow for tubing or canoeing.

NORTHWEST

PEN MAR CLUB

Sixty-eight country acres with pool, volleyball, playground. Tent and RV sites, showers, community kitchen. May–Sept. weekends. P.O. Box 276-WG, Hancock, MD 21750. Phone (717) 294-3262.

Take time to drive down WV 522 to historic Berkeley Springs State Park, where hot mineral springs are diverted to individual baths, pools and the Old Roman Bath House. Suits required. Phone (304) 258-2711.

CAPE COD & THE ISLANDS

CAPE COD NATIONAL SEASHORE

The National Park Service's only special regulation anywhere to ban nudity—not an offense as such under federal law—doesn't deter thousands of nude bathers annually from seeking their own liberated patch of sand on the Cape.

Many go to the ocean beach of Truro, nearly at Cape tip out Route 6, between Ballston Beach and Long Nook Beach; or for solitude, they walk north from Long Nook Beach. Herring Cove Beach just outside Provincetown also has nude use, much of it gay, and can be reached by foot, bike, or paying NPS daily parking fee.

Need lodging? Horton's Trailer Park & Camping Resort is pleasant and in walking distance of Long Nook Beach. Likewise Truro's American Youth Hostel, where regardless of age, $9 will buy you a night's lodging and use of a community kitchen—phone (508) 349-3889. For a bayside Truro motel complete with friendly advice, Seascape Motor Inn, (508) 487-1225.

SANDY TERRACES

Sandy Terraces owns 10 wooded acres on a spring-fed lake 15 minutes from Hyannis, an hour from the beaches of Truro and Provincetown. Volleyball, tennis, shuffleboard, lake swimming, sauna. Tent and trailer sites; families, couples welcomed.

MARTHA'S VINEYARD

Gay Head Lighthouse. Clay cliffs yield natural pools of clay; soak, daub yourself, but don't be a show-off to casual sightseers on the cliff.

Park in the lot below the lighthouse. Walk back along Moshup Trail and take the first path to right, leading down to the beach. On beach walk right 0.3 miles to secluded nude area beneath the cliffs—or walk left, about a mile, to historically nude Zack's Beach.

Chilmark: Lucy Vincent Beach. This beach, in part zoned nude, is strictly for use of locals and guests of local lodgings.

NANTUCKET: MIACOMET BEACH

Miacomet Beach is the "social nude beach," between Surfside (to the east) and Cisco (to west). Reach it from Surfside Beach by walking to the right (west) past the fences for the bird sanctuary and a bit further. Coming directly from town, bicycle along Atlantic Avenue, noting signs for Surfside Beach, but soon after the High School, find bike path on the right. If you've a car, go on, look for road on right, Miacomet Avenue—do not take it, but a bit further turn right onto a well-maintained dirt road. Go southerly about 1.5 miles. Miacomet Pond will appear on your right, and the road ends at the ocean. You turn left into a small dirt road along the backside of the beach dunes. There are several parking turnouts. Hike through dunes to beach. For more privacy—

Pebble Beach—on the south coast stretching from the old Navy station to the village of Sconset. Reach it with a right off Milestone Road to Sconset, taking Tom Nevers Road to the Navy Station.

Eel Point—on the west side, take Eel Point Road to beyond Dionis Beach, keep walking at end of road, past last beach house, to Eel Point tip.

Nantucket Harbor—offers a wonderful destination for skinny-dipping, the Coatue wildlife refuge of low dunes on the Sound that protects Nantucket harbor. Go by sailboat or 4WD (getting a sand permit) by way of Wauwinet, or from Wauwinet by hiking.

Facing: Peter Simon, Child in Sprinkler.

Ingrid Kemperman/Impact Visuals, Gay Head Beach, Martha's Vineyard.

Madequecham—is a secluded coastal valley near Nantucket Airport. Get an island map (Nantucket Information Bureau, 25 Federal St.) and bike out to the end of Old South Road, and the old rutted track that continues on to shore will take you into Madequecham Valley. No beach stickers needed—but respect every "Private Beach" sign and stay out.

Phone (508) 228-0925 for room rentals and (508) 540-2022 for ferry information. Rent bicycles near the ferry wharf (Young's at the steamship wharf is good; no need to reserve).

EASTERN

PEPPERELL SANDBARS

From Ayer, west-northwest of Boston just beyond I-495, take Route 119 north through Groton, then a right on Route 113. Continue to the crossroads in downtown Pepperell at the Town Hall. Get on Park Street and follow it to Brookline Street, turn left and follow it 0.2 miles and take a right on Simmone Street. Watch for a sign for Nissitsit River Wildlife Management Area and park. The river is nearby.

WESTERN

GREENFIELD: GREEN RIVER

☞ Follow I-91 to Greenfield and exit on Route 2A (Main Street) towards Greenfield Center. Cross the Green River Bridge and at Dunkin' Donuts take the first left (Solon Street). This becomes Elm Street at the first light (about 100 yards). Continue on Elm Street to the end, and merge left on Conway Street, which crosses back over I-91, becoming Leyden Road. Continue on Leyden Road until you've gone 5 miles from the Green River Bridge, and find Eunice Williams Road on the left. Follow it as this road twists down past a brick water-pumping station, to the wooden covered bridge, cross it, and climb the twisting road to the top of a steep hill. Here turn right onto Green River Road. After a short distance find a turnoff parking lot on your right. Park and take the steep path to the pools. This is a privately owned site and the owner requires that you help keep it clean. Upriver are more pools.

BIRCH ACRES

Just over the line from New York State. Birch Acres is the only nudist park in the Berkshires; convenient to Pittsfield, Tanglewood, Williamstown. Grassy mountainous setting; mellow, friendly crowd. Volleyball, pool, sauna, tennis, weekend entertainment, organized activities, full restaurant and bar. Tent and trailer sites with hookups. P.O. Box 392-WG, Lanesboro, MA 01237. Phone (413) 738-5968.

HEAVENLY HIDEAWAY

The Heavenly Hideaway is on Goldmine Brook in the Chester–Blanford State Forest—a half mile of tiny cataracts and pools of clear spring water. Because the stream is diminutive it accommodates couples or at most small groups.

Chester-Blanford State Forest Campground is 1/2 mile west on Route 20. A mile beyond that is Sanderson Brook Falls, a 100 foot high cataract thrilling to see in the spring or after a heavy rain but not suitable for unsuited use.

☞ From Westfield, Exit 3 on I-90, the Mass Turnpike, take US Route 20 west, through the town of Russell to the center of Huntington, a distance of approximately 12 miles. From the center of Huntington, go 1.4 miles and pass the Chester/Huntington town line. Go 1.9 miles, passing the main entrance to the Chester-Blandford State Forest which is on the left, and park in a small dirt turnoff on the right, immediately before Route 20 crosses a small cement bridge. Walk across the highway toward the brook, and follow a trail to the left of the brook, heading upstream. The largest pool is the uppermost one, and the best sunning area is 100 yards further up, where a power line crosses the brook and where the brook becomes completely subterranean for several hundred feet. This in itself is an interesting site to see.

POND BROOK FALLS

Pond Brook Falls has a goodly flow of water over tiny cataracts and into potholes even in time of drought—the water is regulated by beaver dams, located in the mountains upstream.

☞ From Westfield—exit 3 on I-90, Mass Turnpike—take US Route 20 west and go 4 1/2 miles crossing the Russell/Westfield town line, and go another mile, and take a left on Route 23

Lee Baxandall, Cape Cod National Seashore.

Massachusetts

Peter Simon, Beach Gymnasts.

west. Go 6 miles to Blandford. From the only flashing yellow light in the center of town, go 2.4 miles on Route 23 west, to Blair Road, a marked dirt road just over the brow of a steep hill on the right. Slow down, and go 1 mile farther to Hiram Blair Road, a nearly invisible, unmarked dirt road on the left. Turn left on Hiram Blair Road, go 1/2 mile, cross a wooden bridge and park immediately after the bridge on the left. Follow the trail downstream a short distance to Pond Brook Falls.

FORTY FOOT POOL & FLUME

Forty Foot Pool and Flume, Huntington, on the East Branch of the Westfield River, is located in small, well-kept Gardner State Park with a sandy beach, large sunning rocks, fireplaces, picnic tables, outhouses, even a small pavillion. Prior to Memorial Day and after Labor Day, the park is sparsely visited and the unclad as well as the clad appear—the former downriver, the clad gravitating upriver. In the spring and after heavy rains the East and West Branches of the Westfield River offer white water rafting and canoeing—a good time to visit.

☞ From Westfield, exit 3 on I-90, the Mass Turnpike, turn south on Route 10 and 202, to US Route 20 west, which is a right turn. Go for 12 miles to the center of Huntington, and turn right on Route 112 north for 2.4 miles. C.M. Gardner State Park is on the left.

KNIGHTVILLE DAM PONDS

Knightville Dam Flood Control and Wildlife Area is a 12 mile wilderness area along the East Branch of the Westfield River, south of Cummington Gorge of George Schulz fame. No camping is allowed but overnight parking is. Pools and sunning areas are just about anywhere one chooses to go, and wildlife abounds, including bald eagles. Knightville lies directly below Chesterfield Gorge, which is still unsuitable for nude use.

☞ To the main pool: from Westfield, take exit 3 on I-90, the Mass Turnpike; turn right, south, on routes 10 and 202. Go to US Route 20 west, which is a right turn. Go for 12 miles to the center of Huntington, and turn right on Route 112, north. Go for 4 miles, past the main entrance which is on the right, and continue north on 112. Cross a long, narrow bridge which is very high above the river, and go up the long hill and across a cement bridge which spans a small brook. Immediately after the bridge, take a right turn on the old access road which is marked. Go down the hill to the valley floor and go left, which is upstream. Take the first right turn, about 0.8 miles upstream, and cross a narrow bridge. Park near the barricade and walk 0.5 miles farther. Walk 100 yards more and paths down to the pool can be seen on your right.

MOHAWK TRAIL STATE FOREST

The pool and water chutes are used by locals au naturel. Camping, nature trails. From Northhampton: US 91 north to Greenfield, then Route 2 west. Mohawk Trail State Forest is 8 miles east of Charlemont.

MICHIGAN

DETROIT AREA

WHISPERING OAKS

Thirty-five miles north of Detroit—a 52-acre landscaped grounds with small lake, pool, spa, sauna, game room, volleyball, shuffleboard, tennis, playground, snack bar, exercise equipment, softball diamond, dance lounge. Tent and RV sites with hookups. April–October. 5864 Baldwin, Oxford, MI 48371. Phone (313) 628-2676.

SOUTHWEST

SUMMER OAKS LAKES RESORT

Summer Oaks Lakes Resort (formerly Sunshine Gardens) 8 miles from Battle Creek welcomes couples and groups to its 140 rolling wooded acres. Spring-fed pond, fishing, boating, tennis, volleyball, rustic golf, exercise equipment, theme parties, large indoor heated pool, spa, sauna, nature trail, snack bar, game room and TV lounge, baby-sitting available, organized youth program. Cabins, rooms, tent and RV sites with hookups, community kitchen, barbecues, free firewood. Handicap accessible. May–October. 21901 Collier Avenue, Battle Creek, MI 49017. (616) 962-1600.

FOREST HILLS CLUB

A co-op nudist camp, Forest Hills Club has hosted several Midwest Sunbathing Association Conventions on its 45 wooded acres. Heated pool, sauna, hot tub, hiking trails, volleyball, badminton, snack bar. P.O. Box 105-WG, Saranac, MI 48881. Phone (616) 642-9526.

LAKE MICHIGAN

Michigan has 255 miles of dunes along the Lake Michigan shoreline. Despite efforts to protect the largest system of freshwater dunes in the world, they're threatened by development. Private construction is stripping the dunes of vegetation, causing instability and erosion, disrupting century-old scenic wonders for the sake of condominiums and resorts.

SAUGATUCK DUNES

Located south of Holland—the showplace of Dutch ethnic pride in America. While in Saugatuck, Newnham Bed & Breakfast is recommended lodging.

Saugatuck Dunes State Park—an easy drive from Kalamazoo and Grand Rapids. No state park in Michigan is truly secure for nude use and this one is no exception: use discretion. Drive north from Saugatuck on the Blue Star Highway, and look for a sign to the Michigan Dunes Correctional Facilities. Follow those signs until you come upon Saugatuck Dunes State Park signs and parking lot. Park, take the trail to the beach, and walk 1 mile north before you get naked.

Oval Beach County Park—check on current enforcement, where both gays and heteros walk north from the public area before disrobing. Then there's private Oval Beach…

Saugatuck Lodge—a gay resort, 2 hours from Chicago or Detroit. Sunbathing, parties, weekend events, Oval nude beach. Day visitors are welcome for a small fee. Open year-round. 6492 Blue Star Highway, Saugatuck, MI 49453. Phone (616) 857-4269.

HARDY LAKE

Near Muskegon. Only a boat can bring you to the lovely west shore of Hardy Lake, the reservoir created behind the Hardy Dam on the Muskegon River. Owned by Consumers Power Co. and no development has occurred at all. Any quiet cove will serve.

LUDINGTON STATE PARK

Located on Big Sable Point, north of Ludington, this state park is halfway up the Lake Michigan coast. Much of the beach stretches along the highway. The north end is relatively quiet and is the best bet for enjoying the great outdoors in your birthday suit. Care should be taken not to offend the casual stroller, so get as far away from the main beach as possible. One drawback to the northern end is the easy access from the campground, so use caution.

If you go, ask to camp in The Pines. Then, for skinny-dipping, hike or bike out the dirt service road to the lighthouse (this 1.5 mile trek starts at The Pines). Swim and sun on the beach beyond the lighthouse; this gets you away from the casual walkers. The dunes east of the lakeside road are generally deserted and you'll find rain-filled pools among them, sometimes 200 feet long—waist-deep, and warmer than Lake Michigan.

NORDHOUSE DUNES

This is a 5,000 acre area, north of Ludington State Park and south of the Lake Michigan Recreation Area. About 700 acres of open sand, 1200 acres of wooded sand dunes, 4 miles of beach on Lake Michigan—and no vehicle access. Real wilderness camping is permitted in the dunes; fancier but still primitive camping is at Lake Michigan Recreation Area. Best nude sunning: take "Michigan Trail" from LMRA campground to designated beach, turn southwest and walk 2 miles further on trail and/or beach which brings you to Nordhouse Dunes. Most sunbathers go at least another 1/4 mile along beach, then cut into the dunes for a private site.

☞ If driving from the south or east, enter by Nurnberg Road which is crossed by Quarterline Road coming from Manistee, or is 11 miles north on Stiles Road if approaching Ludington on Route 10. If not staying at LMRA site there's trailhead parking—closest vehicle approach to the dunes—at the very end of Nurnberg Road. Take something to drink, it gets hot!

SLEEPING BEAR DUNES SEASHORE: OTTER CREEK

Otter Creek is sand beach with clean water and a great lake view just 22 miles west of Traverse City, the northern Michigan convention mecca. Naturists aren't bothered when no one complains. They're discreet and assist to keep the Seashore clean. Traverse City Naturists, phone (616) 275-7979.

Sleeping Bear National Lakeshore is at Box 277, Empire, MI 49630. Camping is available several miles south at Platte River Campground.

☞ Empire is a village 22 miles west of Traverse City by Route 72. From Empire drive south 4 miles on Route 22 to Esch Road. Turn right, drive to beach and park; walk north (right) on beach for at least 1 mile. The walk does involve some climbing through, over, under and around a jumble of tree trunks and limbs but the high dunes of Otter Creek are well worth the work to get there.

NORTHPORT: CAT HEAD BAY

Cat Head Bay in Leelanau County north of Traverse City has a beautiful beach and great swimming. Find the road from Northport past the airport, take the first left and park in the lot (day permit required) for the new 1200-acre state park. Walk the shortest trail to the beach (20 minutes) and then go north for privacy. Camping available at nearby Grand Traverse Lighthouse.

MICHILIMACKINAC WILDERNESS PARK

West of Mackinaw City, the breathtakingly lovely, secluded Wilderness State Park on Sturgeon Bay is worth any naturist's visit. The little-visited beach is about 10 miles long, on the southside of the Wilderness. The home-cooked Polish specialties at Leggs Inn, Cross Village, will send you to your tent tired but satisfied—or you may lodge at the inn.

☞ Exit from I-75 at Mackinaw City (Exit 338). Go north one long block to Central Avenue. Turn left (west) and follow Scenic Route 1 approximately 20 miles to the Lake Michigan shore. Or, from Carp Lake on US 31, take Gill Road (which becomes Lake Shore Drive) for 9 miles west to Lake Michigan. Park and walk to the Wilderness Park area, about 1/2 mile. The 2 mile, wide sandy beach with low dunes appears when you've walked north 1/2 mile and rounded a large point.

BEAVER ISLAND

Due west from Mackinac Island, Beaver Island is 25 miles at sea, linked by ferry service to Charlevoix on the Lower Peninsula. Airstrips available too. The southwestern third of Beaver Island, undeveloped and uninhabited, is reached by a road from St. James, the ferryport. Car and bike rentals, motels and restaurants in St. James. Bare backpackers will love the pristine isolation and wildlife.

Winter visitors might want to drive to Boyne City at the southeast end of Lake Charlevoix. Starting in 1937, Boyne City fishermen began inventing new ways to have fun while hanging their lines in the frigid waters beneath the shanty-city-on-the-ice, dubbed Smeltania. Soon *Life* magazine came around and took pictures. That cinched it: there had to be a more outrageous Smeltania each year. Nudity got mixed in centrally by the Charlevoix Buffs when the lake refused to freeze in time for the smelt festival one year. A William Underhill allegedly "danced naked in downtown Boyne City to get ice for the ice fishing festival ... It is an old custom and it worked, the lake was frozen the next day." Anyway, these Michigan backcountry sportsmen have unsuspected tricks up their sleeves.

UPPER PENINSULA

HIAWATHA NATIONAL FOREST

A popular spot for the locals is along the Au Train River which flows through the Hiawatha National Forest for 4 miles between two bridges on Route H03 that are 3/4 of a mile apart by road. The river is warm, crystal clear and has a beautiful white sand bottom. Many of the banks are high enough that you are out of sight at water level. One swimming hole has a rope tied 100 feet up in a cedar tree, so you can swing and drop into the center of the river.

The bridges are on H03 just south of Au Train. Access is by canoe from the upstream bridge; and when you reach the downstream bridge, it's only a 10 minute walk back to your car. Canoes can be rented at a resort located at the first bridge. Another way to get there is by hiking an old logging trail that bisects H03 between the two bridges.

The rangers do not patrol this part of the forest and the Scandinavian miners who settled the area are tolerant of nudity—hence, no complaints, no rangers. In fact, almost all of the local resorts have large wood-fired saunas in the yards.

BIG KNOB STATE FOREST

From the Mackinac Bridge take US 2 for 50 miles west of St. Ignace. Then measure 1.5 miles west of junction of US 2 with Route 117, to Big Knob Road on left (south) side. Take it 4.5 miles to campground with 23 sites, pit toilets, sandy beach, dunes, nature trails.

PICTURED ROCKS NATIONAL LAKESHORE

Backpackers enjoy sunning nude on the rocks, and there is a sandy beach area. Multicolored sandstone cliffs, waterfalls, forest and a variety of wildlife. From 12 Mile Beach Campground walk east or west, at least a mile in either direction.

UPPER PENINSULA

In addition to the sites listed here, 'northern' Route 28 east of Marquette (between Harvey and Shot Point on Lake Superior) and further east along Au Train Bay offers numerous opportunities to park and walk a short distance to the water in relative privacy. There are similiar sections of beach along Route 2 east of Naubinway and well west of St. Ignace. There's a small grey road (on the Michigan official state highway map) that runs east from Route 123 toward Bay Mills; here you'll find pleasant sandy beaches, protected from road view, on both sides of Naomikong Point.

Michael Meyer, C'mon, indulge!

MINNESOTA

Jayson Loam, Jerry Johnson Hot Springs, Idaho.

MINNEAPOLIS

TWIN LAKE

Also known as Sweeny Lake, Twin Lake is in suburban Golden Valley west of the Minneapolis city limits. Nudity and top-freedom are common but illegal; plain-clothes police do conduct heavy-handed surprise raids. All things considered, it is a lovely and appropriate site—ducks and geese, reeds, cool and spring-fed, little algae even in late summer—and if you paddle out on a raft to strip and sun, there's little the boys in blue can do.

☞ Take Highway 55 west from Minneapolis past the traffic light at Wirth Parkway. Continue on 55 another 1/2 mile to the service road exit near the motel on the right. Double back on the service road to Ottawa Avenue and park in the rear of the parking lot behind the motel. Walk north on Ottawa 1/4 block to the railroad tracks. Follow the tracks to the right for about 1 block. At this point there will be a well-used path on your left. Follow it to the lake. Or, on the service road, go past Ottawa to the first business on the next block. Park behind the building. Follow the path up the hill, past the radio tower. Across the tracks, the path will lead to the lake.

Or take Highway 55 to Indiana Avenue (off the frontage road). There is parking here. Then cross over the railroad cars that are always parked in the yard. Continue on the other side of the cars to the main railroad tracks. At the tracks, head left (west) for 1/4 mile. It's a nice amble down the train tracks, then through a woods, to the small lake. If you reach Ottawa Avenue, go back 50 yards. There is a forked path, take the left fork and walk 5 minutes to the lake. A lakeside trail leads to several coves.

MINNESOTA NATURISTS

For clothing-optional sites and travel information, contact the Minnesota Naturists—a friendly group that enjoys regular statewide activities. As usual, enclose a SASE with inquiries. P.O. Box 811-WG, Minneapolis, MN 55440-0811. Phone (612) 823-8291 ext. 217.

DULUTH AREA

PARK POINT BEACH

Opposite Wisconsin Point, on a Lake Superior breakwater jutting northwest from Superior (WI), is Minnesota Point which reaches southeast into the lake from Duluth (MN).

A sandy beach is at the tip of Minnesota Point. It is isolated by a forest and reached only by an hour's walk that keeps the shore hassle-free for the dedicated hiker and sunbather. The water is never warm—try 42° F—but some days when the wind is right it's just great.

☞ Drive southeast on Duluth's Lake Avenue over the Lift Bridge and another 3.5 miles, as far as you can go, leaving your auto in the Park Point Recreation Area on Minnesota Point near the Sky Harbor Airport.

Walk across the dunes to Lake Superior and then turn right (southeast) traversing a bird sanctuary and two miles of uninterrupted sand beach. The last mile is deserted and many driftwood windbreaks are found for nude sunbathing.

On reaching the end of this beach, you can continue through the forest on a path near the lake to a concrete breakwater. By wading over rocks a brief distance you will reach a final sandy beach inside the breakwater which offers a quarter mile of weekday privacy.

LESTER RIVER WATERFALLS

The locals have made some nice soaking pools at these waterfalls. The area is flat granite, ideal for sunning, but the water is cold.

☞ The Lester River is at Duluth's eastern end. Take Superior St. east from downtown to the stop sign at 60th Avenue East. Go straight another two blocks, crossing over the Lester Avenue Bridge, looking for the Lester Park Golf Course sign on your left.

Turn left from Superior Street onto Lester River Road. Check your odometer: Go exactly 1.2 miles. Look for a small car park on the left-hand side of the road. If it is full, park alongside the road but well onto the shoulder.

Walk down the gravel road from the car park until the gravel stops. Take the path to the right down to the waterfalls of the Lester River.

SUPERIOR NATIONAL FOREST

BOUNDARY WATERS CANOE AREA

In northeast Minnesota at the Canadian border, Boundary Waters Canoe Area offers days of delight to canudists. Canoes can be rented from many outfitters. Access permits are obtained in Ely at the conjuncture of scenic Routes 169 and 1. Once licensed, your fantasy is your freedom, find your natural self in the backcountry. Remember bug repellent.

Ron Marsh, Parachutist.

MISSOURI

SOUTHEAST

JOHNSON'S SHUT-INS STATE PARK

Lustrously smooth rocks shaped by water flowing over them attract 100 plus clothed people on weekends. On weekdays, go 1/2 mile past the clothed area where there are sunning rocks and pools of water about 5 feet deep. Be discreet; avoid weekends.

☞ From St. Louis, take Route 21 south to Glover, Lesterville, and turn right on N to entrance of park. Or take I-55 south to Route 67 south to rendezvous with Route 21, continue west past Lesterville and look for signs to the park. Park in any of several large lots.

BLACK RIVER CANUDING

Black River originates out of the Clearwater Lake reservoir and after a few miles flows through the Mark Twain National Forest to the city of Poplar Bluff and beyond. The stretch below the Clearwater Dam is little-used due to a shortage of commercial canoes and poor vehicle access. You can put in just opposite the Clearwater store below the dam and enjoy canuding.

SOUTH CENTRAL

OZARK NATIONAL SCENIC RIVERWAYS

Canuding is an emergent sport on the waters of the Current and Jacks Forks Rivers. It has been noted in the Round Springs area, a state park on the Current River, and Highway 19 about 12 miles north of Eminence or 31 miles south of Salem.

PULASKI COUNTY: GASCONADE RIVER

Drive I-44 to St. Robert, take Fort Leonard Wood exit, drive north for 5 miles. Turn right where the road forks, drive to Riddle Bridge and park in public lot to the left. The Gasconade is a clean, shallow river with many gravel bars. Bring lounge chairs for sunbathing, or use tubes or rented canoes to head downstream. Use discretion, take litter upon leaving.

CENTRAL

MEXICO GRAVEL LAKE

Actually two lakes, side-by-side; both are suitable for nude use. Plenty of grassy area to grill out and soak up some sun.

☞ On I-70 through Columbia, take Highway 63 south exit north, crossing over interstate to unpaved road PP. Stay on PP for 1 mile, turning left from PP east to PP north. Drive 2 miles and turn left on Mexico Gravel Road and continue 1 mile to low-water bridge. Turn right onto the gravel road at the end of the bridge. Travel 2 miles and watch for an opening in the curve on the road. You can park on the curve and walk in, or drive in on the dirt road just past the curve. Go up the hill 50 yards and you will be at the first lake and beach area.

ST. LOUIS AREA

HAWN STATE PARK

In the peaceful Ozark Mountains this scenic, moderately-rugged 10 mile trail offers small creek pools to dip in. The park receives little use during the week. Most people stay in the picnic area and very few reach the last 5 miles of the trail. From St. Louis, take I-55 south to Route 32. Go west on Route 32 for 10 miles to Hawn State Park. Park in the main picnic area, where you'll find the trailhead.

ROYAL LANDING BEACH

On the Mississippi River in Calhoun County just 50 minutes from St. Louis, this one mile stretch of secluded, beautiful beach isn't specifically nude, nor is it established as gay; rather it is a free space for those who've found it. Come weekdays to avoid the clothed family boat outings.

☞ Take Highway 55 north from downtown St. Louis to the Salisbury exit, and follow signs that take you across McKinley Bridge and to Highway 3 north. Keep on Highway 3 through Granite City, Wood River and by the by-pass route around Alton, coming to the River Road. Take it for about 6 miles along the Mississippi, through Grafton, to the Brussels Ferry. It's free and takes you over to Calhoun City. From the ferry drive 3 miles to a turnoff marked "Royal Landing," go left here, take the dirt road about 1 mile to the parking area. On the beach walk down as far as needed to establish privacy. Then you'll probably only see the occasional fisherman or barge. Be discreet to 'keep it bare.'

FORTY ACRES

Forty Acres—the club name and ground's size—is 45 miles southwest of downtown St. Louis, near Six Flags, Onondaga Caves and Meramec Caverns. Wooded grounds include a large clubhouse, in-ground pool, fishing pond, trails, volleyball and tennis courts, playground, community kitchen. Tent, trailer sites and rental cabins. No singles. P.O. Box 309-WG, Lonedell, MO 63060. Phone (314) 629-0176 or 629-9916.

NORTH CENTRAL

GRAND RIVER

The Grand River offers lots of secluded sandbars for camping and skinny-dipping. The river runs shallow to deep to shallow again. Canoes are necessary when traversing the waters where the Grand River and the Thompson River join. The canuding is excellent and several campgrounds exist in the Chillicothe area.

☞ Go 3 miles west of Chillicothe on US 36 to the bridge crossing the Grand River. Park on the northwest side of the bridge, between the highway and the old abandoned railroad. Proceed west upstream about 1,000 yards to where the rivers meet and to the sandbars.

MONTANA

MISSOURI RIVER CANUDING

While Montana offers few amenities to a sedentary nudism, the wild and scenic Missouri River is terrific for canuding—with towering snow-white sandstone cliffs, badlands and forests. A good put-in spot is Coal Banks Landing, near Fort Benton, with take-out 130 miles below at Fred Robinson Bridge. A road crosses the river only once and discretion might be advised there, and at 2 or 3 other permanent settlements. However, it's possible to canude for days and not see another party, and camping is at your whim. From mid-July through August the river is lower, slower, lukewarm and nice for swimming.

Outfitters offer canoe rentals and shuttle service. Write: Bureau of Land Management, District Office, Airport Road, Lewistown, MT 54957, phone (406) 538-7461. BLM puts out waterproof maps that explain the trip well.

NEBRASKA

EASTERN

PLATTE RIVER

Although the popular site for east Nebraska is actually across the Missouri River in Iowa (see Glenwood Sandpit, Iowa listing), almost any portion of the slow-moving Platte River can be used for skinny-dipping.

The most popular area is just outside Two Rivers State Recreation Area. The spot is accessible from June to the end of September. For at least 20 years, it has afforded hassle-free sunbathing on white sand; and in the hot Midwestern weather a cool dip in the admittedly brown Platte feels awfully good! Watch for the deep holes in the river bottom; go with friends.

☞ West from Omaha on I-92 (Center Street and West Dodge Road) about 20 minutes. Then south at the Venice Inn, where double yellow overhead lights flash and a sign announces the Two Rivers State Recreation Area. Follow the signs, pay the fee, turn left (south) just past the entrance, and go through TRSRA to a camping area where parking is available under the shade trees. Then walk further down a dirt road at least 1 mile southwest and onto the sandbars, outside the TRSRA, where you feel comfortable. On this private property you needn't look for the game wardens.

Dave Patrick, Frankie & Dougie Beach, Lake Tahoe.

NEVADA

LAS VEGAS AREA

NUDIST APARTMENTS OF NEVADA

A very selective, discreet clothing-optional apartment complex with 1 or 2 bedroom units, heated pool, gas barbecue area, laundry. Shown by appointment only. P.O. Box 43824-WG, Las Vegas, NV 89116. Phone (702) 594-FREE.

LAKE MEAD RECREATION AREA

Sprawled out behind Hoover Dam, Lake Mead supports a wealth of recreational boating and with it much skinny-dipping and sunning. Rent a boat, pick a secluded cove, and enjoy. Road-accessed coves are limited. Also check out the Colorado River hot springs below the dam.

☞ Take I-93 for 2.3 miles past the Hoover Dam toward Kingman (AZ), look for a road leading to the left, take that 3.6 miles to a small parking area. The nude beach coves are there.

Or take Lake Mead Boulevard out of North Las Vegas to North Lake Shore Road. Turn left on your way to Calville Bay. Drive 4.7 miles to 8.0 Road. Turn right. Follow the unpaved road all the way down to the beach, turning left at every left turn it takes. Park, then walk east to the beach.

RINGBOLT (ARIZONA) HOT SPRINGS

Among the hot springs along the Colorado River, Ringbolt is one of the easiest to reach. Located above a waterfall, a ladder has been provided by the Lake Mead administration for convenient access.

☞ From Las Vegas take Route I-93 south to Boulder City and Hoover Dam. At the 4 mile-marker south of the dam, park on the east side of the highway in the open space. Walk west from the mile-marker down an unimproved dirt road, which ends between two washes. Proceed down the left wash for an hour until you reach the Colorado River. Bear left between the bushes and the cliff until you see a trail in the sand. Follow the trail over two ridges until you come to the next canyon. Go up this canyon to the pool above the waterfall.

You can more easily reach Ringbolt by water. Rent an outboard-powered boat at Willow Beach Resort, off I-93 13 miles south of Hoover Dam, and go upriver. If you've already been here once on foot, you'll recognize the approach from the water. If you haven't and you miss it, continue on until you see a sign on the left bank of the river, "Caution–Rocks and Reefs Beyond This Point"; or beach your boat about 200 feet beyond the sign for another good soaking point. Yet another good site is 1/2 mile past the 1-mile river marker where three springs of interest feed into the water. One comes out of a tunnel like a steam bath, another is too hot to get into and the third is a series of springs and pools descending a canyon that includes a three-foot-deep pool inside a cave formed by massive boulders.

COLORADO RIVER: LAKE MOHAVE

Cottonwood Cove, where outboards to visit the Colorado River hot springs may be rented, has a sandy beach among small hills and trees. From Las Vegas, the turnoff eastward from I-95 is at Searchlight. Just before you reach the marina, turn right onto Power Line Road and drive to mile-marker 4. Turn left to reach the secluded and nice area.

PAHRANAGAT REFUGE

Isolated Crystal Springs make an oasis of vegetation and birds in Pahranagat Valley to delight any naturist. Tremendous flow of warm water forms a stream, flume and soaking pools, completely undeveloped. Off Highway 93 in Lincoln County, just west of the turnoff for Route 375, about 100 miles north of Las Vegas.

LAKE TAHOE

LAKE TAHOE

The California side of Lake Tahoe did have nude bathing sites, but these dwindled as the Nevada side became popular. The US Forest Service has jurisdiction from Incline Village to Cave Rock and its rangers are unconcerned about discreet sunbathing. Following are some established sites, but they are not limiting; anywhere you see a cluster of cars parked alongside the road, you are likely to find nude bathers. Note: Douglas County in 1979 banned public nudity but added that no action would be taken unless a private citizen makes a complaint.

A Tahoe City boat livery offers naturist canoe and kayak trips on the east shore of Lake Tahoe, with departure from Sand Harbor; contact Phil Segal, Tahoe Paddle and Oar, P.O. Box 7217, Tahoe City, CA 95730. Phone (916) 581-3029.

☞ The area of major use. From Spooner Summit (US 50), drive north 5 miles on Nevada 28 toward Incline Village. From this point to the junction of the dirt Forest Service Road (about 1/2 mile) you may park off the pavement on the narrow road shoulder. Caution: be sure to have all tires off the pavement or you risk a ticket and the possibility of getting towed. Also be sure to remove all valuables and lock your car before leaving.

Walk over the side and down any of the footpaths you will see. Stay on the paths to avoid erosion! The two large dead pines on Nevada 28 can be a good marker. All trails from there intersect the Forest Service dirt road, which has a more gradual descent and is open to foot traffic only. The trails that stem off of it will lead you to a lakeside path that accesses all the beaches. Remember to take all you need as it's a long walk back; and clean up after yourself before leaving.

CHIMNEY BEACH

Part of the Toiyabe National Forest, Chimney Beach is undeveloped shoreline left to the state by millionaire George Whittell; it is named and marked by a remnant of Whittell's estate. The northernmost free beach on the shoreline, Chimney Beach has been quite popular—up to 1,000 visitors on a good day—and clothing is optional. The nude area was formerly in the north end by the old chimney, but lately it has shifted to the south. Find it 2.3 miles south of the car entrance to Sand Harbor. Park along the road and follow the trail down to the beach (20 minute walk).

Another popular spot within walking distance of Chimney is Black Sand Beach, 15 minutes to the south. Large boulders for sunning; can be crowded.

PARADISE COVE

Known also as either Secret Cove or Frankie Loves Dougie Beach (for the graffiti on a large grey boulder that used to be on the east side of the road), Paradise Cove is well-hidden with shallow warm water and large rocks for sunning. It is also the closest beach to the Forest Service dirt road (see above) and requires the least amount of walking to get there. Find the two trails on the Forest Service dirt road that are on either side of the trash cans. Take either trail (they intersect further on) and a short walk of 10 or 15 minutes will lead you to the stairs that descend to the beach.

SECRET CREEK BEACH

Secret Creek Beach has been under the care of a local nudist group which takes great care to conserve the area. Hiking, volleyball, paddleball, frequent cookouts. The water is not as warm as Paradise Cove or Whale Beach but the friendly atmosphere and family-oriented activities make this the most popular of the beaches.

☞ Located on the southeast shore, access can be gained by docking at Boat Beach and hiking a few minutes south, or by way of several paths that lead to the beach from the Forest Service Road. The main trail which begins by the two dead pines on Nevada 28 will get you to the beach in 15 minutes but is quite steep. An alternative is the Forest Service Road, a slower descent to lake level.

WHALE BEACH

Named after boulders that resemble curious sperm whales nosing in to have a look. Whale Beach offers warm, shallow water for sunning on rafts or rocks. South around the bend from Secret Creek Beach, and two miles from the beginning of the Forest Service Road.

Eugene Brousseau, At Top of Clear Pond Mountain, Adirondacks, New York.

NEW HAMPSHIRE

Fully 12 percent of the "Live Free or Die" state is federally-owned land. It includes most rivers and mountains, notably the White Mountain National Forest. Splendid sites are available for discreet skinny-dipping—with emphasis increasingly put on caution and discretion. Rangers have found too much casual uncovering offensive to some visitors. As a result, even appropriate sites for nude use have received increasing requests from the Smokies for dressing. Federal law includes no general prohibition of nudity, and usage patterns in New Hampshire scarcely justify a jurisdictional ban based on conservation or other ennobling grounds. Cooperation of naturists with the rangers and avoidance of offending the clothes-compulsive visitors can preserve the more secluded sites.

SOUTHERN

CEDAR WATERS VILLAGE

Near the New Hampshire coast, with almost 400 acres of woodland and a 20-acre lake with small beaches, Cedar Waters Village is the largest U.S. nudist park. Founded 40 years ago. Miles of nature trails, sauna, swimming, boating, windsurfing, volleyball. Sunday services, new rec hall. Tent and trailer sites with hookups, 4 rental cabins. Couples and families only. R.F.D. #1, Durham, NH 03824. Phone (603) 679-2036.

ODIORNE POINT STATE PARK

Route 1A along New Hampshire's abbreviated coast offers numerous secluded areas where nude use is possible on and off the beach. A rugged area of nature and bicycle trails, rock outcroppings and wild vine profusions, abandoned military bunkers, etc. Get a park map, check it out then explore.

CONCORD: TURKEY POND CREEK

Secluded, mellow; a muddy but pleasant swimming hole. Take Clinton St. west from Concord 1 mile to Route 98. Creek crosses just before; strike off to left and follow it 200 yards to the pond.

COLD RIVER

Too many heedless partiers—please, set an example to remove trash. From I-91, north of Brattleboro (VT), take exit 5 onto US 5, and go south following signs for Walpole (NH). Cross the Connecticut River bridge when you reach it, continue to Routes 12/123 and turn northeast. When you reach Whitcomb Construction Route 123 turns inland (away from the river). Follow it for slightly less than 0.2 miles then turn left on the "unmarked" Wold Road. The Cold River will be parallel on your right. Just short of 2 miles on this road is a small parking lot on the right, alongside a small tributary to the Cold River. Park and wade 50 feet upstream to a sand beach. Or walk back to the road, cross the bridge, and take the path along the field to the river.

CENTRAL

WHITE MOUNTAIN NATIONAL FOREST

This national forest preserves some of the best New England wilderness. Nudity remains a matter for appropriate areas away from the casual visitor. The Kankamagus Highway is a fine access and the Pemigewasset River, north of it, for adventure.

Pemigewasset River. Hike the Wilderness Trail for access to the river, taking this old lumber route to where it follows the river. Skinny-dipping is perhaps 10 minutes from the highway, and a great site is only a mile's walk (20 minutes), at a bend of the river, which has large flat rocks and a sandbar for sunning amid the chilly waters. A bit beyond, there's a natural flume, or slide.

Sawyer Pond. Route 302 brings you to the Sawyer River, which puddles into a number of pools that are preferred for skinny-dipping and sunning. Park at the first wide parking area you reach at the river, and walk a mile up the dirt road, where you'll find the river forms a deep pool. If swimsuits prevail here for the day, just go upstream. A half mile up is a former logging settlement. You'll reach a waterfall, and at the road's end a trail leading to Sawyer Pond. It's 1 1/2 hours in all to the six-site campground.

GORDON POND

Choose this for a premiere, all-day experience. The Gordon Pond Trail is 4.5 miles, requires 3 hours and is Class 1. Find it off

Peter Simon, To the House.

Route 112, 1/7 mile west of North Woodstock. It shortly bears right on an abandoned railroad track, crossing and then recrossing a powerline swath. Soon the trail switches to the north bank of Gordon Pond Brook and parallels the brook at a gentle grade. At the head of the valley the trail crosses the brook again, just above the beautiful Gordon Falls, and in a short time reaches Gordon Pond.

FIELDS BROOK WATERFALLS

On the east side of Lake Winnipesaukee near the Ossipee Ski Area, Fields Brook Waterfalls has cold, clear and drinkable water, and several very nice camp-sites. No one knows who owns the property but there are no signs barring its use. Take Route 109A north from Wolfeboro, to Tuftonboro. Turn left on 171 and follow it 3.5 miles to the brook crossing. Turn right just before crossing a stream and park. (If you reach a junction on the left, you've passed the turnoff.) There's a log across the path, preventing vehicle access. Walk about 1/4 mile to the first site. More falls and bigger pools are located upstream.

GEORGIANA FALLS

Hardly known even to local people, and yet in the White Mountain National Forest and Lincoln township. Not on the Wilderness Trail or the usual hiking maps, so skinny-dipping may have a long existence here. The access is unmarked, so if you like company bring your own. Georgiana Falls is a 1 1/4 mile walk off Route 16 at the southern end of the Franconia Notch: a series of cascades dropping into pools and falling over ledges a vertical distance of about 350 feet. Water supply is steady, coming from a pond, and quite cold. The best pools are near the top of the falls, as are the best sunning rocks.

☞ Drive north on I-93 and exit at the (temporary) end of the highway, joining US 3 northbound. In less than a mile Hanson Farm Road (hard to spot) turns off to the left opposite the Longhorn Restaurant. (Just beyond the restaurant is a Chamber of Commerce information booth—if you reach it, you've gone 75 yards too far. Fantasy Farm on the left is also beyond the turn.) Go 50 yards down Hanson Farm Road and park at its end; don't block driveways. Ford the stream (or cross the bridge, if the owner looks benign) and head across the field on a logging road. At far end of the clearing, before reaching another stream, take a sharp right onto another logging road that enters the woods. This road follows the second stream, Harvard Brook, for a half mile, ending in a clearing. A footpath continues upstream to the falls. The walk along this rushing mountain stream is attractive and litter-free.

NEW JERSEY

New Jersey, the most densely populated state in the Union, is a mixed bag of conflicting attitudes. Liberalization seems blocked, yet people don't lightly yield what they do have. We're betting on the skinny-dippers. Under the leadership of Tri-State Metro Naturists, they are beginning to carefully target sites and the laws that need correcting.

SOUTHERN

WHARTON STATE FOREST: PINE BARRENS

The dirt roads of the Pine Barrens receive few visitors but the rivers often are brimming with canoers, especially the Mullica and Wading Rivers. Result: much barren pine country, and limited bare skin. Your best put in may be Skit Branch—don't forget insect repellent!

☞ From US 30 (the Philadelphia/ Atlantic City connection) take US 206 north for 7 miles to Atsion. About 1,000 feet north of the entrance to Lake Atsion (a formal recreation area, pass it up) is a bumpy dirt road to the right (east). Take it cautiously 3.2 miles to an open field and park. Walk further along the road as it curves to the right, crosses the Batso River, and passes building ruins on the right. Another 100 feet and the road forks; take the right (wider) fork and continue a half mile to the crossing of Skit Branch. Across the plank bridge is a small sandy beach. You'll probably have it to yourselves. Wade downstream for deeper water. Other opportunities in the area.

SOUTH JERSEY

HIGBEE BEACH

Revived use of this once established if unofficial nude beach seems possible—before going, phone (609) 794-3423.

Richard Zachman No Problems, Sandy Hook

NORTHERN

GATEWAY NATIONAL RECREATION AREA: SANDY HOOK

This is now the principal nude beach for the Middle Atlantic states. Thousands attend on a warm, sunny weekend.

☞ Take the Garden State Parkway to exit 117, then Route 36 east following signs to Sandy Hook (about 12 miles). At Sandy Hook follow signs to North Beach until you come to the Old Gun Battery on the right (about 5 miles past the park entrance). Park here in lot G or H. Follow the boardwalk past the gun battery to the beach. Head south (turn right as you face the ocean) along the beach for about 1/4 mile to the nude area.

By public transit: you can get a bus from the Port Authority Terminal in New York to Highlands, NJ; bus stops at Sandy Hook Bridge. Walk 2 miles to Seagulls Nest and 2 more miles north to the nude beach.

SKY FARM

Operated continuously from 1932, cooperative Sky Farm is America's first nudist park, founded by Karl Barthel. Heated pool, hot tub, sun lawn, volleyball, clubhouse. Prospective members allowed 3 trial visits. West of Newark. P.O. Box 17-WG, Basking Ridge, NJ 07920.

ROCK LODGE CLUB

An hour from New York City, with 100 wooded acres and a 5-acre private lake, a sandy beach and sunning lawn. Tennis, volleyball, boating, sauna, whirlpool. Rental cabins and rooms. No tent or RV sites now available but campgrounds are nearby; day visitors are welcome. P.O. Box 86, Stockholm, NJ 07460. Phone (201) 697-9721.

GOODLAND COUNTRY CLUB

Goodland Country Club and Spa welcomes families, couples, and singles. Sunning lawn, woods and creek, pool, sauna, whirlpool, and tennis. Cottages and camp-sites available. Waterloo Village, several state parks nearby. P.O. Box 575-WG, Hackettstown, NJ 97840. Phone (201) 850-1300.

DELAWARE RIVER GAP NATIONAL RECREATION AREA

Delaware River Islands. A 300-acre haven in the Delaware River is Minisink Island, a canuder's delight you can moreover hike to on the Jersey side. Take NJ 206 to the Delaware Toll Bridge, joining Milford, PA and Montague, NJ. From it take NJ 521 south 1.95 miles, find milemarker 39, park and hike over to the river. Kittatinny Campground is north of Milford. Many state parks and other attractions in the area.

Crater Lake. Although it's reverting to wilderness status...an inhibited home owner remains in this lightly-visited park, and other, easily-startled types might appear at any time. Do use a secluded area. From NJ 94 at the Fredon Township School, about 3.5 miles south of Newton, take the county road west and follow signs for "Fairview Lake–YMCA." At Fairview Lake continue another mile, and turn right onto a dirt road near the top of the mountain. Go 2.2 miles to the end of the road, park, and walk right to privacy.

TRI-STATE INFORMATION

Tri-State Metro Naturists—New Jersey, New York, Pennsylvania—best regional source of information and activities. P.O. Box 1437-WG, Doylestown, PA 18901, phone (215) 348-5607. Sandy Hook information: (201) 833-4162. Southern New Jersey: (609) 794-3423. Northwest New Jersey: (201) 689-1048.

Tri-State Sun Club sends information on regionwide events. P.O. Box 532-WG, Broadway, NJ 08808.

Jerry Derbyshire Western Landscape With Janet

NEW MEXICO

SOUTHERN

GILA NATIONAL FOREST

Lightfeather Hot Springs—is a half-mile hike north from the Gila Visitors Center on the Middle Fork of the Gila River—north in turn on Route 16 from Silver City. The spring flows into Lightfeather at 150°F and cools moving to the outflow, so pick your ideal spot by its poaching temperature. A nice treat after visiting the Gila Cliff Dwellings National Monument!

Meadows Hot Spring—another 9 miles hiking up the Middle Fork. First get a wilderness permit at the Visitors Center. The trail fords the river, so neither hot spring is accessible in the rainy season.

San Francisco Hot Springs—on the east bank of the San Francisco River, a soaking pool large enough for a dozen people, a water temperature of 97°F. Accessible year-round. Driving northwest from Silver City on Route 180, about 3 miles before Pleasanton you'll cross a bridge over S. Dugway Canyon. Go 1.4 miles further and, just before a curve in the highway to the right, turn left onto a gravel road marked #519. Three miles to San Francisco Hot Springs. If river isn't high most prefer to walk a mile downstream to Bubbles Hot Springs, which has a large sand-bottom pool.

NORTHERN

ALBUQUERQUE: RIO GRANDE RIVER

Nudity is often found at the Rio Grande River, for instance at North Beach, great for sunning and wading (the water depth ranges from 6' in spring to 6" in the late summer).

☞ Take Alameda Exit on I-25 North and go west until you get to the river. Just before you go over the Barralas Bridge, there is a gate to the right for Rio Grande Recreational Area. Make a loose right through the gate, go down the hill, and follow the dirt road for about 100 yards to the parking area. Walk at least 1/4 mile north before stripping down.

ALBUQUERQUE: TEN THOUSAND WAVES

Similar to the great hot spring resorts of Japan, Ten Thousand Waves offers hot tubs, saunas, massage, acupuncture, yoga and facials. Although kimonos, towels and sandals are provided, the grounds are clothing-optional. Three and a half miles from downtown Sante Fe. P.O. Box 6138, Santa Fe, NM 87502. Phone (505) 982-9304.

SANTA FE NATIONAL FOREST

McReady Hot Springs—close by Spence Springs, more isolated and larger (30 to 40 foot diameter), with an average temperature of 88°F that is more apt for summer soaking.

☞ Either (a) find Battleship Rock Picnic Grounds on Route 4, a couple of miles below Spence Hot Springs; hike a trail along the stream for five minutes or so, then take the trail up the hillside for 1/2 hour to the springs. Or (b) take a much more clearly defined access: Drive over a rough 2 mile road from Route 4 to Jemez Falls Campground. From there, a 2.5 mile trail will get you to the hot spring in about 40 minutes.

Spence Springs—on the southwest slope of Valle Grande, one of the world's largest volcanic craters. The 104°F pool accommodates 15 people maximum in a 10 foot diameter. USFS here first set precedent of a clothes-optional policy in the early 1970s.

☞ From the north: Route 4 from Los Alamos to La Cueva Junction (30 miles). Turn left on H-4 for 1.6 miles, to the large white mound of pumice gravel on the left side of the road, which marks the parking area. From the south: Route 25 from Albuquerque to Route 44 to San Ysidro, where you turn right on Route 4 and proceed north to Jemez Springs. About 7 miles beyond Jemez Springs, you will reach the white mound of gravel with parked cars. If you come to mile-marker 25, you've gone too far.

From the white construction gravel mound, follow the trail around to the right which leads in gentle switchbacks down the canyon, about 5 to 10 minutes. At canyon bottom turn left and follow the stream to the fallen tree. Cross the stream here and follow the trail uphill to the spring, about a 15 minute walk.

TAOS: BLACK ROCK HOT SPRING

Black Rock Hot Spring—a.k.a. Hondo Hot Spring, the 10 foot diameter unimproved pool has 97°F waters, sandy bottom. Camping is okay, everything must be carried in from Arroyo Hondo. Since the spring is adjacent to the Rio Grande it doesn't maintain its temperature when the river is high in the spring. Local custom is night use; bring a flashlight!

☞ Drive north on Route 3 from Taos toward Questa. At Arroyo Hondo, take the turnoff to the left (west) and follow it for a little over a mile. Its terminus is a gravel road going both right and left; take a right and follow this for 1.1 miles to the Rio Grande Gorge. Coming up the far (west) side of Rio Grande Gorge, find the small parking area at the end of the first switchback mounting the west face. The trail starts in the parking area and leads to the southwest for 1/4 mile.

Stagecoach Hot Springs—named for the old ruts that lead to it, this spring has two unimproved pools which hold 5 to 6 people each; 90°F water. Same route as for Black Rock Hot Spring, but instead of turning right at the gravel road, take the left southwest for 2.3 miles to pools on the east side of the Colorado River Gorge in the ruins of the old Sante Fe stagecoach buildings.

TAOS WATER GARDEN

Several hot tubs (indoor and outdoor). Massage, art gallery, beautiful grounds. Clothing-optional around the pools. Pueblo Alegre Mall, #5, Taos, NM 87671. Phone (505) 758-1669.

Peter Simon, Winter Play.

NEW YORK

New York State is swift to hand hard-working special interests their requested legislation—then, to let citizens do much as they like anyway! It surely is the story of the 1984 state anti-nudity law. The provocation was exceedingly narrow. Nude bathers in Bay 1 of Riis Park federal beach in New York City were visible to nearby home owners. Some of them wanted to end the nudity. Failing to gain any federal court or National Park Service help to screen or to relocate these beach users—which most Naturists believed should be done—the neighbors enlisted their state legislator. In classic favor-trading, Gerdi Lipschutz in turn repaid a few dozen of her supporters for their votes and contributions—by getting fellow legislators to hastily back a statute denying nude recreation to millions of New Yorkers!

A series of 'mere nudity' decisions upholding the Gerdi Lipschutz statute confirms that in present Constitutional law, interpreted by New York State appeals courts, the expression of body acceptance with body nudity in appropriate circumstances is literally indefensible...except, of course, in commercial venues where men charge for live 'nude' shows.

Naturists today seek to alter the Exposure of a Person law to eliminate gender discrimination (only males may be topfree) and to permit consensual nudity where communities approve it. Of course, much gender equality and much community support give substance to the nude beach listings that follow. Nonetheless, as long as right treatment remains arbitrary and 'illegal,' body acceptance will not come to New York State. Contact Tri-State Metro Naturists, below, to help.

NEW YORK CITY

TRI-STATE METRO NATURISTS

The best Middle Atlantic source of information and activities. Publishes excellent booklet of update listings for the Tri-State area. Call Northwest New Jersey: (201) 689-1048, Eastern PA: (215) 348-5607, Northeast MD & DE: (302) 762-0969, Delaware: (302) 422-3980, Fire Island: (516) 775-5147, Westchester: (914) 941-9152, Rockland: (914) 352-5258. Or send SASE for information. P.O. Box 436, Monsey, NY 10952.

STATEN ISLAND

This 1840s farmhouse B&B on Staten Island offers the quiet seclusion of tall trees, evergreen hedges and lilac bushes for local and visiting naturists. The huge yard is perfect for sunning. Coming by air, train, bus? Your transportation may be met. Venturing into the Big Apple? Your hosts can provide information on what to do, where to go and how to get there. White Pickets, 67 Brewster St., Stapleton, NY 10204. Phone (718) 727-9398.

LONG ISLAND

JONES BEACH

A very popular beach for those with autos. In the dunes of the Tobay Beach area a mile to the east of Lot 9, sun worshipers have long congregated. It's a very sociable group, with the clothed and the nude, the gays and straights, mixing easily.

☞ Take any freeway from New York City out to Long Island. Turn off going south on Meadowbrook Parkway and follow it to Jones Beach. Park in Field 6 near the east bathhouse. Walk east along the beach about 30 minutes. Since Field 6 may be filled by 8 a.m. on weekends, consider using Field 5. In this case, drop passengers and equipment along the beach road between the light poles marked 248 and 260, drive to Field 5, and walk the 3 miles back.

The beach is also accessible by public transportation; Long Island Railroad to Freeport, then bus to the beach from the station. From the beach, walk east, past the obelisk and Field 6 (last stop for refreshments) for about 20 minutes, passing the old Field 9 and a bird sanctuary, until you see other naturists.

FIRE ISLAND

FIRE ISLAND

A low-slung barrier reef 32 miles long and 900 yards to less than 200 yards wide. Fire Island is reached from the southern coast of Long Island. For those who choose to visit the several sections where nudity is not uncommon, it offers an exciting experience of wind, surf, sky and one's own natural being. The Fire Island National Seashore rangers are responsible for preserving the dunes and vegetation, and they are generally of assistance to the nude as well as the garmented visitor. You may drive to Smith Point and to Lighthouse Beach only. To reach the other destinations, you must take a ferry or perhaps a private boat or seaplane; no roads serve most of Fire Island. Most people go by the Long Island Railroad, phone (718) 217-5477, from New York City, connecting by taxi to the correct ferry. Taxis meet the train.

New York

FIRE ISLAND LIGHTHOUSE BEACH

An attractive nude sunbathing site, which US Secretary of the Interior Manuel Lujan and his wife have viewed and pronounced a "no problem nude beach." Please respect the efforts of naturists to avoid lifestyle conflicts. Contact: Friends of Lighthouse Beach, P.O. Box 571, Babylon, NY 11702.

☞ Drive east on Long Island by Southern State Parkway, Sunrise Parkway, or Montauk Highway. At West Islip turn right (south) on Sagtikos State Highway and Robert Moses Causeway to Robert Moses State Park. Drive left (east) and park in Field 5. Hike east 1/2 hour to Lighthouse Beach and 200 yards beyond, to be out of sight of casual tourists at the restored landmark. Avoid Kismet residences to the east. Memorial Day to Labor Day. You can also take the Long Island Railroad to Bay Shore, then taxi to the Kismet ferry, and on Fire Island walk a short distance west.

WATCH HILL

For access, see Davis Park. The Watch Hill attraction is the beach—and a visitor center and campground where you must reserve. Four-night limit. Phone (516) 597-6633 for family camping or (516) 289-4810 for group camping. Showers, picnic tables, snack bar, groceries and ice. From Watch Hill it's a 7 mile wild beach east to Smith Point Park, much of it hikable au naturel.

DAVIS PARK

Couples, singles, and families enjoy the clothes-optional beach to the west of Davis Park. The curious clothed may wander over to check the scene, but they're harmless and some stay to join. Food and drink pavilion at the ferry arrival point.

☞ Ferries from Patchogue run to both Davis Park and Watch Hill. Take the Southern State Parkway to exit 44 east; follow the Sunrise Highway east for 9 1/2 miles to South Ocean Avenue in Patchogue. Take a right onto South Ocean for 2 miles to Maiden Lane. A right again onto Maiden Lane (it jogs into Brightwood Street) will bring you to the ferries. Davis Park and Watch Hill schedule: phone (516) 475-1665.

POINT O'WOODS

East of Point O'Woods, clothed and unclad bathers generally coexist amiably. If you experience difficulties, hike further east past Sunken Forest and Sailors Haven to Cherry Grove. Road connection and ferry schedule from Bay Shore to Ocean Bay Park.

CHERRY GROVE & FIRE ISLAND PINES

These twin communities—favorite celebrity havens—are known for the most extravagant personalities on Fire Island. Clothes-optionality was pioneered here. Many summer visitors rent cottages together, summer after summer, forming a stable and strong-minded community that sets, for National Park Service purposes, "the community standard" of dress (or undress) code. Gay is prevalent with heterosexual concentration on the beach west of Cherry Grove or east of the Pines.

☞ Ferry service is from Sayville. Schedule: for Fire Island Pines, (516) 589-0810; Cherry Grove, (516) 589-3622. Driving, exit 44 east from the Southern State Parkway. Follow Sunrise Highway east about 4 1/2 miles to Lakeland Avenue. Go south on Lakeland (which runs into Railroad Avenue) for 1 1/2 miles to Main Street. Take a left on Main for 50 feet, then bear right on Middle Road 2 blocks to Foster Avenue. Right on Foster for 7 blocks to Terry Street. Left on Terry 1 block to River Road, then right on River Road to the ferries.

SMITH POINT COUNTY PARK

This remains a delightful haven because nude recreation—accepted alike by federal rangers and Suffolk County deputies—begins 1 mile west by foot from the parking and concession stand. A red post at the dune line is the apparent demarcation. The beach is then wild for 6 miles west to Watch Hill, and with some tact may be hiked nude. Gawkers usually lack fortitude to hike in.

☞ Take the Southern State Parkway to exit 44 east; follow the Sunrise Highway east for over 17 miles to the William Floyd Parkway (Route 46) in Shirley. Go right on William Floyd

Peter Simon, Each Is Brave.

Parkway 5 miles across the bridge over Narrow Bay to the Smith Point parking lot. Park in the west end and follow the boardwalk west. Distance from Manhattan: 74 miles and worth it, with no ferries to hassle. Information phone: (516) 597-6455.

SOUTHERN

MINNEWASKA STATE PARK

Acquired by the State of New York in 1987 were 1,200 acres of woodland surrounding Lake Minnewaska, combining for a 17,000 plus acreage now forming Minnewaska State Park. The NYS Office of Parks, Recreation, and Historic Preservation (OPRHP), administrators of the Minnewaska park through their staff at Bear Mountain Park, have never appeared permissive. Fitfully the rangers have interfered with nude bathing along the Peterskill Stream running through state property. Generally the ranger will move on if presented with a show of compliance. Money is very short, so enforcement is generally an early-season show of authority, followed by absence.

Nude swimming is a tradition in the run-off falls and streams of Lake Minnewaska—a lovely spot on top of the mountain—and skinny-dipping and sunning in this beautiful woodland continue to flourish.

☞ The prime dipping spot is reached by driving west from New Paltz on Route 299, then turning right onto Route 44/55 and up into the mountains in the direction of Kerhonkson. Route 44/55 essentially splits the mountain in two, creating an uphill section and a downhill section. Downhill are Lower Falls; uphill lie Minnewaska and Peterskill parks.

For Lower Falls, stay on Route 44/55 to Ski Minne Restaurant and camp-sites. You'll probably be charged to park. Just beyond, on the right, begins the trail leading downhill to the Lower Falls.

Minnewaska and Peterskill parks are the sites upstream. Plenty of nice pools with sunning rocks. Reached by staying on 44/55 to 0.2 miles past the main entrance to Minnewaska State park, to a smaller state park sign and entry gate to a larger parking lot (fee may be charged). Walk south past the gate for 15 minutes on a shale road. Find a footpath down to the Peterskill Stream on the east side of the road and stake your claim to the site you like best.

MINNEWASKA: MOHONK PRESERVE

Privately-owned 5,400-acre resort. Parking on Clove Road next to the stream has a $3 fee and the lot fills up fast so arrive early. Since it's not state land, the patrolling ranger has no dress code hang-up and is concerned mostly by glass and noise. Many of Smitty's regulars have shifted here—it's just upstream—since Smitty's was sold.

☞ Drive west from New Paltz on Route 299, then turn onto Route 44/55 and up into the mountains in the direction of Kerhonkson. Exit right on a dirt road from 44/55 where it levels out after climbing the mountain, bearing right on this dirt road where it forks, and park in the pull-off area for day parking of the Mohonk Preserve ($3 fee). Hike downstream on the right bank for several hundred yards until you reach a wide area of the flat rock stream bed. There you will find the kindred folk.

WEST POINT: BLACK ROCK FOREST

Black Rock Forest is a 3,600-acre, Harvard-owned, experimental area just west of the West Point Military Reservation, with a maze of lightly-used hiking trails and 8 wilderness lakes. Swimming is allowed only at Sutherland Pond. Skinny-dipping should be done from the rocks to the right of the main swimming area, separated from it by trees and bushes. The other lakes are reservoirs and are attractive and more private locations for picnicking and sunbathing. Hiking should not be done without a trail map, which can be obtained from *Walking News*, Box 352, New York, NY 10013.

☞ Sutherland Pond is about a mile from the nearest trailhead, but this mile includes an initial steep climb. This trailhead is reached by going east from Route 32 in Mountainville on Angola Road and then south on Mine Hill Road to a parking area at the trailhead. Another access is from Route 9W several miles south of Cornwall-On-Hudson. Here you can turn onto a dirt road at the sign for Black Rock Forest and drive to a small parking area by the gate at the Upper Reservoir. From here you can take longer and more interesting hikes to Sutherland Pond.

Lee Baxandall, World Trade Center Beach Picnic, 1978.

New York

CENTRAL

FULL-TAN SUN CLUB

Fishing pond, small in-ground pool, golf, sauna, luncheonette. Archery, volleyball, sunning lawn, hiking. Tent and trailer sites. Sixteen miles from Amsterdam and 3 miles from Canajoharie, in the heart of the beautiful Mohawk Valley. Route 1, Box 34, Sprakers, NY 12166. Phone (518) 673-2886.

WESTERN

EMPIRE HAVEN

Heated pool, spa, sauna, restaurant, volleyball, tennis, congenial atmosphere, mountain air and scenic setting. Empire Haven's 97 acres in the Finger Lakes near Cortland make a base for area day trips. Rooms, tent sites. May–Sept. Box 297, Sun Lane, Moravia, NY 13118. Phone (315) 497-0135.

SUNTAN CLUB

Ninety acres near Finger Lakes. Hiking, fishing on rustic grounds, tent and camper sites; day visitors welcome. R.D. 4, Box 51-B, Bath, NY 14810. Phone (607) 776-9703. June–August.

ITHACA: SIX MILE CREEK

The ban on college students and others swimming in the dangerous reservoir waters is strictly and wisely enforced by rangers, and should be respected. Sunning continues on the lovely wooded banks and is ignored by the rangers.

☞ From Ithaca take Route 79 out State Street southeast. It parallels Six Mile Creek. Look for parking between the Second (Thirty Foot) and Third (Sixty Foot) Dams; the area now used nude. The Thirty Foot Dam can be reached by a 20 minute hike upstream from the parking lot at Van Natt's Dam off Giles Street. Sixty Foot Dam is a few minutes down from the cars parked on Route 79 east of Pine Tree Road. Another good site is the Potter's Falls stretch, a walk of about 7 minutes from below the top reservoir dam.

WESTFIELD: CHAUTAUQUA GORGE

Local residents posted a 2 mile stretch of the gorge for clothes-optional use. Skinny Dip Falls is especially popular with young hikers and campers. Weekends are best. The local Chautauqua Institute has many cultural events and there is a spiritualist center at Lily Dale Assembly in Cassadaga.

☞ From Buffalo, follow I-90 south to Westfield and switch to Route 20. From Route 20 find Chestnut Street (the next after Welch's) and follow it uphill (away from Lake Erie) for 3.4 miles to Ogden Road. Turn left on Ogden and go 1.5 miles to a dirt road marked only by a snowmobile trail sign. Turn left on it, go 0.6 miles to the end and park off-road or in the parking area at the top of the trail. Although the trail is rough in places, with a 4WD one can drive down to the stream. For those on foot, take the trail that leads down to the steambed, then follow the gorge downstream 1 mile for the best spot, Skinny Dip Falls.

ZOAR VALLEY SHALE BEACH

In the mid-60s the "hippie" movement brought hundreds of people to gather in this Buffalo-area river site. It has remained liberated. State police occasionally pass through but have never hassled anyone, and when, as is expected, Zoar Valley becomes a state park, its status as a nude recreation site will remain. No facilities, no camping, and the park closes at sunset. It is a good hiking area, with both forest and plains.

You can camp out at Evangola State Park, along Lake Erie near Angola, 25 miles south of Buffalo, beautiful in its own right and with skinny-dipping possibilities.

☞ From Buffalo, take Route 62 for 40 miles south to Gowanda. Ask for directions to the Zoar Valley, about 4 miles from town (there are no directional signs; it's a county park). The important thing is to get onto Forty Road, which is a dirt road off Point Peter Road, where Point Peter Road crosses the South Branch of Cattaraugus Creek. It's a barely-improved gravel road that twists and turns through the hills. You may park where Forty Road crosses the creek, and walk downstream along (or in, if the water is high) the South Brook for about a mile to a small beach along the water. Above you will be shale cliffs over 100 feet high and downstream there will be pools.

SOUTHWICK BEACH STATE PARK

Known even by rangers as the "natural beach" section of Southwick Beach State Park, this is a secluded nude area on Lake Ontario that delights its users.

☞ From Syracuse take Route 81 north to exit 40 (Mannsville/ Pierpont Manor). Make a left at the end of the exit ramp and find the sign for Southwick Beach State Park. Follow Route 193 west about 5 miles to the intersection of Route 3 and the park entrance (there is a parking fee). Drive to the beach and clubhouse, park, walk left (south) about a mile to "natural beach."

STEPH'S POND

Beautiful pond in 65 acres of near wilderness. Swim, canoe, raft, camp, go for a hike or join a game of volleyball. Camp-sites have water, showers; no hookups. Family-oriented but most singles accepted. Reasonable fees, laid-back atmosphere with some social activities coordinated by Naturist Rochester. P.O. Box 195, Ontario, NY 14519. Phone (315) 589-9646.

NATURIST ROCHESTER

A small but dynamic naturist club which reflects the interests of founders Mary Lou and Morley Schloss—in whose basement, members enjoy a clothes-free pool, sauna and hot spa. Topfree civil disobedience is pursued as necessary to gain court decisions regarding topfree legalities. 237 Vassar St., Rochester, NY 14607. Phone (716) 244-1219.

DURAND EASTMAN BEACH

Durand Eastman Beach lost bathers a decade ago when pollution and high water levels all but destroyed the beach. With revitalized concern for conservation, the beach has been reborn. Lakeshore Boulevard runs parallel to this area. Park in the most easterly parking spot on Lakeshore Boulevard. Walk through the underpass under the high bank, then to the right on the beach until you reach the area just beyond the steep steps to houses on the hillside. This beach area is ideal to develop for clothing-optional use. Take out more trash than you bring in.

BARE ASS BEACH

Bare Ass Beach, a.k.a. Dutch Street Beach, is mostly pebbles with some sandy places. From Rochester: take Route 104 east to Huron. At Huron, take old Ridge Road east to Dutch Street; go north on Dutch Street 5 miles to the end, where you'll find the beach.

Peter Simon, On the Threshold.

NORTHERN

ADIRONDACK HIGH PEAK

New York's vast Adirondack Park project offers possibilities for nude recreation. The High Peak Area is of particular interest—well-marked trails crisscross a number of creeks with crystal clear water and warm sunning rocks. Owners support skinny-dipping and despise litterers.

☞ Twelve minutes east of Lake Placid on Route 9N, about 1 mile west of Keene, look for turnoff to north, Alstead Hill Road. Follow it 1.5 miles to end of pavement. Turn right on unmarked dirt road. After less than a mile it branches three ways. Take sharp left onto Lacey Road, drive half mile to iron bridge. Park off road and don't block driveway at end of road! Follow short trails south to a series of small falls and pools.

Adirondack Park also boasts the St. Regis Canoe Area; 58 bodies of water for canoeing, fishing, hiking and camping. Camp-sites available at Fish Creek Ponds off Route 30. Adirondack Park phone (518) 457-2500.

INDIAN LAKE

In Adirondack Park (phone 518-457-2500), Indian Lake island camp-sites—accessible by boat only—are a natural retreat and a treat. Access is by reservation from Ticketron. Take I-87 to the junction with I-90, continue north on 90 beyond Albany to Amsterdam. Then Route 30 north through Speculator to Indian Lake. Park at the main gate, present your permit, and paddle away to your naked hide-out.

NORTH CAROLINA

OUTER BANKS

There's a stark, seemingly desolate, light-drenched and humidified beauty to the Outer Bank Islands—a timeless quality that draws many to experience the sand and sea. The Cape Hatteras and Cape Lookout National Seashores between them preserve 120 miles of magnificent beach. Ferries service most islands. Unfortunately, the state passed a vague and overbroad law in 1985 criminalizing consensual nudity. While it is aimed at the commercialized sleaze trade in women's nudity, some religionists and parks officials believe it is their duty to enforce it against skinny-dippers.

CAPE HATTERAS NATIONAL SEASHORE

Cape Hatteras has long stretches of lovely uncrowded barrier island—for many the best in the Middle Atlantic states, ideal for enjoyment au naturel. Sadly the two most popular areas, Pea and Ocracoke Islands, are subjected to zealous Seashore enforcement which assimilates revised NC nudity regulations that require covering the genitals in public in the presence of the opposite sex without exception.

However, being topfree or in a g-string is legal! Indicative of the mood on Ocracoke: a woman was reprimanded by a ranger for walking her dog without a leash. When she told him she didn't have a leash, he told her to use her bikini top.

Until 1985, nudity on Ocracoke was tolerated from a mile or so northeast of the campground north to Hatteras Inlet. It cannot now be recommended. Until 1990, Pea Island was still enjoyed by the initiated. Its USF&WS management is now replaced by CHNS policy and must be avoided until political changes are achieved.

CAPE LOOKOUT NATIONAL SEASHORE

Cape Lookout National Seashore is a 58 mile, mostly day-use barrier island, sparsely visited on weekdays. Most visitors head for the southern tip to go shelling, conceding the wild area north of the lighthouse, and Shackleford Banks too, to the occasional stroller and the naturists. Shackleford Banks currently has no rangers and no ferry access—bring-or-rent-or-hitchhike with a private boat.

The ride to Core Banks from Harkers Island takes about 45 minutes. For another fee, the Park Service will carry you and your gear in a tractor-drawn wagon 1/4 mile to the lighthouse point or a few miles down the beach. Go at least 1/2 mile north of the lighthouse to avoid the clothed. Take everything you will need including water. The last ferry returns to the mainland at 4 p.m., keep an eye on the time as well as the horizon.

Consider launching a boat from the mainland—or ferry over a johnboat and light trailer with your vehicle from Atlantic (this will pull best in the damp sand of low tide without 4WD)—then, you can drive to the Cape's far north end, where Portsmouth Island has its own ghost town, Fort Portsmouth, and Ocracoke Inlet offers many fascinating creeks and channels; the price of this adventure is that strong insect repellent is absolutely essential.

☞ Cape Lookout National Seashore is accessible by a passengers-only ferry from Harkers Island Marina, south on US 70 from New Bern and east of Beaufort; the turnoff at Otway is well-marked, reservations are a good idea: (919) 728-3907. (Another ferry, this to central Cape Lookout—$55 round-trip for a vehicle—runs from Atlantic at the very end of I-70.) The ferries cost $10 per person round-trip.

HAMMOCKS BEACH STATE PARK

The park on Bear Island is reached by a 20 minute ferry ride from Swansboro. Take Route 17 or 258 south to Jacksonville and then Route 24 east. Ferry runs from June through August, usually 9:30 a.m.–5:30 p.m. Vehicles not permitted.

Rangers have acted against nudity only on complaints as long as it is well away from the clothed beach. From the ferry follow the path to the right 1/2 mile over the dunes to the ocean. Then go left up the beach another 1/4 mile or so to be out of view of the textiled. Beach facilities include bathhouse and refreshment stand.

WILMINGTON: WRIGHTSVILLE BEACH

A shallow-draft boat, rented at one of the Wrightsville marinas, plus a high tide and some skill at negotiating muddy channels, entitles you to the widest selection of fine beaches across the Masonboro Inlet. Any boat at all, and no skill at all, will still get you to Masonboro Island with its 8 miles of wonderful beach (choose north or south end), or to Hutaff or Lea Islands (reached best by launching at Scotts Hill, Hampstead or Topsail Beach). Get skilled quickly—pick up Salt Water Sport Fishing and Boating In North Carolina ($13; phone 703-750-0510).

Of course, going is the fun—channel navigation makes you feel like a skipper, spartina grass varies with the seasons, the egrets, herons and ibises abound, ghost crabs are amusing, ospreys are breathtaking, and you may see dolphins from the outer beaches. Camping is permitted.

☞ From Wilmington follow Routes 17/74 east, then Route 74 leading to Wrightsville Beach. Continue south to the Wrightsville marinas, rent a boat. Go out Banks Channel behind the north end of Masonboro to find your private cove, or at least a harbor to begin your walk to a trackless hideaway.

From Carolina Beach you can take the Intracoastal Waterway north to green marker #155A. Turn right into the Carolina Beach Inlet channel. Moor the boat in the sheltered water of south Masonboro Island and again walk off 10 minutes to your private paradise.

A shallow-draft boat will open up much of the leeward side of marshy Masonboro Island. Try at high tide to navigate into Dick Bay, opposite red marker #152, or John Creek, near red marker #150.

SOUTH COAST

WHISPERING PINES

A 27-acre campground and nature reserve close to N. Myrtle Beach. Pond, spa, sauna, trails, playground, volleyball, snack bar, clubhouse. Tent and RV sites with hookups. P.O. Box 148-WG, Longwood, NC 28452. Phone (919) 287-6404.

INLAND

DURHAM: NEW HOPE CREEK

Large sunning boulders, shady areas and a swimming hole. From Durham, take Highway 15-501 and exit onto Highway 751. Turn left onto Erwin Road (Route 1306). After passing a country store on the left and then a bridge 1/2 mile later, turn right onto Whitfield Road (Route 1731). Continue 1/2 mile to the first gate (two poles and a locked chain across the road), and park on the side of the road (do not block the gate or the road). Go down the path, walk down some steps, turn right and continue 1/4 mile to a big rock overlooking the creek. You are there. Take out your trash!

RALEIGH: FALLS LAKE

Recommended as the sunbathing area is not visible by Falls Lake boaters. In Wake County on Highway 98, go 0.8 miles west of US 1 and turn left onto SR 1967. You will pass Keith's Country Store on your left at the intersection with SR 2000. Continue on SR 1967 until you come to a red and white barricade; go around it and proceed to the barricade at the end of the paved road. Park and walk down the trail over two dirt banks toward Falls Lake. Turn left onto one-lane road and walk over two more dirt banks. At the top of the hill (in woods) there is a cable between two trees blocking an old road. Go right on brown dirt trail to small field. Go left on trail in field, about 3/4 mile from parking area. An alternative site is to continue past the cable and past one dirt bank to a cove, about 1 1/2 miles from the parking area.

MIDDLE OF NOWHERE

Near Triangle. It's 127 acres of meadows, pines and hardwoods, brooks, pond, hiking trails. Pool, deck, volleyball. Restored tobacco farm manor is clubhouse/restaurant. Tent and RV sites. P.O. Box 248-WG, Kittrell, NC 27544. Phone (919) 690-0000.

PISGAH RANGER DISTRICT: CANTRELL CREEK

Serving Asheville with secluded skinny-dipper pools and easy access. Take Highway 280 for 18 miles south from I-40, to Henderson-Transylvania county line. Turn right onto Forest Road 297 (Turkey Pen Road) and follow it about 1.5 miles until you reach South Fork Mills River. Walk down Trail 133 to Swinging Bridge and follow river until you reach the former site of the historic lodge. Just after the lodge site, turn right (NNW) onto Trail 148 which parallels Cantrell Creek.

BLUE RIDGE PARKWAY: FLAT LAUREL CREEK

Flat Laurel Creek is a classic with sunning rocks and pools deep enough for swimming. Near mile-marker 422 of the Blue Ridge Parkway, turn north on Route 215 and go 3.3 miles to a stone bridge. Cross and park on the right side of the road. Descend beside the bridge and follow the stream downstream, around a bend, and to a small spot with rocks to sunbathe on. For larger rocks and deeper pools, drive past the rock bridge to the first gravel turnout (about 1/2 mile) and park. Nearby is a sign; enter the woods here (no visible trail), and continue for about 5 minutes to the creek.

PISGAH NATIONAL FOREST: JONAH HOLE

About 70 miles by road northeast of Asheville, a semivertical Blue Ridge wilderness site to delight skinny-dippers. Awesome Jonah Hole is at least 1,800 feet deep.

☞ From Morgantown, north 22 miles on Route 181. Or turn southeast onto Route 181 from Blue Ridge Parkway at Pineola and drive just beyond Jonas Ridge. Go 1 mile northwest of Barkhouse Picnic Area, park by guardrail on right side of road, step over guardrail and take nearest trail you find there for 1 mile. All trails join and lead to top of a waterfall. Cross stream on rocks, go upstream to 3rd or 4th pool. Or descend to lower creek trail where there's a slide rock. Nonnaturists have found this site, so assert skinny-dipper manners.

GREENSBORO: BAR-S-RANCH

New 180-acre club in the Piedmont, with a 7-acre pond, sun lawn, pool, snack bar, tent sites. Route 2, Box 402, Reidsville, NC 27320. Phone (919) 349-8976.

NORTH CAROLINA NATURISTS

North Carolina Naturists will provide detailed, accurate maps to over 50 sites across the entire state. $12 complete. P.O. Box 33845-WG, Charlotte, NC 28233. Phone (704) 872-4536.

TRIANGLE AREA NATURISTS

Triangle Area Naturist—concerns range as widely as the Outer Banks. SASE brings newsletter. P.O. Box 33612, Raleigh, NC 27636.

Bern Loibl, Fishing, Sandy Hook, New Jersey.

OHIO

CINCINNATI AREA

PARADISE GARDENS

Thirty-five acres and 18 miles from Cincinnati. Olympic 'greenhouse' pool, volleyball courts, fishpond, playground, rec hall. RV hookups, tent sites, snack bar, store, community kitchen. 6100 Blue Rock Road, Cincinnati, OH 45247. Phone (513) 385-4189.

COLUMBUS AREA

ALUM CREEK STATE PARK

Alum Creek State Park provides Columbus with nude sunning sites. G-string and thong suits are popular at the beach, rangers react only to disorderly conduct; the pond sees little use by anyone clothed or otherwise. Info from Buckeye Naturists, P.O. Box 14753, Columbus, OH 43214.

☞ Five miles east of Delaware on Route 36, use small parking area east of the bridge over Alum Creek. Take path south between the two wooden posts at the small parking area. Go 50 feet, selecting the next path to the left, through the field and to a home. There take the road south to the pond and pick your spot. North side preferable.

SUMMIT LODGE RESORT

Clothing-optional resort in the Lake Logan-Hocking Forest area. This 400 wooded acreage offers a pool, sauna, hot tub, gym, lounge, rec room, miles of hiking trails, and full food service. Overnight facilities include tent and trailer sites, cabins and rooms. Canoe livery, horseback riding, state park and golf course located nearby. Open year-round; singles and families welcome. P.O. Box 951C, Logan, OH 43138. Phone for reservation: (614) 385-6822.

CLEVELAND AREA

ALPINE RESORT

Twenty miles from Wooster, 70 acres, rustic. Volleyball, rec hall, hiking trails, pond and playground. Tent and trailer sites. Open year-round. P.O. Box 110-WG, Millersburg, OH 44654. Phone (216) 674-6856.

GREEN VALLEY OUTING CLUB

Akron–Cleveland area. Thirty wooded acres. Heated pool, diving board, water slide, pond, Frisbee golf, volleyball, rec hall. Tent sites and RV hookups, rental trailers. P.O. Box 740-WG, Bath, OH 44210. Phone (216) 659-9934.

OKLAHOMA

TULSA AREA

SUN MEADOW

Oklahoma's naturist park, 20 minutes from downtown Tulsa. Heated pool, spa, sauna, volleyball, children's play area, party pavilion with juke box, jogging track and a community kitchen. Tent and RV sites. Must reserve in advance. P.O. Box 521068-WG, Tulsa, OK 74152. Phone (918) 266-7651.

Sheryl Campbell, Mother and Daughter.

OREGON

Oregon was the first state to pass legislation that explicitly acknowledges the right of citizens to appear in the nude. The scope of nudity is, of course, limited in practice. Lewd nudity for commercial exploitation is curtailed. Cities, and the three home rule counties—Washington, Multnomah, and Lane—are permitted to pass nudity ordinances if they wish. And beyond this, offensive flaunting of the nude body is subject to disorderly conduct provisions.

In practice, social recreational nudity is curtailed by participants themselves to secluded settings or a few locales where recreation managers have provided services and security. This is a reasonable and desirable development of the legal entitlement, most Oregonians believe.

For the state is by no means the "hippie haven" it has been called. Natural priorities are strongly espoused by many citizens, but a conservative streak of another kind is equally evident. Nonetheless—other states, counties, municipalities and parks departments may look here for positive practical experience in managing the nude recreation of large numbers of citizens.

EUGENE AREA

McCREDIE HOT SPRINGS

A cluster of natural thermal pools in the Willamette National Forest, 9 miles southeast of Oakridge on I-58 at Salt Creek, is traditionally nude and much appreciated by long-distance drivers. One mile from a Forest campground.

Based at McCredie, Alida Reyenga's "Friends of Primitive Hot Springs" newsletter is dedicated to preservation of nature in all respects at undeveloped thermal sites. Send SASE to P.O. Box 1174, Oakridge, OR 97463.

☞ To the north bank—drive from Oakridge on Route 58 past Blue Pool Campground. Just after mile-marker 45, turn south (right) into a large oval truck park near the creek and walk upstream. Water cools from 120° F.

To the south bank—go 0.5 miles further east on Route 58, turn right across the bridge and stay right on Forest Service Road 5875. Park at the first curve, walk to the creek and head downstream. Spring temperature here is 140° F before mixing with Salt Creek water. Warning: DO NOT try to wade across Salt Creek—it's deep with a strong current.

COUGAR SPRINGS

University of Oregon–Eugene students frequent this hot spring 50 miles east of Eugene. The five creek pools surrounded by big boulders, wildflowers and forest are accessible year-round. Nearby lake fishing, swimming, water-skiing. Please leave a donation for the caretakers. Camping nearby but not at the springs.

☞ East from Eugene on Route 126 to about mile-marker 45. Turn right at the sign "Cougar Reservoir" (not dam), pass the bridge, turn right and go three miles to the dam, bear right and drive about four miles until you a see a small lake on your right. It has a waterfall on the right shore. Park on the left side and walk back to where a trail begins on the north side of the lake. The trail is 1/4 mile long and somewhat steep. Look for the pools in the center of a small creek.

WILLAMETTANS

Amid Douglas firs, in the Cascade Mountains foothills 15 miles northeast of Eugene, this friendly 40-acre co-op naturist park has pool, whirlpool, playground, restaurant, rec hall, volleyball and tennis. Rental units, ample camping with hookups, open year-round. P.O. Box 969, Marcola, OR 97478. Phone (503) 933-2809.

SALEM AREA

BREITENBUSH HOT SPRINGS RETREAT

Clothing is optional at the meadow hot springs for guests of the Breitenbush Community, which often hosts workshops and retreats for up to 200 in the Cascade Range east of Salem. Natural mineral steam sauna, tubs, cabins, vegetarian restaurant, hiking and cross-country skiing in an ancient forest to lakes and river; massage, yoga, aerobics, aroma and hydrotherapy, herbal wraps. P.O. Box 578, Detroit, OR 97342. Phone (503) 854-3314.

☞ From Salem, Route 22 to Detroit. Left on Route 46 at gas station. Ten miles to Defor Bend Campground. Just 100 feet past it, take a right over bridge across the Breitenbush River. Follow signs, taking every left turn after the bridge, to Breitenbush parking. Please phone to reserve.

PORTLAND AREA

SAUVIE ISLAND GAME REFUGE

Sauvie Island's north end—about two miles long!—is a popular family recreation magnet capably managed by the state Dept. of Fish and Wildlife. People fish, wade, swim, hike, chat, sunbathe—nearly all, au naturel. Sauvie Island is west of Portland and doesn't have the Columbia River Gorge cool breeze that bothers some at Rooster Rock. Yet it's still the beautiful Columbia River...with hidden drop-offs, so children should be watched. Parking for 1,000 vehicles ($2.50 daily/$10 seasonal). Some regulars put their boats in the water at Ridgefield, WA to come over. Security and portapotties are provided. There is a 10 p.m. curfew.

☞ Drive 4 miles north of Portland's Saint Johns Bridge on US 30. Turn right over the well-marked Sauvie Island bridge. Take the left (north) fork that follows the Columbia River slough, passing some houseboats. At 2.3 miles turn right on Reeder Road and go 4.5 miles to Gillihan Road. Turn left here, along the river past both Reeder and Marshall beaches (privately owned). At 6.5 miles

Gillihan Road turns to gravel and dirt; go another mile to the opening on right through the woods, which will put you in the middle of a 2 mile nude beach. Park only on the left (west) side, lock well, walk in. RVs will find the narrow roads difficult and the oversize parking is scant on weekends.

Are you a joiner? Two nudist clubs visit Sauvie Island and other public sites: Sun Rovers, P.O. Box 3183, Portland, OR 97208, and Hidden Springs, P.O. Box 17600, Portland, OR 97217.

ROOSTER ROCK STATE PARK

Rooster Rock State Park on the majestic Columbia River is the state beach with the longest record of large-scale, legal, clothing-optional use anywhere in the USA. Clothes-optional and mandatory beaches are side-by-side, with the official line the stairway at the east end of the parking lot. Sand Island, opposite the nude shore, is the place to socialize in times of low water. Toilets, snacks at central building.

☞ Drive 25 miles east from Portland on I-84N, turn off at Rooster Rock State Park (exit 25), proceed to the far east end of the parking lot ($1 fee charged in summer and on holidays) and walk eastward down to the river.

INNER CITY HOT SPRINGS

This holistic health center 10 minutes from downtown Portland has a sauna and clothing-optional hot tubs on a secluded deck open to the elements. Massage therapy, nutritional counseling, wellness workshops and classes, floatation tank. Open daily. 2927 N.E. Everett, Portland, OR 97232. Phone (503) 238-4010.

NORTHWEST: RESTFUL HAVEN HEALTH CLUB

A pleasant base while visiting Portland—it's 30 miles southeast. The 100 wooded acres has tent and RV sites/hookups, heated pool, sauna, hot tub, snack bar, community kitchen, rec hall. Many residents, open year-round. P.O. Box 248, North Plains, OR 97133. Phone (503) 647-2449.

BAGBY HOT SPRINGS

A "world-class soaking opportunity"—according to Jayson Loam, our geothermal guru. Two hours east of Portland in Mt. Hood National Park. An exceptionally beautiful, volunteer-tended public resource reached by a 1.5 mile hike through a rain forest. The Friends of Bagby Hot Springs rebuilt and maintain the three bathhouses and expect visitors will help to do the same.

☞ Trailhead is reached by driving Route 224 to 40 miles southeast of Estacada, then follow Forest Roads S-46, S-63, and S-70 to the southwest end of the parking lot of Pegleg Falls Campground. Weekends and holidays are always crowded. The Friends welcome donations: P.O. Box 15116, Portland, OR 97215.

Squaw Mountain Ranch is on the way to Mt. Hood. The West's oldest (1933) nudist club has 19 rustic acres, a hot tub, sauna, pond, volleyball, tent and RV sites, community kitchen. Turnoff is from Estacada. Plan ahead: phone (503) 630-6136 and leave message, or write P.O. Box 4452, Portland, OR 97208.

Facing: Sheryl Campbell, Rooster Rock State Park, Oregon.

Jayson Loam, Cougar Hot Springs, Oregon.

EASTERN

HAMBURG: LITTLE SCHUYLKILL PARADISE

A splendid natural site with only moderate use. From Allentown, go west on Route 78. Exit onto Route 61 north, and at Route 895, turn east. In Drehersville, turn right at sign for Albany and Hawk Mountain Sanctuary. Cross the tracks and park almost at once on the left, then walk further 1/2 mile to the Little Schuylkill bridge. Paradise begins here, find an enjoyable spot.

LANESBORO: DEVIL'S PUNCHBOWL

A roughly triangular pond with nearly vertical sides. The two creeks that cascade down the cliffs make it a delightful spot in spring. Best swimming is in early summer; late summer brings murky waters.

☞ From Binghamton, NY (the nearest city) take NY 17 to exit 80 and follow the signs towards Lanesboro (you will be parallel with the Susquehanna River). Look at your odometer as you pass into Pennsylvania, and take the dirt road on the left 0.6 miles from the state line. Follow the road over the railroad tracks and park just beyond. Trails lead from here to Devil's Punchbowl. Be careful descending the cliffs to the water's edge, and know that some locals tend not to be too tolerant of nudity.

BERWICK: POWDER HOLE

A small, wild gorge for skinny-dipping, sunning and hiking. From I-80 go northeast on Route 11 along the Susquehanna to Berwick. Downtown, turn right on Route 93, cross the bridge and go 1.8 miles, turning left at the bottom of the hill. Go 4.2 miles and turn right (gas station is on your far right-hand side). From this point you'll be going up into the gorge area. All along are access points, however, to get to the uppermost falls continue 1.1 miles on curvy road and take a sharp right. Go 1 mile past a farm with a house on left and a barn on the right. Park on the road where the woods begin, and take the path to the falls. Most nude use is here.

PENN SYLVAN HEALTH SOCIETY

Fourteen miles from Reading. Camping with hookups, pool, sauna, whirlpool, volleyball, tennis, rec hall. Eighty acres. R.D. 3, Box 3770, Mohnton PA 19540. Phone (215) 445-6330.

SUNSPOT

Secluded 135 acres north of Scranton. Heated in-ground pool, hot tub, sauna and pond. Volleyball, horseshoes, badminton, Ping-Pong, nature hikes. Tent/RV sites with hookups. Rental rooms, playground, snack bar. May–Sept. P.O. Box 211-WG, Susquehanna, PA 18847. Phone (717) 853-3060.

SUNNY REST LODGE

A 115-acre site in the Pocono Mountains. Pool, tennis, volleyball, whirlpool, sauna, exercise room, restaurant, game room, nightclub. Air-conditioned motel, campgrounds with hookups. May–Sept. Palmerton, PA 19071. Phone (215) 377-2911.

BEECHWOOD LODGE

Thirty-five acres 2 miles from Lehighton near Appalachian Trail. Pool, sauna, whirlpool, playground, restaurant, volleyball, tennis, rec hall, exercise equipment. Rental rooms, tent sites, RV hookups. P.O. Box 145-WG, Ashfield, PA 18212. Phone (717) 386-4449.

CANUDING THE DELAWARE RIVER

The Tri-State Sun Club regularly organizes canuding trips on an 8 mile stretch of the Delaware River. P.O. Box 532, Broadway, NJ 08808.

WESTERN

BELLEFONTE QUARRY

Serving Penn State University students, the quarry is often, but not always nude; exercise tact if others already there are clothed. Route 150 intersects I-80 near State College. From I-80 drive north on Route 150 for 1.2 miles, passing the Cero Metals plant on your right. Take a sharp right onto a dirt road alongside the plant fence. Continue to where the road widens and a quarry is visible on the left. Park and continue on foot as the road curves around to the left. After about 10 minutes you will reach the swimming hole. Take a path to the left, just before the water, and follow it down.

SPROUL STATE FOREST: YOST RUN

A large waterfall with lots of rocks, ledges, pools and hemlocks; the area is largely deserted in summer—but is popular with hunters during deer season.

☞ From State College follow Highway 26 north 14 miles to I-80. On I-80 go west 12 miles, exit at Highway 144 north. Follow Highway 144 through Moshannon and 13.5 miles past the intersection of highways 144 and 879, through Sproul State Forest. Park at a large turnout on the left side of the road. Walk back (south) on Highway 144 about 0.3 miles to a dirt road on your right. Follow this road 1 mile downhill past Camp Bloom (usually closed until fall) to Yost Run. The trail follows Yost Run down the narrow, wooded canyon to the waterfall.

WHITE THORN LODGE

Volleyball Superbowl tourney is the weekend after Labor Day. Co-op club is 1 hour from Pittsburgh. Pool, shuffleboard, hot tub, tennis courts, snack bar. Tent and RV sites with hookups; rental rooms. R.R. 1, Box 242-WG, Darlington, PA 16115. Phone (412) 846-5984.

RHODE ISLAND

SOUTH COAST

SOUTH KINGSTON: MOONSTONE BEACH (NENA BEACH)

In 1986 the piping plover, a beach-nesting shorebird, was identified by the US Fish & Wildlife Service as an endangered species requiring extraordinary protective measures. Several of the birds nested on Moonstone Beach, then the leading clothes-optional beach of New England.

The nude beach was first relocated within Trustom Pond National Wildlife Refuge—then, all public use of Moonstone Beach was banned. Resident nudists organized as the New England Naturist Society leased a private shore property adjoining Moonstone starting in 1990. This has become known as NENA Beach.

☞ Most parking is at Roy Carpenter's Beach (fee charged; restrooms and showers are free). Do not attempt to park roadside or on private land.

Access from north is via I-95 through Providence to the split at Route 4. Exit left on Route 4. Route 4 narrows to a two-lane highway, and after a traffic circle becomes Route 1. Follow Route 1 and look for exit signs for Trustom Pond NWR on left. You must execute a U-turn on Route 1 and then turn right onto Moonstone Beach Road. Follow it as it winds left then right, across E. Matunuck Schoolhouse Road, to Camp Pond Road. Turn left to find Roy Carpenter's Beach on the right.

From the south, follow signs in southern Rhode Island from I-95 to Westerly on Route 2, becoming Route 1 going east through Charlestown to Moonstone Beach Road off to right.

NEW ENGLAND NATURIST ASSOCIATION

The long-established group providing Rhode Island with clothes-optional beaches. Membership, or visitor privileges—NENA, P.O. Box 5369-WG, Wakefield, RI 02880. Phone local: (401) 789-7850; U.S. and Canada (800) 722-NENA. Ask about their excellent booklet of listing updates.

DYER WOODS

A quiet, family-oriented campground on an old farm with 200 beautiful acres of meadows, woodland and a beaver pond. Sauna, hot tub, pond, volleyball, playground, clubhouse. Tent and RV sites. Visitors must prearrange. 114 Johnson Road, Foster, RI 02825. Phone (401) 397-3007.

BLOCK ISLAND

A low-cost, less-developed alternative to Martha's Vineyard and Nantucket. "Sun Your Buns on Block Island," some local t-shirts promise. Accessible by ferry from Montauk Point, New London, Providence and Galilee. Ferry tickets are reasonable and bicycles are allowed. Mopeds may be rented on the island. Try following the road to the abandoned North Point Lighthouse, then south along the east coast to the clothes-optional beach below the clay cliffs. Or try Black Rock Beach, or any of the secluded coves, at the base of the Mohegan Bluffs. The climb down and up is steep; use the wooden stairway close to the Mohegan Bluffs lighthouse. Check out the many lakes here as well—good spots for skinny-dipping.

SOUTH CAROLINA

CHARLESTON COAST

FRANCIS MARION NATIONAL FOREST

Ten miles north of Charleston, opposite coastal Bull Island, lies this 250,000-acre federal refuge from dress codes. Many unimproved roads, trails throughout. Permit is needed for overnight camping. Along the northern boundary meanders the Santee River, the flowage from Lake Marion; it has many sandbars, a fully wild river.

OFFSHORE NUDING

Charleston's barrier reef islands give a boat skipper and a friend the option to find a 'deserted' island and strip down… sort of a Robinson Crusoe with a witness!

Truth to tell, nothing's deserted any more. But try Capers Island, a fish and wildlife refuge. It permits overnight camping. The south end draws a number of boaters and campers, but further up, oceanside, is generally hassle-free.

Dewees Island, privately-owned, has only a few homes on the southwest side. Land to the southeast or north and you should trouble no one. Better, land on the small uninhabited island at Dewees' north end; its dunes prevent a view from the inland waterway if you choose the ocean side.

Edisto Island is reached by a causeway, but a cut separates the northerly 2 or 3 miles from ready vehicle access, although anyone on foot can wade (or at high tide, swim). There are many beautiful shells, even live conches, but they're sharp—bring sneakers. A commercial center south of this state park includes restaurants, groceries, fish stores, even a golf course. To Edisto: at Walterboro (off I-95), take Route 64 to US 17, then Route 174. Park at picnic area or 100-site campground, walk north along the beach 1 1/2 miles.

Bull Island also has a nice beach for collecting shells and sun's rays. Moores Landing is the point of departure for the island at 8 a.m., with a return pick up at 4 p.m. Friday-Sunday; $12 per person. Call for reservations, phone (803) 928-3368; bring a lunch. To reach Moores Landing, turn east off US 17 onto Doar Road (20.8 miles north of the Cooper River Bridge that connects Charleston and Mt. Pleasant) and follow signs. Tent and RV camping 6.8 miles north of Doar Road at the Buck Hall Recreation Area.

CENTRAL

CEDAR CREEK

New, 50-acre woodland park convenient to Augusta, planning pool, spa, restaurant, rental units. Spring-fed creek, nature trails, landscaped grounds, a friendly welcome to a rustic, relaxing naturist getaway. 260 Gantt Mill Road, Leesville, SC 29070. Phone (803) 894-5159.

WESTERN

REMICK'S HAVEN

Located off Cherokee Foothills Scenic Highway, Remick's Haven is 80 acres—indoor heated pool, hot tub, volleyball, clubhouse, 6-acre lake, sandy beach. Tent camping and cabin rental available. 9 Remicksville Drive, Cleveland, SC 29635. Phone (803) 836-3447.

Jerry Derbyshire, In the Grand Canyon, Arizona.

Greg Price, Family Camping.

SOUTH DAKOTA

BLACK HILLS NATIONAL FOREST

DEERFIELD LAKE

Deerfield Lake, seldom visited by the tourist, is scenic and safe for skinny-dippers. From Rapid City take Route 44 west to Route 385 to Pilot Knob on the County Line. Turn left (west) here on Route 237 to Rochford, where you take Route 17 south toward Deerfield. About 1 1/2 miles before Deerfield you'll find the road to Deerfield Reservoir; turn off left onto it for about 2 1/2 miles on gravel to the parking area, where mostly fishermen with family RVs are found. You can walk around the lake on a well-maintained path and find an appealing cove to bathe and sun in.

TENNESSEE

Creeks, cricks, sundry ponds and TVA flowages are the best that skinny-dippers now expect in Tennessee. Strong personalities in some respects, Tennesseeans have yet to establish their nude recreation needs in a social setting.

EASTERN

CLEVELAND: UPPER OCOEE RIVER

Take Route 64 east about 28 miles from Cleveland in the extreme southeast. The first half mile of the Upper Ocoee is a very popular area for the locals and the first few large pools are generally filled with clothed visitors. As you go further up the river you should see only an occasional hiker. Take a maintenance road that is 1 mile east of the first parking area; the road is steep in some parts, and should only be attempted with 4WD and high-clearance vehicles. Parking areas at top and bottom of this road, which is less than a 1/2 mile long. Several camping areas nearby. Ocoee No. 2 Dam is a popular launch point for white water rafting.

TIMBERFELL LODGE

Gay, clothing-optional resort on 250 acres in the Appalachian Mountains between Knoxville and Johnson City. Three-story stone lodge with guest rooms and bunkroom. Pond, streams, large pool and sauna, jacuzzi, gym. Breakfast included, catering available. Camping and RV sites. Open year-round. Ideal for large groups. R.R. 11, Box 94A, Greeneville, TN 37743. Phone (800) 437-0118 or (615) 234-0833.

CROSSVILLE: VIRGIN FALLS

One of the best hiking, camping and swimming areas in Tennessee is in White County and it gets little use. From Crossville, take US 70S west to DeRossett. Turn south at 1000 Oaks Grocery on the DeRossett-Eastland-Pleasant Hill Road (4385). After 5.9 miles turn right on a gravel road, and follow it 2.2 miles to the Virgin Falls Trailhead. Go 3.5 miles down this trail where a stream pours out of a cave over a cliff and vanishes into a sinkhole. Below the falls the trail descends into the canyon of the Caney Fork where there are numerous campsites and secluded pools suitable for swimming.

CROSSVILLE: CANEY FORK RIVER

From Crossville, go 10 miles west on US 70S to the second Pleasant Hill exit, a paved road 4385 (known locally as Browntown Road) and go 4 miles south. Just past the 4-H Camp go west at the fork, travel 3 miles, and turn left just past a large yellow storehouse. Follow this unpaved road 7 miles to Clifty. Go through this hamlet and down to Blue Hole Falls Bridge. The Clifty turnoff is the first road on the left after 4385 makes a sharp right turn and begins to head west.

PINEY RIVER SWIMHOLES

Several swimholes can be found in the first 3 miles of the Piney River Trail in Rhea County. Go west on Route 68 about 1 mile from US 27 near Spring City. Turn left on Shut-In Gap Road (the last street to the left before the bridge over Piney River), and proceed 1 mile to a picnic and parking area on the right side of the river. Piney River Trail begins across from the picnic area.

SAVAGE GULF STATE NATURAL AREA

At the southern end of the Cumberland Plateau, the Savage Gulf preserve in Grundy County is reached by taking Route 127 south of I-40 to park headquarters. Walk 3/4 mile to Stone Door. There take the Big Creek Gulf Loop Trail west along the canyon rim, descending into the canyon after about 4 miles of easy walking. Leave the trail to descend to the creek bend at the first opportunity. Rock hop about 100 yards downstream to a large secluded swimming hole.

Additional site: drive east from Grundy County Courthouse in Altamont to the end of the dirt road (if impassable because of mudholes, park beside the road and walk to the end). Take a trail down to an old mill hole on Firescald Creek. This pool is frequented by Altamont residents, as is the downstream Greeter Falls, and it is not advisable to skinny-dip if locals are in the area. However, with reasonable discretion nude hiking should be safe on weekdays.

FALL CREEK FALLS STATE PARK

North of Savage Gulf on the Cumberland Plateau, this state park straddles Van Buren and Bledsoe counties. Cane Creek has a rarely-visited, delightful pool. From the foot of Fall Creek Falls, go 1/4 mile down Fall Creek and Cane Creek, occasionally scrambling through or under a rhododendron thicket, to a deep pool where Cane Creek falls 4 feet over a shelf of bedrock cutting diagonally across the stream bed. Approaching visitors can be spotted some distance away.

For even greater privacy, a second swimming hole can be found 2 miles further downstream at the junction of Cane Creek and Piney Creek, with an excellent camp-site nearby. Easier access to this spot is from a park trail which crosses the canyon a 1/2 mile downstream from the pool.

COOKEVILLE: ROARING RIVER

About halfway between Nashville and Knoxville. Take Route 136 north from Cookeville, pass the Overton County line and over the "new" Roaring River Bridge. Take the first good gravel road to the left and go about 2 miles to the fork, bear right and park. Walk upstream to the good sunning sites. Popular with fishermen on weekends.

Or take Route 136 from Cookeville and about 12 miles out of town look for Hardys Chapel Church and turn right on the next paved road. Go about 3 miles. When the road curves right, take the dirt road that leads to the left. Continue for about 1/2 mile to the next road and take the left fork. At the river, go downstream.

TIMBERLINE LODGE

Equidistant to Nashville and Knoxville off I-80. It is 150 acres of woods, lake, pool, hot tub, trails, tent and RV sites, dining area, lounge. Fishing, hiking, sailing, volleyball. P.O. Box 1173-WG, Crossville, TN 38557. Phone (615) 277-3522 or (800) TAN-NUDE.

BIG SOUTH FORK NATIONAL RIVER AND RECREATION AREA

Big South Fork offers over 120 miles of streams which feature waterfalls, gorges and rock arches. A true delight for those who enjoy outdoor recreation, Tennessee's newest national park has something for everyone. For invaluable maps contact park headquarters at Oneida, TN 37841.

CENTRAL

ROCK HAVEN

A 25-acre park 40 miles south of Nashville. Pool, spa, rec hall, snack bar, nature walk. Volleyball, tennis. Cabins, tent sites, trailer hookups. April–October. P.O. Box 1291-WG, Murfreesboro, TN 37130. Phone (615) 896-3553.

WESTERN

MISSISSIPPI RIVER

Whenever the Mississippi is running low, sandbars emerge that extend for miles and miles—putting the beaches of California or Florida to shame for sheer length, natives like to say. And they're clean. The water may be muddy but it's not polluted. The river is under federal jurisdiction and you should have no problems with the law for that reason, as long as you're discreet. You do need a boat to get to your sandbar; try the boat launch ramps north of Memphis at McKeller Park or Martin Luther Park and tool upstream. You'll enjoy solitude if you don't bring your own company.

Craig Busch, Ponderosa Ranch Nudists visit MacGregor County Park, Lake Travis.

TEXAS

EASTERN

SOUTH PADRE ISLAND BEACH

This South Gulf Coast is becoming known to students on spring break and to their parents (snowbirds) for gentle breezes, sunny skies and abundant shells and fishing. You can try windsurfing, water-skiing, sailing, parasailing, jetskiing, bicycling, four-wheeling, wade fishing, horseback riding, snorkeling and scuba diving. And then there's nuding to factor in...

☞ From Port Isabel, take Highway 100 to the Island and then left, up the Island. Beyond the city limits, on your right, find a beach access road leading out onto the wet sand, extending another 14-17 miles north. You will pass the end of the road (the original Highway 100) about 7.5 miles after you have turned onto the beach. Beyond that, the dunes are only 55 feet from the Gulf. Two miles further will be a salt flat that is actually an inlet established by hurricane Camille. This area will "flood" with the Gulf when it rains a lot or when the tides get high. About 3 miles further is a stacked pile of timbers for a road that would lead to an old gas well. Next, you will notice what was probably a freshwater tank from a shrimp boat. From that point and extending for a few miles is the nude area.

McALLEN: SANDPIPERS HOLIDAY PARK

Near Mexico and South Padre Island. Rent mobile home suites and RV lots. Restaurant. Large heated pool with diving board, water slide, toddlers pool, jacuzzi, hot tub. Lighted tennis, volleyball, shuffleboard and horseshoe courts. Golf nearby. R.R. 7, Box 309-WG, Edinburg, TX 78539. Phone (512) 383-7589.

SOUTH PADRE ISLAND NATURISTS

South Padre Island Naturists can provide beach information, help in arranging land transportation from the airports, or accommodations on the mainland in Port Isabel or on South Padre Island. P.O. Box 5603, Port Isabel, TX 78578. (512) 943-7534.

PADRE ISLAND NATIONAL SEASHORE

Access PINS from Corpus Christi. Pick up your food and drink needs at Bob Hall pier area, drive 20 miles south, park car at the barricade and walk into "wilderness" area. Take care to remove litter and preserve the dunes.

A ranger impelled by church imperatives has spearheaded nudie citations—so check with other users on current enforcement. In truth, PINS has no legal basis to cite discreet sunbathers; certainly not under the Texas law which condones Hippie Hollow.

SAN ANTONIO: RIVERSIDE RESORT

Twenty-five minutes south of the Alamo on the banks of the San Antonio River, Riverside Resort has 17 wooded acres. Hot tub, rec room, restaurant, playground, volleyball and camp-sites. P.O. Box 14413-WG, San Antonio,TX 78214. Phone (512) 393-2387.

TRAVIS COUNTY: McGREGOR PARK (HIPPIE HOLLOW)

When the Lower Colorado River Authority transferred the regulation of Hippie Hollow to Travis County in the '80s, this new entity, McGregor County Park, was at last extended the support services that citizens have a right to expect.

The basics—sparkling Lake Travis, a rocky shore and dirt parking, nothing more—were improved. The County asphalted a perimeter trail, providing handicapped access. A large new supervised parking lot, deputies on horse patrols, trash receptacles and toilets: these were unheard-of amenities in a skinny-dipping haven.

The Travis County attorney had first done his homework and issued an opinion. The County would not enforce the state lewd and lascivious statute at the park, he said, reasoning that a public facility where signs prepare the public for the fact that nudity may be encountered, cannot be "reckless and offensive."

The signage announcing the nude custom is at the entrance of all major trails. The shore is patrolled to ensure law and order. Gays gather at the far end. In the spring and early summer, the lake is high but cold, and many visitors bring raft floats. In the late summer and fall, the water is low but warmer. Do not dive recklessly from the limestone ledges, people have died doing it.

Open April–October. 9 a.m. to 8 p.m. No overnighting. Phone (512) 266-1644.

☞ From Austin, take Route 2222 for 15 miles northwest to Route 620. Turn right at the "Hippie Hollow County Park" sign (Comanche Trail). After 2 miles and a steep decline, look for the park sign and the abrupt entrance on the left. Pay the $3 parking fee (gates lock at 8 p.m.), park and lock, and walk down the paved trail in the southwest corner of the parking lot to any of the several cliff-side paths that lead to the beach. Remove litter.

TRAVIS COUNTY: TOM HUGHES PARK

Like Hippie Hollow, the shore is limestone rock but has more privacy, lots of litter, and no gawkers. A portable toilet has been installed, as well as a few trash cans. Access to water is difficult because of the steep decline.

☞ Follow the route to Hippie Hollow, but instead of turning in on Comanche Trail, continue another mile and turn right at the sign (several bends past the modernistic church that overlooks Lake Travis).

TRAVIS COUNTY: PALEFACE PARK (PACE BEND)

Officially, it's Pace Bend Park, and it lies beyond Lake Travis (coming from Austin)—on the Pedernales River—but its cleanliness and the limestone cliffs make it special. Take your choice of several coves (the furthest end is clothed). Most prefer those on the left for nude use. Coves one through five all have steep cliffs from which the clothed daredevils like to leap. The sixth, Gracy Cove, is slightly less steep, with camping at both the road and the lower levels. The lower level, out of sight of the road, is freely used nude, while the campers at road level now largely shield themselves from road view with tents and vehicles.

Terry Blum Barton Creek Austin Texas

The nude tradition is now threatened by a church agitator who wants the public to confuse skinny-dipping with pornography. Facilities are primitive (outhouses). Water is very warm in August. Vehicles $2/day. $2/overnight fee, 7 days max.

☞ Take US 290 west from Austin, crossing Ben White Boulevard to route 71, which forks right. Follow it several miles to FM 2322—there is a general store at the corner—if you come to the Pedernales Bridge you've gone too far. Turn right on 2322 and follow it for perhaps 2 miles north. Just after entering the park, go left at the fork and look for a cove that you like.

AUSTIN: BARTON CREEK POOL

Barton Springs Pool, a spring-fed creek recreation facility within city limits, offers a haven for women who prefer topfree sunning (legal throughout Austin, by the way). While not as prevalent as in the '70s, it remains an option. Full nudity occurs discreetly in wooded areas upcreek from the pool.

☞ Cross the Colorado River from downtown Austin on Lamar or Congress. Find Barton Springs Road and proceed north to Zilker Park, where you angle left to Barton Springs Pool Parking Area (pool fee charged). Alternately, take I-35 across the river and Riverside Drive, then right on Barton Springs Road.

SAHNOANS (STAR RANCH)

Forty miles from Austin, Sahnoans Star Ranch provides nude living for families. Pool, tent and trailer sites, volleyball, tennis. Very low profile resort; send SASE for additional information. P.O. Box 4261-WG, Austin, TX 78765.

HOUSTON: LIVE OAK RANCH

Large and growing club with live oak trees and rolling green grass. Pool, whirlpool, volleyball, rec hall, rental cabins, tent and RV sites with hookups, laundromat, restaurant, playground, 25 acres. North of Route 290 by Route 6 from Houston or Austin. R.R. 1, Box 916-WG, Washington, TX 77880. Phone (409) 878-2216.

KILLEEN: DANA PEAK PARK

The small cove is closed on three sides, providing privacy from passersby. Camping, fishing and swimming. Take the Harker Heights exit from Highway 190 onto Farm Market (FM) 2410. Proceed east 8 miles to the Dana Peak Park sign, turn right, continue 1 mile to the park entrance sign on your right. Continue 0.2 miles and park on the right, straight in against the wood and wire barrier. The site is 1/4 mile from the road walking through a wooded grassland.

DALLAS: BLUEBONNET

Dallas, Fort Worth and Denton are within an hour's drive. Has 67 acres of rolling hills, oaks and meadows with nature walks. LBJ National Grasslands adjacent. Tent camping, RV hookups, hot showers, laundromat and snack bar. Playground, pool, sauna, jacuzzi, volleyball, tennis, shuffleboard, horseshoes. R.R. 1, Box 146-WG, Alvord, TX 76225. Phone reservation (817) 627-2313.

PONDAROSA RANCH

Sixty acres near Dallas in pine country. Horseshoes, pool tables, dance floor, volleyball, shuffleboard, large pool, sauna and spa. Tent and trailer sites, rental trailers. Hosts nude pageants. P.O. Box 133-WG, Wills Point, TX 75169. Phone (903) 873-3311.

RIVER HILLS RESORT

Among sandstone hills and oaks overlooking Lake Ray Roberts Dam near Dallas-Fort Worth. Pool, volleyball, dances and cookouts. Day visitors and singles welcomed, children are free. R.R. 2, Box 242-B-WG, Aubrey, TX 76227. Phone (817) 365-9571.

WESTERN

AMARILLO: PALO DURO CANYON STATE PARK

This lovely part of the Panhandle has so many canyons and other isolated areas a ranger, or anyone else, is unlikely to stumble upon you. A wonderful place for nude swimming and hiking. South from Amarillo on Route 27, east on Route 217 from Canyon, to the park headquarters for directions/trail maps.

BIG BEND NATIONAL PARK

Primitive camp-sites along the Rio Grande at the Mexican border are very remote and spaced miles apart, permitting nude and natural highs for the friends you assemble to bring in. The park's higher desert also has many camping areas with beautiful vistas. Primitive areas can be reached only with high-clearance vehicles. Bring plenty of water and food as it is a long, slow and rough drive back to the ranger station. Maps and information from Big Bend National Park, TX, 79834.

Terry Blum, Clothes-Optional Apartments, Austin.

UTAH

SOUTHERN

LAKE POWELL HOUSEBOATING

Outside of private homes, Lake Powell is the sociably naked place to be. Folks who don't normally recreate au naturel may camp or float nakedly in one of the many secluded coves. Choose a marina and a speed or houseboat to fit into your pocketbook.

Jim and Yvonne Coffman are experienced nude houseboating skippers. Fantastic scenery including Indian ruins, dramatic canyon walls and the famous Rainbow Bridge. Their 52' 'Kachina Cruiser' docks at Wahweap Marina, Page, AZ. A 4-person minimum, price includes all meals, wine, 16' runabout for sidetrips, and water-skiing. Three, 5, or 7 days. April–October. P.O. Box 1193-WG, Page, AZ 86040-9998. Phone (602) 622-5122.

MOAB AREA

CANYONLANDS NATIONAL PARK (NEEDLES DISTRICT)

This has to be the greatest sandbox for adults anywhere on earth. Replete with beautiful red rimrock and alternate red and white layers of sandstone, a very warm beauty, and a myriad of trails and paths through an infinite variety of scenery.

The area south of the campground is limited to foot traffic and includes dozens of miles of easy-to-hike trails, marked simply by rock cairns. Skinny-hiking on the established trails poses no objection unless it's done in sight of the campground.

There are no fuel, food or other facilities in the park, but water is available within a mile of the campground.

☞ Needles District of Canyonlands National Park lies southeast of the Colorado River. Drive 40 miles south of Moab on US 163 or 15 miles north of Monticello to the park entry. Drive west 37 miles on Route 211 to the Ranger Station and 3 miles further to the Squaw Flat Campground. A handout schematic map is available. It's all one needs to guide oneself to several days' adventure.

MILL CREEK CANYON

From downtown Moab go east on Center Street 4 blocks to 400 East Street, then go south a similiar distance, and turn left (east) onto Mill Creek Road. In about 1 mile, turn left onto Powerhouse Lane and go to the end. Park and continue on foot up Mill Creek Canyon past the dam. About a mile upstream the canyon forks; the north fork leads to beautiful waterfalls and pools well worth a dip. It is unlikely you will run into anyone easily bothered by nudity, but when in doubt, ask first.

NEGRO BILL CANYON

A beautiful box canyon spanned by Morning Glory Arch. Remember to bring drinking water; at least 1/2 gallon per person. From Moab take Main Street (Route 191) north 2 miles, turn right (east) onto Route 128 and follow it upstream along the Colorado River for 3 miles. Park in the lot 100 yards past mile-marker 3. Hike up the canyon about 2 miles; follow the right (south) fork of the canyon another mile to Negro Bill Canyon. Along the hike you'll find many pools to cool off.

ARCHES NATIONAL PARK

Most areas of Arches National Park are approachable by car—easy hikes to relatively secluded and beautiful red rock landscapes that defy description. A short scramble off any established trail can provide privacy. Cross-country hiking off the trails is readily available. This always sunny area is great except mid June–August, when it's too hot for the comfort of most. Water is scarce away from the campground, and the few swimholes are difficult to find. Firewood gathering is prohibited and you need a permit to camp in areas other than the designated campground.

☞ About 28 miles south of I-70 and 4 miles north of Moab on US 163 is the entrance. Arches National Park personnel can provide directions to the trails.

NORTHERN

INLET PARK HOT SPRING

On the north end of Provo's Lake Utah, a sand-bottomed pool 15' across and about 3' deep with a sundeck is surrounded by willows and cattails. Take the road west from Lehi and turn south at road sign 6800 North and Saratoga Road. Park on the south side of the road at the ditch crossing west of the Inlet Park entrance (1/4 mile east of the locked gate at Saratoga Springs) and follow the trail south for 100 yards to the pool. The trail crosses the ditch several times.

GREAT SALT LAKE NUDE BEACH

The eastern beach of Great Salt Lake is shallow, and muddy in spots. You may wade out to better water. It's an alternative to standing by your car like many do.

This is stark basic beaching—dead flat with no facilities, and lots of users don't like to go in the saltwater. It's what there is in the Bee Hive State and has an existential aura as if Samuel Beckett scripted your visit. Relax and go with it.

Never walk barefoot. The salt is merciless in cuts. If you plan to go into the lake bring a gallon of fresh water to wash off, and remove all salt from your body, clothes and car before leaving.

Local and county white patrol cars, always white, may patrol despite the long tradition of nude use, but can be seen far off if you're on the flats.

☞ Take I-80 west from Salt Lake City, then exit 111 and get onto the north side frontage road alongside I-80 for about 2 miles. Turn right on a gravel road that goes north past the radio transmitter towers. One mile brings you to a T intersection and you turn left (west), and go a mile to the end of the fence on the north side of the road.

Here begins a maze of dirt tracks. Don't enter, even with 4WD, if wet. Drive only on compacted tracks 1 mile north to a ditch, crossable by going 1/4 mile west. Cross and you're 'there.' Park and lock. Hike west to the shore or northwest to the stuck barge before removing your shorts.

UINTA MOUNTAINS

Hundreds of miles of trails meander among scores of alpine lakes. It is not unusual to be in the mountains for a couple of days without sight of other hikers. For a couple seeking solitude, or a group outing, this summertime splendor is a must.

☞ Wasatch National Forest near the Wyoming border. Along Route 150, find signs that lead to the park entrance, or consult a local map.

NATURIST TOURS

Utah Naturists—organizer of Southwest river rafting trips. P.O. Box 9058, Salt Lake City, UT 84109. Phone (801) 278-9740.

Wildernaturists—organize clothing-optional hiking, camping. Evergreen, CO 80439-0845. Phone (303) 674-9724.

HOME
BROTHERS AND SISTERS !
Rainbow INFO
PLEASE FEED US TREATS
HAPPY NAKED DAY!

VERMONT

Vermont's attorney general in 1973 issued a memorandum of enforcement policy on nudity that seems to sum up the live-and-let-live tolerant attitude of Vermonters:

The state has no legitimate interest in nudity on private land out of public view. Nor has it a nudity interest in public if secluded areas—unless a citizen should complain, in which case the person shall be asked to dress.

The then attorney general is now U.S. Senator Patrick Leahy. If only all North America were to be "Vermonticized!"

Any lake, pond, or stream in Vermont that is away from thoroughfares is likely to have its share of skinny-dipping. To locate sites not mentioned here, simply watch for the telltale parked cars on roadsides near water. If you're a boater or hiker, you will find many more suitable sites.

The standard guide is *Vermont Unveiled* (1989) by Jim C. Cunningham, $5.95, P.O. Box 452, Enosburg Falls, VT 05450.

One word about quarries. They offer sunning rocks and cold refreshing waters; if you find a "No Trespassing" notice sign be aware that owners often post them to shed liability if anyone is injured on the property. An owner determined to get rid of swimmers has more than mere signs available. Swimmers emerging from a quarry covered with drain oil might surmise it was poured there on purpose. If you find manure laid out along the quarry perimeter, that could be because it draws a large number of vicious horseflies. When you do find a quarry whose owner is tolerant of visitors, be a responsible guest; closing access gates behind you, etc., and you will seldom be turned away. Just know that your safety is your concern. Look before you leap.

Nick Novick. On the Long Trail, Vermont.

Joseph Luczynski, The Ledges, Vermont.

SOUTHERN

HARRIMAN RESERVOIR: THE LEDGES

Close to Massachusetts. The Ledges is cherished by many skinny-dippers as the premier site of Vermont as well as being what a more body-tolerant America should support and enjoy in its natural preserves.

Located on private property of the New England Power Company (NEPCO) adjacent to the company's picnic grounds and a portion of the Green Mountain National Forest, large flat rocks usually offer ample sunbathing space. The level of the Harriman Reservoir is higher early in the season. Nude windsailing and water-skiing are possible. Some folks paddle a raft in, rather than hike the shore trail.

☞ From Brattleboro: take Route 9 west toward Wilmington, and bear left onto Route 100 south. Watch for the NEPCO sign on right and bear right up the dirt access road, passing a few homes and continuing almost a mile to the picnic grounds. Once there, park as close to the lower right parking and picnic area as possible. Continue to the right along the shore until a well-trod path becomes evident, and follow it 5 minutes to The Ledges. It's close enough to carry lounge chairs and coolers. Portatoilets at the picnic grounds. The Ledges can also be accessed by boat from a launch site in Wilmington at the north end of the reservoir.

SOMERSET RESERVOIR & GROUT POND

Over 250 square miles of wilderness controlled by NEPCO and the Green Mountain National Forest. Hiking trails, windsurfing, powerboating and water-skiing, canuding, camping—all clothes-optional. Rangers don't hassle nudity. Cliffs, waterfalls, boat launch. Over 30 camping areas (14 night maximum) in Grout Pond area. Long Trail and Appalachian Trail cross it. It's a new listing—and wonderful!

☞ From Wilmington, go west on Route 9, and enter Searsburg. Take first right turn—Somerset Road, marked with sign: "NEPCO Picnic Area 10 Miles." Take it for 8 miles, cross Deerfield River, turn left on FH-71 toward Airfield, following it to the end and Grout Pond for nude camp-sites with swimming and hiking.

Follow Somerset Road 2 miles farther to end and park, walk the well-marked trails north for a nude paradise. Maps are available at several points.

LYE BROOK FALLS

Lye Brook National Wilderness Area has a winding brook that cascades for 2 miles. You'll catch the sun at one pool or another at any time. The water is crystal clear and potable. Walking the rocks in the gorge is fun. Litter here is nonexistent so take your trash out.

☞ Richville Road south from Route 30 in the center of Manchester, and turn left on East Manchester Road. Go to the first underpass and cross underneath US 7. Immediately take a right on Lye Brook Falls Access Road, and follow it to the end, which is a large cul-de-sac. Park and follow the well-defined trail to Lye Brook. Walk in the direction of water noise and you'll find it on the right. Follow the brook upstream for as far as you like.

BRANDON: SILVER LAKE

Route 7 to Route 53 east, exit between Brandon and Middlebury. South on Route 53 to Branbury State Park. Park and follow signage on east side, hike up 10 minutes to Falls of Lana picnic area and pools. A further 30 minute steep hike brings you to the clean sandy beach, primitive camping and toilet, freshwater well with hand pump, and large swimming area of Silver Lake.

LUDLOW: BUTTERMILK FALLS

Icy water and little privacy have not stopped dauntless Vermonters from enjoying these several cascades, pools deep enough for diving, and large rocks for sunning au naturel. Drive northeast on Route 103 from Ludlow towards Rutland. Watch for a turnoff on the right for Route 100, but go past it and turn right onto "Old Route 103" (large white building on the corner). Proceed 1.3 miles, past the VFW Post, to the several paths down to the water on the right side of the road. The road ends at a washed-out bridge at the top of the main falls. All paths are an easy 5 minute walk down the slope.

WALLINGFORD: LITTLE ROCK POND

North on Route 7 from Manchester Center towards Rutland, this Green Mountain forest pool beneath a 50 foot rock accepts 25 or so skinny-dipping hikers. Access by the Long Trail where it crosses Forest Route 10, east of Mount Tabor. Hike the trail north for 2.5 miles. Or turn east off Route 7 just south of the South Wallingford Congregational Church, cross a bridge and follow a curve to the right. On the left is South Wallingford Community Center. Park there, find Homer Stone Brook Trail at the driveway to the right of the next house (don't park near this house), and hike this route 2.5 miles—a bit steeper than the Long Trail.

RUTLAND: MILL RIVER

South from Rutland on Route 7 past junction with Route 103 and a rest area on the right, take the next left. Immediately take the next right, and drive on this dirt road to an old steel bridge and park. Most bathers at the bridge wear suits. Trails leading upstream along Mill River a half mile bring you to a skinny-dipping site, or you can sample the pools along the way.

STOCKBRIDGE: WHITE RIVER

Annabelle's Restaurant is an elegantly restored 18th Century farmhouse—and the landmark for a secluded section of the White River, near Pittsfield, used for skinny-dipping by a few careful and responsible people.

☞ Take Route 4 east from Rutland into the mountains. Near Bill's Country Store go north on Route 100 through Pittsfield to the intersection with 107 near Stockbridge. Annabelle's will be on your left. Bear right on 107 a few hundred yards over the bridge, take a dirt road to the left following the cornfield until you come to a log cabin. Park there and enjoy a gorgeous mountain stream deep enough and long enough for a good swim. The owner of the cabin does use the stream occasionally and may ask you to leave, but your chances of being evicted are pretty slim.

PIKES FALLS

A beautiful area of cascades and small waterfalls with many potholes to dunk in, and one very large pool at the bottom of the main falls. Usually clothed and nude mix fine. If crowded you can always retreat upstream.

☞ From Brattleboro, Route 30 will take you past Jamaica State Park to Bonville. Go about 2 miles up Stratton Mountain Ski Area access road, turn left onto Taylor Hill Road, and go 3.5 miles to a one-lane bridge. Cross it, drive around corner and park on right. Follow footpath down to falls.

FELCHVILLE: READING SWIMMING HOLE

Between Springfield and Woodstock on Route 106, find Felchville. You'll know it by the Reading Country Store with a big Shell sign on the west side. Turn west here, towards South Reading and Tyson. Go exactly a mile and park on the crest of a small hill—along the road, not blocking any driveway. Paths lead down to the left: first a 50 foot scramble, then 20 foot high cliffs, and at the base, a blue-green pool in the North Branch of the Black River, known as Twenty-Foot Pool. This site is usually clothed; but a hundred yards downstream is Ten-Foot Pool where clothing is optional. So too further on at Fifteen-Foot Pool.

NORTHERN

WOODBURY QUARRY

Midday sun balances the quarry's icy water with its sunning rocks. Horseflies can be thick in early summer. Take Route 14 from Barre or Hardwick and in the village of Woodbury, with a white United Methodist Church on west side, take the facing road to Cabot eastward. After road climbs for 3/4 mile turn left on a dirt road. At the fork stay right. At 3/4 mile from the road to Cabot is the entrance to a working quarry on right. Go past, for another 1/2 mile on the worsening road, to the swimming quarry with spectacular cliffs and shelving ledges.

STOWE: BINGHAM FALLS

The West Branch of the Waterbury River offers easy access to lovely falls and pools where the unclad and clad frequently mingle. No one questions their nude use. No sandy beaches, only rocks.

From Waterbury on I-89, north on Route 100 to Stowe. North on Route 108 towards Mt. Mansfield. Just past "The Lodge" hotel on your left, park in the turnout on the same side of the road. The trail down to the falls is opposite the turnout, on the right (east) side of the road.

WATERBURY: MAD RIVER PUNCH BOWL

Privately-owned and supervised, the Punch Bowl is opened to the public and offers a litter-free beach, sunning rocks, no gawkers, good diving, a small waterfall and an island. Take I-89 to Waterbury. South on Route 100 to Irasville. Take first right after sign for "Alpen Inn & Restaurant" onto a dirt driveway that leads along the Mad River to the end of a field. Park and walk left down to the river. Take home your trash when leaving.

TAFT CORNERS QUARRY

This is perhaps your model skinny-dipper quarry pond—with clear water, sandy beach, sunning rocks, low diving cliffs, a rope swing, surrounded by groves and meadows with trails.

From Burlington, leave I-89 at exit 14 and continue 3.4 miles on Route 2, then turn south on South Brownell Road opposite O'Brien's Getty & Quick Shop. Go 1.2 miles, just over the I-89 overpass, you'll find parked cars and the quarry road on right. Block no road when you park and walk in (drive in if gate is open). Coming from the east, you'll find the O'Brien sign 0.8 miles west of Taft Corners (the intersection of Routes 2 and 2A).

BURLINGTON: RED ROCKS PARK

Lake Champlain has many boaters who sail au naturel or look for a quiet cove to enjoy as nature intended. Shelburne Point has some of the more popular coves where you might find like-minded naturists. If landlocked, the startling bluffs at the north end of Red Rock Park are established for social sunbathing.

☞ Route 7 south (Shelburne Road) from Burlington. After I-89 intersection take right turn at Mobil station (Queen City Park Road) for a mile, across a narrow one-lane bridge, and the next left (Central Avenue) to the park entrance. Pay to park or park outside fence. At shore, clothed sandy beach is at left. You go right (north) about a mile on a broad bicycle path to the accepted nude use area just before the cliffs.

BURLINGTON: GRAND ISLE STATE PARK

Grand Isle State Park's south beach on Lake Champlain is developing a clothes-optional area. Skinny-dippers remain discreet especially in heavily-used areas. To get from Burlington to Grand Isle, take Route 89 north to Route 2 west and follow the well-marked route.

FOREST CITY LODGE

Milton is close to Lake Champlain and to Canada, on Route 7 north of Burlington. Forest City Lodge on Long Pond is 6 miles west of Milton—rental cabins, trailers, camping, recreation hall, volleyball, water sports on private spring-fed lake. 260 Beebe Hill Road, Milton, VT 05468-9726. Phone (802) 893-4513.

MAPLE GLEN

Close to Lake Champlain near Canada east of Swanton. Begun, as was Forest City Lodge, for the French-Canadians to avoid a Catholic orthodoxy which governed Quebec into the '60s. While Quebec now has nudist parks Maple Glen keeps a French-speaking membership. Beaucoup acreage, tent and RV sites with hookups, volleyball, tennis,

pool, rec hall. P.O. Box 445, Sheldon Springs, VT 05485. Phone (802) 933-7753.

JEFFERSONVILLE: BREWSTER RIVER

Route 15 northeast from Burlington to Jeffersonville. Turn south on Route 108 as if to Smuggler's Notch—just out of town on your left, you'll see Brewster River Mill Gift Shop. Take the next left towards a covered bridge but instead of crossing it, turn right onto a narrow dirt road upriver. Go past the first pools on the left to park at turnabout and stroll the broad trail further upstream, wading the stream once. Away from the suited, and to the better bargain, a nude pool and waterfall. Early afternoon has best sun. The bold may clamber further up the gorge.

BARTON: LAKE WILLOUGHBY STATE PARK

Hassle-free, sandy wading beach for children and water sports; clean but chilly water with fine trout fishing and water-skiing, and spectacular view of Mt. Pisgah. North on I-93 or I-91 and exit from I-91 at Lyndon. Route 5 north to West Burke, then bear right onto Route 5A to south end of Lake Willoughby. Park either at clothed beach by the road, or about 200 feet south of this on the left. A trail from the latter leads down to the lake at Cunningham Cove around a small point from the clothed beach. Named for Jim Cunningham whose family pioneered nude use.

White Caps campground and store is a a few minutes on foot. Motels, restaurants nearby.

BOLTON SKI AREA: JOINER BROOK

I-89 to Waterbury. West on Route 2 towards Richmond. A paved road on right leads up to Bolton Valley Ski Area; take it, and look for 'Bolton Valley Resort' sign on right. Just 1.5 miles beyond, another sign urges: 'Steep Hill Use Low Gear.' Park in the next turnout on right. Cross the road, cross Joiner Brook, and follow trail upstream to the mother of skinny-dipper pools on this stream. You might also check other turnouts with parked cars descending to Route 2, as many will beat trails leading to nice parts of Joiner Brook.

Fred Gerty, The Ledges, Vermont.

VIRGINIA

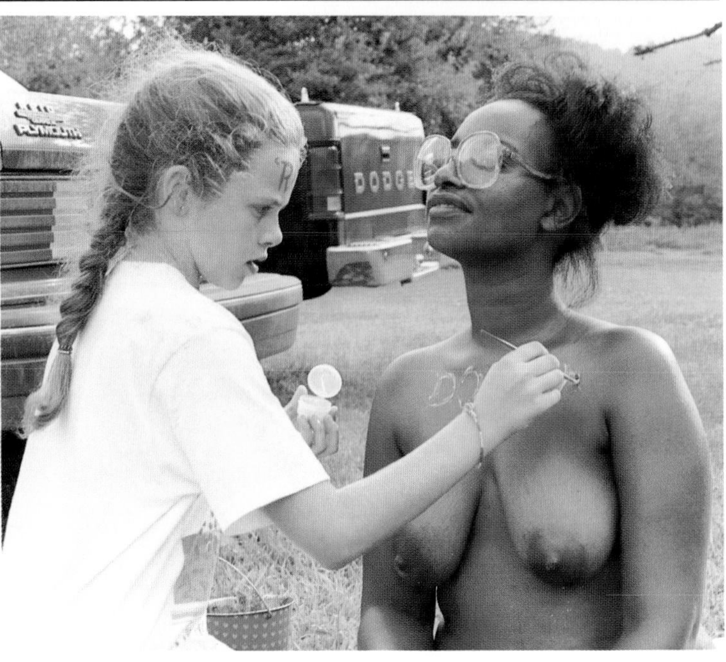

Vic Blandburg, Avalon, Virginia.

Up to the early Eighties, the Assateague Island National Seashore and Chincoteague National Wildlife Refuge were the seat of a world-class naturist beach. A mile and a half shore hike north from the parking, it was kept pristine by its few dozen daily visitors. The federal manager had no cause to eliminate it under federal code. Virginia statutes gave him no handle with which to hammer down. Stymied? No way. The civil servant conspired with local Baptist body-rejecting extremists, in control of the county, who passed an anti-nudity regulation! Federal Seashore but local bigotry, and the courts have let it stand. No wonder Europeans look at Americans as backward.

SOUTHERN

WHITE TAIL PARK

Family-oriented resort of 550 members. Trails, pool, hot tub, snack bar, rec halls, playground, volleyball, with 160 wooded and cleared camp-sites. Near Williamsburg, Jamestown, Virginia Beach. P.O. Box 160-WG, Zuni, VA 23898. Phone (804) 859-6123.

NORTHERN

POTOMAC RIVER: SHERWIN ISLAND

From I-495 take the George Washington Memorial Parkway west to Cropley and park. Sherwin Island is due west in the Chesapeake & Ohio Canal National Historical Park, easily hiked to by the C&O towpath. Recommended maps are USGS Quadrangle for Falls Church, VA and Potomac Appalachian Trail Club Map "D." Swim and sun on the river side of the island.

AVALON CONSERVATION CLUB

At the foot of the Blue Ridge Mountains, family-oriented Avalon ("place of apples") offers camping, a cement-bottomed pond, hiking, volleyball. Less than two hours from the Capital Beltway and within an hour of Shenandoah National Park. P.O. Box 763, Madison, VA 22727. Phone for reservation (703) 923-4316.

SHENANDOAH NATIONAL PARK

A number of large streams suitable for impromptu dipping: pick up Circuit Hikes in Shenandoah National Park from the Potomac Appalachian Trail Club, 1718 N St., N.W., Washington, DC 20036 or any outdoors store.

Overall Run has been popular, with its rock bathtubs and slides, especially weekdays. Big Blue Trail will also delight the naturist backpacker, with its frequent remote streams, ponds, and lakes, as it follows a 144 mile route from Hancock, MD, south through West Virginia, then east across Shenandoah Valley into the north part of Shenandoah National Park.

Other recommended spots include Rose River-Dark Hollow Falls Trail at Fishers Gap, mile 49 on the Drive; Big Rock Falls on the Rapidan River-Mill Prong Trail at Millam Gap, mile 53; and Jones Falls (especially the pool 3 miles from the trailhead), reached by the exit Drive near Loft Mountain Campground (mile 81) and follow Jones Falls Trail. Weekdays are best at all of these sites for uninterrupted enjoyment.

VIRGINIA CONTACTS

VIRGINIA CONTACTS

National Capital Naturists, serving DC–VA–MD–DE to inform the public and to preserve clothing-optional recreational areas. P.O. Box 3122-WG, Fairfax, VA 22038. Phone (703) 241-BARE.

Blue Ridge Naturists, active in preserving VA–NC clothing-optional recreation. P.O. Box 3201, Lynchburg, VA 24503.

Bare Buns Travel—arranges trips to clothes-free destinations for Washington area naturists. Frequent introductory workshops. P.O. Box 11-WG, Oakton, VA 22124. Phone (703) 281-7736.

WASHINGTON

EASTERN

SPOKANE: PEOPLES PARK

The bus from downtown Spokane stops a mile west on the corner of Riverside and Clark, and some who get off hike through a reforested area to Peoples Park. One of the nation's best-established nude beaches, its origin was the Spokane Expo '74. Homes in the area were condemned to enlarge High Bridge Park. Workers at the Expo set up rough camping. Skinny-dipping was part of it, and never has gone away. In 1982, prudes invoked the Spokane lewdness ordinance and several citations were issued before an ACLU lawyer (with aid from the Naturist Society) stopped the nonsense that nude was lewd.

After nearby residents pushed for a traffic closure, the park board installed a concrete barrier and the number of complaints regarding parties and traffic decreased considerably. The user group has asked for portable toilets, another garbage dumpster, more parking and a pay phone but the city is reluctant to provide these as it may be viewed as encouraging the nudity that goes on there.

☞ A 15 minute walk from downtown Spokane. Go west on Riverside Avenue for 1/2 to 3/4 mile. At the bottom of a long hill, where Riverside intersects Clarke (the concrete road barrier was installed here), you will see the Spokane River curving around to the right. Hike through 1/4 mile of reforested area, beneath the bluffs where Hangman Creek meets the Spokane River, until you reach the parking lot. The nude beach runs along Latah Creek at its intersection with the Spokane River. Or take bus #10 to the park entrance.

CENTRAL

COLUMBIA RIVER: WANAPUM DAM RESERVOIR

Located upriver from the Vantage Bridge at I-90 on the Columbia River. Families and singles sun nude without hassles weekdays. Weekends, it may be wise to use the farthest beaches. Volcanic basalt rocks, good sailing, swimming, Frisbee.

☞ Five miles east of Vantage on I-90, take exit 143 and turn left onto the Champs de Brionne Winery Road. After 0.5 miles (mostly north) you will reach a T-intersection. Turn left, following the signs to the Wanapum Dam Reservoir on the old highway (no road name) for 5 miles, passing a "dead-end" road sign. The road ends at a boat landing and parking lot with an outhouse. A sand road on the left continues downstream past two trees with nice beaches and on to the bluff. People with trail bikes ride the sand roads and trails.

MOSES LAKE: POTHOLES RESERVOIR

Potholes Reservoir is ideal for amphibious naturists, for hundreds of sand islets are closely spaced over 10 square miles in the northwest half of the reservoir. The shallows keep the motorboats at bay, providing the desired privacy. A shallow-draft kayak or canoe is recommended but not mandatory: you can easily reach the island of your preference by wading. Indeed, nobody congregates here. Nude use is growing but it is dispersed. Free overnight camping with no facilities.

☞ West of Moses Lake on I-90, take Route 17 exit, get on south frontage road. Go west 2.4 miles to gravel road marked D5-N.E. Take it for 3 miles and a series of forks going down to the lake appear. Explore; find your spot.

YAKIMA RIVER SITES

Between Ellensburg and Yakima snakes Canyon Road alongside the Yakima River. Numerous turnouts permit the skinny-dipper to refresh almost at whim.

WENATCHEE: DOUGLAS CREEK

Spring-fed creek offers many pools as it flows through a lovely sandstone and basalt canyon on BLM land. Most nude use is weekdays as non-nude picnickers emerge on weekends. No harassment.

☞ From Wenatchee take Route 28 east past Rock Island State Park to Palisades Road, turn left and follow it to town of Palisades. Where Palisades Road cuts east away from Douglas Creek you soon turn left, follow creek (6 or 7 miles beyond Palisades town) to picnic and parking areas alongside County Road I (rough road).

WESTERN

SNAKE RIVER DUNES

In southeastern Washington the Snake River dunes are a game preserve which has been getting nude use. The size of the beach varies according to the amount of water held back by the dams downstream, but there is almost always some beachfront available. Boaters and water-skiers pass by frequently on weekends; weekdays are quieter.

☞ From Colfax or Pullman, follow the signs to "Boyer Park," "Almota," or "Lower Granite Dam." When you reach the river go past Boyer Park and Marina and cross over the dam to the south or opposite shore of the river. Follow the road for 2–3 miles downstream. About 1/2 mile past a small trailer park, you'll see a small parking area on the right. Park there and pick a trail to the beach. Please don't contribute to the litter problem.

SNOQUALMIE FOREST: GOLDMYER HOT SPRINGS

The fabled Goldmyer Hot Springs has been reopened by the private owner. A rugged 7 mile hike north of Snoqualmie Pass on the Cascade Crest Trail. The 120°F water provides an oasis of relief for the trail weary. A quota of 20 visitors per day is established. Nude use is permitted as long as others in tub do not object. Reserve before coming to be assured entrance. Midweek is best, Summer–Fall; do carry out your trash. P.O. Box 1292, North Bend, WA 98045. Phone (206) 888-4653.

LAKE BRONSON CLUB

Private, clothes-optional 320 acres of lush forests northeast of Seattle with warm 7 acre lake, grassy beach, trout stream, high waterfall and hiking trails. Fishing, canoeing, tennis, volleyball. Snack bar, cabins, tent and RV hookups. East of Everett. P.O. Box 1135-WG, Sultan, WA 98294. Phone (206) 793-0286.

GLACIER PEAK WILDERNESS: KENNEDY HOT SPRINGS

Located at 3300' in the Glacier Peak Wilderness, a 5 mile hike from Owl Creek campground. The 96°F hot springs fill a 4 x 5' soaking pool that is traditionally clothing-optional and extremely popular. Open all year. In summer a park ranger lives on-site. Overnight permits from the Mt. Baker-Snoqualmie National Forest ranger station.

☞ I-5 north from Seattle. North of Everett, take Route 520 east to Darrington. There drive on Forest

D.W. Thorne 4WD In the Northwest.

Service Road 20 southeast for 8 miles to FSR 23. Turn on FSR 23 and go to its end—trailhead for 643 up White Chuck Canyon, to spring. Seek map and conditions at the ranger station in Darrington.

OLYMPIC PENINSULA: FOREST MURMURS

Across Puget Sound from Seattle, Forest Murmurs welcomes visiting naturists. The nudist park sits on 10 acres of forested grounds with a cleared area that offers a sunning lawn, clubhouse, hot tub, sauna, volleyball, pool, RV and tent sites. P.O. Box 51-WG, Silverdale, WA 98383. Phone (206) 692-7257.

OLYMPIC PENINSULA: COOPER POINT

Evergreen State College students use Cooper Point Beach right on campus. From I-5 take Route 101/401 to the campus, then Cooper Point Drive to Driftwood, and left to parking lot F. Nature trail starts at rear of lot. Go right at each fork of the trail to the beach.

DUNGENESS WILDLIFE PRESERVE

From Sequim near Port Angeles drive to Dungeness Recreation Area, a county fee park contiguous with the Dungeness Wildlife Preserve. Take a path down the bluff to the beach and turn left (west). Within a quarter mile you should be far enough from the crowd that no one will be bothered by your unclothed condition.

In about a mile you will cross a creek where on weekends you may meet people picnicking. Beyond the creek are several miles of almost deserted beach backed by a 100 foot bluff. This beach changes from sandy to partially sandy to rocky overnight. Sandy spots for sunning can usually be found next to the bluff.

OLYMPIC HOT SPRINGS

Olympic National Park removed the hot springs from its introductory map. No doubt, this action reduces the visits by shockable, casual tourists, and a good thing. The dedicated hot spring user will not be daunted—not even by roadblocking boulders which ONP dumps across the access road during the winter months to discourage vandalizing teenagers.

Cross from Seattle to the Olympic Peninsula by the ferry or by driving through Tacoma and north along the Hood Canal. Take Route 101 along the north shore to Port Angeles and 8 miles further west to the Elwha general store. Here turn south following the Elwha River Valley into the mountains. At the ranger station take the right fork up Boulder Creek to the head of the road. Should the road (Elwha River Road) be closed, park and hike an easy 2.5 miles to the springs.

FRATERNITY SNOQUALMIE

Forty acres, modern camping facilities, heated pool, whirlpool, sauna and outdoor games. P.O. Box 985-WG, Seattle, WA 98111. Phone (206) 392-NUDE.

SEATTLE: CARKEEK PARK

North of Carkeek Park is a 1.5 mile stretch of beach backed by a bluff with heavy tree cover, ideal for nude use with only an occasional passing train or boat. Leave car in upper lot at Carkeek Park, cross pedestrian overpass, walk north 1 mile and you're at the start of the beach. Check your newspaper or tide chart: with a 10' tide there's no beach, at 5.5' or less it's a splendid sand strand.

EDMONDS: POINT WELLS

This fine beach is in Edmonds just north of the Standard Oil dock. The nude part of the beach is usually to the tank farm. Drive to Richmond Beach and walk about a mile north along the railroad tracks. Or park in the beach lot immediately south of the Edmonds yacht harbor (open 6 a.m. to 8 p.m.), and walk 1 1/2 miles south along the tracks. Whichever way you come, walking the tracks can not be avoided. It also filters out the Yahoos who would make this beach a mess otherwise.

SOUTH WHIDBEY: DOUBLE BLUFF BEACH

Double Bluff Beach (South Whidbey) is privately-owned. The owner has no problem with beach nudity but litter really bothers him. Take home your trash. And don't go nude on his beach when the whole family gathers there; they're not all into it.

NORTH WHIDBEY ISLAND

Bare 300 foot cliffs add a dramatic touch to a beach experienced by some au naturel. The water's cold, as everywhere on Puget Sound, and the surf can sometimes be tricky—but the swimming is good. Sun's best in the afternoon.

Take I-5 to exit 227 just north of Mount Vernon. Follow the signs to Anacortes which will lead you onto Route 20—look for signs "Oak Harbor/Coupeville." From there proceed exactly 12.4 miles until you reach Ault Field Road, Whidbey NAS; turn right. Take the second left onto 80 NW Street, which is unmarked, then turn right at Crosby Road (also 1050 Avenue West) and proceed east of the beachhouses until you reach an extensive parking lot (capacity 200 cars). Walk 1/2 mile south from the lot until you reach the first broad sandy spot and strip down.

SAN JUAN ISLAND

A number of fine beaches from South Beach to Eagle Cove get very little use, and yet they are within the San Juan Island National Historical American Camp Park—making them virtual havens for skinny-dippers.

☞ From the ferry landing in Friday Harbor drive up hill on the main street a couple of blocks, to where the street branches into a Y. Take the left branch, Cattle Point Road, south past the county fairgrounds. Cattle Point Road makes several right-angle turns but eventually arrives at the southern tip of the island, rightly named Cattle Point. Just beyond the American Camp (6.7 miles from the ferry) make a right turn off the main road, and take this new road over the low ridge and down to South Beach. Park in the lot and walk west, either on the beach or in the meadow above the bluffs, to your pick of coves (they keep getting nicer). Rangers don't see any problem with the nude use.

ORCAS ISLAND

Often called the best of the San Juan Islands, 56 square mile Orcas Island is a naturist's delight. Animal life and wildflowers are abundant everywhere, isolated pebbly beaches are all along the 125 miles of coastline, and Mount Constitution offers a spectacular view. Secluded beach areas on the southeast side of the island hold nude possibilities and 106°F clothing-optional hot tubs can be found in Doe Bay Village, where overnight lodging ranges from $30–$65. Nearby Moran State Park has over 150 camp-sites and the arts and crafts town of Deer Harbor has a luxury hotel.

☞ From Seattle, drive north to the ferry terminal in Anacortes. The ferry arrives daily from Anacortes to Deer Harbor town on the southwest side of Orcas. Bicycles are available for rent and cars are allowed.

BELLINGHAM: TEDDY BEAR COVE

Nearly to the Canadian border, Teddy Bear Cove has a sandy beach with granite and conifers around, and a regular skinny-dipping clientele. Friendly, mellow crowd.

☞ Take Route 11 from I-5 just south of Bellingham, or State Street from downtown Bellingham going south. Both intersect the major ocean frontage, Chuckanut Drive (which becomes Route 11). Take Chuckanut south to the city limit sign, also marked as milepost 18: look for the parked cars and park. Hike the trail in a zigzag fashion down the steep hillside and at bottom, cross the Amtrak tracks and go 20 yards beyond to reach the cove. About 100 yards to the south is another nude beach about 3 times as large. One can reach both beaches by boat, but watch for shallow spots and hidden rocks.

Robert Kelty, Blimp Over Bonny Doon Beach, California.

WEST VIRGINIA

EASTERN

POTOMAC RIVER HEADWATERS

From Berkeley Springs, take Route 9 west thru Great Cacapon. Go 2.1 miles and turn right on County Road 18. Continue 6.6 miles (some parts are rough) to County Road 12, make a sharp right and go 2.3 miles to Magnolia. Turn left over the railroad tracks and then right (a sign says "Private Road"—it belongs to the railroad). On the left is the Potomac River. Parking is off-road. Many grassy and shade areas to enjoy—if you don't like one spot, find another.

CENTRAL

TYGART LAKE STATE PARK

Discreet skinny-dipping from the shores of this large lake. From Clarksburg, take Route 50 east, pass under I-79, and continue to Grafton. Here follow US 250 south toward Philippi until you come to the Arden turnoff, marked "Arden 6." Follow this road about 4 miles to Arden. Cross the bridge here and turn left downstream. This section of road is not paved. Cross a small bridge and continue another 1/4 mile or less. Park along the road anywhere for the next couple of miles, and choose among the several spots which are secluded from the road. You might also drive to the next bridge across the Tygart, park, and hike downstream for more privacy.

Local police are said to act only on complaints; they'll ask that you cover up. From a tavern near the falls (about halfway between the first two bridges), liquid refreshments may be purchased. Camping is available near the falls or in the national forest area 25 miles east.

SENECA ROCKS

Climbing is exhilarating at Seneca Rocks with Spruce Knob the highest point in the state. Seneca Falls are cold—go down to the deep swimming holes, rapids, lots of sunning rocks. For map, brochure: Monongahela National Forest, Elkins, WV 26241.

☞ From Washington, DC: take I-66 west to I-81, north on I-81 and exit on US 50 at Winchester, VA. Take US 50 west 50 miles, then left (south) on US 220 to Petersburg, WV. Turn right on WV 28 (west and south) 20 miles to US 33 at Mouth of Seneca. Then US 33 west 5 miles to secondary Route 7 on left, follow it 2 miles past campground to trailhead on left. Park either at trailhead or campground. Falls and rapids are 3–4 miles up trail following Seneca Creek.

RED CREEK CANYON

Red Creek descends in rapids and waterfalls for 3 miles through a canyon. Many flat rocks for sunning, deep swimholes at base of falls. No trail in the canyon—wade or walk upstream or down.

☞ To Petersburg per Senaca Rocks route. Then WV 28 for 10 miles west, turn right on secondary Route 4 and 1 mile to Dolly Sods Road on left. Take it 6 miles to intersection at top of mountain, turn right there, follow ridge–top road 4 miles to Fisher Spring trail (on left) or 6 miles to Red Creek Trail (on left). Both trails lead 2–3 miles into the Red Creek Canyon; the rapids, falls and rocks are between the two trails.

CHEAT RIVER

RIVER OUTFITTERS

Mountain Streams and Outfitters recommends the Cheat River during quieter midsummer months for that all-over tan. "If it is 80 degrees and sunny, you can wear as little as the traffic will bear" the brochure advises. Rafts, all gear supplied. Mike McCarty, P.O. Box 106, Ohiopyle, PA 15470. (800) 245-4090, (412) 329-8810.

Sheryl Campbell, Washington Seen From Rooster Rock.

WISCONSIN

Wrote Catholic priest Louis Hennepin in his *New Discovery of a Vast Country In America* (1698): "THEY GO STARK NAKED IN SUMMERTIME, wearing only a kind of Shoes made of the Skins of (Buffalo) Bulls."

Father Hennepin was describing the indigenous Americans of the western shore of Lake Michigan, near present-day Milwaukee. Sweltering in the robes of ecclesiastical authority, Hennepin must have appeared as strange to these "Indians" as they surely did to him. In the late 20th Century, the controversy continued on this Lake Michigan shore over the propriety of dressing appropriately.

People sometimes ask what Naturist headquarters is doing in Wisconsin? We answer, it's a cool and quiet place to get the work done. If we could just bask in the sun all day too, who would take care of the description and the advocacy?

SOUTHEAST

RACINE COUNTY: SUN RAY HILLS

Near the Wisconsin-Illinois border, Sun Ray Hills is the largest nudist retreat in either state. Its many acres of rolling woodland and ample birdlife combined with a modern pool and picnic grounds, make Sun Ray Hills an attractive spot for couples to visit for a day or camp for a weekend. P.O. Box 246-WG, Burlington, WI 53105. Phone (414) 539-2592.

MILWAUKEE: PARADISE BEACH

A secluded beach to enjoy the morning sun all-over; on Lake Michigan a half mile north of Bradford Beach. A good mix of singles and families; inappropriate police visits could be in the past.

☞ From downtown Milwaukee follow Lincoln Memorial Drive north. Park where it passes the water filtration plant and curves away from the shoreline on an upgrade. Walk parallel with the lake northward past a chalet-like county works building to the University of Wisconsin-Milwaukee Kenwood Conference mansion. Before reaching it, turn to the lake and scramble down a gravel slope to the lake. Turn left and walk a few hundred feet, past a concrete wall with "Private Beach" written on it. You are there.

MILWAUKEE ATHLETIC CLUB ROOF

MAC has a world apart from clothing-compulsive values on its 12th floor roof deck. Here in years past, bankers, executives, lawyers and Judge Seraphim would

Lee Baxandall, Mazo Beach, Wisconsin River.

Mary Wells, Stretching The Season, Wisconsin.

lounge totally exposed to the sun, snickering at troubles on proletarian Paradise Beach 2 miles north. A "No Women" sign has protected the screened area.

DANE COUNTY

WISCONSIN RIVER: MAZO NUDE BEACH

Very popular, wild and scenic, this clothing-optional site in the Mazomanie State Wildlife Refuge seems immune to lifestyle complainers—the core users have high moral, etiquette and conservation standards. Cooperation with authorities is a constant and National Nude Weekend is a big event. Badger Naturists, P.O. Box 55346, Madison, WI 53705.

No glass. No overnight camping or parking. Nearby on Route 12, newly state-acquired Blackhawk Ridge has a remote camp-site loop favored by the Mazo Beachers. Ganzer's Motel in Sauk City is naturist-friendly.

Canuding the Wisconsin River is quite popular. Rent your canoe early, as outfitters often run out of canoes on hot summer weekends. Sauk City to Arena is a nice 1/2 day trip; picnic on a grassy sandbar or explore a wooded bluff. If camping on the river, take long tent stakes (the soft ground doesn't hold short stakes well), lots of bug spray and protective clothing from poison ivy. As usual, remove your trash.

☞ From the Northeast: off Highway 41 to right on Route 26. Right on Route 151, and continue south to Sun Prairie. Here turn on Route 19 west to Route 12. Turn right (north) for 9.1 miles to County Y. (It's really Y only if you get to the top of the hill before turning left.) On County Y drive west and north exactly 5.2 miles, and turn left on blacktop Laws Road, which leads left in 1/2 mile onto gravel Conservation Road along the Wisconsin River. The nude beach is where all the cars park. If you reach the boat landing, you've gone too far. Take short path to the beach, stay to the north end (right), and avoid affronting the passing canoeists.

From northwest. Off I-94 at the Baraboo exit. Highway 12 south 20 miles to Sauk City. Cross river and right on County Y, to Laws Road and right.

From Madison. Highway 14 west to Mazomanie. Turn right (north) on County Y. Go 4 miles and turn left on Laws Road, and as above.

VALLEY VIEW RECREATION CLUB

Rustic cooperative club, 25 miles east of Madison, 40 wooded acres. Day visitors welcome. Cottage, RV hookup, tent site rentals. Sun meadow, solar above-ground pool, rec hall, volleyball, community kitchen, playground. May–October. P.O. Box F, Cambridge, WI 53523. Phone (608) 423-3060 weekends.

DOOR COUNTY

NEWPORT STATE PARK

Door County is Wisconsin's thumb in Lake Michigan. And Newport State Park is at its northeast tip, one-hour drive north of Sturgeon Bay. Newport State Park rangers don't bother discreet skinny-dippers at Europe Bay. Food and lodging nearby. Roads are less crowded on weekdays.

☞ Drive to Ellison Bay then east on Route 42 and where it again swings north, continue east on Europe Bay Road to its end; park. Walk to the shallow Europe Bay, then north (left) to the seclusion of fallen trees where the beach is the best. Behind this beach is Lake Europe, warmer than Europe Bay with a shallow sandy bottom. Bring a float.

TOFT POINT

Not as far up Door County peninsula is little-visited Toft Point. This wildlife sanctuary was acquired by the Nature Conservancy and turned over to the University of Wisconsin-Green Bay. Old growth makes you think of Canadian forests. Dilapidated wood buildings have a ghost town appeal. UW groups sometimes visit as do New Age folks from The Clearing. The most relaxed, lovely nude sunbathing spot in northeast Wisconsin, with a rocky shoreline on chilly Lake Michigan; a reedy bay with sandy shading to muck; and grassy sunning lawns.

☞ Route 57 to Bailey's Harbor. At Sandpiper restaurant, east on Ridge Road for 1 1/4 miles. Where the road forks right for Bailey's Harbor Yacht Club, you go left and soon pass through the Toft gate. Another mile brings you to a small parking lot area (if filled, you must park at the gate). Walk a mile further to Moonlight Bay Beach.

MISSISSIPPI RIVER

LAKE PEPIN BEACH

Convenient and pleasant for Twin Cities. Avoid in spring flood season when the beach disappears. From Minneapolis take I-94 east to US 61 south. In downtown Red Wing turn onto US 63 north and cross the Mississippi River to Wisconsin side, go 3 miles and turn right on Route 35. Proceed 11 miles to County Road A; a large blacktop parking lot is on your left. Park here! Now, pick your poison: (a) walk down the Rush River, it's right under the bridge just south of the parking lot. Mostly shallow, spring-fed, the path takes you to Lake Pepin in 15 min. Or (b) cross railroad tracks, follow a path through the woods that somewhat parallels the Rush River on its north side. You'll probably get into mud and/or itchweed. Either route, on reaching Lake Pepin walk right along shore to sandy beach. The yacht set simply cruise over.

WYOMING

YELLOWSTONE NATIONAL PARK

THE OTHER SIDE

There was a time when federal park officials let you reach your own understanding with Nature—including the geothermalities of Yellowstone. Many a taxpayer soaked au naturel yet safely in the Gardiner River Boiling Spring and others in the Madison Hot River.

Recently federal managers ruled out these activities for our own good. In getting to hot water as to mountains, the oath of admission is to hold onto their handrails. Is a sanitized Yellowstone becoming Washington's Nature theme park?

In sadness, we dropped Wyoming from this Guide.

Barely in time, #17 of Roger Phillips' *Hot Springs Gazette* arrived (12 S. Benton Ave., Helena, MT 59601, $4.75 or $15/yr) to rescue Yellowstone's reputation with revelations of "The Other Side of Yellowstone" where it's even legal to skinny-dip, as posted signs advise!

If you know how to hike, camp, and apply for a permit, go now.

☞ In the rectangle that is Yellowstone, head for the southwest quadrant by the Idaho border for a camp-site reservation and map from the Bechler River Ranger Station. You must book within two days of entering; you may not reserve earlier; after Labor Day is best. Choose campgrounds up Silver Scarf Creek or the Bechler River. On the north fork of Mountain Ash Creek the Union Falls is a 45' high, 100' wide torrent of 82°F water! These wonders still await the energetic camper.

Ron Marsh, USF&WS At Moonstone Beach, Rhode Island.

CANADA

A thinly populated rural expanse of forests and countless lakes offers many tempting chances for small parties to skinny-dip while hiking or canuding. However, do note that particularly, but not only while in Ontario, citizens of other countries should be aware of Canadian legalities.

The United States federal criminal code does not contemplate or penalize nakedness. Disorderly conduct or lewdness—if such behavior might be exhibited by nude bathers—yes. But not nudity, practiced by discreet recreationists. In Canada it is different. Section 170 (i) specifically bans nudity in public places, and defines nudity as being "so clad as to offend against public decency or order." This is ultimately a community standards regulation, and on appeal, most nudity prosecutions have been reversed. Yet that has done nothing to alter the fundamental law in Canada. Unlike the United States' higher court jurists, those of Canada are strict constructionists, leaving to Parliament the opportunity to remake policy. Only the original intention is considered. The Supreme Court could redirect the notion of current "public decency"—but perhaps that would yield too mixed a result as long as attitudes are formed in Yonge Street as well as the town quarry.

For the present, there is a saving grace in Canadian law: "No proceedings shall be commenced without the consent" of the attorney general of the province where the arrest occurs. The Ontario attorney general always consents to prosecution. The attorney general of British Columbia is convinced that provincial law contravenes the federal code, and he never gives permission to prosecute.

The result is that any poor devil who tries to dip his naked bottom in the icy waters of Georgian Bay may be hauled off to a $100 fine; while 5,000 happy sun worshipers may throng Wreck Beach in Vancouver the same day with impunity. "Skinny dipping in a moderate sense is something that has been a bit of a way of life in Canada," said British Columbia Attorney General Gardom in 1977. So much for federal consistency; in some provinces, notably Ontario, you take your chances.

For a more detailed listing of Canadian sites, the FCN and FQN are currently producing a guide which will list the naturist resorts, clubs, groups and free beaches of Canada, including maps, photos, and a full listing of resort facilities. English/French text. Newsletters also available from both organizations. Write: Federation of Canadian Naturists: P. O. Box 186-WG, Islington, Ontario M9A 4X2. Federation Québecoise de Naturisme: 4545 Avenue Pierre-de-Coubertin, C.P. 1000, Succursale M, Montreal, Quebec H1V 3R2.

ALBERTA

JASPER NATIONAL PARK

Tomahawk Canoe Trips arranges expeditions in Jasper National Park wilderness areas well suited for nudity alone or in a group. Indian-style sweat lodges prepared. 11035 - 64 Avenue, Edmonton, Alberta. Phone (403) 436-9189.

FQN Photo, Weathering Winter in Quebec.

BRITISH COLUMBIA

KOOTENAY MOUNTAINS

HALCYON HOT SPRINGS

For centuries access to the "Great Medicine Waters" of the Halcyon Hot Springs has been contested. The Washington and Kootenay Indians periodically fought over them, then the white man came to develop the springs, charging admission to anyone who would use them. At last the springs flow free for all to enjoy. The bathhouses have long since burned down, leaving the small concrete retaining walls open to the skies.

☞ From Nakusp take Route 23 north for 33.6 km until you reach lot #100, a large open meadow. The retaining walls are visible from the road. The temperature ranges from 115° to 122°F. All pools are excellent for naturist enjoyment.

FAIRMONT HOT SPRINGS

The high-class resort at Fairmont Hot Springs has long serviced the needs of those people who enjoy hot soaking best when accompanied by all the comforts of home. We've discovered a way for free spirits to enjoy the use of these same springs in a more natural setting. Above the hotel on Indian Reserve land, the Native People have built a stone bathhouse that is both charming and free. Four separate rooms, each 4' x 6' with a concrete bathtub, give ample opportunity to enjoy the 120 degree waters.

☞ From Cranbrook take Route 93/95 north to Fairmont Hot Springs. Once in town park at the resort and walk upstream along Fairmont Creek to the bathhouse. Show respect for others and enjoy!

VANCOUVER AREA

CHILLIWACK LAKE

From Chilliwack, east of Vancouver, follow signs 50 km to Chilliwack Lake. Parking is beside road with many private beaches in coves around the perimeter. Nearby Vedder has food and lodging. The outstanding scenery draws canuders, hikers/backpackers, campers. Clad and unclad share without offense.

SUNNY TRAILS CLUB

Twenty minutes from Vancouver, 13-acre grounds, 20 resident members. Pool with jacuzzi, sauna, volleyball, shuffleboard, horseshoes, rec hall with video, cabins, restaurant. Reasonable rates. 9900 162A Street, Surrey, BC V3R 4R6. Phone (604) 481-1353.

MOUNTAIN HAVEN

Sauna, 18 foot diameter pool, tenting area. 36111 Ridgeview Road, R.R. 3, Mission, BC V2V 4J1. Phone (604) 820-0100.

WRECK BEACH

Wreck Beach is a Naturist success story. At first the haven of a few guarded sun worshipers, Wreck is now home to 8,000 laid-back nude bathers on a hot weekend. Much credit goes to the Wreck Beach Preservation Society (WBPS), a coalition of ecologists and naturists.

The first victory came in 1981 when WBPS convinced University of British Columbia not to go ahead with a $12 million erosion-control scheme that would have ended the nude bathing at Wreck. Instead of destroying the cliffs that are the beach's backdrop, replacing them with manicured grass-covered hills—and perhaps a four-lane shore highway from airport to downtown—the UBC built berms to control erosion at the foot of the bluffs. The scheme is working.

A second victory is now unfolding as WBPS defends the beach at Parks hearings against the calls for a ready access road or curtailment of clothing-optional status.

Extending from the Musqueam Indian reserve is 6.5 km of clothes-optional beach at the mouth of the north arm of the Fraser River, to West Spanish Banks. Since 1970, no nude bather on Wreck sands has been hassled for it by the law—the provincial attorney's policy has been toleration, albeit in 1983 several people were arrested for brazenly undressing in full view of Marine Drive.

The Greater Vancouver Park Board allocated no support services to Wreck. So entrepreneurs have packed in food and drink. Police and rescue, when required, have come by Hovercraft over the waves. When drug vendors also began showing up, the Wreck Beach Preservation Society was ready to call for police work. WBPS urges visitors to strictly avoid lighting fires on the beach and not to camp, cause erosion or leave litter.

WBPS has evolved from Citizens Concerned for Cowards Cove, to Marine Drive Foreshore Users Advisory Committee, to the Wreck Beach Area Advisory Committee (appointed for one year by the Park Board), to the Wreck Beach Committee (reformed in 1978), and into the WBPS.

Down the years the Wreck Beachers had to fear the contamination of the Fraser River, University of British Columbia's effluents, and now a sewage plant immediately across the North Arm of the Fraser that is scheduled to release primary sewage with no chlorination or secondary treatment.

Support the Wreck Beach Preservation Society. Send a donation for its work and its newsletter. P.O. Box 602, Delta, BC V4K 4J7. Phone (604) 946-7545.

☞ From the United States take Route 99 northward, past the airport entrance, and immediately get off at the river's far side onto Marine Drive. You'll have to exit going east and double back, passing under Route 99 and threading through some small streets until you're on Southwest Marine Drive going west. Continue for several miles; once at Wreck, you'll have a choice of several parking areas and access trails.

If you park near the green sign with white letters announcing Wreck Beach, take the macadamed path off to your left from the sign and follow a brook. At the bottom of the bluff, walk right at the huge rock partly painted red and continue along the shore for two city blocks until you reach a small beach. Turn inland at the large fallen pine tree hanging out over the water and take the trail at the foot of the bluff that Gerhard Schulz constructed a decade ago to ease your walking on otherwise difficult terrain.

If you drive on past the first sign, you'll enter the UBC campus. The next beach access is at the intersection of Marine Drive and University Boulevard. Gate 6 of UBC (known as Trail 6), Gate 3 (Trail 3) and Trail 4 (directly south of the Museum of Anthropology) will lead through the woods to the beach. Finding trails going back up can be difficult. Trail 3 goes up at the more northerly of two WW II searchlight towers on the beach. Trail 6 goes up about a mile down the coast at Coward Cove, which faces the stone breakwater, just east of an outleaning spar pine.

Access to Wreck Beach from the north is by way of the Spanish Banks Public Beach. This access is recommended for those wanting to avoid the strenuous climbs required for the various trails. From downtown Vancouver, take Route 99, turn off into Fourth Avenue, head west into Northwest Marine Drive. Follow it west several miles onto the university grounds. Where the road begins

Wreck Beach Preservation Committee, A Fine Day

to climb, get off and park; you're 100 yards or so from Spanish Banks Beach. Walk left a couple hundred yards.

LILLOOET RIVER HOT SPRINGS

British Columbia has a wealth of hot springs for the intrepid skinny-dipper to enjoy. Though most of the easily accessible springs have been commercially developed—to the dismay of many naturists and naturalist soakers—a number of springs in the backcountry are well worth the trek. Of note in the Vancouver area are the Meager Creek and Skookumchuck hot springs along the Lillooet River.

☞ From Vancouver take Route 99 north to Pemberton; for Meager Creek follow the logging road northwest along the Lillooet to where it meets Meager Creek; the springs are a 10 km hike up the creek bed. For Skookumchuck continue on Route 99 to Mount Currie, then south along the forest road for 54 km until you see the BC Hydro tower #682. The spring is located between markers 22 and 21.

BRUNSWICK BEACH

"Little Wreck Beach" (as Whistler Mountain ski buffs have dubbed Brunswick Beach) has caused problems for its namesake. Problem is the Canadian Criminal Code still treats nudity as illegal although provincial policy autonomy in the matter has been tolerated since the 1960s. Wealthy Brunswick Point neighbors want the code enforced.

☞ From North Vancouver, northwest on Route 99 (the road to Squamish) to 1 mile north of Lions Bay. Take trails towards Brunswick Point, go to clothed public beach (500' long) on south (Howe Sound) side of point, then walk east, cross 5' high rock groin to 1000' nude beach, a mellow place.

VANCOUVER ISLAND

THETIS LAKE PARK

The capital of British Columbia, Victoria is a charming city on the southern tip of Vancouver Island. Victorians (at least those who do not live up to their name) established a free beachhead at Prior Lake in Thetis Lake Park. In July 1978 city officials conceded it would be pointless to enforce laws against nude bathing.

☞ From Victoria take Route 1 west for about 12 km to Highland Road, about 1/2 km before the main entrance to Thetis Lake Park. Turn right and continue 1/8 km. Just 1.1 km beyond the spot where the paved road becomes gravel, look for Prior Lake on your left. Or look for the Thetis Lake Park-Prior Lake sign while on Highland Road and backtrack the 0.1 km to Trillium Trail, which leads after a 1.5 km hike to a number of secluded beaches on the eastern end of Thetis Lake where nudes often gather.

ISLAND VIEW BEACH

Large beach area, the water is cold and there are no facilities. In 1987 the Victoria parks committee asked staff to prepare a management plan "to separate nude bathers, rather than banning them," as numbers grow. Accessed by Island View Road off Highway 17. Take the foot trail to the park and walk north along the beach or take the trails above the beach. The optional area is below the Indian reserve. Walking distance is about 0.5 km.

PACIFIC RIM NATIONAL PARK: LONG BEACH

From Victoria, Route 1 to Parksville then Route 4 past Port Alberni to Pacific Rim National Park. North end of Long Beach is used nude—past the camping towards Schooner Cove. Couples, gays, a beach backed by tall trees.

SOOKE RIVER POTHOLES

The Sooke River Potholes are well-known to clothed visitors, especially for the waterfalls. The hike along the river involves scaling rocks and wading waist-deep in chilly water. Skinny-dippers just go a bit farther along before stripping down.

☞ About 30 km from Victoria. Drive west on Route 14 almost to the town of Sooke; turn right on Sooke River Road and then into the parking area. Hike 1 km beyond the clothed beach to the nude zone.

WITTY'S LAGOON BEACH

Accessed off Metchosin Road. Take the footpath and wooded stairway to the beach. Turn right and proceed west along the beach beyond the overhanging trees which delineate the boundary between the clothed and optional areas. Walking distance is 0.5 km; the water is cold and there are no facilities.

ALBERT HEAD BEACH

Less then 30 minutes from Victoria, Albert Head Beach is accessed from Farhill Road off Metchosin Road. Park at the Albert Head Lagoon Wildlife Sanctuary and walk north along the beach toward the gravel loading dock. Best area is about halfway, where gravel turns to sand. Walking distance is about 90 m.

QUALICUM BEACH

By train: take the Esquimalt and Nanaimo Dayliners (the E&Q) from its Victoria station at 450 Pandora Avenue. The train makes a round-trip daily, leaving at 8:15 a.m. and traversing Vancouver Island's eastern seaboard. Reservation required: 383-4324 or toll-free 800-665-8630. This is Canada's fourth-shortest line with marvelous wild scenes and terrifying trestles. Cost to Qualicum round-trip is Canadian $20. You'll have two hours there, time for a midday swim, sunning and a picnic or restaurant lunch.

HORNBY ISLAND

From Victoria, Route 19 north. From Denman Island, take ferry to Hornby Island. Drive to Little Tribute Bay, where nude use has been established.

KELOWNA AREA

KELOWNA BEACH

The lake beach is rocky into the shallows. Used by a mix of families, couples and gays. Because many trees were cleared from behind the beach, nude use has shifted further north. From Route 97 (Harvey Avenue) turn south on Pandosy Street. This becomes Lakeshore Road. At intersection with Swamp Road turn right (which is still Lakeshore Road), go exactly 3.2 km, turn right and park in the lot above the beach. Walk well past a small white building to the nude area.

MANITOBA

CROCUS GROVE SUN CLUB

This 60-acre club has a dining hall and lounge, pool, volleyball, tent and RV sites. P.O. Box 314-WG, Winnipeg, Manitoba R3C 2H6. Phone (204) 338-0802 winter, 265-3469 summer.

NEW BRUNSWICK

KOUCHIBOUGUAC NATIONAL PARK

Kouchibouguac National Park offers 40 kilometers of sandy shore on the Northumberland Strait. Of the four areas (dunes), only two are accessible by car. The main dune, South Kouchibouguac, is 7 kilometers long, ample to accommodate the clothed and the nude sunbather. The best weather is from mid-June to the end of August, with the water reaching its warmest temperatures (58° to 60°F) at the end of the season.

☞ Take Route 11 from Moncton to Kouchibouguac Park. Park at Kelly's Beach; walk along the boardwalk to the dune, about 15 minutes. The main bathing area is at the end of the boardwalk; go about 1.5 km farther south before stripping down.

NOVA SCOTIA

HALIFAX AREA

CRYSTAL CRESCENT BEACH

The capital of this eastern maritime province, Halifax has its own formal nude ocean beach—recommended to visitors who ask the Tourist Bureau. Great scenery, up to 300 friendly people on a weekend.

On the weekend of August 4, 1990 the Royal Canadian Mounted Police told people they'd better cover up or be arrested. The beachgoers at once formed a committee and contacted officials, and the incident was not repeated.

☞ From Armdale Rotary at the head of the Northwest Arm in Halifax, drive south on Route 349 for 2.6 km, and turn right following the Old Sambro Road for 18.1 km via Harrietsfield. In Sambro at the stop sign and Harts Store, turn right and drive 2.4 km, following the signs to park at Crystal Crescent Beach. From its lot to the right you'll see the first two beaches which are clothes-required. Walk 20 minutes south, past the second beach to the third, whether by shore or overland path. Starting with the third beach and south along the rocks, the entire coast and peninsula are openly clothes-optional.

GASPEREAU RIVER

If you're in the old French area, about 2 hours directly west of Halifax by freeway, and it's a hot August day, try the pools on the Gaspereau River above the power generating plant. Wolfville is the center of this lowland country reclaimed from the Bay of Fundy with elaborate dikes. Gaspereau Avenue, starting at the Wolfville library, will lead you to the bridge over the Gaspereau. Cross to the east side, turn south, then almost immediately, at a church on the left, turn right again, and follow the Gaspereau upstream a couple miles to where the power plant dams the stream. Here cross to the west side, continuing upstream a half mile to the high-voltage lines. Park, follow them east down to the wooded, cooling pools. Or walk upstream from the power plant.

SUZIE'S LAKE

Very secluded, Suzie's Lake is still lightly used. If driving Route 102 south from Exit 2, stop and park at the first green highway sign you find (about halfway to Exit I) and descend the path to the west to the Birch Cove Lakes (opposite side of Centennial Drive from the Bedford Basin); about a 10 minute walk to Suzie's, the first lake you'll reach.

BAY OF FUNDY

ANNAPOLIS RIVER ISLAND

On the Bay of Fundy find the historic town of Annapolis Royal, then take the road toward Bridgetown. About 5 to 6 kilometers on your way, an inconspicuous dirt road leads from Route 201 down to the beach at the island. If in doubt, ask for directions. The beach is lovely, on the shore of a dammed causeway of the Annapolis River. Long used for skinny-dipping. Heavy river traffic on weekends, so be discreet.

CAPE BRETON ISLAND

INVERNESS BEACH

On northernmost Cape Breton Island, Inverness features a waterfall that crashes down into the ocean. A virtual paradise that resembles Big Sur, it's a favorite spot with the locals.

☞ Take Trans Canada Route 2 from Moncton, New Brunswick, to Amherst, Nova Scotia, then Route 104 to the Canso Causeway. From here take Route 19 along the western shore for 85 km. Just before crossing the railroad tracks into Inverness, take a left onto Sight Point Road. Follow this road for 10 km and park along the side near the farm buildings. Walk an additional 1.5 km until you see the path that leads to the beach.

ONTARIO

Ontarians at home are forced to toe the mark of clothes-compulsive moralism. The provincial attorney general, with his anachronistic crusade against naturism, has launched an annual exodus to the Caribbean which costs the nation dearly in foreign exchange, while encouraging salacious commercial entertainments at home on Yonge Street.

EASTERN

BUFFALO'S GETAWAY: LILLY VALLEY PARK

An all year naturist resort just across the international bridge, providing relief for snowbound Buffaloans with indoor pool, sauna, spa, camp-sites. P.O. Box 261, Fort Erie, Ontario L2A 5M9. Phone (416) 871-4208.

LAKESUN NATURIST RESORT

An unspoiled large lake with wilderness hiking. To protect the loons, no motor boats are allowed. Sailing, fishing, camping. Families and singles welcome at this family-operated resort with European tradition (the first in North America to call itself 'naturist'). It is 25 miles north of Kingston; near Watertown, NY; reached by US 81 north. R.R. #1, Perth Road, Ontario K0H 2L0. Phone (613) 353-2463.

THE GRAND BARN

The 220 foot renovated Grand Barn—between Ottawa and Montréal on cross-Canada Route 417—has 150 acres of its meadows, ponds and woods available for nude sunbathing, hiking and camping. Plus, a grounds-wide, clothing-optional "Nature's Way In the Nude" is held each July 17-25 and Sept. 5-9. Please call by June 1 to reserve. Art events and music performances are the main attraction. Combine with popular Rivière Rouge gorge, north by ferry across the Ottawa River. 777 Barb Rd., R.R. #1, Vankleek Hill, Ontario K0B 1R0. Phone (613) 678-3453.

EAST HAVEN SUN CLUB

70 acres bordered by the South Nation River, providing excellent fishing and canoeing. Volleyball, pool, tent and trailer sites. 50 km from Ottawa; 130 km from Montreal. English, French and German spoken. P.O. Box 440, Casselman, Ontario, K0A 1M0. Phone (613) 764-3187.

GATINEAU PARK: OLD MILL (QUEBEC)

Gatineau Park lies within Quebec, but serves the nation's capital. The Old Mill is a popular site and the oldest established nude beach in Eastern Canada. The name conjures up images of a 17th century grinding mill, but don't be fooled. This is an abandoned hydroelectric power station and 'old' is circa 1914. Oh well! at least the pond is nice, and the surrounding mountains are authentic. Camping is at the north end. As to nudity, in 1977, the local press said that "Royal Canadian Mounted Police and Gatineau Park rangers usually have an easygoing attitude toward offenders, mainly because nude bathing is confined to secluded areas." In 1984 Kevin Hogan was brought to court for nudity at the Old Mill. The reasonable judge dismissed the case, and there's been no hassle since then. However, the National Capital Commission has announced plans to develop the area, turning the Old Mill into a regular stop on their visitor tours—we wonder just which tourist attraction will be the big draw.

☞ From Ottawa drive Route 105 north to Gatineau Park, locate Meach Lake, park, and walk up the winding trail for 1.5 km to the Old Mill site.

Another site in Gatineau Park is Lake Lapêche. Take Route 105 from Ottawa through Hull, Chelsea, and several small towns to St. Cecil. In St. Cecil look for a dirt road turnoff to the left for Lake Lapêche. Park at the lake, and walk past the restaurant and picnic tables and around the peninsula by way of the lake to the nude bathing zone, where you may find up to a hundred fellow naturists.

WINDSOR-CHATHAM AREA

Ontario has a long shoreline on Lake Erie, and several informants report most of it hassle-free—partly because it isn't the warmest or most desirable water. But that doesn't stop those who would like to sun themselves—all the way from Detroit to Buffalo, on both the U.S. and Canadian shores.

DETROIT GETAWAY: POINT PELEE NATIONAL PARK

The east beach of Point Pelee National Park on Lake Erie is a great getaway spot not far from Detroit. Drive to Windsor, take Route 401 east and exit onto Route 77 south towards Leamington. Beyond Leamington look for the Point Pelee signs.

Featuring a nature center, marsh boardwalk, and numerous woodland trails, the main attraction is 22 kilometers of beach. With all that sand there is room enough for the clothes-optionals to have established a delightful beach, located 2 km north of the East Beach change house. The adjacent Red Head Pond is also used by skinnydippers. An entrance fee is charged. Camping is available at nearby Wheatley Provincial Park, or find food and lodgings in Leamington.

TorStar, Scarborough Bluffs, Toronto.

SLEEPY HOLLOW BEACH

Used by Detroit, Sleepy Hollow Beach is in the Chatham area, Raleigh Township. Drive 16 km south from Chatham to Route 3. Then take Route 3 west from Cedar Springs for 2.4 km to the Crawford Side road. Park at its end, walk to the left through a gulley, and continue along a clifftop to a sandy slope that you descend to the beach on Lake Erie.

SUNNY GLADES NATURE PARK

Located near junction of highways 79 and 2 between Chatham and London, 80 miles from Detroit/WIndsor. 40 trailer sites, pool, sauna, hiking trails, flower gardens, lovely restored barn as rec hall. ASA and TNS membership cards honored. P.O. Box 309, Bothwell, Ontario N0P 1C0. Phone (519) 695-3619.

TORONTO

Toronto police and judges have been acting against the personal freedom of citizens at Hanlan's Point and Outer Harbour beaches. The most secure site for sunning seems again to be the beach below Scarborough Waterworks, reached by a steep descent.

Other sites sought out by harried Toronto landlubbers are the distant dunes of Pinery Provincial Park on Lake Huron and the dunes of Sherkston Beach Park on Lake Erie. Torontonians with boats can usually enjoy a skinny-cruise on Lake Ontario.

GEORGIANA ISLAND

Bare boaters are reported along Georgiana Island's south shore, making Lake Simcoe one of the more popular nude recreation spots for Torontoans. Take Route 404 north to the launch points.

N.U. RECREATIONAL RESORT

Welland is around the byte of western Lake Erie from Toronto. Pool, hot tub, sauna, snack bar, lawn sports, playground, nature trails and picnic areas. Niagara Falls excursions. Rental rooms, tent and RV spaces. Open year round. R.R. 2, 1782 Turner Road, Welland, Ontario L3B 5N5. Phone (416) 384-2632.

FOUR SEASONS NATURE RESORT

10 miles from Hamilton, an hour southwest from Toronto. Luxurious Four Seasons has 50 acres, three lighted tennis courts, volleyball, indoor and outdoor pools, whirlpool, sauna, restaurant and night club. Tent and trailer sites, rooms. P.O. Box 9-WG, Freelton, Ontario L0R 1K0. Phone (416) 659-7784.

PONDEROSA NATURE PARK

100 acres, open all year. Indoor/outdoor pool and whirlpool, sauna, TV lounge, restaurant and snack bar, tennis, hiking trails, dances, playground. Tent/RV sites and trailer/room rentals. Box 501-WG, R.R. #3, Puslinch, Ontario N0B 2J0. Phone (416) 659-3410.

GLEN ECHO PARK

As Toronto Gymnosophical Society's comfortable quarters near Toronto, Glen Echo Park is a welcome stop on a naturist itinerary. Indoor pool, whirlpool, sauna, volleyball, tent and trailer sites. P.O. Box 185, Willowdale, Ontario M2N 5S8. Phone (416) 939-7736.

HANLAN'S POINT

The northernmost beach, adjacent to the airport, has been clothes-optional for years, but police have begun issuing "please dress" passes lately. However, there are many small, secluded beaches to the south of the main beach than can be used au naturel. Avoid any area visible from the walkways.

☞ Access by ferry to Hanlan's Point. Off the ferry, follow the fencing south until it ends at a changing building, where there is beach access.

SCARBOROUGH BLUFFS

A long tradition of nude sunning here, but definitely not the future for Toronto naturism: It's a narrow and stony if picturesque beach, with broken glass and rusty iron underfoot. East of Warden Avenue, avoid on weekends. Few care to swim.

☞ Located beyond the Toronto Hunt Club Gulf Course between Warden and Bluffers Park. Take Kingston Road past Birchmount to Glen Everest, turn right, again at Fisleigh Drive. Proceed to the Scarborough pumping station, and turn right between the two buildings to the parking in the rear. Follow the path to the right, and walk along the bluffs until you see the building at the base of the cliff. Climb down the path (carefully) and use the beach on either side.

Or take the steep path from the end of Warden. A fence appears to close it off, but was carefully constructed so that one can walk around the end of it.

UNICAMP

The Unitarian Universalist Unicamp and Conference Center northwest from Toronto at Honeywood Springs includes a nude beach. Only U/U members and participants in special events at the Camp are welcome to use the beach. Information: Summer, 519 925-6432. Off-season, 416 395-1449.

LAKE CONGO

Excellent camping on the far side of the lake. If you see a float plane, don't be alarmed—it's most likely German people from a nearby lodge learning how to fly on floats who don't mind nudity at all. Used by hunters in early spring and fall, at which time, avoid. Take your trash out.

☞ Route 400 north from Toronto to Route 69 as far as MacTier. Turn left in MacTier and go 18 km from Route 69 down the backroads. Once you have gone through MacTier, continue 6.5 km to the Healey Lake Road and turn left. Go 12.5 km and after passing a marina (Shell), the pavement ends. Continue on the unpaved portion for 4 km. Park on the right side of the road in the small turnout. If you go too far, you'll see water on your right ; go back. Unlatch your canoe or grab your tent and head for the wooded area.

GEORGIAN BAY

McREA LAKE

A nudist haven about 110 miles north of Toronto. Fairly large, with lots of bays and rocky points to camp on. Some of the campsites even have sandy beaches.

☞ Accessible from Route 69 on the east and Georgian Bay on the west, and can only be reached by water which tends to keep out undesirables. Not an organized camping area patrolled by rangers, but rather reasonably remote and unspoiled by cottages. One must portage a canoe over the hill adjacent to the rapids and proceed west along the river to the lake. Don't let the 50 or so cars in the parking lot discourage you; these people use canoes and the lake remains uncrowded.

WOODSBAY LODGE

This rustic resort and fishing base has a designated area for nude sunbathing. Rooms available in the Lodge with Full American Plan. Cabins also available. 2 1/2 hours from Toronto.

Nestled among small lakes, Woodsbay Lodge shows the way to clothing optionality in the backwoods. The area is fine for fishing and canuding, hiking or boating in the buff, exploring the many rock formations and inlets. Float plane, canoe and paddle boat rentals, windsurfing. % General Delivery, MacTier, Ontario P0C 1H0. Phone (705) 375-5395. In Europe: Jan vom Bauer, Kiefernstr. 24, D 4156 Willich 1, Germany; phone 02154-4500.

285919

363082

QUÉBEC

Québec's attorney general does not consent to prosecution of nude recreation. This is a more enlightened attitude than that in neighboring Ontario, and the more remarkable when it is remembered that, until the 1960s, Québec was virtually without individual liberty, bowing to a quasi-ecclesiastical provincial government. The situation has improved so much in recent years that many Montrealers who once journeyed south to Cape Cod and other spots for some freedom now stay closer to home.

Information and membership: The Fédération Québécoise de Naturisme, 4545 Avenue Pierre-de-Coubertin, C.P. 1000, Succursale M, Montréal, Québec H1V 3R2. The FQN enjoys the support of the Regroupement Loisir Québec in maintaining an office and is consulted by the Ministry of Tourism on relevant matters.

QUÉBEC CITY

ÎLES DE LA MADELEINE

In relatively warm waters of the Gulf of St. Lawrence, particularly during August, the Magdalen Islands, Îles-de-la-Madeleine have long been a popular Québec vacation choice. Best bets are Plage de l'Éolienne's south dune, at the end of Chemin de la Cormorandière and facing l'île Shag; and Plage de l'ouest, on the north end of l'Étang-des-caps, beyond the shipwreck.

Also recommended is Plage du Havre. From Havre-Aubert, take the Airport Road leading to a dumpyard and find the clothed beach. From there walk east towards Sandy Hook.

RIVIÈRE DU SAULT-À-LA-PUCE

Rivière du Sault-à-la-Puce, of Château-Richer, near Québec, offers superb scenery and nice falls and cascades. A wonderful area with magnificent sculpted rocks and numerous waterfalls. People walk, swim and sunbathe in the nude.

☞ About 10 miles from Quebec on Route 138 toward Ste.-Anne-de-Beaupré, you enter Château-Richer. Take the route to St.-Achillée. Right after Grenier Camping, park near the dirt road that goes down to your right. Hike down, go to the left and cross the river. Near the big fall, under the Hydro-Quebec pilons, there are clothed swimmers. You can swim in the nude a bit further, or at many places along the river. Nude swimming also takes place up by the municipal aqueduct.

LAC-SAINT-CHARLES

Take Route 73 north which becomes Route 173, in the direction of Lac Delage resort, to Lac-Saint-Charles, suburb of Québec City. In Lac-St.-Charles take 1st Avenue toward Saint-Émile. Turn onto the gravel road on your right opposite the street numbers 1051 and 1053. Park in the clearing or at the end of the road. At the end of the clearing there's a path leading to a sandy beach just big enough for two couples, or a family and a bonfire, on the lazy Rivière St.-Charles.

STE.-AGATHE FALLS

A magnificent site, well worth the trip yet off the tourist map. Several spots suitable to dive and swim in the gorge. Wilderness and commercial camping available.

☞ Take Route 20 from Québec City, to exit 278 (Laurier Station). Take Route 271 South to Ste.-Agathe. Turn right to take Route 218 west, to the first fork to the left. Follow it along the river to the covered bridge. Park, and walk downstream, passing the clothed areas, until you reach the rocks which are the naturist area.

CAP-AUX-OIES

Charlevoix area. Find the abandoned train station, near the shore, and go into the bay (east). Popular.

LOTBINIÈRE: POINTE-PLATON

On the south bank of the Saint Lawrence River west of Québec CIty, drive Route 20 to Laurier Station (exit 171) and north on Route 271 to Sainte-Croix de Lotbinière and continue west on Route 132. On your right find the Chemin de la Pointe-Platon which brings you to the Joly de Lotbinière Manor. Drive onto the manor grounds to your right. Park, follow the road which passes in front of the house and down the slope, until you reach the pier. The beach is fine gravel and the water warm. The best time for swimming is when the tide is high.

VALCARTIER: JACQUES CARTIER RIVER

Drive to Loretteville, where Routes 371 and 369 join west of Charlesbourg. Take Route 371 (Boul. Valcartier) north to the village of St.-Gabriel-de-Valcartier and continue to the bridge over the Jacques-Cartier River. Park by the road, on the west side (the south bank), and take a path down to the river. The island with a long sandpit perfect for nuding and camping is located 700 m from the bridge. The water is warm and deep.

RIVIÈRE BRAS DU NORD-OUEST

The area near Baie St.-Paul is popular without being crowded. Excellent for families with young children and perfect for romantic scenery enthusiasts. The water is a bit cold but drinkable. A nice place to tent.

☞ Coming from Québec City, continue on Route 138 to a turn, Route 362, which descends to Baie-St.-Paul; skip this, keep going until Chemin du Golf. Here turn left, and at Chemin de l'Équerre, turn left again. Follow it to the first left and take it to the end, a plank barrier. You'll now find a wire fence on your left. Park by it and take the path to the left, which leads to a lagoon and through the trees to the river. Settle among the rocks you first find, or the small basins up the river are excellent for swimming.

CLUB NATURISTE L'AVANTAGE

Six km east of Pont-Rouge on Route 358, l'Avantage has 90 acres with a stream and camping, motel, restaurant, bar, laundromat, club house and 2 pools, one heated. 30 minutes from Québec. Bilingual. No singles or pets. 259 Route Grand-Capsa, Pont-Rouge, Québec G0A 2X0. Phone (418) 873-4791.

EAST MONTRÉAL

SHERBROOKE: AYER'S CLIFF FALLS

Between Routes 55 and 143 which both connect Newport, VT and Sherbrooke, on Route 141 at the foot of Lac Massawippi, locate and park behind the dance hall. Take the path that leads to the foot of the falls. On a weekday you should be able to skinny-shower.

160 EXIT QUARRY

Drive Route 20 toward Québec, taking the Route 150 exit and turning right in front of the Petro-Canada station. The first road on your right will take you to

Preceding Page: Greg Griffith/Mountain Moments, Alta Lake at Whistler Mountain, British Columbia, Canada.

the quarry. There is no beach and water depth is 20 to 30 meters.

CLUB NATURISTE LOISIRS AIR-SOLEIL

Club Naturiste Loisirs Air-Soleil is a co-op, youth-oriented resort. On a river near Drummondville, Route 20 east of Montréal. Perfectly kept, 235 sites with full hook-ups. Heated pool, restaurant, rec hall, open-air cinema, campfires, dances. Volleyball, pétanque, archery, ping-pong, shuffleboard, playground. No singles. 28 chemin Allard, C.P. 2, L'Avenir, Québec J0C 1B0. Phone (819) 394-2556.

SOUTH MONTRÉAL

CLUB LA POMMERIE

La Pommerie—Apple Orchard is 35 miles south of Montreal and 30 miles north of Plattsburg (NY). It has 400 acres of cedars and working trees, a getaway with esprit and savoir faire that is favored by many. A trout-stocked quarry pond, pool with sunning lawn, volleyball, massage, shiatsu, yoga, pétanque, ping-pong, aerobics, t'ai chi, ceramics and macramé, archery, campfires, dances. Camping, mobile homesites, chalets to rent, gourmet restaurant, convenience store, fashion boutique. May–August. St-Antoine Abbé, Québec J0S 1N0. Phone (514) 826-4723.

☞ From Montréal, Pont Mercier and Route 138 southwest towards Huntington. At Ormstown turn left on Route 201, and left again at St.-Antoine Abbé on Route 209. Go less than a mile and enter on right.

VALLÉE RUSTIQUE

Club Naturiste la Vallée Rustique is a quaint, well equipped club with friendly atmosphere. Pool, tennis, archery, volleyball, shuffleboard. Just across border from Enosburg Falls. Chemin des Bouleaux, C.P. 89, Frelighsburg, Québec, J0J 1C0. Phone (514) 298-5372.

NORTH MONTRÉAL

DOMAINE DE L'ÉDEN

On the near north of Montréal; restaurant and night club, artificial lake with beach, large pool, tennis, youth club, playground, picnic tables, camping. Rooms to rent. 63 St.-Stanislas, C.P. 1197, Laurentides, Québec J0R 1C0. Phone (514) 478-6012.

SHAWINIGAN: LE CYPRÈS

This 560-acre club is intersected by the unpolluted Batiscan River 2 1/2 hours northeast of Montréal; canuding is part of club experience along with the volleyball, baseball, archery, hiking, community dinners, bonfires, dances. Hundreds of tent/RV sites. Rang de la Traverse, Notre-Dame de Montauban, Québec G0X 1W0. Phone (418) 336-2573 or 647-3887.

WEST MONTRÉAL

RIVIÉRE ROUGE

Just north of the Ottawa River, a 3-mile granite gorge on the Riviére Rouge with whitewater rapids and lovely waterfalls. Above the last falls (30 minutes walk), white sand beaches. In season, rafters come through, don't mind them. Plenty of large smooth rocks for sunning with deep pools upriver for cooling off. Fish for your dinner? Take in a trash bag; carry out some of the garbage. Informal camping.

☞ 75 minutes from Montréal, near Hawkesbury (Ontario) and Petite Nation Provincial Park, midway to Ottawa. The park straddles Route 148 west of Calumet and before Pointe-au-Chêne. Park where the highway crosses the river and descend on the east side to the river. Walk upstream beyond the first rock outcropping to a second rocky zone where the clothes-optional use begins. The walk is moderate to difficult as you continue upstream for the seven waterfalls.

OKA BEACH

Oka Beach use grows, despite official claim of non-condonement. Route 640, Montréal's beltline on the north, will take you 35 km southwest, through St.-Eustache, becoming Route 344, ending at Oka on the Ottawa River. Many nudists arrive by boat. The sandy beach is on the north shore of Lake of Two Mountains—even on a Montréal bus route. Parking was $8 per car in 1990. Nude bathers go to the east end of the 3.5 km strand, beyond the lifeguarded beach.

LA PRAIRIE QUARRY

Swim in early summer before algae growth begins. Easily accessible and nice for wilderness camping. To La Prairie by Taschereau Boulevard (Route 134), then take Route 104 south (toward St.-Jean-sur-Richelieu). At 3 km, right before the bridge, a bumpy dirt road leads to the river. From there, proceed on foot to the quarry, about 5 to 10 minutes.

SASKATCHEWAN

GREEN HAVEN SUN CLUB

This club is very rustic, with some camping and trailer facilities and 25 acres of gentle rolling land with large open grass areas and shade trees. P.O. Box 3374, Regina, Saskatchewan S4P 2H1. Phone (306) 699-2515.

SASKATOON: BARE-ASS BEACH

The Saskatchewan River flows through the capital city of Saskatoon, offering many fine spots for skinny-dippers. Most popular of the "bare-ass" beaches is south of the city on the west river bank. Park on the old Pike Lake Road near the Cranberry Flats.

A native advises that, in the prairie provinces, "every town has a summer skinny-dipping hole—the nearest water, be it the town reservoir or river, lake or slough." That goes for much of Canada, but do remember to check police practice before creating your Eden.

YUKON

WHITEHORSE: EAR LAKE

Ear Lake is close to Whitehorse. The shallow water is relatively warm for the Yukon, another attraction. Sunbathers disperse among the many coves, mostly on weekdays, for they have to allay gossip; Whitehorse has 15,000 curious citizens.

Alternative is Long Lake, also near town. Access at one end. By walking halfway around you find more privacy.

For the Liard River Hot Springs, see Alaska, U.S. listings.

CENTRAL & SOUTH AMERICA

ARGENTINA

BUENOS AIRES

NATURIST ARGENTINA

Cofounder Ramón Rodríguez was the publicly-named officer of the nation's sole naturist club, Primera Asociación Naturo-Desnudista Argentina. Started in 1934, PANDA was by far Latin America's oldest naturist association. The Rodríguez family also owned the land on a Tigre River Delta island 40 km from Buenos Aires where members met for gymnastics and vegetarian repasts.

PANDA's membership as well as rigor declined as the founders aged. In 1985 the family simply took back the land, closing the club.

In recent years those not PANDA members had sunbathed by hiding among public beach dunes. Or they drove to more liberal beaches in Uruguay and Brazil. Six years after PANDA ended Naturist Argentina has regrouped, including some former PANDA members, as NAT. The NAT goal is to win legal nude beaches open to all.

☞ NAT gathers on land owned by Jorge Biagosch at Benavídez, 30 miles north of Buenos Aires. Pool, snack bar, ping-pong. Families and singles welcome. Phone Cristian Vogt, (011-541) 824-7389, or Biagosch, 0327-8566.

Vic Blanburg, Tourists Try Sea Au Naturel.

BRAZIL

SANTA CATERINA

PRAIA DO PINHO

Brazil's southerly state of Santa Caterina is pretty and popular for snowy mountains, natural hot springs, sweeping beaches, chic discos and high rises. German settlers left their influence.

Tourist information in English comes from Florianopolis. Officials accept topfree and some nudity on resort beaches of Camboriú. But the naturist mecca is 4 km south of Camboriú at Pine Beach, Praia do Pinho.

The crescent sand beach lies between rocky points, with good snorkeling, lobsters and shellfish, volleyball, surfing, bonfires. Snackbars, camping, motel with bar/restaurant. Naturists maintain etiquette. Associação amigos da Praia do Pinho, C.P. 272, 88330 Camboriú SC, Brazil.

☞ By air, to Florianopolis. Bus or rental car for 70 km almost to Camboriú. Turn off coastal route 101 at km marker 140. Eight km to the beach on a dirt road.

GALHETA BEACH

Near Ilha de Santa Caterina north of Florianopolis, Praia Galheta is south of Barra de Lagoa (itself near Logoa da Conceição), and north of Fortaleza town—with Praia de Mocambique to its north and Priai Mole to its south. Galheta Beach earlier was a refuge for transvestites and it remains clothing-optional.

PARAÍBA

PRAIA DE TAMBABA

Conde, a city en route to Jacumã on BR-101 from João Pessoa, has a naturist supporter as its city prefect. Aluisio Regis is implementing a plan to transform Tambaba—one of the 10 most beautiful beaches of Brazil, according to Quatro Rodas—into the first Paraíba state legal nude beach.

Lee Baxandall, Pit Stop At The Blue Hole On Hummingbird Highway, Belize.

SÃO PAULO

PRAIA BRAVA

A small remote 'wild' beach usually without hassle, thanks to difficult access. Close to São Paulo between Bertioga and São Sebastiao on the Rio-Santos Highway; look sharp between the towns of Boissucanga and Maresias.

RIO DE JANEIRO

PRAIA GRANDE

An emerging Brazilian clothing-optional site south of Itacuruca. Take Rio-Santos Highway (BR-101) south from Rio. At 92 km mark (7 km past Itacuruca) find turnoff toward beach. Park before railroad tracks and continue on foot.

BÚZIOS

This peninsula fishing village is "the St. Tropez of South America"—a weekend hideaway for hip folks from Rio. Cheap to luxurious lodgings. Euro-Brazilian cuisine in Búzios' many restaurants with muscians strumming bossa nova tunes.

☞ Located 125 miles northeast of Rio. Drive, or take a small plane that soars over Sugarloaf Mountain before landing in a field of wild goats. A Buzios package can be put together for you by Adam Carter at Brazil Nuts, phone (718) 834-0717.

Life begins at 11 a.m. with a stroll to the nude beach. A path up the wooded hill brings you to a small sandy cove, **Ferradura**, or further on, to tiny and isolated **Ferradurinha** beach, encircled by rocks and trees that drop flowers.

Praia de Focas is the 'hot' new beach, already well established. North of those in walking distance, Focas is reached by driving the Estrada de Usina.

Praia Olho de Boi is the next nude beach north from Focas—actually in Cabo Frio—and is also reached by the Estrada de Usina. Just past Forno and Forninho beaches, just south of famous Brava Beach.

Praia Brava is an 'official' nude beach as of 1991, by act of Mayor Ivo Saldanha of Cabo Frio. Control of the use of the beach is entrusted to the Rio De Janeiro Naturist Association–Serbio de Oliveira, Rio Nat, C.P. 136, 20001 Rio De Janeiro.

MATO GROSSO

CHAPADA DOS GUIMARÃES

A beautiful canyon park 68 km from Cuiabá, the capital of Mato Grosso state in west central Brazil. Chapada dos Guimarães has waterfalls and rivers where skinny-dipping has become a tradition. According to the 2-89 edition of *Pinho é*, nude use is well-established and growing due to influence of the nearby "hippie community" since the early 1970s. Camp-sites available. Cuiabá is the gateway to an immense ecological preserve, the Pantanal, well worth a visit.

BAHÍA

TRANCOSO

In the south of Bahía this town on a hill overlooking a beach remains a tranquil place. A few hippies and young people dominate the local population but there is no heavy drug scene. Pousadas offer rooms or you can stay with local people. The beach is located to the south of Trancoso.

☞ Bus to Porto Seguro. Across from its bus terminal, catch the ferry across the river, and then another bus to Trancoso. If you arrive to Porto Seguro at night, stay over and go to Trancoso the next morning. If you know how long you're going to stay, book your return bus from Porto Seguro when you arrive, especially between December and March, and on holidays.

LAGOA AZUL

This Blue Lagoon has a lovely beach as well as medicinal mud baths; described as a nude site in the 1988 Quatro Rodas Guide. Lagoa Azul is near Arrial de Ajuda, across the river from Porto Seguro.

AREMBEPE

Fifty km northeast of Salvador, capital of Bahía, Arembepe was the original hangout for hippies in the late '60s. Now it is quiet and peaceful. The beach is long and lined with palms. You can find lodgings but most people make a day trip from Salvador. The nude portion is 2 km north.

☞ On BR-099. Buses run daily from Salvador at Terminal Franges in Cidaele Baixa (lower city). Best to check with your bus to find out when the last bus returns from Arembepe.

CEARA

JERICUACUARA

Young hip Brazilians put the fishing town of Jericuacuara on their maps. Ringed by sand dunes and lakes in the northern state of Ceara, it lacks electricity or tap water, with only a town pump. Some families convert parlors to restaurants serving catch of the day. No hotels but locals rent rooms. Nude bathing is a 3 km walk west of town.

☞ A bus leaves daily at 8 a.m. from Fortaleza to a town called Gijoca. It is very important that you book in advance and, if you know when you'll be returning, buy your tickets when you arrive in Gijoca. From Gijoca jeeps meet the bus to take you for an hour ride around the dunes to Jericuacuara.

GUATEMALA

EAST COAST

SEVEN ALTARS FALLS

Livingston, Guatemala's ancient port on the Caribbean and former headquarters of United Fruit Co., is now a quiet outpost of 4,800 souls, mostly Carib blacks. You can laze about, consume exotic fruits and bask on the rocks beside a spectacular cascade of 10 to 20 foot falls, the Seven Altars, nestled into the Maya Mountains. The waters then flow through aquamarine pools into the sea while giant trees filter out all but slender beams of sunlight, which dance on the pools and cast pale shadows on the underwater stones. Avoid the dry season when the falls dry up.

In town, be sure to eat at Margoth's and load up on coconut bread, fruit and other goodies. In mid-May, Livingston throbs with reggae and street dancing as other Guatemalans come to help celebrate St. San Isidro Labrador. Cf. *Américas*, March-April 1988.

☞ Seven Altars Falls is reached from the town beach by boating or walking north for 5 miles, past orchids, coconuts and pineapple stands, to the end of the white-sand shore. You must ford the 30 yard mouth of the second of two rivers, wading out. When the beach gives way to rocks and trees, find an overgrown path in the sea grass leading into the jungle. You'll soon hear the falling water.

To reach Livingston, take the bus from Guatemala City to Puerto Barrios and from there take the mail boat north to Livingston. There's no road. La Casa Rosada, on the hill, the only hotel with plumbing, is recommended. Or choose a spartan pensione or the hostel by the harbor.

HONDURAS

NORTH COAST

THE BAY ISLANDS

Las islas de la Bahía, little developed or visited, delight both skinny-divers and honeymooners looking for a quiet spot in the sun to be naked all day. Explore the west end of Roatán Island—rent a boat that will take you and supplies. On Utila, another of the islands, the unfettered can enjoy the sunshine and surf anywhere away from town. The beaches are among the best in the Caribbean and a chartered boat is the best way to enjoy it all.

☞ Lodging and meals are found on the islands of Roatan and Guanaja, rates higher for dive packages. Recommended: Anthony's Key Resort, phone: 1-800-227-3483. Florida: (305) 858-3483.

The Honduran airline, Tan Sahsa, has direct connecting flights to the Bay Islands from Miami, Houston and New Orleans. Phone: 1-800-327-1225. Be sure to bring sun screen and more importantly, bug spray—the no-see-ums can be quite pesky.

Doug Triggs, At a Honduras Bay Dive Resort.

MEXICO

The 16th century Spanish takeover of Central America was enabled in part by a body-rejecting Catholic doctrine that confirms Mexicans in their misery. A new gentry now looks upon nakedness as the evidence and punishment of poverty and unworthiness. Thus does nudity default to the unchurched, desperate status of the *indio*. No wonder Mexicans feel troubled by nude beaches! Before going nude anywhere in Mexico, the visitor must ask at the hotel or police station about current custom, law and enforcement. You may also be helped by the Mexican Tourist Board, phone: 1-800-262-8900.

YUCATAN

ISLA MUJERES

About 6 miles off the coast from Cancún, Isla Mujeres is a mellow fishing village with tourist restaurants, shops and several hotels. On the edge of town, playa cocos (Coco Beach/North Beach) is best for topfree sunbathing—confirmed by the island monthly Isla Mujeres Today. The southern end has good snorkeling and sailing. Prices are cheaper here than in Cancún and many prefer it. Ferry service from Punta Sam and Puerto Juárez and daily boat excursions from Cancún hotels.

CANCÚN

Magnificent Mayan ruins—some of them overlooking the white sand beach and turquoise sea—the superb yet competitively priced hotels, and low-cost air access have coaxed the Yucatan Peninsula into a world-class destination.

The upgrading clientele often request topfree or nude sunning, for which the Mexican tradition is ill prepared. The public beaches of Cancún Island see the topfree option more and more asserted, particularly by European women. And full body freedom occurs at the Cancún Club Med nude sunning zone. Displaced by the Conrad Hotel to its north, Club Med nudity shifted onto the lagoon side just past the windsurfing pavilion.

Beyond this incremental acceptance by Cancún proper, the Playa del Carmen, Cozumel Island, Playa Paraiso at Tulum and Isla Mujeres beckon.

PUERTO MORELOS

Puerto Morelos is just south of Cancún. From the Posada Amor bathers are driven to a deserted nude beach. A room at the inn, including 2 meals, is about $30 per day. Sr. Rogoello Fernandez, Posada Amor, Apartado Postal 806, Cancún, Puerto Morelos, Q. Roo, Mexico.

Mexico

PLAYA DEL CARMEN

South of Cancún–north of Tulum along the coastal highway is the town of Playa del Carmen. Europeans welcome its quiet accepting way. Broad white-sand beach, giant palms, many small restaurants and posadas, plus bus terminal, airstrip and the Cozumel Island ferry. From the pier north for 1/2 mile it's topfree. The next 5 miles often invite clothes-optional use. The water is clear and clean, with sandy bottom and patch reefs and fine snorkeling. Do not leave anything unattended on beach.

☞ Simply drive into town and pick the posada and the price you want.

Best upscale alternative: three intimate package resorts operated north of Playa del Carmen at Punta Bete by Turquoise Reef Resorts, P.O. Box 2664, Evergreen, CO 80439. Phone: 1-800-538-6802 or (303) 674-9615. Fax: (303) 674-8735. Shangri-La Caribe, 2 miles north of town, is right next to the clothes-optional beach described above. Restaurant and bar, palapa bungalows on beach, freshwater pool, dive shop, car rental. Four miles north of Playa del Carmen, also adjoining nude beaches, are the moderately priced deluxe tent hotel KaiLuum; and the upscale resort Cabañas Captain Lafitte.

COZUMEL ISLAND

Directly across from Playa del Carmen is Cozumel Island. If you're lodging at a Cancún hotel you can make a day visit by a cheap 20 minute commuter flight. The 2 hour boat connection leaves Cancún at 9:30 a.m, returns at 5:30 p.m., except Tues. At the Cozumel dock or airport local authorities will direct you to the nude beaches; just ask.

Nudity is accepted at Punta Celarain on the miles-long Southern Lighthouse beach (aka Naked Turtle Beach). Rent a car, or a bicycle or motorbike at Rueben's 2 blocks behind the San Miguel central square. Go south, past El Presidente Hotel, and you'll see the lighthouse from the Coastal road. Access is by a gravel hard right turnoff that doubles back south where the Coastal road angles northward. Nearing the lighthouse, park on its left. The Naked Turtle Restaurant & Bar has good food, cold beer, nice people, restrooms.

Other secluded beaches on the eastern coast are north of where the paved Coastal road ends upon joining the Cross Island road. Take the dirt spur north, stopping at Mescalito's. The owner can suggest good nude sunning spots.

Also recommended on the southwest coast—check it out first—is the little-used area of San Francisco Beach south of the tranquil Presidente Hotel.

TULUM

Starting from the ancient Maya coastal city of Tulum, 75 miles south of Cancún, topfree and some nude use is made of the beach, at El Mirador Campground and further south. A couple of native restaurants, a bakery and other supplies can be found at the ruins; another restaurant, El Crucero, is at the crossroads where the bus stops. Small hotels here, very reasonable, with communal hot showers and other amenities, are Cabañas Don Armandos and Cabañas Chac Mool.

☞ To El Paraiso Beach: From the Tulum ruins parking lot take the paved road south for about 1 km, then from the campground follow a dirt road southward that winds to the beach (after rain it is impassible). Or drive 3 km south from the Tulum ruins by the paved road, until the sea is visible from the highway, park at one of several roadside turnoffs and walk north along the shore.

Along the highway heading south from the parking lot entrance, you'll see signs on roads leading to various cabañas (small cabins with thatched roofs to rent) which are on beautiful beaches that are used topfree. The further south you walk, the more clothing is optional. These beaches south of Tulum are little visited except by the American and Canadian tourists who stay at the cabañas.

AKUMAL

Akumal, south of Playa Del Carmen, has superior diving and is less developed than Cancún. Some topfree sunning. Good accommodations. Club Akumal Caribe phone: 1-800-351-1622.

X-Cacel Beach, 5 miles south, has tent camping, good surf, restaurant. The far north end has parts suited for nude use; topfree is accepted on either end of the beach. $2 entrance fee.

OAXACA COAST

HUATULCO

Mexico's 'new Cancún' is Huatulco—250 miles south of Acapulco and 45 minutes east of Puerto Angel. A village, Santa Cruz Huatulco, has been visited with an international airport and a mammoth, slowly unfolding, development plan.

The Club Med beach facing south, near the putting green, gets nude use. It's not encouraged. Playa El Maguey is a charming beach where nudity is tolerated.

PUERTO ANGEL

Puerto Angel is often described as a left-over hippie town from the Sixties which developers ignored due to its rugged setting–be grateful!

First, get updated in Puerto Angel (and we recommend you rent a room) from a California woman, Susanne Lopez, who runs La Posada Cañon de Vata, A.P. 74, Pochutla, Oaxaca, Mexico; no phone. The Posada evening meal is family style and cosmopolitan. —Deluxe Hotel Angel del Mar, phone: 011-52-958-40397. Both overlook the west harbor Playa del Panteón.

§ The best nude beach is 4 km west of Puerto Angel; you'll need a taxi to Playa Zipolite. Go to the far end, beyond the clothed people and the dangerous surf. The headland marks the end of the beach, and you'll find, up the cliff, a vegetarian food place with camping, run by yet another American woman who is helpful. Suggested lodging is Hotel Gloria at Playa Zipolite.

§ Another nude beach is at Esatcahuites, a 20 minute walk from the bus/taxi stop near the Navy (marina) base. Walk up the highway towards Pochutla for 1/2 km. The dirt road to Esatcahuites is on the right and an 8 minute walk will bring you to several sandy coves. Do not leave your gear unat-

Playa del Carmen, Yucatan. At the Ferry Dock.

tended. Swimming is dangerous. The beach has a refreshment stand.

PUERTO ESCONDIDO

An international airport now makes the access easy. It's still a small town, on a small and now crowded cove. Municipal Playa Marinero separates most town hotels from lightly used Playa Zikatela, which stretches 2 miles eastward inviting nude bathers. Recommended: Hotel Santa Fe, 25 rooms, fine restaurant, fresh-water pool, right at start of Playa Zikatela, phone: 011-52-958-20170.

You may hire a boat to go north around the point to Playa Sin Ropa (naked beach) or to the best surfing beach.

You may also take the interurban bus 50 miles south to Puerto Angel for a few day's visit.

ACAPULCO

You won't choose to go to Acapulco if a great nude beach is your priority. Once there, enjoy the best of what there is.

BOCA CHICA

Boca Chica is a fine hotel of 40 rooms with excellent food, lush grounds, a good pool, and a private swimming/snorkeling cove. The resident boatman will take you to the deserted beach of a nearby island. Reasonable rates include breakfast and dinner. Hotel Boca Chica, Playa Caletilla, Acapulco. Phone 748-26014.

HACIENDA INN

Hacienda Inn, at Los Magotes, 25 km north of Acapulco, is operated and visited by fun-loving French Canadians. Price in 1991 season: Canadian $200 per week, includes room and breakfast. Quiet 17 km clothes-optional beach with palapas; hike to waterfall. Information: Michel Lauzon, 6000–29e Ave. No. 20, Montréal, Québec, Canada H1T 3G9. Phone: (514) 721-4678.

IXTAPA

POINT IXTAPA

Located 240 km northwest of Acapulco on Mexico's Pacific coast, served by its own international airport, Ixtapa is targeted for a great future. For the present, visitors are still limited and it's easy to find a secluded stretch of sand to enjoy naturally.

Recommended is Cuata Beach on Point Ixtapa; a Club Med lies just around the tip and the atmosphere is easy going. The starting point for the beach is also the public access point to the Club Med beach and the take off point for the Ixtapa boats. Other secluded beaches see nude use as well. Bathe nude only in areas you know are secure, or in sufficient numbers to discourage hassles.

☞ To Cuata Beach: From the Los Cuatas Cafe—which is just across the narrow tip of Point Ixtapa from the Club Med's tennis courts—walk down the shore to your left as you face the water. Cross two coves and follow an easy trail across a rocky promontory to the third beach, a 100 yard heaven of soft sand with waves perfect for bodysurfing and a late afternoon sun and view you will not forget. The water is much cleaner than in front of Club Med. You may wish to arrive early so as to establish the nudity usage for the day.

MANZANILLO

TENACATITA BAY

Surrounded by lush jungle, Manzanillo is a Pacific fishing port with white sand beaches and a sunny climate, suddenly becoming a world-class destination. Located an hour from the airport is the Fiesta Americana deluxe resort overlooking Tanacatita Bay, popular with Canadians and Americans.

The beach in front of the hotel is textile; topfree sunning occurs at both ends. South of the villas are large rock formations, and beyond the rocks is a large beach used for nude sunbathing. But not swimming! There is a strong undertow, and the beach can only be reached at lowtide.

PLAYA BLANCA

On Chamela Bay in Colima province, Club Med Playa Blanca is a huge complex designed for 660 guests. Scuba, sailing, snorkeling, tennis and more. Topfree, sometimes nudity occurs on the large, high, private terrace above the dock next to the beach, with a great view. Many French guests. Side trips to Guadalajara and Puerto Vallarta. Guests fly into Manzanillo for a 1 1/4-hour bus ride to the club.

Green Tortoise Tour of Baja California.

Mexico

PUERTO VALLARTA

YELAPA & QUIMIXTO: UPPER FALLS

Located near a charming seaside town of the same name, reached only by sea, Yelapa Waterfall is well-known in town. Intrepid naturists learned of a lovely pool at the top of the falls, deep enough to allow you to relax in without worrying about being carried over the top. Surrounded by lush vegetation, skinny-soakers enjoy an unobstructed view of the bay below.

Your access is through Puerto Vallarta, Mexico's most popular resort with Californians. Take the 9 a.m. tourist ferry to Yelapa, walk through town and ask for the waterfall. Climb the path up the right side of the falls, and you'll find access to the pool.

Better, take the midday supplies boat, chat with the boatman, and plan to stay overnight at the Lagunita Hotel or in a local palapa or a U.S. expatriate's house.

A similar waterfall, with little-visited pools above the falls for skinny-dipping, is at Quimixto. Rental horses can be used to go 20 minutes from beach to falls.

You may find that Yelapa or Quimixto is what Puerto Vallarta is all about! Leave your hairblower home, there's no electricity in the coastal villages.

SAYORITA

About 46 km north of Puerto Vallarta—1/2 km north of Sayorita; the turnoff is inconspicuous—used clothes-optionally by Canadian and other families and couples. Non-naturist camper park and restaurants in Sayorita.

GUADALAJARA

RIO CALIENTE

The Rio Caliente, a hot mineral-water river, flows through a lush valley 20 miles northwest of Guadalajara at 5000' elevation. Revered by the Huichol Indians of a thousand years ago as a holy place with curative powers, the Rio Caliente is appreciated by modern folk as well. Natural soaking pools, rocks for sunning, swallows swarming overhead and some small falls make this a delightful spot to rest and recharge. Some will camp; others stay at Rancho Rio Caliente.

☞ The sensuous wonder of a hot river valley is at your doorsill at Rancho Rio Caliente. Vegetarian meals, massage, yoga, horseback riding, thermal pool, herbal baths, all at low rates. One hour from Guadalajara, served by nonstop flights. Rancho Rio Caliente, Apto. 1-1187, Guadalajara, Jalisco, Mexico; no phone. Reservations: 1-818-796-5577.

MAZATLÁN

ISLA DE LA PIEDRA

Mazatlán people encourage the gringo to go desnudo offshore at Stone Island on weekdays, since weekends they want to have well-dressed picnics on those beaches!

☞ On a weekday, find the Mazatlán Navy Yard; just to the north is "la barca a Isla de la Piedra," a 20' rowboat with motor and awning. A 5 minute ride deposits you opposite the cruise boats on Stone Island; walk inland along the harbor edge and then follow the main (dirt) road around the hill, bringing you to the beach by a restaurant with great smoked fish. Here, you walk left, out of sight of the restaurant, and strip down. Sometimes a horse cart is available to la playa desnuda.

BAJA CALIFORNIA

BAJA PENINSULA

Ah, Baja! The word evokes its rough and exotic terrain, true southwest—unspoiled, untamed. Naturists have explored its desert, beaches and hot springs and recommend these sites to the clothes-optional:

§ The hot springs 50 miles south of San Felipe on the Sea of Cortez, where the sea rushes in to mingle with the hot water (ask a local boy, when you're near, to direct you there, as no map includes them).

§ The rocky beach near Hotel Solmar in Cabo San Lucas, at the tip of Baja, a vast stretch of land with room for every mood. Go left from the hotel and squeeze through the rocks to a beautiful cave and nude beach, 200 yards from the Baja point. Great sports fishing.

☞ It's 1000 well-paved miles, Tijuana—Cabo San Lucas by MEX-1. Or fly cheaply from Tijuana to the Cabo. Ferry service is Mazatlán—La Paz or Puerto Vallarta—Cabo.

Hotel Cabo San Lucas illustrates topfree beach use in recent ads. Phone: 1-800-282-4809. Younger, less posh set stays at Hotel Mar de Cortez off the beach.

BAJA TOURING

Enjoy a Baja vacation more, by booking on the live-aboard bus operated by the Green Tortoise. They attract mellow, clothes-optional vacationers to sail, windsurf, explore, just hang out—or whale watch from November to March.

It is not your average bus trip. Green Tortoise shows that public transportation can be fun, with travel from major stop to stop at night, so passengers can make the most of daylight hours. Sleeping is on the bus itself, which has been converted into comfortable, living-room style space. Passengers are encouraged to bring musical instruments and additional sporting equipment. Average age of passengers is 20-30 but all ages have participated; singles, couples, families alike.

☞ Green Tortoise picks up in Seattle, Portland, Eugene, San Francisco, or Los Angeles. Write: Box 24459, San Francisco, CA 94124. Phone (415) 821-7922.

PLAYA GRANDE

Fifteen miles north of San Felipe is a huge stone sign for Playa Grande on the east side of the highway. Two miles down the road is a a caretaker's shack. Turn right at the beach beyond. Drive a mile south in your beach buggy to the sand dunes and several permanent camp trailers, Campo Hawaii—a community of several families enjoying the nude life. When you leave, don't forget to pay the caretaker $3 per person per day.

BAHIA DE LOS ANGELES

Five hours south from San Diego on a fine paved highway, find Bahia de los Angeles on the shore of the Sea of Cortez. Hot days of nude snorkeling in warm clear waters; nights are wonderful. Spectacular scenery, sparsely populated, with no hassles from the local people. Bring your own water!

For an inexpensive naturist boat excursion on the Sea of Cortez, write Capt. Johnny Ramos, Yacht Hay Chihuahua, c/o Port Capitan, Mulege, B.C. del Sur. Ask him to phone you collect.

URUGUAY

PUNTA DEL ESTE

PLAYA CHIHUAHUA

Chihuahua Beach is a broad white sand beach on the Atlantic Ocean that is backed by woods and accepted for full nudity. While it is convenient to Argentina, 90% of users are Uruguayan according to Noticias of Buenos Aires (Feb. 2, 1991).

The thriving nude beach apart, Punta del Este is an international resort. Hotel guests may be topfree. Fernando Barcia, police superintendent of Punta del Este, emphasized a decade ago: "The Prefecture will not take anyone into custody for being topless. Topless is not authorized–neither is it prohibited."

☞ At kilometer 124 on the Montevideo—Punta del Este highway, turn on a dirt road towards the ocean. Park, wade the lagoon. Is waist-deep wading unacceptable? Get off instead at marker 125. Park at the hotel named Cabaña del Tío Tom. Walk back along the beach, to reach the clothes-optional zone without hassles.

VENEZUELA

ISLA DE MARGARITA

MARGARITA ISLAND

The Venezuelan Traveler, a national newspaper for English-speaking tourists, states: "As for nude beaches, they're anywhere you find them. Technically, it's illegal in Venezuela, but there are many great hidden coves on Margarita Island that permit its private fulfillment."

During the week even the nicest coves may (with discretion) be used nude: Playa Puerto Cruz or Playa Puerto Viejo on the north coast, or the Big Sur-like string of white sand beaches at the foot of rocky cliffs as you drive a new mountain road from Manzanillo to Pedrogonzales.

Even the popular beaches–Playa Caribe, Playa El Aqua, and the Hotel Concorde beach–now get topfree women sunbathers, the *Venezuelan Traveler* concludes, saluting their "courage."

A few kilometers east of Juangriego is Playa Piel where nude use occurs. Playa Piel is on the far southwestern end of Playa Caribe near the outcropping. Or try the beach at El Saco; it's usually deserted, and extends for more than a mile.

MAINLAND

MAINLAND BEACHES

Venezuela has laws prohibiting nudity but enforcement is another story; the police do not patrol tourist-zone beaches. "Along the coastline of Venezuela there are hundreds of beaches," which "range from vast public grazing grounds to secret coves and harbors, where even the faint of heart can dare to skinny-dip," states the *Venezuelan Traveler,* and hotels are beginning to cooperate:

Barcelona—Puerto La Cruz. Puerta La Cruz can be combined with a visit to Margarita Island. The Doral Beach Hotel assists guests to enjoy beaches on ten islets au naturel. You will be taken to a deserted beach. A driver will leave you there and return to pick you up. Cost is $5; bring everything you'll need.

Visas are required to visit Venezuela and must be obtained prior to arrival. To avoid having your papers reissued at every major stop, list your last intended port of call on your papers.

Lee Baxandall, Source of the Rio Caliente; Guadalajara.

THE CARIBBEAN

THE CARIBBEAN

For the pale-skinned, inhibited denizens of eastern North America, the Caribbean beckons like a paradise from autumn to springtime. The constant sweet warmth, the palms, the white sand beaches, the lilting rhythms spell relief from rules and schedules. The anonymity of a distant resort is often as important as its beauty; it permits experiments with one's life-style.

Have you ever wondered what skinny-dipping for adults would be like: lounging without clothes, a soft trade wind stroking flesh that has never been exposed, with families and couples mixing unashamedly beneath a forgiving, embracing sun? Numerous resorts—principally on Jamaica and St. Martin—now cater to this wish.

If you, a spouse or child are not confident about choosing a clothes-optional adventure, remember that the accented word is *optional*. Remain clothed at the destinations described here without embarrassment. . .just as you may remove most or all of your clothing.

Another way to be clothes-optional in the Caribbean is to make up your own small party on a sailboat with a capacity of four to 15. Most likely there'll be a couple to host and skipper you to skinny-dip beaches of the Bahamas or Virgin Islands.

Moreover, the clothes-optional, week-long chartering of major cruise ships is now popular; whether the quaint windjammers, or the 'loveboat' cruise ships that offer water sports.

In addition to direct connections, these travel agencies specialize in packaged tropical nude vacations ashore and afloat:

- Caribbean Travel Naturally—Box 897, Lutz, FL 33549. Phone 1-800-462-6833 or (813) 948-1303.
- Bare Necessities Tour & Travel Company—1502 West Avenue, Austin, TX 78701. Phone 1-800-743-0405 or (512) 469-0092.
- Skinny-Dip Tours & Caribbean Hideaways—R.D. 1, Box 294, Bloomingburg, NY 12721. Phone 1-800-828-9356 or (914) 733-4596.

ANTIGUA

HAWKSBILL BEACH

Antigua's chief clothes-optional beach is the furthest of the four maintained by Hawksbill Beach Hotel, 3 miles southwest of St. John. It has several sandy areas and a hotel "beach officer" from 8 a.m. to 4 p.m. to provide security. There are fine coconut palms and the hotel supplies umbrellas and chaises. Bring any food or drink you need, and definitely use footwear along the quarter-mile path over two hills going left (south) from the hotel. Close cattle gates behind you. Meals at the Hawksbill are tasty and lodgings convenient. Phone: (809) 462-0301. Air travel from Miami to Antigua is quite reasonable.

ARUBA

MANCHEBO BEACH RESORT

Aruba shines among the former Dutch Antilles largely with its fine beaches. While it has a desert climate and more cacti than palms, a constant breeze keeps things comfortable.

Hotels line the 4 mile Palm Beach, on the western coast north from Aranjestad. Among them, Manchebo Beach Resort, a Best Western Hotel, supports topfree sunbathing. It may open a clothes-optional beach to better serve a European clientele. Expensive, with an excellent restaurant. Aruba phone: 23444. Reservations: 1-800-334-7234.

Recommended for 'wild' nuding with a friend are the dunes 2 miles north of the hotels—around California Lighthouse at Aruba's north tip, and the rocky area beyond the lighthouse. A rental car is needed to get there. Beware getting stuck in the sand.

BAHAMAS

North from the Caribbean Basin. The large islands are heavily developed but the Out Islands—some only 50 miles from the Florida coast—have gorgeous, deserted beaches. Many small yachts are available for day or week charter to reach these sites; a small party can easily handle the cost. Be sure to tell the captain that you want to sail as well as swim nude.

CRUISE SHIPS

NORWEGIAN CARIBBEAN

Three of the four Norwegian Caribbean Lines boats sailing from Miami take the passengers ashore to a company-owned Bahamian Out Island with a nude beach.

Disembarking, walk down the beach to the right until the sand gives out and you're on the rocks (sneakers are a plus!). Keep going past a second rock break; after a total 15-20 minutes be rewarded by a beautiful white sand cove, the best beach on the island!

NCL is a first-class cruise operation—the only Miami departures making it easy to go nude. Ask your travel agent about 'guaranteed' fares, with a 99% chance of an accommodations upgrade.

NEW PROVIDENCE

PARADISE ISLAND

Under control of Resorts International, this enclave, until 1960 known as Hog Island, has been remade for pleasure. Across a bridge from Nassau, four miles long and a mile wide, nine resorts on a perfected beach, plus golf, casino, many restaurants and nightclubs.

For nude use, enter the Paradise Public Beach, reached by cab from Nassau or the Paradise Island hotels. On paying a fee ($5) the Public Beach official assigns you a locker and a rum punch, and you have shower privileges. (Some avoid the fee, entering through the Holiday Inn.)

Walk left down Public Beach past Club Med, and the Yoga Center where g-strings and topfree are ok, to the open beach. Nudity occurs on Lighthouse Beach on the western tip, before the rock jetty. It gets very hot so bring sunblock and plenty of drinking water. Be wary of sea currents, thieves and gawkers. Do not swim after sunset when the local sharks feed.

Walking from the Sheraton Grand Hotel to the eastern point, Cabbage Beach is at times topfree (no more) at the tip.

You may also hire a small boat at almost any hotel to take you to either point or to a deserted offshore islet eastward from Nassau Harbor and Paradise Island.

From Cable Beach, in high season a scheduled boat runs day trips with lunch barbecue to offshore Balmoral Island and its Pirates Cove, "so secluded a bathing suit feels like formal wear." Inquire at Balmoral Beach, Emerald Beach, Ambassador or Nassau Beach hotels for pickup.

GRAND BAHAMA

FREEPORT

Drive or motorbike to 3 miles east of the Holiday Inn. Turn right on a small dirt road that leads to El Club Carib, a honky-tonk bar and restaurant on Fortune Beach. You can pitch a tent nearby, or just take a taxi there for a few dollars, and enjoy the huge Fortune Beach in your choice of dress code. The stretch from Holiday Inn to Club Carib, Churchill Beach, can be used with caution too.

The beach at the Xanadu Hotel can be reached conveniently by a shuttle bus from the Bahama Princess or Bahama Towers hotels. At Xanadu, walk east (right, as you face the water), past three stone breakwaters, to a quiet spot of your choice or as far as the water cut, a half mile.

The East side of Grand Bahama is undeveloped and largely open to nude use.

CAT ISLAND

CUTLASS BAY

Fifty miles in length, with many small Bahamian villages, this narrow, hilly, perhaps most beautiful island in the Bahamas was a pirate haven.

Cutlass Bay Club abuts a beach that many guests use au naturel. The shallow warm beach extends for 10 miles long with few neighbors. You may ask Robby for a convenient villa. Freshwater pool, snorkeling, beach barbecues, dancing, island tours, tennis, volleyball, bicycling. Port Howe, Cat Island, Bahamas. Phone (809) 359-3534.

FERNANDEZ BAY VILLAGE

Fernandez Bay Village near New Bight rents housekeeping villas. Each with maid service, windsurfer, small sailboat, and secluded by vegetation for deck sunning. Beach permits nude swimming at either end. Airfield, anchorage, sunfish, windsurfers, minimart, restaurant, bonfires with local musicians, air transfers. Phone: 800-940-1905 or (305) 792-1905.

ANDROS ISLAND

SMALL HOPE BAY LODGE

Andros is a low-slung coral island on which little grows large but casuarina trees. Comfortable cottages are lined up by the shore facing the main attraction, the fabulous sea. A small rock islet with a hot tub that you may use 'starkers' also looks out. Scuba, snorkel, bicycles, minimart, air transfer from Nassau. Small Hope Bay Lodge, Fresh Creek, Andros. Phone 809-368-2014 or 305-359-8240.

GREAT EXUMA

PEACE & PLENTY BEACH

George Town is a laid-back, friendly spot to forget time. Direct flights from Miami and Ft. Lauderdale. Gentleness on its unspoiled beaches, which admittedly don't have the bright lights and concrete of Nassau and Freeport.

On Elizabeth Harbor are several inns—try Peace and Plenty Hotel. Pool, lounge, restaurant, pier, scuba, windsurf, 32 air-conditioned rooms. Phone (809) 336-2551.

Peace & Plenty operates a Beach Club on Stocking Island a mile across the harbor. It provides transportation; you do not have to be a hotel guest. A clothes-optional beach is to the left of the club as you go ashore, past the rocky breakwater.

LONG ISLAND

STELLA MARIS INN

At the north end of 90 mile Long Island, between Exuma and Cat Islands. Scheduled Bahamasair service from Nassau and George Town.

The German managers support free body culture, if integrated with vacation activities—not as 'cult' behavior in itself or on the grounds. Shark feeding is a specialty (integrate that, scuba-dippers!). Three-mile beach extending east is in au naturel use. Scuba, snorkel, jet ski, windsurf, bone fishing, tennis, 6 beaches, 3 pools, 120-guest capacity. Bungalows, hotel rooms; superb cuisine. Phone 800-426-0466 or (305) 467-0466 or (809) 336-2106.

ELEUTHERA

CLUB MED ET AL

An island, 120 miles long, named with the Greek word for freedom. Rightfully, if eleuthera consists of the solitude to go nude and not see a soul for days, selecting from hundreds of beaches with powdery white sand and clear warm water under sunny skies.

Choose a boat or small hotel as your base. Or Club Med Eleuthera: it's set on traditionally clothes-optional French Leave Beach. Club personnel now deny—at government request—knowledge that nude sunbathing occurs starting 100 yards to the left outside the club's (topfree) enclave.

Some vacationers sun on this beach while lodging at Governor's Harbour a short walk away.

BONAIRE

SOROBON NATURIST RESORT

On the south end of the Caribbean 'lake,' close to Venezuela, is the small Dutch island of Bonaire. It's quiet, dry and temperate. Flamingos wade in salt ponds and offshore reefs are protected.

An upscale clothes-optional resort with 20 single-bedroom units built in 1984, new owners in 1991 began a policy of all-inclusive pricing which includes all meals. Fine sand private beach, windsurfing and snorkeling with Scuba options. Superb reef life you can wade to across Sorobon Bay.

It's not for partiers and it is praised and promoted by Bonaire officials. Sorobon Naturist Resort, P.O. Box 14, Bonaire, Netherlands Antilles. Phone 011-599-7-8080 or 1-800-828-9356.

Peter Simon, A Venusian Moment, Orient Bay, St. Martin

CAYMAN

THE CAYMAN BANKS

We're often asked what causes travel to the Caymans. Surely it's not the small dive resorts or the arid beaches! Indeed not. What you will find is over 250 banks and a resident population of 15,000; this British Crown Colony's institutions do not cooperate with any inquiring government. The attraction of the Caymans is tax evasion.

Because the Caymans are so disreputable it's amusing that a bill was introduced to the legislative senate which required that "both residents and visitors are attired in such a manner that their bodies are properly clothed, and that no parts of the body are exposed to view which ordinarily should be covered, and that beachwear is worn only on beaches." Rep. Annie Huldah Bodden explained: "A lack of proper clothing can only lead to the moral decay of this once highly respected community." We feel that the banking laws might first bear some scrutiny.

☞ If you insist on making a bank deposit on Grand Cayman, Little Cayman and Cayman Brac—both 80 miles away—are superior for diving. Discreet nudity should be possible, especially on Little Cayman, pop. 20.

CUBA

Said Fidel Castro, "We have to exploit the sun, and even the moon shining on us. We do not live in either the North or the South Pole; we live in a warm country. That is wealth." (July 1988, Santiago de Cuba).

His speech launched an initiative to bring tourists to Cuba that the world-famous white sand beaches deserve. The Cuban spotlight is on Varadero Beach, which is getting an international airport and new hotels. Foreign help is at hand—SuperClubs of Jamaica, owners of Hedonism II, has two hotels in Cuban construction.

Clothing-optional beaches are an important element of the tourism project. Flights are conveniently arranged for U.S. citizens through Toronto, Montréal, Mexico City, or Meridá in the Yucatan. With Magna Holidays (through Toronto) the package price includes round-trip air with weekend departure from Toronto, transfers between Havana and Cayo Largo, and seven days at the Villa Capriccio with meals and many extras included.

Magna Holidays (phone: 416 665-7330) has early-evening flights to Havana with a hotel overnight before transfer between 8 a.m. and 9:30 a.m. to Cayo Largo. Other visitors to Havana join this morning flight, returning the same afternoon.

Through Mexico: Mexico Airlines, phone: 1-800-555-1212. Through Montréal: Champagne Tours in Mirabel, phone: (514) 866-3695. Flights depart early, arrive the same day.

CAYO LARGO: PLAYA SIRENA

Cuba's island for nude beaches attracts many Canadian and European travelers. U.S. citizens are joining this adventure, including it with a brief or longer stopoff in Havana, through which all flights must pass.

Yachters also continue to sail into the Cayo Largo marina without a customs fuss as long as they don't try to go to Havana.

The earliest (and largest) hotel on the Cayo Largo beach, located nearest to the airstrip and harbor, is the Cayo Largo Isla del Sur. It has freshwater pool, squash and tennis courts, restaurant, shop, sailing, scuba, snorkeling, fishing, water-skiing, bicycles and horses. Dive master is Pipin Ferrera who holds the world record for depth immersion without equipment (67 meters).

Iguana Hotel offers town house suites on two levels. Villa Capriccio, a few minutes' further walk, has beach palms, thatch roof huts with ceiling fans as well as usual amenities—the right tropic comfort.

Cayo Largo is renowned for 'venusian sunsets' where the light is dart-shaped. Monkeys and iguanas inhabit nearby keys. In the hot afternoons the chilled Blue Marlin Club is a social center.

A bus takes guests to a boat commuting to Sirena Beach, ideal for nudity with miles of powder white sand and a restaurant featuring huge lobster tails.

John Wull, Bare Bottom Boat.

CURAÇAO

CORAL CLIFF HOTEL

On Santa Marta Bay, towards the little-developed, picturesque western end of the Dutch island near Venezuela in the south Caribbean, Coral Cliff Resort reserves a third of its beach for nudity and its charter boats welcome nude scuba charters. There are 35 villa units with sea view, air conditioning, kitchenette; patio restaurant, tennis.

An islet, Little Curaçao, is host to nude beach picnics that originate at Coral Cliff's sister hotel, The Curaçao Caribbean. Ask the clerk how to connect.

Divide a visit in the south Caribbean between a Coral Cliff base for Curaçao's activities and nightlife, and laid-back, naturist Sorobon Beach Resort on Bonaire.

DOMINICAN REPUBLIC

Locating a third international airport on the Samaná Peninsula in the lushly tropical northeast, the Gulf & Western-advised Dominican Republic would provide access to fine beaches where nudity has much more than a toehold.

The airport is a top priority; La Samaná could be another Negril success story. Naturists might speed the clothes-optional trend, in this development-hungry tourism destination, by offering to build or manage a naturist facility, and by patronizing hotels which do presently offer aspects of nude recreation.

Don't hesitate to express your interest to the Dominican Consulate: (212) 768-2480.

LA SAMANÁ PENINSULA

EL PORTILLO BEACH CLUB

El Portillo on the north shore of La Samaná peninsula has 75 hotel units. The management takes pride in its food and the beautiful Las Terrenas coast where guests may stroll 10 minutes down the soft-sand beach (to the left) to get naked.

Prices are welcoming—little more than half what Jamaica charges, with all meals, drinks and cigarettes, watersports, horse back riding on the beach and entertainment included. Mostly Germans now have the good sense to revel in this bargain.

In mating season, whale watch cruises are rewarding. Fishermen are for hire.

An hour drive from Samaná, El Portillo is 3 1/2 hours by rental car or transfer van from Puerto Plata international airport. Charter aircraft landing strip. El Portillo Beach Club, Playa Las Terrenas, Samaná, Dominican Republic. Phone (809) 688-5715.

BAHÍA SAMANÁ: CAYO LEVANTADO

The small and friendly community of Samaná, with its simple hotels and eating establishments, has long enjoyed a nude beach on Cayo Levantado. Unlike most such getaway keys, this one has refreshments and cabanas to rent for the day. It's 30 minutes by ferry from Samaná town, or by courtesy transfer from nearby Bahía Beach Hotel—which should probably be your hotel of choice for its pool, tennis, open-air night club and many doings. 105 air conditioned rooms. Phone (809) 685-4020. Another option is the informal Hostal Cotubanama. Cruise ships sometimes come.

Many Canadians vacation here. Archaic English is spoken by many Samaná descendents of freed slaves, spirited away from their masters in the Old South in the decade prior to the American Civil War via the 'underground railroad' connection at Philadelphia. You'll absorb a different slant on American history here!

Dave Patrick, The Surf's Fine

GRENADA

Since U.S. intervention to remove a revolutionary government, Grenadian tourism made a comeback. A 7,000 ft. runway to serve international flights, begun by the Cubans, is now complete and with a new terminal building. Grenadians speak English which gives many a tourist a comfortable feeling in comparison to the French islands. Nude and topfree bathing is not practiced openly by the locals. Neither is it discouraged for the tourists.

THE BEACHES

Most beaches are of black volcanic sand where foot protection is needed in the day.

The first bathing on Monruge Bay is BBC Beach: highly commercial, no nudity. At the south end is a large area of rock which stops walkers on the shore. Beyond this rock and continuing to Point Salines (where the invasion took place) are: Two Minute Beach, Dr. Grooms Beach, Penguin Beach, Point Salines Beach. All have white sand with clean warm waters for swimming and snorkeling.

All beaches are accessible by road or water taxi. Denim "Commodore" Peters operates a water taxi for St. George Harbor. He will take a party of six for a day trip (8 a.m.-4:30 p.m.) to any of the beaches for about $100 U.S; price includes lunch.

Uninhabited Calivigny island is another day trip.

Inland, Concord Falls and Seven Sisters Falls have pools ideal for hikes that may end with skinny-dipping.

The paved road going from the Caribbean side to the ocean side leads to a tree-lined beach suitable for suitless sunning.

Grenada's satellite island, Carriacou, about 20 miles north, has okay beaches that may be used for discreet nude bathing if they are distant from the main town of Hillsborough. Boat building is an ancient craft here.

THE GRENADINES

PALM ISLAND

Palm Island owner John Caldwell speaks plainly about nude sunbathers: "We don't mind."

Welcoming its nudity-positive attitude and "string of comfy, breeze-conditioned cottages designed for privacy," author Peter Passell in his 1987 book *The Best* nominates Palm Island Beach Club as "the world's best nude beach."

Since leasing the 110-acre island 30 years ago, Caldwell and his wife have made it into a paradise. The shoreline is virtually all sandy beach, and topfree is allowed everywhere. There's a lovely windward shore designated for nude sunbathing, where showgirls of the visiting Princess Line maintain their all-over tans. Under St. Vincent jurisdiction, the government hassled John about the nudity. Because there had never been complaints, the law is not enforced. If you visit, ask Caldwell about his "crazy" lone sail in a 29-foot ketch across the Pacific. He was hit by a hurricane that left him without food for 22 days (described in his book, *Desperate Voyage*). How many actually realize their dreams? Caldwell does, and he shares this one with you.

Your party may fly to Barbados, arrange a charter flight to Union Island's Funny International Airport, then a launch for the 1-mile crossing to Palm Island. Or just sail your charter boat to anchorage. Lovely stone cottages, water sports, tennis, boutique and grocery store. Palm Island Beach Club, Grenadines, St. Vincent, West Indies. Phone (809) 458-4804.

UNION ISLAND

Union Island, at the bottom of the Grenadine Islands, is a great place to sail nude and Chatham Bay on the east coast is used by many nude bathers. Sailing cruises from Union Island can be arranged over to the Tabago Cays, where the majority of users are nude. The beautiful palm-fringed beaches on these 7 or 8 isolated islets have an abundance of marine life.

CANOUAN ISLAND

One of over 100 islands in a chain linking St. Lucia with Trinidad, Canouan was long the exclusive retreat of yachters. No longer. With the opening of the Crystal Sands Beach Club, we commoners may enjoy the gorgeous white sandy beaches, described as among the most beautiful in the Caribbean. Nude beaching has been accepted here, if discreet.

PETIT ST. VINCENT RESORT

"Some of our guests never put on any clothes until dinnertime," or so the advertising goes at Petit St. Vincent Resort, a bungalow complex on this 113-acre private island in the Grenadines.

Each bungalow has its own sundeck where many guests prefer to spend their time—when they're not in one of the secluded coves. An exquisite spot, arranged with care and taste to satisfy the hedonist in all of us and with a price tag to match. Petit St. Vincent, St. Vincent-Grenadines, W.I. (U.S. office: P.O. Box 12506, Cincinnati, OH 45212).

Len Feinberg, Good Catch from Orient Bay, St. Martin.

GUADELOUPE

Guadeloupeans are not the most devil-may-care of Caribbean peoples. They're industrious and extend a welcome to naturist tourists. Indeed, Guadeloupe recognized the first official nude beach of the Western Hemisphere in 1964, owed largely to the initiative of Jean Rocquemont, a French engineer who has since returned to France.

Guadeloupe is worth an extended stay. Miles of beaches, all of them topfree at least, and lava-formed peaks of lush rain forest, waterfalls and fumeroles, offer a stimulating range of tropical experiences. Climb Mt. Soufriére, Guadeloupe's ever-smoldering volcano, for stunning views on a clear day. (Soufriére is often cloud-covered, so you have to watch carefully; get up early each morning to see if the top is visible; if it is, jump into your car, stop at a bakery for a baguette or two and set out immediately... it's the only way you'll get a panorama of this wonderful butterfly island, which also is très gastronomique.)

The Guadeloupe Naturist Association is at B.P. 44, F-97118 St. François, Guadeloupe, French West Indies.

GRANDE-TERRE

STE.-ANNE: JEAN ROCQUEMONT BEACH (CLUB MED CARAVELLE)

The finest beach on Guadeloupe, many agree, is also the most nude. Backed by groomed palms and lawns, with a gorgeous view across a protected bay to the cloudcapped Soufriére volcano, Plage Jean Rocquemont adjoins and is somewhat maintained by Club Med Caravelle. Access is open to the public under French law, but a fee is charged if you use Club Med facilities. The entire white-sand Anse Bourdel is topfree and the nude portion normally extends to the berm. Architecture of the Club Med is spectacular, you will agree, and you may wish to attend as a week-long paying guest. The air charter arrangements are now convenient.

☞ From Pointe-á-Pitre take south coastal Route d'Argent (RN 4) 18 km east. Just 1 km west from the limits of Ste.-Anne, find the Shell station on your left. The access road to Jean Rocquemont Beach is just opposite. Drive in and, if you are not a guest, curve left along the outside of the Club Med fence to the east end of the beach. Or park further out and walk in. You may also ride the bus that runs often to St. François and ask to be dropped at the Caravelle entrance. Walk right onto the Jean Rocquemont Beach from the east end fence, where a native snack bar serves nonguests. While you may mingle with the Club Med guests, remember that the Anse Bourdel beach, not the grounds, is public domain. Your cooperation with the club is recommmended.

Make Club Med Caravelle reservations through the usual travel agencies.

Comfortable bungalows 2 minutes east along the beach may be rented from Mme. Giroux, Le Barrière de Corail, Durivage, F-

Lee Baxandall. Club Med Caravelle, Guadeloupe.

97180 Sainte-Anne, Guadeloupe, French West Indies. Phone 88 20 03.

The Motel de Ste.-Anne (F-97180, Guadeloupe) is comfortable, with a good restaurant. Turn left beyond the Esso station, next left after the Shell station. Mme. Giroux's is 200 m further on the right, the first of two gates in a low stone wall, just before a bridge and cemetery beyond on the left. Other low-cost accommodations also available.

Le Rotabas is located between the cabins rented by Mme. Giroux and the nude beach fronting the Club Med. Featuring 20 rather tiny but air-conditioned, double-bedded rooms, each with a shower and phone, the hotel has its own restaurant, au Matete, with native Creole as well as continental French cuisine and bar. Clothing required everywhere except the beach. Le Rotabas, B.P. 30, F-97180 Ste.-Anne, Guadeloupe, French West Indies. Phone 88 25 60. Telex ROTABA 919 445 GL.

HOTEL TOUBANA

Toubana accepts full nudity in and around the pool, cottages, and tiny beaches at the foot of the cliff. Price includes full use of tennis courts, canoe, sailboard, catamaran or pedalboat; horseback, fishing and scuba are extra. Brochure from Hotel Toubana, B.P. 63, 97180 Sainte-Anne, Guadeloupe, French West Indies, Phone (590) 88-25-78 or 57. Telex GL 919434.

POINTE TARARE

Eight kilometers east of Saint-François—on the north shore of the Pointe-des-Châteaux, at the eastern tip of Grande-Terre—is Pointe Tarare, first legally designated nude beach of the Western Hemisphere.

Pointe Tarare often has wild surf breaking on its protective reef and is very picturesque, with firm sand for wading. Palms provide nice shade from the sun. On weekdays, there are a few dozen people on the whole beach, some clothed. Weekends the beach is entirely nude with 50 or 60 users. You also may climb the bluff of Pointe Tarare in the buff, to enjoy a great view down to the Pointe-des-Châteaux, itself a mandatory visit.

☞ Continue beyond St. François on the coastal highway, past the airport and Hotel Méridien on your right, over the narrow single-lane stone bridge. At this point check your odometer; the turnoff to the Point Tarare Beach is a one-lane gravel road on the left 3 km from the bridge. A vine-covered steel cyclone fence is on the left, but is now virtually obscured by growth. The best way to find the correct turnoff is to look for a Creole restaurant sign (painted with a large shrimp) on the left side of the road. The top of the sign reads "Plage Tarare" and the other side of the sign reads "Plage Naturiste Ici Tarare." A white turnoff stripe marks the rock-strewn lane that leads to the small parking lot. Park at the lot and walk the 100 m to the beach.

Leif Heilberg, Jean Rocquemont Beach, Guadeloupe.

Or try the beach near the Pointe-des-Châteaux parking lot. Cross to the far (north) side of the entry road, walk west and wade through ankle-deep water to the beach which extends for 2 miles west. Do not use the small crescent beach directly at Pointe-des-Châteaux; it is dangerous as well as too public.

BASSE-TERRE

PIGEON CAY: SCUBA AU NATUREL

The French view diving as a naturist activity and even have an organization for it, Nautena. Now divemaster Guy Genin lets the day-tripper to Pigeon Cay follow the bubbles of Cousteau while dressed in the costume of Adam. (Cousteau proclaimed this reef a world resource.) His 45' live-aboard dive ketch will go to Les Saints, Dominica, Marie-Galante, even Martinique and the Virgin Islands for diving, while the day-trip boat departs Malendure Beach at 10, 12 and 3. Auberge on premises.

☞ Contact Guy Genin at Caraibe International Plongee, B.P. 4 Pigeon, F-97132 Bouillante, Guadeloupe F.W.I. Phone 9–5: 98-91-72 or 98-85-84.

LES SAINTES

TERRE-DE-HAUT: ANSE CRAWEN (HOTEL BOIS JOLI)

Terre-de-Haut is one of 8 islets in the Les Saintes group south of Basse-Terre. Its charming harbor has a fine view of Mt. Soufriére and is remarkable for fishermen who preserve ways learned long ago in Brittany.

Nudity is at Crawen Beach on the west end—400 ft. behind Bois Joli, the casual hillside hotel with fine Creole seafood, water sports and trips into town, which was the first in the Caribbean to foster nude recreation.

Direct phone 590-995038; U.S. reservations (212) 840-6636.

Cheaper is Jeanne d'Arc near the pier; direct phone 590-995041.

☞ Drive to Trois Riviéres on the south of Basse-Terre island, 1 1/4 hours from Gosier. From Trois Riviéres take the 40-minute ferry (which leaves in the morning and the afternoon) to Les Saintes. Air to Terre-de-Haut connects with international flights several times daily.

Jamaica could be your perfect getaway—with family or friends—for a first exposure to social nudity. A week in Negril has led many into a life of body acceptance.

An English-speaking Eden by the sea, Jamaica causes the feeling of nakedness to feel almost like a destiny. "No problem, mon, do what you like!"

Holiday nudity is tried by about half of the vacationers where it is permitted, especially on a number of hotel beaches.

It's not really expensive. Air Jamaica competes against U.S. airlines, which improves your choice of departure cities, times and fares. Pick an upscale or a bargain package, an all-inclusive resort or improvise as you travel. Stick to a beach or venture to the mountains, rivers and islets.

SENSE ADVENTURES

No matter where you plan to stay for your main Jamaican vacation, make it a point to also meet Sense Adventures guides for a day or more. They're trained by the originator of 'adventure travel' to Jamaica, naturist Peter Bentley. They'll drive you to canude on a little-known tropical river, hike the high Blue Mountains, or visit remote beaches, as naked as you desire.

You might stay at Maya, SENSE adventure's clothes-optional villa, Bentley's headquarters on Jack's Hill, a half hour from downtown Kingston. Mountain cottages, rasta hideaways, seaside lean-tos also available.

☞ Contact SENSE Adventures, Box 216, Kingston 7, Jamaica. Phone (809) 927-2097. US $15 service fee brings full information and the necessary personalized attention.

WESTERN

NEGRIL BEACH

Six miles of superb white beaches overlook the wadeable turquoise sea and world-class sunsets that are applauded at Rick's Cafe. Equally classy resorts offer sports and partying while bungalow colonies feature relaxation. All of them benefit from Negril's lively Afro-Baptist-Rastafarai community.

The tourists who forget their swimsuits? They descend from the North American hippies of a generation ago—college and corporate dropouts who wandered to Negril. There they found the sight, sound, and spliffs of Rastafarai's different drummers and dj's.

The hippies contributed a white-race body confidence to the mix. And Negril became an influence on its time.

☞ Beyond the listed resorts, some bungalow colonies in the west end, including Drumville Cove, permit nude sunbathing. Spartan guest rooms can be rented in some Negril homes.

Some of the west end families cater to tourists with savory chicken or fish grill dinners served in their parlors.

Be sure to patronize the Paradise Yard Restaurant, 600 yards down the road to Savanna from the Negril Roundabout. Marsha, its busy owner, takes vacations to Florida and Kansas as a naturist.

HEDONISM II

The original "Nude or Prude Beach Choice" getaway is SuperClub's Hedonism II. A single fee covers air, transfers, lodging, sumptuous meals, sports, gymnastics, entertainment and drinks.

Not 'covering' you in unwanted garments is the SuperClubs philosophy of personal freedom. There is no mandated nude beach, and you may, in principle (although it is rare in practice), initiate nudity anywhere you and others are comfortable with it.

There is a nude beach area by consensus. It has its own bar and hot spa, nice lounge chairs and shade trees too. Its fans return repeatedly. P.O. Box 25, Negril, Jamaica, W.I. Phone (809) 957-4201 or 1-800-858-8009, or through your agent.

GRAND LIDO

On Negril's Bloody Bay, this newest, most upscale of inclusive-price resorts has Jamaica's best-developed nude beach. The 200 rooms (110 face the beach) have TV, stereo, separate sitting area, porch or deck. Exercise room, tennis, scuba, sailing. Clothing isn't required between the 'nude beach zone' rooms and their shore, pool, jacuzzi, bar and sundeck complex. Lido guests also have access to Hedonism II next door. Brochure, phone: 1-800-858-8009. In Canada: 1-800-553-4320. All travel agents can book Grand Lido.

NEGRIL CABINS

Negril Cabins are budget lodging only 100 yards from nude-use Bloody Bay on the east end of Negril Beach. Across the road from Grand Lido, comfortable Negril Cabins are raised on stilts and nicely designed. Phone (809) 957-4350.

Janis Foore, Topfree on Negril Beach.

FIREFLY COTTAGES

Nudity on its part of Negril beach, also windsurfing rental, bar. Studios, housekeeping cottages. Food staples sold nearby; many restaurants. A budget base to explore the area. Reservations: (809) 925-5728 or 927-4358.

MONTEGO BAY

SEAWIND BEACH

If not quite a first-class resort, Seawind draws many young people—Canadians and others—with bargain horseriding, tennis, sailing, waterski, scuba, nightly entertainment, dances and beach bars. Hotel or villa accommodations.

Secured on a peninsula jutting into Montego Bay, Seawind gets local bus service to shopping and night spots.

The nude beach is on the point. Any oglers are chased off by a guard. Nudes may relax and watch MoBay air traffic. Any travel agency books Seawind.

RUNAWAY BAY

CLUB CARIBBEAN

Attractive north coast cottage resort between Montego Bay and Ocho Rios. A clothes-optional beach fronts some bungalows: be sure to request these, nudity is prohibited elsewhere. Restaurant, disco, pool, tennis, scuba, volleyball. Children welcomed and provided for—unusual in the Caribbean. Reasonably priced. Reservations: 1-800-221-4558 or (212) 355-6605.

JAMAICA JAMAICA

Jamaica Jamaica is a SuperClub and its west beach and jacuzzi are in nude use. Nor are they screened from the 'prude' beach.

Jamaica Jamaica is a class act: a gourmet restaurant offers native cuisine, exotic birds, a Nautilus and spa in the main lobby, clean convenient rooms, snorkeling, catamaran, windsurfing, sailing, soccer, tennis, golf, cricket all with instruction available. Any travel agency can book.

OCHOS RIOS

COUPLES

SuperClub Couples Resort is spotless, dining superb, drinks free-flowing. Nudity is restricted to an offshore islet with open bar, hammocks, mats, on-call boat shuttle. Rocks discourage swimming. A pleasant spot to get basted while dozing or chatting. Adult couples only; no singles. Do not confuse SuperClub resorts with their archcompetitor, the prudish Sandals resorts. Any travel agency can book.

EASTERN

MAYA LODGE

Sense Adventures headquarters provides guest lodging, hostel-style. Maya is just down the Skyline Drive from reggae-king widow Rita Marley's home, with a sweeping view of the Blue Mountains. Only 20 minutes from Kingston, Maya is a great place from which to explore Jamaica. You can hike from your cabin door to a secluded pool, breathtaking waterfalls, or a tropical rainforest. The area is a naturist's heaven.Tents for rent, meals cost additional. Rasta guides available. Nude camping permitted. Write Sense Adventures (see listing) or phone (809) 927-2097.

PORT ANTONIO: NAVY ISLAND

A cove for nude use on 64-acre Navy Island, described by the Admiralty Club brochure, confirms a reputation for sophistication set by former owner and film swashbuckler Errol Flynn. The lodge has a 30 person capacity, pool, restaurant and bar. A quarter mile offshore from bustling Port Antonio and its reggae disco, The Roof. Ferry is about $4.

☞ Admiralty Club Resort & Marina, P.O. Box 188, Port Antonio, Jamaica. Phone: (809) 993-2667.

REACH FALLS

Reach River is a refreshingly cool stream that flows from the mountains, cutting into limestone. Delight in nakedly entering the cave under Reach Falls, and riding the sluiceways downstream. Hike upstream a half mile to where Reach River emerges from a 'blue hole'. Or 2 1/2 miles downstream to the coast road where you may be picked up. Visit on a weekday morning to minimize user conflict possibility.

☞ Six miles south from Port Antonio on the coastal road then 2 miles inland. A highway sign announces it. Check your way with locals as you probe the roads. Tell caretaker Frank Clark we sent you: he's naturist-friendly.

MARTINIQUE

Martinique is sister-island to Guadeloupe. You may even be able to visit both on a single ticket. The island is rich in history and natural geography.

Be advised however that its aristocracy—unlike that of Guadeloupe—survived the purges of the French Revolution and, 200 years later, still exercises an authority and emphasizes a conservativism that is based on large landholdings. A consequence evidently is that nude beaches are not tolerated.

The public relations firm representing the French West Indies Tourist Office advises: "On all of the French Caribbean islands topless sunning and bathing is not only permitted but is the general rule for Europeans staying at the hotels, large and small."

Indeed Martinique has topfree sunning. One site is Ste.-Anne in the southeast; especially Club Med Martinique, where the small section in topfree use is located beside the inner, warm-water bay.

PUERTO RICO

A big tropical island often inspires tourists to try out being nude on remote beaches. However, in Puerto Rico, the tourists who strip down are often noticed; they draw 'bushwackers', as surely as cows draw appreciative egrets. The voyeur hidden in a mangrove morass does inhibit one's fantasy of playing in "From Here to Eternity".

Do drive about the splendid mountains but consider the beaches not worth the hassle. The islands listed below are the exception.

Topfree for ladies is tolerated, if discreet, at the El San Juan hotel and The Sands. Special police trained for tourist areas (they wear white caps) usually don't bother the topfree or at most ask them to dress.

VIEQUES ISLAND

Off Puerto Rico's southeast coast, Isla de Vieques is reached by a two-hour ferry ride from the Port of Fajárdo or a 30 minute flight from Isla Grande charter airport. Deposited at Isabel Secunda, take the publico van to the south shore's Sun Bay Beach. Visit its bathhouse then walk to the right for 10 minutes or so to an area generally enjoyed nude. Walk another 20 minutes to the town of Esperanza with dining and lodging facilities.

USMC Camp Garcia, also on the south coast, gets nude use. (The U.S. military controls much of Vieques.) Show the gate guard an ID. A bumpy 2 mile drive takes you to a fork. Go straight and you'd be at Blue Beach, known for snorkeling and surfing. Instead bear right, and drive to Red Beach with nude use if you walk to the right.

Garcia Beach is reached by turning right on a gravel road just before Red Beach. It's seldom used and offers many shade trees.

CULEBRA ISLAND: FLAMENCO BEACH

Isla de Culebra is midway between Puerto Rico and St. Thomas. It is conveniently reached by air from San Juan's Isla Grande charter airport or by ferry from Fajárdo in eastern Puerto Rico. Its 3,000 residents are friendly. About 1,500 of its acres are included in The Roosevelt National Wildlife Refuge; you may share a beach with a sea turtle.

On the north shore the picture-pretty sugary sand of Flamenco Beach is easy to get to and weekdays you might have it to yourself. The 2 mile crescent was used for gunnery practice by the military until local protests. Shot-up armored tanks still sit on the beach to the left, as you walk down for sunbathing. To the right is Flamenco Beach Resort, a great place to stay for your nude holiday.

Other lodgings, all reasonable, are Posada la Hamaca (809-742-3516) in Dewey; Coral Island Guest House (617-545-5120) overlooking the town pier; and Seafarer's Inn (809-742-3171) with 15 basic rooms. Most hotels provide transportation to the beaches. The Culebra Underwater Diving Association offers scuba and snorkeling trips.

The Fajárdo–Culebra ferry is $27 round trip for auto and passengers, or $5 per person. Auto reservation needed: phone (809) 742-3161.

ST. BARTHÉLEMY

It is commonly known as St. Barths—smallest of the French island departments. You can drive around it in an hour. It is the only one with a predominantly white population, mostly descended from settlers.

A New Jersey reader calls St. Barths "the low-key alternative to the boorish throngs of New Yorkers who overrun Sint Maarten."

St. Barths may be reached from Guadeloupe or St. Martin by a heart-stopping STOL aircraft flight, or with one of the many boat charters at St. Martin. A sign at the airport warns, "Nudisme est interdit à St. Barthélemy," yet almost all the hotels permit, even advertise, topfree; and most of the beaches get extensive nude use.

The island is notable for expensive secluded inns such as the Emeraude Plage Hotel on an excellent beach of St. Jean Bay. The hotels and bungalow and villa rentals are surveyed in *Vendôme Guide: Saint Barthélemey* ($8 from West Indies Management Co., P.O. Box 1461-WG, Newport, RI 02840. Phone 1-800-932-3222).

COLUMBIER BEACH

The most memorable beach is Anse de Columbier at the northwest tip near the Rockefeller estate. A taxi may take you as far as La Petite Anse just past Anse des Flamands; or perhaps to the village of Colombier. Trekking from either trailhead (wear boots and long pants) is 30 minutes. Stunning views make it worth while. Or have a small boat rented in Gustavia take you.

ANSE DE GRANDE SALINE

Anse de Grande Saline is a delightful beach on the east coast, only a five minute drive from St. Jean Bay. Long accepted as a nude haven, its long crescent never is crowded. Every cab driver knows the way. The bodysurfing can be great.

ANSE DU GOUVERNEUR

Anse du Gouverneur gets nude bathers. Remote and beautiful, this south coast beach has a sharp dropoff near the shore. It can be very windblown. It is reached by 10 minutes of driving a very steep, winding road from Gustavia via Lurin. A regular vacationer to St. Barths says the biggest change regarding nudity is that the local residents now outnumber the tourists.

ST. JEAN BAY

Baie de St. Jean is called a Caribbean St.-Tropez—better than the original, because not really exploited. The topfree beach of picture-perfect St. Jean Bay has attracted investments in wonderful inns and restaurants. Golden youth of French and international origin sip aperitifs and glance at the STOL arrivals to the nearby airstrip.

A recommended hotel on St. Jean Bay is Hotel Filao Beach. Fresh water pool complex with decking and lounges, huge palms, deep baths in each of 30 bungalows. B.P. 167, St. Barthélemy FWI-97133. Phone 011-(590)-276484. Fax 276224. See Vendôme Guide for full selection.

Villa and studio rentals here and island-wide: Sibarth, Box 55 Gustavia, St. Barthélemy, FWI-97133. Phone 011-(590)-276238. Fax 276052.

Leif Heilberg, Papagayo at Club Orient, St. Martin.

ST. MARTIN

Saint Maarten—Saint Martin. The Dutch and French divide this smallish, sunnily dry and temperate island. This sparks a concurrence, beneficial to Naturisme, because Dutch-side hoteliers and investors are acceptive of the French tolerance.

You fly into Philipsburg on the Dutch side. Casino hotels generally have abundant rooms. Electronics and other buys are touted by duty-free shops. Rent a car, and on the French side find small green farms and the tiny restaurants, in Marigot and Grand-Case, with cuisines très chic et cher. Theft's a problem–don't walk away from valuables on a beach or in a car. Visas aren't required. English is lingua franca. US$ OK partout.

ORIENT BAY

PLAGE BAIE ORIENTALE

Plage baie orientale—Orient Bay Beach, on the northeastern coast—is reknowned as a top beach of the Caribbean. Gentle transparent water, white sand bottom, protective reef and offshore islands delight all swimmers. The view of the green hills, until recently undeveloped, can't be beat.

Leif Heilberg, Orient Bay, St. Martin.

Cruise ships that stop in Philipsburg pay the tribute of sending their guests here for a first glimpse of naturism. Orient Beach is open and free to the public. Rental sailing/snorkeling/windsurfing gear, and snorkel/sail day-cruises available.

Go first class 'as the Romans do' : reserve at the pioneer, all-clothing-optional Hotel Club Oriënt and enjoy all of its perks (next entry).

Or stay at a non-naturist resort and 'try Orient Beach for a day'. Bring a lunch; dine at Club Oriënt's moderate-price restaurant; or perhaps at low-cost Pedro's Barbeque on the beach.

Budget-to-luxury non-naturist lodging near Orient Bay has arrived.

¶ Budget-minded travelers might stay at non-naturist Huckleman's Hideaway on the east end of main street in Grand-Case (west of Orient Bay). Hitchhike to the beach. 8 dbls with fridge, about $40 a night. Minimart shopping, or dine with locals for $4 to $6.

¶ A major luxury resort new to Orient Beach allows topfree at pool and beach, but not full nudity. The 227-unit Hotel Mont Vernon management would do well to revoke its ban on clothes-optionality. Mont Vernon's niche and destiny, as 'the other anchor' of Orient Beach, is to enhance value for all clients, creating synergy for a low-concrete Caribbean version of Cap d'Agde.

¶ In mid-Orient Beach, Esmerelda Resort has built 53 villa-style suites on 100 acres; pools, restaurant, lighted tennis courts and still a clothes-optional beach.

¶ Other non-naturist lodging options near Orient Bay include upscale Alizea (a long walk from the nude beach), and budget-kind Sunrise Hotel (across Orient Bay, but you'll want a car). The hotel resorts are booked by Caribbean Travel Naturally: 1-800-462-6833 (in Canada, 1-800-548-6833).

☞ Take the island's circle road westerly from Philipsburg's airport, passing Marigot and Grand-Case. Beyond the Grand-Case airfield find a sign for Club Orient, turn left on a paved road and then another left, following signs and a dirt road. From Philipsburg's port area, take the circle road north to Orleans; Club Orient turnoff lies beyond.

HOTEL CLUB ORIËNT

Hotel Club Oriënt is the Caribbean's first fully clothes-optional resort—dreamt, designed, constructed and up to a point financed, managed, promoted by self-made Dutch millionaire Reint 'Ray' Brink.

The idyllic Baie orientale, the watersports, tennis and volleyball, bar-restaurant, boutique and Finnish-log bungalows make this a destination that draws back its naturist patrons. Auto rentals on premises. In nearby Cul de Sac is Mark's Place with Creole food at reasonable prices. L'Orientíque, Club Oriënt's clothes-optional store, carries basic food items and fresh French baking.

F-97150 St. Martin. Phone: (590) 873-385. Fax: 873-376. Skinny-Dip Tours reservation: (914) 733-4596 or 1-800-828-9356.

WEST PENINSULA

CUPECOY BEACH

Backed by low sandstone cliffs, the more remote, always nude Cupecoy Beach gets up to a dozen folks together. At times the beach just northwest of the Cupecoy Villas is also nude—early-comers set the dress code.

Cupecoy Bay is on the Dutch western coast of the farflung west peninsula of St. Martin known by locals as the lowlands or terres basses. Cupecoy is a mile west of Sheraton's huge Mullet Bay Hotel.

For Cupecoy Beach Hotel reservations: (215) 885-9008. A Naturist agent for discounted Cupecoy Villa rentals: J. Casacio, (215) 885-9008.

☞ Drive west from airport, and just past the Treasure Island Casino and the Cupecoy Beach Hotel and Villas, take a dirt road to the left. Park here to try the close-in beach for clothes-optional mixed use, descending the shore steps furthest from hotel.

Or continue on your left-turn dirt road, 1/2 mile to where it takes a sharp right. You go left, and at once park along the concrete wall. Take the steep trail to the beach and continue to the north end. Beyond the point, La Samanna begins.

PLAGE LONGUE

A long (1.5 km), wide sandy beach—one of St. Martin's finest—convenient for those who stay in Marigot or at Mullet Bay/Cupecoy Bay hotels. Rough ocean at times, a strong undertow and rocky bottom. Walk past "No Nudity" sign to far west end, which is by custom au naturel. Swimming and snorkeling are good here. Large sunning rocks.

☞ Drive the island circle westerly from Philipsburg or the airport past Cupecoy Beach and the welcoming French border sign. At top of the hill, turn left on a paved road marked Baie longue. Turn right just before the entrance to La Samanna Hotel, go 1 km to a parking area on the left.

Or drive a mile further on Long Beach Road—cutting back towards the beach on a fork, where the loop angles back to the main road—for the smaller, beautiful Plum Bay Beach. It sees light nude use.

BAIE ROUGE

At Pointe du Bluff ('the Bluff') Red Bay is a beautiful small beach for those coming from Marigot–they drive only 5 minutes west instead of 25 minutes to Orient Bay. Breathtaking rock formations, lively beach scene. Ample parking.

☞ Starting westward from Philipsburg on the circle road, at 4 km beyond the French border—between la Samanna and the PLM St. Tropez Beach hotels—find the sign for Baie Rouge. Turn left and follow dirt road to parking. The area to the right (east) is topfree; a plage naturiste is 100 yards to the left (west).

Leif Heilberg, Club Orient Bungalow. Lee Baxandall, Ray Brink and Guests.

THE VIRGIN ISLANDS

Tourist experience in the English and American Caribbean seems to turn out more prudish and packaged than the ambience that tourists can find in the independent Caribbean nations and the French islands.

Travelers to the Virgins find it enhances their safety and convenience to be cocooned on a boat or in a bungalow or tent colony or a rental villa.

This generalization is only partly true; it is truer of St. Thomas than of St. John.

Still, the contemporary Anglo-American tourism packaging and marketing do respond effectively to the restive racial and economic underclass in the Virgin Islands. Anger, theft, riot and murder encourage keeping a distance: the cocooning truism is fairly true.

In what follows we recommend the cocooning options because that's what the Virgins do best.

Start with villa rentals in the British and U.S. Virgins. *The Vendôme Guide* costs $8 from West Indies Management Co., P.O. Box 1461-WG, Newport, RI 02840. Phone 1-800-932-3222.

THE BRITISH VIRGINS

Cottage colonies flourish in the British Virgin Islands. The proprietors focus their services on a handful of guests. Now just think of the growing fleet of charter boats in these islands only 60 miles east of Puerto Rico. They're a floating 'cottage' industry. The skippers outdo themselves to please their guests. Check listings in *Nude & Natural* magazine.

VIRGIN GORDA

Virgin Gorda makes a memorable day-trip by air from San Juan. North end nude sunning centers on one-mile Savana Bay and neighboring Pond Bay. Walk to Savana Bay around Blowing Point from Little Dix Bay Hotel. Or from the airport proceed straight to a T-intersection, go right, continue past Olde Yard Inn another 2 km. Valley Trunk, also at the north end, is an alternative.

Devil's Bay is your best south end bet, and it's next to a boat landing for The Baths. Drive to Baths roadhead; instead of taking that trail, slip under barbed wire and angle off to right and downhill for 10 minutes. Turn left at shore to Devil's Bay. Discreet nude use. Bring snorkel gear.

TORTOLA

Many natives on this most populated BVI take a dim view of naturism. Avoid any busy beaches or anchorages. Green Cay offers hope. So too Josiah's Bay, going by 4WD.

Long Beach on the north shore is recommended. Walk to right on Long Beach to the end of the bay. Fine swimming and snorkeling. The guests of Marine Cay Hotel cross over to Great Camanoe island offshore for private sunbathing.

Or go to east point, cross the bridge onto Beef Island, pass the first road on the left, then a pond, to find doubtful-looking tire tracks. They take you across sand (it's firm) until you must park. Go another 100 yards on foot.

ANEGADA

Anegada Island, alone among the BVI, has a coral, not a volcanic origin. Its 23 mile, lowslung, little-visited shore allows you to doze au naturel on sand, instead of on sharp rocks. Its one lodging, Anegada Reefs Hotel, is reasonable and recommended.

THE U.S. VIRGINS

Over time they have been held by Spain, France, England, Holland, even the Knights of Malta. Eventually, Denmark sold them to the U.S. for $25 million; our military sought a presence in the eastern Caribbean.

ST. JOHN

Virgin Islands National Park holds 9,500 acres of St. John, two-thirds of its area. Packaged activities include underwater reef 'trail', tours of a Danish plantation, tours through lush tropical forest.

Check with a shuttle driver on arrival for the best available skinny-dipping; many visitors to St. John quietly skinny-dip.

'No nudity–NPS' signs prevent aggressive nudity. Rangers just wave to discreet and deferential sunbathers–who strip again when the ranger goes.

Jumbaie Bay, the first cove west of Trunk Bay on the north coast, has shade, snorkeling and a great view of Trunk Bay. The 100 yard beach at the 3 mile marker on the north shore road is the local naturists' favorite and St. John's best. Limited parking (3-4 vehicles) prevents crowding. Arrive by 9:30 a.m. for your pick of parking and dress code.

Solomon's Beach is another option. Go east on North Shore Road from Cruz Bay; at top of first hill, turn left on paved road that goes to NPS housing. Opposite the second house from the end, take the trail to the right. Proceeding across two intersecting trails, the trail then bears right along the shore and emerges at Solomon Bay, which is regularly clothes-optional. The beach is a 20 minute walk from the center of Cruz Bay. Or park in the Caneel Bay Plantation lot and walk west from Honeymoon Beach.

Jumbaie Beach is in easy reach of Cinnamon Bay Campground, a reasonably priced tent and cottage establishment. Each unit comes complete with cots, linen, picnic table, charcoal grill, ice chest and cooking utensils. Cinnamon Bay Campground, P.O. Box 120, Cruz Bay, St. John, VI 00830. Phone (809) 776-6330; 776-6458.

Maho Bay Camp, an inexpensive resort has grown to 102 units, and the naturist use of Francis Bay to the east is increasing. The permanent tents are comfortable and place little barrier between you and a felicitous nature. You'll also observe new minimalist technology in use: compost toilets, an energy-generating windmill and an elaborate sys-

Preceding pages: Lee Baxandall, Goofing On Orient Bay, St. Martin.

tem that utilizes the water from sinks and showers for irrigation and freshwater pools. No hot water available. Bring repellent against the sand flies that you may encounter. Maho Bay Camps Inc., 17 E. 73rd St., New York NY 10021, Phone (212) 472-9453.

ST. THOMAS

There's trouble in paradise. Tensions are on the rise. It is not advisable to visit any secluded beach without companions.

A sure solution to the safety problem is to charter a small craft with several other people for a day or a week. Boats are advertised in the Yellow Pages. For a reasonable sum you can snorkel and sunbathe to your heart's content. Just make certain before you hoist anchor that you have a congenial skipper and fellow passengers; even one prude can spoil the day.

Magens Bay on the central north coast focuses landlocked nude beaching. Platform Beach was liberated by cruise ship and airline staff—weekday use only—it's well down the road to the right beyond Magens Bay Beach. However, Peterbourg Beach on the south shore of Magens Bay continues as the primary nude beach of St. Thomas.

Lee Baxandall, Jean Rocquemont, Anse Bourdel, Guadeloupe.

EUROPE

EUROPE

Europe's naturist beaches, campgrounds and resorts have multiplied. No longer can our introductory, illustrated guide hope to include all the worthwhile sites. Our aim, for Europe, is to survey the most popular and the best.

OTHER INTERNATIONAL GUIDES. Experienced travelers will want the *World Handbook of Naturism*. Europe-based, the International Naturist Federation abstracts encyclopædic data for 850 INF clubs and resorts. Omitted from the listings are a number of unaffiliated clothes-optional resorts. Moreover, the beach information is spotty and slight.

A compilation of European nude beaches is provided by Englishman Phil Vallack. *Free Sun Beaches* includes crude small map sketches. Being frequently unverified, the reports sent in by travellers on which Vallack relies involve a wide margin of vagueness and inaccuracy.

These key references, and some of the single-nation guides, are available from The Naturist Society, P.O. Box 132, Oshkosh, WI 54902, USA. Phone: (414) 426-5009 for a catalog.

NATURIST TRAVEL AGENCIES. Clothes-optional and naturist resorts and campgrounds are a unique niche of travel —and often a complete mystery to a general travel agency. You'll benefit by going to the specialists.

At this time one North American agency stands out for experience, range of European and world naturist destinations offered, and full-service competence: Skinny-Dip Tours, R.D. 1, Box 294, Bloomingburg, NY 12721. Phone 1-800-828-9356 or (914) 733-4596. Their full-color offerings 'magazine,' priced at $20, orients the first-time and experienced traveler alike.

Other agencies specialized in naturist destinations advertise their varied and changing offerings in *N (Nude & Natural)* magazine (see introductory offer, back of this book).

AUSTRIA

The mountain lakes and streams are frequently used au naturel by campers and local people. "Topfree *(oben ohne)* is practiced nearly everywhere," reports the ÖNV journal *Nahtlos Braun* (Seamless Tan). Austrians did not lead in the early FKK movement, but tourism to Yugoslavia's Istrian Coast after 1960 exposed many Austrians who caught on.

Austrian campgrounds listed in the INF *Handbook* have no rental lodgings, only empty sites. Information: Österreichischer Naturistenverband (ÖNV), Postfach 88, A-1024 Vienna. Phone: (222) 218-0831.

VIENNA (WIEN)

Beginning in 1981 the City Council has turned over recreational facilities to topfree and clothes-optional use.

DANUBE ISLAND

Danube Island is more or less in the center of Vienna. A flood control project mandated this 22 km 'fill' in the famous river creating a separate Drainage Canal (sometimes called the New Danube). Tens of thousands enjoy the setting on warm summer days.

In clothes-optional use are both sides of the north and the south ends of the Canal—about 15 km of pebbly river beaches in all, with barbeque pits, meadows, woods and trails. Fine restaurants are at hand. A mobile Konditorei with petits fours and ices, coffees and liquors, might drive right up to your cove! Bask or swim, play cards or picnic, it's your free choice.

Topfree (oben ohne) is accepted almost anywhere that bathing costumes are worn in Vienna. It was officially adopt-

Preceding pages: Durand Stieger, Beach at Cap d'Agde, France.

ed in 1981 at the popular Gänsehäufl bathing island, on an arm of the 'old' Danube. In 1982 FKK areas were extended to Gänsehäufl and the Danube Island.

☞ Autos are allowed on the Island but parking is very limited. The bus system requires more study than you may have patience. The subway carries you in minutes from the western or southern peripheral districts to the Island. The tram and inter-city Schnellbahn have stations on or near the island. A ferry across the Danube is a pleasant access.

DANUBE FLOAT

The Viennese love to take outings by auto up the gorgeous Danube River to enjoy a fine day. Some will make this 80 km excursion by train so as to float home to the metropolis on an air mattress, sunbathing on the way (watch out for the steamers). Check the shores as you go for the nude beaches—there's one on the sandspit in the Danube between Melk (with its famous monastery) and Aggsbach, on the right bank as you float.

☞ From Vienna take the Melk train, or drive A-1 to Melk. Exit at Wachaustrasse, follow the signs for Krem for 7 km and then take the lefthand fork, which will bring you to the beach. No facilities, and no camping.

KÄRNTEN

CARINTHIA PROVINCE

Kärnten–Carinthia, the southern province of Austria, bordering on Yugoslavia, is a sunny region of small lakes and large mountains. Major naturist resorts nestle among the Alpine meadows and forests. Day trips will include castles, cathedrals and chateaux. The provincial capital, Klagenfurt, is of interest as are many towns that retain medieval qualities. If possible, attend the Carinthian Summer Festival, July–August in Ossiach and Villach. Mention your naturist interests if you contact the Austrian National Tourist Office, 500 Fifth Avenue, New York, NY 10110. Phone: (212) 944-6880.

KEUTSCHACHER SEE

The free beach adjoins a huge naturist campground with showers, sauna, sports field, restaurant. RV rentals. Camping Sabotnik, Dobein 9, A-9074 Keutschach. Phone: (4273) 2509.

Next door is FKK-Camping Müllerhof, Dobein 10. Phone: (4273) 2517. With 350 campsites Müllerhof is less crowded than its older and popular neighbor.

Take E-94 south from Klagenfurt. Turn west to Wörther See and continue on to the southwest shore of Keutschach Lake.

TIGRINGER SEE

West of Klagenfurt, north of Moosburg, is Tigring Lake. Again a popular nude bathing site adjoins a large and impressive naturist campground. F. Kogler, Tigring 19-a, A-9062 Moosburg. Phone: (4272) 83542.

RUTAR LIDO

On 25 acres with 347 campsites, 28 rental RVs and a magnificent view of the mountains. Tennis, hiking, fishing, water gymnastics, indoor wave pool, outdoor heated pool, massage, sauna; volleyball, chapel, facilities for children and the disabled; restaurant and minimart; a large artificial lake. No single males—otherwise it is a small luxurious smoothly regulated city. Located 22 km east of Klagenfurt. English-language brochure from Rutar Lido, A-9141 Eberndorf. Phone: (4236) 2262.

FORST SEE

An Edenic site near Wörther See. Forst See (lake in the woods) can be reached by well-marked hiking trails. Flat sunning rocks and sandy beaches at this large former quarry cause picnickers to get naked. No facilities on site.

☞ From Velden on the west end of Wörther See, go 3.5 km east along the north shore to the aluminum works. Turn left, drive 1.5 km, hang a left and after 500 m park on the shoulder. Or hike from Unterwinklern (eastern Velden) for 90 minutes uphill on trail number 5, 15, following signs to Forst See.

HELIO-CARINTHIA

Helio Carinthia Naturist Park has tent and RV camping, bungalows, playground, grocery store in an awesome natural setting on a mountain. Hike nude for hours or visit the nearby town of Gmünd for the Porsche car museum. Familie de Graaf, Pressingberg 31-32, A-9861 Eisentratten. Phone: (4735) 268.

PESENTHEIN

This health facility on the Milstätter See has a public beach with a section reserved for naturist use. Strandbad Pesenthein, A-9872 Millstadt. Phone: (4766) 2021/44.

STEIERMARK

THERME LOIPERSDORF

In the verdant, hilly Styrian countryside east of Graz, a hot spring site has been wedded with modern architecture to provide vast indoor and outdoor pools, 'brooks', 'waterfall', waterslides, spas, saunas, and sunning areas for the clad and semi-clad. Plus restaurant, children's rooms, steambath, massage, solarium, and sports and exercise programs.

The Schaffelbad, a smaller area with indoor and outdoor decks, spa and sauna, offers FKK use on Fridays 5–9 p.m. Schaffelbad continually provides a huge lawn for nude sunbathing.

Contact: Therme Loipersdorf bei Fürstenfeld, A-8282 Loipersdorf 152. Phone: 33 82-8204.

RABNITZBACH GELÄNDE

About 10 km northeast of Graz, Rabnitzbach is set in a rich agricultural valley of rolling hills. Its 17 acres include two sunbathing meadows, sports fields, tennis and volleyball, a pond surrounded by woods, playgrounds, swimming pool, a canteen with a sun terrace. Visitors are always welcome. Rabnitzbachgelände, Elisabethstr. 23, A-8010 Graz. Phone: (316) 37983.

TIROL

VÖLS CAMPGROUND

Völs' convenience to Innsbruck makes it popular despite being crowded. You need your own tent or RV. Pavilion with snack bar, fine swimming pool, very friendly. Reservations: LffL Innsbruck, Postfach 17, A-6022 Innsbruck 3. Phone: (512) 303145.

SALZBURG

HALLSTÄTTER SEE

Local initiative succeeded in gaining a section of Hallstätter See at Untersee for naturist use. Open to all; facilities nearby. The best access is Route 145 from Bad Goisern toward Pötschenpass. After St. Agatha, bear right toward the lake and the FKK area. Phone (6135) 8166.

GASTHOF NEUHAUSEL ALM

Frau Janisch is the friendly host at this inn on the road from Kirchberg to Aschau, approached from Munich or Salzburg via the famed winter resort Kitzbühel. About 5 km south of Kirchberg look for the sign on the right of the road, a bit up a hill. This driveway leads to the 17-bed pension with small FKK sign by the door. Reasonable. Solarium, sunning lawns, sauna, fitness equipment, hiking trails, nearby skiing. A-6365 Kirchberg bei Kitzbühel. Phone: (5357) 8161.

J. C. Lavoix, Diving.

LESSER RHINE

BREGENZ

In western Austria the Lesser Rhine flows into the Bodensee (a.k.a. Lake Constance) north of Lustenau. Its delta forms a wetland with sandy 'islets.' Here the town of Hard has a nude recreation area with lockers, showers, a marsh walk and a buffet-biergarten!

☞ Take B-202 (Rheinstrasse) for 7 km west from Bregenz. Go all the way through Hard and at the city limit of Fussach, after the bridge over the so-called "New Rhine," turn right and follow signs for FKK beach. After the gravel plant look for the reception area. Adjoining guesthouses.

BELGIUM

Since 1981, Belgium has permitted a topfree option, but not full nudity on its haute coûture but cheek-by-jowl North Sea beaches.

The development of landed nudist clubs goes forward; they were long banned. Belgium is up to 20 clubs and 12,000 FBN members. Many of these naturists still go only on holidays to the French and Spanish beaches, which were long their only option. FKK is now an option at some inland hotels.

Contact: Fédération Belge de Naturisme, B.P. 66, B-1000 Brussels 22. Phone (03)325-3970.

A Belgium-Luxemburg guide, *Benelux-gids Naturisme*, is available from SNU, Antwoordnummer 4058, NL-3500 VB Utrecht, Netherlands.

LANDED CLUBS

The clubs came first. Land later, when possible and if allowed. Many clubs developed ties with South European FKK campgrounds; others with Dutch ones. Contracts for winter use of municipal pools are a later and now widespread practice.

Sustained naturist club activity appeared in Belgium only with Robert Lambrechts who started the Athena Club (1955). Lambrechts was to become a dynamic INF president. For safety, early Athena Club members had to cross an international border to their club grounds at Ossendrecht, Netherlands.

Lambrechts later established native Athena terrains for Brussels, Liege, Ghent and Hasselt. The Antwerp terrain, 16 km distant at Ossendrecht, has 350 member sites, 50 rental units and a proud tradition.

☞ For a landed club experience in Belgium begin with the prime mover: Athena Club, St. Thomasstraat 24, B-2018 Antwerp. Phone: (03) 239-1287.

DOMAINE LES CASSEROLES

Looking to the future, Domaine les Casseroles is a large inn with some FKK tent and RV sites in the Belgian Ardennes between Luxembourg and Liege. Nude-use pool, sauna; clothed tennis, hiking, skiing, playground, restaurant. English spoken. Baraque de Fraiture, B-6690 Vielsalm. Phone: (80) 418808.

BULGARIA

Organized social nudity came about at the Black Sea by the mid-1960s: Balkan Tours gained hard currency by promoting FKK vacations to the West Germans. Sites at Nessebâr and the Ropotomo River were controlled to serve only these tourists. But conservative Bulgarian elements soon forced even the tourists to cover up.

Today, beach freedom rules. The modern hotels, and 120 mostly modern campgrounds, remain inexpensive and private rooms are often rented by local fishermen.

Contact the Bulgarian Naturist Association % Dr. Todor Bostandjiev, Lenin Blvd. Bl. 112–B, BG-1113 Sofia. Bulgarian reservations (including good AYH facilities): Pirin Travel, 30 Al. Stamboliiski Blvd., Sofia.

US visitors are not required to obtain a visa.

THE SUN COAST

VARNA–BURGAS

The clear, warm Black Sea between Varna and Burgas has a Sun Coast tourist section—80 km from Varna, 30 km from Burgas—5 km of hotels, night clubs, shops and restaurants.

☞ The FKK area is 4-6 km north of this sunny shore near Nessebâr, designated by UNESCO as a World Heritage city and now an artists/writers hideaway. The beach is just past the Morski sanatorium; the Dolphin Restaurant abuts it. Another FKK beach is 1 km north of the Vlas textile campground.

The big, clean Varna hotels that you may use upon arrival have topfree and some nudist activity. Or choose a quiet Bulgarian retreat, such as the historical garden town, Balcîk, north of Varna.

SOUTH COAST

SOZOPOL–KITEN

Tourists who come for FKK beaches from Eastern Europe often choose the South Coast—many exquisite coves to receive individuals and couples.

Here, south from Burgas, the Sozopol peninsula is 'a natural' for nudity and the town is an artist colony. Near Arkutino, the oak forests march down to the sea. Kiten Beach is in an exotic nature park at the delta of the famous Ropotamo River. Hospitable fisher families take in guests as far south as Ahtopol, and there are fine campgrounds—all FKK-friendly.

Illiana Gencheva, Sun Coast, Black Sea, Varna, Bulgaria.

CZECHOSLOVAKIA

PRAGUE

SEBERÁK

Seberák, slang for the quarry *Seberovsky rybník* in the southeastern suburb of Kunratice, has an FKK sector which in the Eighties became the first legal nude beach in Czech history. It is fully enclosed to control gawkers and keep nudity mandatory, collecting a 3 kr. fee. Volleyball, toilets, buffet. 9 a.m.–7 p.m. daily.

☞ Take the Metro (subway), line C, to Kacerov. Transfer to bus 114 which runs at 13 minute intervals, 8 a.m.–6 p.m. Kunratice–Seberak is its last stop. The bus halts at the textile beach entry; walk another 200 yards to naturist access.

Other Prague area sites, briefly noted:

The Union of Naturists of Bohemia and Moravia (Unie Naturistú Cech a Moravy), publishers since 1990 of *Naturista*, have a campground 60 km south of Prague on the road to Príbram, at Hrímezdice–Slapská prehrada. Write UNA, P.O. Box 96, Olsanská 9, CS-13000 Prague 3. Restaurant, bar, sauna, small pool, minigolf, playground, volleyball.

A lawn for nude sunning is available at *Podolí* south of Prague, a public textile pool.

At *Lhota u Brandyse nad Labem*, 20 km northeast of Prague, is a clearwater pond where the public and the nearby campground users skinny-dip in numbers up to 6,000 on hot days!

Northwest of Prague, in Central Bohemia at *Vokovice, Lake Dzbán* has an official nude facility back of Pavilion A. Naturists often camp at TJ ARITMA Dzbán, Nad Lávkou 3, CS-16000 Prague 6. Phone: (42) 02-368551. Rental tents; buffet, sports equipment. June–August.

BRATISLAVA

RUSOVCE STRKOVEC

Bratislava, capital of Slovak province, has expanded to incorporate the village of Rusovce where there is a nude swimming quarry or "strkovec," easily reached by urban transport.

The Union of Naturists of Slovakia (Únia Naturistov Slovenska) federates with the Czech UNA while pursuing Slovak goals with a magazine and facilities. UNS is at P.O. Box 14, CS-94603 Kolárovo.

NATURA CAMP

Opened in 1991, the first Slovak naturist campground has 2 hectares on the Danube River. Four km from Komárno, midway between Bratislava and Budapest on Route 63. Rental tents, sites, cabins, buffet, and terrace restaurant with local and vegetarian specialties. Thermal spas nearby. June 1–Sept. 15. CS-94611 Nova Stráz. Phone (42) 819-82119.

BRNO

BRNËNSKÁ PREHRADA

Brnënská prehrada, the Brno dam site below Osada (Pod Osadou) on the left side of the lake, is long in FKK use. From Brno center take tram # 10 or 18 northwest to Bystre, walk to the main harbor (Bystre) and board a lake steamer to its third stop, Osada. Steamers leave every half hour.

Contact in German: Dr. Dusan Rysánek, Vránova 55, CS-62100 Brno.

Leif Heilberg, Beach at Ostrava, Czechoslovakia.

DENMARK

Here is a true complete list of the public beaches where nudity is ILLEGAL in Denmark: Aabenraa and Holmsland–Klit.

The remaining 4,700 kilometers of Danish coast are authorized for public nudity.

This acceptance was not initiated by the government. It needed major lobbying and educational efforts by Danish naturists. These culminated with a public, then-illegal, "wade-in" by some 300 nude beachers—finally jump-starting a transformation of public policy in 1969.

A number of beaches were then posted as officially nude. The Danish Tourist Board emphasizes: "Public nude beaches are open to everybody whether they want to bathe with or without clothes, but only a few of these beaches are specially marked by signs."

At all other beaches too—with the two exceptions noted—*nudity which does not lead to complaints* is permitted. A sensitivity to others' comfort level is the key.

If you choose a beach that is not specially posted for nudity, watch others' behavior. Perhaps ask Danes for advice. At some mixed-custom beaches it's okay to lie down without covering oneself but it's not acceptable to get up and stroll to the water nude. Considerate behavior is a small price to pay for extensive freedom.

For a map of the coastal accesses, contact any Danish Tourist Office. For some Naturist clubs and campgrounds contact the Danish Naturist Union, % Ella Pihl, Fuglebakkevej 103, I th, DK-2000 Frederiksberg.

Jess Jessen, Tisvildeleje Beach, Sjaelland, Denmark, 1986.

Denmark

JUTLAND

RØMØ ISLAND

Rømø is the most southerly vacation island on Jutland's west coast—popular with naturists from all of northwestern Europe. Those who tire of Sylt may move to Rømø by a 45 minute ferry ride. A causeway connects to Denmark's autoroute A-11. Rømø's wide open spaces, quaint Frisian villages, shepherds and modern hotels are easily reached. Contact: Tourist Offfice, Rømø, DK-6791 Kongsmark.

The most popular free beach is Sonder Strand, 1,500 m long, located near the hotels and campgrounds of Havneby, the port for the ferry from Sylt, on the southeastern shore. Drive A-11 to Skærbæk and take the Rømø Island exit.

FANØ ISLAND

North of Rømø, Fanø Island has 18 km of fine sandy beaches and dunes that stretch from Vesterhavsbad in the north to Sønderho in the south.

Most beach nudity is at Søren Jessens Strand, at the island's north tip. Take A-12 into Esbjerg, where a ferry connects to Nordby. Contact: Tourist Office, Torvet 21, DK-6700 Esbjerg.

WEST COAST

The Jutland Peninsula is Denmark's leading choice for vacation campers, being inexpensive and convenient to the Dutch and Germans. The surf of the North Sea crashes onto wide sandy beaches. Grass-covered dunes and vast moors also make it a romantic sight. But not only can strong currents drag the swimmer out to sea—bathers are sometimes kept on shore by frothy fish-killing yellow sea algae.

Take A-11 north past the Rømø and Fanø island accesses, to the 40 km of North Sea beaches which stretch from **Kærgard** beach north to Skalingen, with Kærgard the most popular. Beyond Esbjerg take the Varde exit and drive west to Oksbøl. Past Oksbøl, where the road angles south, continue west to Grærup, where you take the coastal road north, past Børsmose, to Kærgard.

North of Kærgard beach is the town of Henne with its **Houstrup** nude beach touted by the tourist office. Its dunes are wildly romantic. The Blåbjerg Plantation is here, and Lyngbo naturist campground is in walking distance of the beach. Curiously, Holmsland–Klit beach to the north is one of two in Denmark that forbid nudity.

On Jutland's northwest coast, find the Jammerbugten. Coastal A-11 diverges from the main A-11 at Østerild, rejoining it beyond Fjerritslev. Shortly before Fjerritslev take another road leading northeast to Hjortdal. Then follow the signs to Svinklov and Slettestrand—Jammerbugt Beach lies between the two.

From Løkken on A-11, drive north 7 km to just before Gølstrup, and turn west to the coast between Rubjerg Knude and Nørre-Lyngby-Molle. The road to a nude beach begins from the restaurant at Molle.

Lee Baxandall, Danish Naturist Elders On Hyldeholm Island, 1987: Soren Sorensen, Erik Holm, Eila Pfeiffer.

LYNGBO PARK

Lyngbo Park, West Jutland, has naturist camping for US $200 or 1400 kroner a week, electricity included. Nudity is not required and activities such as volleyball are clothing-optional. Restaurant, laundromat, minimart. Young members are made welcome by getting lower rates and use of a special camping area where radios and late partying is okay. May 1—Sept. 15. Strandfogedvej 15, DK-6854 Henne. Phone: (05) 25 50 92.

BALTIC COAST

Skagen, at Jutland's northern tip, faces Sweden to the east. Its 65 km of windswept dunes and sands are clothing-optional. Reach by A-10 along the Baltic Coast.

North of the Fin Island causeway, the tourist board recommends a site on the southern hook of Vejle Fjord. Take A-18 south from Vejle to the Vinding exit; then east to Trelde Næs. Or from Fyn Island, take A-1 northwest across the causeway; at the Erritse exit, go north, through the city of Fredericia, to Trelde.

BALTIC ISLANDS

Most of us visualize the Jutland Peninsula when we think of Denmark. In reality, industrial activity and population are centered on Denmark's Baltic Islands.

ANHOLT ISLAND

Anholt is small and remote with a fine, unspoiled shoreline. Reached by a 3-hour ferry from Grena or by air. A free beach on the eastern shore is popular.

BORNHOLM ISLAND

Bornholm is a 7-hour ferry ride southeast from Copenhagen or 2 1/2 hours by ferry from Ystad, Sweden. Air travel is available. Nudity at the Dueodde, Jomfrugaard and Vester Somark beaches.

FALSTER ISLAND

Falster Island is en route to Copenhagen, if you take the auto ferry from northeastern Germany. Boto Strand is 18 km south on A-2 from Nykøbing, the principal city. Between Boto and Marielyst, look for the large graphic sign.

FYN ISLAND

Fyn Island is linked by causeway to Jutland and to Langeland Island and by ferry to Sjælland.

Thurø By beach is on a cove just east of the A-9 causeway from Fyn to Langeland Island. It's pebble-free and safe for bathing.

Hverringe Skov beach, near Kerteminde to the northeast of Odense, is 800 m long with parking at the Forest of Hverringe.

LOLLAND ISLAND

From Nakskov, drive southwest to Lange and make your way to Albuen at Lolland Island's western tip. Albuen is a hamlet on a sandspit in Nakskov Fjord.

SJÆLLAND ISLAND

Sjælland is largest and most populous of the Baltic Islands.

☞ A designated nude beach is on **Køge Bay** 15 km south of Copenhagen between Ishoj and Brondby Strand. The suburban train goes to Ishoj (with bus connection to Ishoj Strand) as well as to 'youth' beaches some 10 km north at Helsigor and Klampenborg.

A more southerly nude beach is at **Feddet** on Fakse Bugt. From Copenhagen take E-4 south to Tappernøje. Turn off in the direction of Orup. The Feddet Peninsula is accessible to the east about halfway to Orup.

The most popular nude beach—recommended by the tourist board—is near **Tisvilde**, bordering Troldeskoven (the troll forest). Tisvilde is special in Sjælland for its beauty and the quality of the sand and water. Drive northwest on A-16 to Frederiksværk, then A-205 N to A-237, then to coastal Tisvildeleje and the nude beach 3/4 mile to the west. Closest parking is Stangehus P-Plads. Camping facilities in Tisvildeleje.

The westernmost free beach, **Vesterlyng**, is reached by A-4. Follow signs for Kalundborg and take the exit after Viskinge to Eskebjerg. From Eskebjerg take the road west toward Alleshave; Vesterlyng will be on your right.

Another beach, **Ordrup Naes**, offers a solitary naturist idyll within a state park 60 miles from Copenhagen. Lush meadows back a part sand, part gravel beach. Take A-4 west to Holbæk. Five miles outside of Holbæk—while following signs to Kalundborg—turn right toward Gislinge and Fårevejle. In Fårevejle drive past the train station and turn left for 100 yards at the main intersection in town, then right again in the direction of Ordrup Næs. After 2 miles, look for the village store and the Blaa Ged Restaurant. Turn off the road at Næsvej about 600 yards beyond the park and walk to the beach.

WHERE TO STAY

The hotels of *København* (Copenhagen) are expensive and often full. The Sleep-In is an adventurous, unadvertised alternative. Those who arrive in the summer without a bed can ask for it. About $4 a night buys a private bunk, toilet and shower use, and breakfast. Some 250 travelers comfortably share this converted ice rink nightly. Children under 12 free.

Coastal areas feature Vacation Villages, liked by European visitors. Rental about $25 per night. Write Vacation Centers Inc., Box 186, Spring Lake, NJ 07762.

Country inns and farms are another cost-saving option. Write for a list to Danish Tourist Board, 75 Rockefeller Plaza, New York, NY 10019.

Solvennerne offers a relaxing naturist base in a piney woods as you visit Copenhagen. It's 10 km due west on A-1 and off onto E-4 N at Glostrup. It's even near Copenhagen's suburban tram. Community kitchen, large pool, volleyball. May 1—Sept. 15. **Tysmosen**, Nybøllevej 21, DK-2765 Smørum. Phone: (42) 97 34 02.

Further west on A-1, 22 km beyond Roskilde, *Naturistforeningen Sjælland*—or **Solbakken**—welcomes foreign visitors. Rental chalets, community kitchen and clubhouse, fjord waterfront. April—Sept. Klitrosevej 6, Kyndeløse Sydmark, DK-4070 Kirke Hyllinge. Phone: (42) 40 56 07.

North of Kirke Hyllinge at Skibby is a popular winter solarium-pool-sauna for naturists, *Hellas*.

Roskilde Fjord harbors *Hyldeholm*—from 1936 the 'naturism on one island' project of Søren Sørensen and Eila Pfeiffer (see photo).

Jerry Derbyshire, Among the Islands.

FINLAND

With thousands of small lakes, Finland offers a plethora of sites for enjoying the great outdoors in the altogether. The Finns are sometimes misunderstood. The sauna is their invention and gift to the world, yet traditionally they do not practice mixed-sex nudity except among family and close friends. Every household has its sauna. The result is a dearth of public naturism, with the exception of municipal and hotel saunas.

The small but energetic Finnish naturist group is reached through Kalevi Rantanen, Killintie 3, 45200 Kuovola, Finland. Phone: 358-51-120353.

ÅLAND ISLANDS

MOCKELO BEACH

The thousands of southwestern Finnish islands in the Åland archipelago—formerly Swedish—have become a sunbathing haven. Even Swedish nationals boat and ferry over to Åland to enjoy camping/sunning. A social nude beach has emerged and is advertised in tourist brochures at Mockelo—on the first peninsula west of the principal Aland town of Mariehamn. Offical camping is adjacent.

PUNKAHARJU

KULTAKIVI HOLIDAY VILLAGE

Punkaharju offically established the first Finnish inland naturist beach in 1986 for Kultakivi Holiday Village, a 3-star resort offering 4 moraine lakes with beavers, restaurant, bar, disco, cottages and tents, minimart, saunas, boats, bicycles, velos, tennis, fishing, riding, volleyball, hiking. Only 43 miles from Savonlinna, famous for open-air performance of modern Finnish operas in July. Direct rail link to Helsinki, 330 km southwest. Contact Kultakivi, Heikinpohjantie 18, 57100 Savonlinna 10, Finland. Phone: 957-13640.

Leif Heilberg Sauna

FRANCE

France followed Germany's lead in establishing organized Naturism and was the second nation to do so with significant numbers. Today, perhaps 80,000 belong to the Fédération Française de Naturisme.

Kienné de Mongeot, a naturalized Frenchman, was primarily responsible for this early development. A tall, aristocratic free spirit, he edited *Vivre* (later *Vivre d'Abord*), the focal nudist magazine of the 1930s and 1940s. De Mongeot also founded the Sparta Club, near Paris, where a classic Greek norm of social nudism was developed, acceptive of the male and female singles and not family-oriented. Like other European clubs of the time, Sparta Club set rigorous codes of nudity.

Albert Lecocq, de Mongeot's disciple and successor in French naturism, was not, at heart, more Christian or family-oriented, but he made more concessions to the popular prejudices in the interests of popularizing Naturism. The era of Lecocq is still with us: the terrain he founded, Club du Soleil; the ocean resort, Montalivet and the journal, *La Vie au Soleil* continue, if they have changed hands.

Some FFN club naturists resisted the rise of nude beaches and resorts in the 1970s while other FFN members helped create public clothes-free zones. The private clubs are presently losing members; they seek to extend the education and benefits to reattract members. The FFN is at 53 rue de la Chaussée d'Antin, F-75009 Paris. Phone: (1) 42 80 05 21. Brochures in major languages.

The non-FFN monthly magazine *La Vie au Soleil* is available in North America from Express Magazine, 4011 Boulevard Robert, Montréal, Quebec H1Z 4H6, Canada. Sample, $7.

NORTHWEST

DUNKERQUE TO NORMANDY BEACHES

Nord—Ghyvelde. Municipal nude beach, east of Zuydcoote Marine Hospital. The deprived next-door Belgians benefit. Access by coastal N-1 or D-60 then north on D-947 to park at Bray Dunes.

Pas-de-Calais—Berck-sur-Mer. At 42 km south of Boulogne, turn off N-40 west onto Blvd. de Boulogne, then right on Chemin des Anglais to sea. Park at Dr. Calot St. lot. Cross to Terminus Beach, walk north 15-20 minutes for nude beach. Stay out of the handsome dunes.

Somme—Quend Plage Rue. Enjoy the Channel dunes north of Abbeville. From Rue drive by D-940 to Quend then D-102 to Quend Plage; walk south towards Le Crotoy.

Manche—Hatainville. Drive south from Cherbourg on D-904 to just north of Le Moitiers d'Allone, then D-242 west through Hatainville to the beach. Walk 1 km south to halfway to Cap de Carteret.

Manche—Agon-Coutainville. From Granville take D-72 north. Turn left on D-44 to Agon. There go south onto the hook. Just before the lighthouse, take a sand road on the right (just before the Lechanteur monument), park, walk north to the huge sand beach. Note that low tides go far out.

Manche—Bréville-sur-Mer. Exit D-971 (Graville-Constances Road) at Grand Chemin heading for the Bréville airport (D-236). Take this road over the dunes to the beach, then continue left. The beach is north of Vanlée Camping and opposite the rifle range.

BRITTANY BEACHES

Cote d'Emeraude—Crique de Fréhel. From N-786, east of Pluvien, take D-34a northeast via Pléhérel-Plage. Follow signs for Cap Fréhel and park atop Trou du Poulifer. A goat path leads down to Port-du-Sud-Est beach, on the east shore of Cape Fréhel, halfway between the point and La Guette beaches.

Cap d'Erquy—Le Lourtuais. Leave N-786 at Erquy, direction Cap d'Erquy. Take the right-hand road at the ruins. Park when the road becomes too steep; walk to the gathering spot, east of Cap d'Erquy, a large beach of black rocks backed by hilly pinewoods.

St.-Brieuc—Plage des Rosaires. Easy access. From St.-Brieuc drive northwest on D-786, turn right (north) at Piérin to Gréve des Rosaires. Walk right.

Lannion—Beg-Léguer. At the mouth of Le Léguer river, 10 km west of B-786, is Beg-Léguer and Mez an Aod beach. Take D-21 north from Lannion and exit left at Le Raudour, direction Pointe Servel. Confusing intersections abound—follow your nose, due west. Past Beg-Léguer Church and before the lighthouse, turn left at the road with a stone marker. Park your car here on the side of the road. Walk 10 minutes west to a small cove surounded by granite boulders. Walk north over the rocks to Mez an Aod. Try Camping Beg-Léguer, F-22300 Servel-Lannion. Phone: 96 48 75 20.

Quimper—Cap Sizun to Tregunc. North of Audierne, Pors-Péron beach at Beuzec-Cap-Sizun has a nude cove beyond the rocks on its west end. On the Bay of Audierne, naturists use the ends of Prat-ar-Hastel beach, southeast of Treguennec; D-156 east from Plonéour-Lanvern goes there. For Treffiagat beach: take D-102 coastal route south from Pont-L'Abbé, and 1 km beyond Lesconil (going west now) turn left onto a dirt road. Camping des Dunes, Phone: 98 87 81 78. Tregunc's Plage de Kerouini is south on D-1 to Pointe de Trévignon.

Lorient—Ploémeur. From Lorient drive south then west on the D-152 loop to Plage des Kaolins near St.-Jude Church.

Morbihan-Erdéven—Kerminihy Beach. Easily reached and popular. Via

Durand Stieger, French Family Camping.

Auray or Ploemel to Erdéven (where D-781 and D-105 meet). At Erdéven Church go due west to Kerminihy, drive through, turn left at last house and go to the second right. Beach is between the rivière d'Etel and Roche-Sèche World War II gun blockhouse. Lodging: Association Naturiste Morbihannaise, B.P. 8, F-56106 Lorient.

KOAD AR ROC'H

Koad Ar Roc'h is a chateau in the Brocéliande Forest 50 km west of Rennes, now a magnificent naturist park. Rolling woods and fields, lakes, restaurant, bar, crêperie, disco, handicrafts, yoga, volleyball, soccer, canoeing, riding. Rental RVs, stone-built bungalows; a fine base for visiting Brittany. June 15–Sept. 15. Chateau de Bois de la Roche, F-56820 Néant-sur-Yvel. Phone (97) 74 42 11.

PARIS AREA

HELIOMONDE

Huge outdoor heated pool, volleyball, tennis, restaurant, bar, clubhouse and library, on wooded 45 ha. Rent a bungalow or 'caravan' (RV). South 50 km from Paris, close to N-20, with metro bus and rail only a mile away at St.-Chéron. Open all year. La Petite Beauce, F-95130 St. Chéron. Phone: (1) 64 56 61 37.

An innovator and paragon among the federated clubs, Heliomonde faces a crisis of function and identity. Costs are rising, and consumer tourism values impact the naturist market and current members' attitudes.

ATLANTIC COAST

TURBALLE TO VENDÉE BEACHES

La Turballe—Pen-Bron Beach. Brittany's most popular nude beach: sunny, fine sand, good swimming, boating and fishing. La Turballe is west-northwest on D-99 from Nantes, near the mouth of the Loire River. From La Turballe take Route D-92 south. Drive 1 km past signs for Village Vacances Famille to the T-intersection, and park on left. Walk in entrance and through forest for 10 minutes, past the lifeguard station, then right over dunes to beach. No lodging within 30 km.

St.-Nazaire—Les Jaunais. Pointe de Chémoulin. West on D-92 from St.-Nazaire, south on D-292 through St.-Marc. Ask, and perhaps stay just beyond the nude beach, at Camping des Jaunais–St. Marc, F-44600 St.-Nazaire. Phone: 40 45 92 60.

Île de Noirmoutier—Luzéronde Beach. Nudity is long established on the island's west coast between L'Herbaudiére and L'Épine among free spirits who mostly stay at Camping de la Bosse (phone 39 01 07) or Camping de L'Oasis (39 09 77) in L'Épine, or Camping de la Pointe (39 16 70) in L'Herbaudiére. Île de Noirmoutier can be reached by D-38 via Fromentine.

Fromentine—La Barre-de-Monts. Just south of Île de Noirmoutier, another well-known free beach. La Barre-de-Monts is at the center of a pine shaded, undeveloped 7 km beach from La Barre-de-Monts to Notre-Dame-de-Monts. At hamlet of Les Lays on D-38, park and follow trail across dunes.

St.-Gilles—Brétignolles-sur-Mer. On D-38 south of coastal St.-Gilles, west of La Roche-S-Yon. Access to a splendid 2 km beach is at L'auberge du Petit-Pont (La Rhumerie) just north of Brétignolles. Drive around the inn, park and walk 1 km west to the beach. Camping Les Cyprès, Phone: 52 55 38 98.

Olonne-sur-Mer—Sauveterre Beach. International set enjoys sun and seclusion. North on D-32 from Sables-d'Olonne, then west on D-80 to Sauveterre and continue west through the Olonne Forest to parking on the sea. Walk 1 km north.

La-Faute-sur-Mer—Pointe d'Arçay. A bird sanctuary runs the length of this wild and calming sandy beach. Approach by N-746 west through L'Alguillon. Park at sanctuary entrance, walk 2.5 km south to naturist portion. Or drive full length south, park and cut west across woods to the beach. Phone: 51 56 45 19.

CHARENTE-MARITIME BEACHES

La Rochelle—Île de Ré. Popular beaches are Lisay and Petit-Bec on the island's north shore, and between La Couarde and Bois-Plage-en-Ré at the gun blockhouse on the central southwest coast. Causeway is from La Pallice near La Rochelle. Information: 46 29 46 09.

Royan—Île d'Oléron—Oléron Nature. The Saintes–Royan area accepts a number of naturist sites inspired by the FFN success south at Montalivet. On Oleron Island there is naturist camping at Oléron Nature. Rental RVs, restaurant,

Domaine de Belezy, Avignon area. The Family Pool

minimart, pool, tennis, volleyball. F-17190 St. Georges d'Oléron. Phone 46 76 50 20. From the campground you might walk to naturist beaches on the northeast coasts both west and south of Fort Boyard.

Point d'Arvert—Tremblade Beaches. On the west coast of the peninsula, which juts above the Gironde River mouth, a large free beach extends along coastal D-25 from Pointe Espagnole south. Northern access is via the parking lot at Pointe Espagnole (Pointe d'Arvert). From the south look for the ranger station Bouverie at the junction of D-268 and D-25. It's a long hike in. Nudity resumes further south at Pointe de la Coubre and at La Palmyre/Plage de la Grande Côte. Close to it all is naturist camping at Atlantique Soleil, F-17570 Les Mathes. Phone (46) 22 40 35. Two pools, restaurant, volleyball, playground, activities, rental bikes and RVs. April–Oct.

GIRONDE PENINSULA

The Gironde Peninsula was 'liberated' by naturists after World War Two. With a pleasant climate, and rather convenient to Paris and much urban FFN membership in a time of more difficult travel, the Gironde was attracting campers to its sandy pine woods and Atlantic beach surf. A bid to buy land seemed right.

Today the resorts of Montalivet and Euronat mark the success of organized naturism. But many families still drive to the area for no-frills clothes-free camping—at Naujac-sur-Mer (northern part, from Pin Sec); Hourtin (south); Carcans (south and right of the ranger station Alexander); and Lacanau.

Also of interest are the northernmost and southernmost points of Gironde. Just 10 km from Soulac-sur-Mer, the former is Le Gurp, named for the street which leads to it. The high dunes provide a beautiful backdrop and ensure that naturism is widely practiced. At the southernmost tip is Cap Ferret and the campground Truc Vert (F-33979 Cap Ferret). Though not a naturist campground it does boast a naturist beach.

EURONAT

South of Royan and the Gironde River lies Soulac. South from Soulac via D-101, amid coast pines and dunes, is Euronat with double the area of its model, Montalivet, on a 1.5 km, broad sand beach. English-speaking assistance at check-in. Bicycle a necessity, may be rented. Rents 50 RVs and 300 bungalows fully supplied, and 790 tent/RV sites. Camping rated ****. Baker, butcher, deli, wine and fish shops, minimart, restaurant, boutiques, newsstand, bank, post office. Huge all-year heated indoor pool, with child's section, and special camping area for ages 16–25. Riding stable, all sports. Thalassotherapy spa and fitness program. From the Bourdeaux airport, 90 km. Centre Naturiste 'Euronat', F-33590 Grayan-l'Hôpital. Phone (56) 09 33 33. In USA, 1-800-828-9356.

MONTALIVET

Montalivet—the premiere campground of the Fédération Francaise de Naturisme—dates from 1949. Albert Lecocq and his FFN colleagues intensively negotiated with a Vendays mayor and councilmen, who were sceptical of admitting nudists to their community, yet fearful—after a forest fire charred the sandy coast—that no sensible person would bring money into a devastated region.

The FFN accepted strict conditions: nudity was confined at first to areas screened by scrub pine. They began reforestation and built primitive bungalows and common buildings. The numbers increased until, by 1970, Vendays was overshadowed by its stepchild. Now, over 20,000 vacationers come to Montalivet each year, many repeaters, spending two to four weeks.

Montalivet now offers its own 2 km nude beach with much spillover at the ends, tall pines, 1,250 chalets (200 for rent), 1,200 tent/RV sites (camping rated **). Children's pool and club, 16 volleyball courts, 8 tennis courts, heated pool, sauna, massage, spa, ping pong tables, amphitheater, films, crafts, library, TV, disco, bakery, wine and fish stores. All year. It's 80 km from Bourdeaux airport. Avenue de l'Europe, F-33930 Vendays-Montalivet. Phone 56 09 30 47. Paris phone (1) 42 46 43 87.

☞ From the north, take ferry at Royan to Pointe de Grave. Continue via Verdon to Soulac, and take D-102 south through Vendays to the coast and Montalivet. Rail to Bordeaux and then Queyrac, 14 km distant. Couples and families only. INF membership required, may be purchased at gate.

GIRONDE BEACHES

Lacanau—Bunker Beach. During its Occupation, the German army laid a road from Lacanau south to the defensive bunkers. Ask for 'l'Route Allemagne.' The 15 km beach—59 km due west of Bourdeaux via D-2—has a naturist B&B, 'La Forestière,' phone 56 03 20 50. Otherwise lacks facilities. Good surfing.

Arcachon—La Test-de-Buch Beach on the Dune du Pilat Lagoon. A very popular, superb naturist zone of dunes and pines. Reached by D-63, southwest from Bourdeaux to Arcachon, then D-112 south, towards Biscarrose-Plage; a km past Petit Nice Camping, turn in to Parking 'La Lagune'—safe, with hotels/restaurants; try 'Le Sablonney', phone 56 22 71 01.

LA JENNY

An elaborate and popular naturist complex between the Médoc and the Arcachon Basin 50 km west of Bourdeaux, La Jenny has 300 acres of pine forest on the coast. Opened 1983, 300 fully-equipped (including mopeds), self-catering rental chalets for 2 to 7 persons—and no tents or RVs. With 4 pools, 10 tennis courts, trails, surfing, archery, yoga, sauna, cultural evenings, newsstand, terrrace restaurant and bar, food shops, fitness center. Many children's activities. June–Sept. La Jenny, Route de Lauros, F-33680 Le Porge. Phone 56 26 56 90. Fax 56 26 56 51.

LANDES BEACHES

Biscarosse Beach. Nudity on north and south ends of Biscarosse Plage, which is reached by D-146. Coast road D-652 connects Biscarosse to La Teste-de-Buch to north and Mimizan to south.

Mimizan Beach. Nudity south of Mimizan Plage entrance from the shipwreck almost to the Maison forestière de l'Espécier, which is a good spot to park.

From Lit-et-Mixe to Vieux-Boucau-les-Bains. Lots of skinny-dippers along the coast from Cap-de-l'Homy in the north (D-88 west from Lit et Mixe), to St. Girons Plage, Huchet Plage, Moliets-et-Mas Plage—and especially, walking north on Vieux-Boucau Plage.

Vieux-Boucau-les-Bains is an old-time resort with pensions, small hotels, and a large campground to the north ('Camping municipal des Sablères', phone 58 48 12 29) close to the nude zone. A tolerant and lively town, easily reached via the Bordeaux-Biarritz highway.

Soorts Hossegor Beach. Signage tells the tale north of the main beach: "Nudists Can Be Expected Beyond This Sign."

Capbreton Beach. Naturists meet south of the main beach. From Capbreton, take N-652 to Labenne then D-126 west to Labenne Océan. Behind the shore turn north, following signs for l'Institut Héliomarin. Beyond it, park at Ste.-Therese chapel, walk to beach.

ARNAOUTCHOT

Family camping, rated ****, in a pine forest between the Landes and Basque country. Atlantic sandy beach of 1.5 km.

Heated indoor pool, playground, golf, 4 tennis courts, riding stables, watersports, films, disco. Canuding in Hutchet River reserve nearby; excursions to Pyrenees and Basque country. Rental chalets, RVs, tentsites. Minimart, bakery. Biarritz airport 65 km. May-Oct. Domaine d'Arnaoutchot, F-40560 Vielle St.-Girons. Phone 58 48 52 87.

MEDITERRANEAN COAST

PYRENEES ORIENTALES BEACHES

Argelés-sur-Mer—Bocal del Tech. Near the Spanish border is a magnificent expanse of beach at the 'mouth of the Tech River.' The cleanest water on the French Mediterranean coast; swimming is encouraged. Catalan and Sardice folklore shows two nights a week in town and the Festival de Prades at the end of July–start of August.

☞ Drive north from Argelés-sur-Mer and turn off D-81 on its west side between le pont de la Ribérette (Riberette Bridge) and le pont du Tech (Tech Bridge). The turnoff soon loops back under D-81, and east a mile to the coast. Drive carefully across the sand. When it gets treacherous do park, walk 5 to 10 minutes. Naturists often stay at the nearby (clothed) 'Le Soleil' campground, rated ****, phone 68 81 14 48.

Torreilles—Bourdigou Plage. Exit D-81 between the Bourdigou and Agly rivers, drive to Torreilles' Village des Sables on the coast and then south, staying north of the Bourdigou River.

PORT LEUCATE

Quartier Naturiste Port-Leucate was built (1976) as a nude-use zone, anchored by the resort-villages Aphrodite and Ulysse. A 2 km, clean, windy, unvegetated beach framed by jetties that stop beach walkers. With an INF card you may ask for a free day pass. Common amenities include pools, tennis and volleyball courts, water ski, windsurfing, balneotherapy, children's activities, minimarts, restaurant and bar with beach terrace, newsstand, discos. Since 1989, the quartier has been expanded.

Aphrodite Village has 546 garden villas and apartments around a marina. **Oasis Village**—of classy design, and on the beach, with a pool–palm 'oasis'—now extends Aphrodite. F-11370 Port Leucate. Phone 68 40 90 42.

Club Nature 'Ulysse' has 130 studios and apartments, and features 150 tent/caravan sites rated **. New **Eden** apartments extend the Ulysse holdings. F-11370 Port Leucate. Phone 68 40 86 58.

Les Maisons de la Jetee and **Poseidon** are to complete the construction.

☞ Thirty km north of Perpignan and 50 km south of Narbonne. Turn off A-9 at Leucate, and then by RN-9 on the left after 200 m take D-627.

LANGUEDOC–ROUSSILON BEACHES

Port-la-Nouvelle—Les Montilles. A posted, public nude beach south of Port-la-Nouvelle, most often used by visitors to the naturist campground Le Clapotis, 7 km away. Directly on the lagoon (Étang) of Lapalme, Clapotis has 220 campsites rated ****, a restaurant, bar, supermarket, sauna, boat rentals, lagoon beach, volleyball and basketball courts. Le Clapotis, F-11480 Lapalme. Phone 68 48 15 40.

☞ To Les Montilles Beach from Port-la-Nouvelle: South on B-9 from Narbonne, off at Sigean, then N-9D east. Drive south to the nude beach on a dirt road that is 500 m behind the shore. Park and continue walking.

For Le Clapotis: from Port-la-Nouvelle drive south on D-709 to Lapalme and beyond, hugging the Étang de Lapalme on your left. Its campers have walking access to Les Montilles beach via Camping Côte Vermeille, off D-709.

Gruissan—Fleury d'Aude. Between the beach villages of Gruissan-Plage and Les Cabanes de Fleury is a breezy, lovely strand of campgrounds and naturist beaches. Since 1974 it's legal. The tarmac road to St.-Pierre-le-Mer offers convenient entry. So too from Gruissan via Blvd. de Pech-Maynaud towards Narbonne-Plage, taking the first exit to the right at the traffic circle, continuing on to sand tracks, angling north. Write: Camping municipal de l'Étang, F-11560 Fleury-d'Aude. Phone only: Gruisson Promag, 68 49 09 00. Campgrounds: Les Ayguades, 68 33 81 59 (rated ***, on the nude beach). Naturist Camping Grand-Cosse, 480 RV/tent sites, where migrating shorebirds are an off-season attraction. F-11560 Fleury-d'Aude. Phone 68 33 61 87.

Grau-du-Roi—Espiguette Lighthouse. Directly east of Montpellier. The local FFN club was instrumental in gaining this lovely beach as an official naturist site. The club now maintains it as a first-class beach with ample parking and signs. Take D-62b out of Grau-du-Roi, circle around the Arena, exit with the Port Camargue on your right onto Route du Phare de l'Espiguette. Go straight past the lighthouse to the natural parking lot. Beach vendors bring refreshments.

SÉRIGNAN

West of Agde, this official naturist beach was restricted to guests of the Clos-du-Ferrand and Gymno-Club Méditerranéen campgrounds when decreed in 1972. The general public now uses it, entering by public Sérignan-Plage. Better, park on the right 100 m before Gymno-Club gate, for direct access onto the nude beach. Refreshments on beach.

Gymno-Club Méditerranéen, F-34410 Sérignan. Phone 67 32 18 47. Rated *** with 300 tent/RV sites, restaurant, all watersports, volleyball, clubhouse, disco. Right on the beach, 10 ha, open all year.

Le Clos Ferrand, F-34410 Sérignan-Plage. Phone 67 32 15 59. Rated ***, a small and satisfying naturist campground on the beach.

CAP D'AGDE

Begun as a small naturist campground in 1956 by the Oltra family on their coastal farm, Cap d'Agde now covers 90 ha—truly a naturist city and a model for developers internationally. Government investment was vital to make Cap d'Agde what it is today. The four distinct complexes each accommodate thousands as well as a wealth of enterprises. The unique aspect of Agde is the integration of naturism with everyday town life. Only here can you do all your shopping, banking, garage visits, and other daily business in the nude. This lends a tremendous sense of freedom, and causes one to wonder what a clothes-optional world might be like.

Centre Helio-Marin is the campgrounds—with 3,000 sites. March 15–Oct. 15. Agence Oltra, BP 545, F-34305 Cap d'Agde. Phone 67 26 33 78. If your notion of camping is to get away from it all and commune with nature, this isn't for you. The French like to bring their surburbia with them when they camp, including social events such as Tupperware parties and niceties such as garden fences. It's a good thing that the visitors aren't all that interested in nature—the beach that serves the Naturist complex is only 3 km, hardly adequate for all those bodies.

Hotel Eve, near the entrance, built 1983, rated ***, offers convenience, a heated private pool and terrace, solarium and full services. BP 654, F-34308 Cap d'Agde. Phone 67 26 71 70.

Cap d'Agde can accommodate up to 40,000 persons, and indeed does in the peak season July 15–Aug. 20. The international clientele creates a cosmopolitan atmosphere. The last few years have seen an increase of Japanese and American naturists. Readers may obtain a brochure in English about the rental agencies, RV/camp-sites, hotels, area attractions. Office Municipal du Tourisme et des Loisirs, BP 544, F-34305 Agde Cedex. Phone 67 26 38 58. Fax 67 26 22 99.

Travel consultants for visiting Agde include: Skinny-Dip Tours (1-800-828-9356) in association with Peng Travel, and Pangaea Travel (1-800-248-8980) in association with Pru & Larry Beck, an

Lee Baxandall Petanque at Belezy

American couple at Agde who can make your on-site and travel reservations: 34 Helio Village, F-34308 Cap d'Agde, phone 67 26 03 41, fax 67 26 03 41.

Emsdale Travel (phone 44-1-514-0005) and Peng Travel (both London-based) welcome newcomers to Agde with parties.

☞ Driving: Take motorway A-9, exit Agde/Pezenas southwest of Montpellier. Road signs to the Quartier Naturiste. Rail: Agde Station has direct day/night connection with Paris, Nice, Bordeaux, Strasbourg, Spain, Switzerland, Germany and Italy. Air: Air France, Air Inter and other airlines have daily flights from Paris and London to Montpellier, 50 miles from Agde. Transfer service is available, airport and rail, with Agde.

BOUCHES-DU-RHÔNE BEACHES

The Camargue—Saintes-Maries-de-la-Mer. From Arles south via Albaron on N-570. Drive east from Stes.-Maries to this vast delta beach of the Rhone River; passing 5 km of parking to the last lot. The eastern 9 km are a clothes-free utopia—look for the lighthouse, 'phare du Rousty,' and the FKK signs are located to its right. The farther you stroll the more naked and clean you and the beach get. Beach camping is now banned. There's a big campground at the beach entrance. Provisions in town. In August, the gypsies gather. Office de Tourisme, Ave. van Gogh, BP 34, F-13460 Saintes-Maries-de-la-Mer. Phone 90 47 82 55.

Salin-de-Giraud—Arles Beach. A vast flat like Stes.-Maries to its west; with a 5 km designated-nude zone signaled (still?) by the sculpture of a naked couple! Follow the south bank of the Rhône southeast from Arles for 35 km to Salin-de-Giraud (get your water here; last chance); there's also a ferry here for cars to cross from D-35 (direction Marseille, Aix). Continue southeast past salt flats and bird marshes for 11 km, and turn right at signs to Le Grau du Piémançon. Just short of the sea turn left, drive on hard sand to signs for naturist zone. Camping okay. Office de Tourisme, esplanade des Lices, F-13200 Arles. Phone 90 96 29 35.

Marseille—Martigues. A small cove of sand and large, flat rocks, at the Plaine de Bonnieu, south of Martigues, which isn't far west of Marseilles. Reserved for card-carrying (sneaker-wearing) naturists. The local FFN club provides for amenities and vets INF cards. Bring snorkel and mask—good waters to catch your next bouillabaisse. Map: Naturistes de Martigues, BP 123, F-13695 Martigues Cedex. Camping l'Arquet, phone 42 42 81 00.

Marseille—Southeastern Calanques. The lovely secluded coves east of Marseille draw au naturel picnics. Hire a fisherman at Morgiou to take you to the calanque of Pierres Tombées, Sugiton, or Port-Pin, picking you up hours later. You can also hike from Morgiou but it's rugged. From Marseille by N-559 and les Baumettes—but driving to Morgiou is chancy—controlled access. Drive on a weekday mid-morning, or better, try public transportation.

TOULON BEACHES

La-Seyne-sur-Mer—Le Jonquet. West of Toulon, approached by paths through the sloping Cap Sicié woodlands, then over rocks between the seven small coves. Each interesting and unique, some have natural springs. Signs limit naturism to between Point Malpasset and Point St.-Selon. Jonquet is much loved. Parking lot above beach, off the Route de la Corniche opposite a fire lane leading inland. Office de Tourisme, 6 rue Léon Blum, F-83500 Seyne-sur-Mer. Phone 94 94 73 09.

Carqueiranne—Bau-Rouge. Unblessed with a sand coast, Toulon makes do with Le Bau-Rouge's pebbles—bring portable comfort. From Carqueiranne take N-559 toward Le Pradet, exit at D-86 south, follow signs for Le Bau Rouge. At the hilltop settlement take the somewhat treacherous path to the beach. The FKK section is clearly marked.

ÎLE DU LEVANT

This earliest naturist seaside colony owes its establishment to a decision of two doctors, the brothers Durville, to purchase a large section of the rock island of Levant when it was discontinued as a penal colony in 1930. They installed carefully selected naturists on subleased plots, creating a community dedicated to harmony with the elements and simple living. The French military stepped in and built a naval base in World War II, disrupting the hegemony of health and limiting the recreation and lodging to only 220 acres.

You must wear *le minimum*, a kind of g-string, or another *cache-sex*, everywhere when off the beach. The "Levantines" even dress formally for dinner.

The "village" awaits its rebirth, with its makeshift provisions for water and light and failure to develop with clothes-optional popularity.

France

Yet even the rockiness of the shoreline (except in a sandy cove) doesn't daunt devotees, who return year after year to this sun-baked island. Lodgings are booked far in advance. Naturists interested in a living 'museum' of the movement's past might take the ferry over for a day, lodging on the mainland.

Lodge at **Lavandou**. It's a ferry port to Île du Levant. East of Lavandou on D-559 around the Pointe du Layet, there's a good nude beach—Plage du Layet—down a stairway painted green. Look for the iron walkway, park there. The path to the beach is 100 m in the direction of Lavandou. Two stone markers are at the entrance. This nude beach has a restaurant! It rents umbrellas and chairs too.

☞ Hotels, restaurants, bars, shops, campgrounds, windsurfing, discos, are described by information from Union des Commercants, F-83146 Île du Levant.

CAVALAIRE–CANNES BEACHES

Cavalaire—Pointe de La Nasque. Cavalaire (not to be confused with nearby Cavaliére) has a nude beach accessed across from the Bon Porteau Campground (rated ****, 94 64 03 24). Take N 559 south from Cavalaire-sur-Mer, park at Bon Porteau and walk to the beach over a very stony path—so rugged that many choose to enter the water at the family beach, to swim around the rocks. The nudes gather toward La Nasque Point to the south.

Ramatuelle—Plage de Pampelonne. The ancient fishing village St.-Tropez set an example to the youth of the Côte d'Azur in the mid-1950s thanks to Brigitte Bardot, rock musicians and other creative rebels. Nudity was a big part of the 'St.-Tropez scene,' started by topfree women at Plage de Pampelonne in 1964. Bardot fled the tourist throngs in 1990. The new St.-Tropez mayor caters to conservatives and has 'banned nudity'. Is naturism finished? No, it's just that ignorant journalism thrives.

Clothes-free fashion was rare enough, in this style-setting town, even at its media zenith. Topfree cannot be stopped in St.-Tropez. And full nudity occurs just east, on the Ramatuelle peninsula where it has flourished since the mid-1960s (Plage de Pampelonne, at the restaurant Le Blouch, served by bus; Cap Cartaya, Cap Taillat–Plage de l'Escalet, Baie de Briande).

St.-Tropez Camping Ltd. is convenient to the clothes-optional beaches and offers frame tents, ferry service, some amenities, and the cheapest accommodations in this expensive resort area. Write 4 Greenwood Ave., Poole, Dorset, England. Phone (0202) 70 94 17.

Leif Heilberg, The Discreet Charms of les Francaises d'Outremer. Pointe Tarare.

Fréjus—St. Aygulf Plage. From the road from Fréjus to Fréjus-Plage turn south on D-98, cross two bridges to town line with St.-Aygulf. At Camping Sammoa instantly turn around, park in lot on right, walk 300 m north to official Fréjus naturist beach—of fine sand and lifeguarded, posted for nude recreation, and nice rollers come in. Shallow enough for children to enjoy, sandy all the way out to where you can swim. Neat backdrop of a high-rise coastline eastward towards Cannes.

Cannes enforces a nudity ban. This limits seamless tanning to la Pointe du Dragon on l'Île Sainte-Marguerite, reached by boat from le Suquet. There's also Pointe Fourcade between Cannes–Golfe Juan.

CAP DE NICE

On the old Riviera, Cap de Nice gets the most nude exposure, partly because Nice is a port from which many sail to that nude haven, Corsica. Recommended is the Eze-sur-Mer beach. Follow the road to Monaco. The clothes-optional beach, Plage Pissarelle, is reached beyond the Eze-sur-Mer exit on the way to Cap d'Ail, 1 km from Cap Estel. Bus 100, which goes along the Lower Corniche from Nice to Menton, will drop you about 100 m beyond the Fina station (where mineral water can be purchased). Walk directly opposite the station to a road, signed Pissarelle, leading down to above the beach. If driving, there is parking for only a few cars. Park and walk 40-50 m to the beach where singles and families can be found relaxing in the nude.

Youth hostel in Cap d'Ail, the convenient rail station and 35 minutes walk from the beach. Naturist camping, 45 minutes from Nice International Airport at Club Origin Côte d'Azur, % Nat'Azur, 23 Ave. Jean Médecin, F-06000 Nice. Phone 93 05 06 00. Want to rub bare elbows with the yacht set? Neptune III, 20 Quai Lunel, F-06300 Nice.

AVIGNON AREA

CÈZE RIVER CAMPING

Europeans since prehistoric times have enjoyed clothes-free campgrounds along the cliff-lined, sandy banks of the Cèze River in the foothills of the Cévennes.

Northwest of Avignon, 120 km from Cap d'Agde and 30 km south of the Ardèche river gorges—the naturist camps have a 'lock' on their part of the Cèze, freeing a 530-acre, 3 km zone for canuding, rafting, fishing, hiking, rock climbing, caving and swimming. Pleasant into October.

La Genése is on the south bank—drivers note, as the others are by north bank access! It's a most sophisticated Cèze naturist center, 30 ha, 400 sites. Pool, volleyball, tennis, Ardèche excursions, craft workshops, archery, playground, minimart, restaurant, creperie, fine new bungalows. Rated ****. May–Sept. F-30430 Méjannes-le-Clap. Phone 66 24 51 73. Reservations: SOC-NAT, 16 rue Drouot, F-75009 Paris. Phone 42 46 43 87.

Les Bois de Sablière offers 300 campsites on 60 ha, rated ****. Ecology emphasis. Canuding beneath a towering rock face. Pool, sauna, fitness gym, tennis, disco, restaurant, bar. Rental RVs, bungalows. April–Oct. 15. St.-Privas-de-Champclos, F-30430 Barjac. Phone 66 24 51 16.

Le Martinet de L'Elze, on 15 ha, borders the Cèze atop the Cévennes plateau for 1,300 m. Rated ***, 132 sites. Pool, children's playground, clubhouse. Aujac, F-30450 Genolhac. Phone 66 61 12 37.

DOMAINE DE BELEZY

Drawn to France and the beach-city of nudists, Agde? Do also visit Belezy, an energetically bucolic retreat for family naturist camping; you'll enjoy making the comparison. Olympic pool, smaller heated pool, tennis, volleyball, soccer. Over 35 workshops in high season: archery, aquatics, French, astronomy, photography, computer use, sculpture et al. Child care, youth programs. Choral and instrumental performance. Restaurant/bar on terrace. Minimarket, massage, yoga. 25 ha. Camp-sites, dormitory, bungalows, RVs. East of Avignon and Carpentras, below Mont Ventoux; great area for excursions. May–Oct. Domaine Naturiste de Belezy, BP 3, F-84410 Bédoin. Phone 90 65 60 18.

FRANCE-CORSICA

After World War Two, naturists were still seeking the rare sundrenched strands where officials would accept their social nudity. Corsican developers were trying to think of a tourist market that could be attracted to this somewhat remote destination, off the Côte d'Azur but closer to Italy, where rugged terrain makes farming and manufacture difficult.

Voilá! Vacationing Naturists! The east coast around San Nicolao (central) and Porto Vecchio (south) was given over to clothes-free campgrounds. Northern Europeans flocked in, enchanted by snow-capped peaks, meadows of wild flowers, ancient ruins, yet lovely beaches.

Rarely do Americans visit Corsica; we miss some of Europe's finest long sand beaches, great weather lacking mistral gusts, and low prices. Skinny-Dip Tours books Corsica: phone 1-800-828-9356.

Fly into Bastia or Figary—not Ajaccio, it's on the wrong side of a 10,000' mountain range. Perhaps hire an airport car or book a car ferry; you'll want to see the island. Be sure to go nude only where prescribed. Corsican nationalists fiercely dislike foreign tourists especially the naked ones.

NORTH COAST

BAIE DE GIUNCHETU

Along the north coast from Cap Corse west to Calvi are many secluded lovely coves, including a favorite, Baie de Giunchetu, west from L'Île-Rousse.

The train from L'Île-Rousse to Palaga takes you to Baie de Ginchetu beach; or by auto, follow N 199 from L'Île-Rousse to Algajola, then signs for Le Bodri campground. Park at Le Bodri and walk to Botre Beach, then by goat trail over the rocks southwesterly; the naturist cove is at the tip of Punta di Ginebre. Another recommendation: Anse de Peraiola, near Santo-Pietro-di-Trenda, east of L'Île-Rousse. Follow D 81 to where it bends with an overlook of the water; park well off the road and descend to the beach, then walk out of sight of this road. Or continue on D 81 and exit at Casta, following directions to Saleccia, and then find the turnoff for Faggiola Cove, reached by a 12-km trail.

Karl H. Reddies, The Beach at Club Corsicana.

Top: Richard Pasco. Baskin-Robbins. Bottom: Lee Baxandall. Mini-Mart Shopping. Cap d'Agde.

NORTHEAST

CLUB CORSICANA

Club Corsicana is the largest Corsican naturist facility with 530 chalets, largely filled by German tour organizers. Guests share a 4 mile beach with Tropica and other naturist resorts—there's enough beach, and beach restaurants, for everyone!

☞ (Cf. *N*, 9.3) Club Corsicana: Linguizzeta, 20230-San Nicolao, Corse, France. Phone (95) 38 80 25. Or Tropica, 20230-San Nicolao, Corse, France. Phone (95) 38 80 71.

SAN NICOLAO

North of Aleria, the town of San Nicolao focalizes a number of naturist campgrounds. Access is by ferry or airport via Bastia. Drive 60 km south on Route 193 to 198, and look for signs to the campgrounds on your left.

Continuing south beyond San Nicolao find the friendly **Chez Mathieu** (formerly Club Baghera) and **Rivabella**, with lodgings, restaurants and minimarts that U.S. travelers usually require. Chez Mathieu, 20230-San Nicolao, Corse, France. Phone (95) 38 83 47. Rivabella, 20270 Aleria, Corse, France. Phone (95) 38 81 10.

SOUTHEAST

PORTO VECCHIO

High-priced, well-appreciated for its efficiency and development by largely German clientele, **La Chiappa** resort has panoramic restaurant, sauna, barber, laundromat, minimart, water sports, lawn games, nightly dances. 20210-Porto Vecchio, Corse, France. Phone (95) 70 00 31.

Aptly-named, Porto Vecchio harbored **Villata**, the earliest naturist camp on Corsica. Primarily a campgrounds for the young on a beautiful beach, with some bungalows, Villata is tranquil, self-contained. Villata, 20144-Ste. Lucie de Porto Vecchio, Corse, France. Phone (95) 71 62 90.

Ten kilometers inland is U'Furo, formerly Le Moulen; the only naturist complex that is not on the coast. The "wild" landscape of water and rocks rewards a drive even if you do not stay at the Mill. U'Furo, Route de Muratello 20137 -Porto Vecchio, Corse, France. Phone: (95) 70 35 10.

GERMANY

Bone-chilled Germans began some 1,800 years ago to rush to the Mediterranean climes. This dedication recycled in the last 40 years, as an estimated 12 million Germans now seek nude beaches for their holidays.

Innkeepers and tax collectors of Yugoslavia, Corsica, Turkey, the Baléaric and Canary Islands, southern France and Italy are pleased.

Increasingly, Germans also look to the Caribbean, even to repressive Florida, for Freikörperkultur—FKK, or free body culture—vacations. They also visit their own lakes and north coast for sun. Not to overlook the luxurious indoor/outdoor, sauna/swim/fitness leisure centers that now serve many German cities.

Acceptance grew during a century. In 1904, Richard Ungewitter wrote the manifesto, *Die Nacktheit* (Nakedness). It grew out of 19th Century health ideas and focused an organized movement worldwide. Ungewitter put morals and history, art and health in a new light.

By 1990 some 55,000 West Germans belonged to FKK organizations. Now the East Germans, equally enthusiastic naked people, will join and be counted.

For more information, obtain a current *FKK Reiseführer* (Verlagsgesellschaft R. Glöss & Co., Hamburg); *ADAC-Reiseführer: FKK Badeplätze* (P.F. 700126, D-8000 Munich 70) or, for data in symbols and English, the *INF Guide*.

Deutscher Verband für Freikörperkultur E.V, Uhlemeyerstrasse 14, D-3000 Hannover 1. Phone (0511) 34 22 33. Its magazine is *Freikörperkultur*.

NORDSEE

EAST FRISIAN ISLANDS

Borkum Island. Westernmost of the East Frisian Islands. Easily reached from Holland, Borkum has a 1,200 m FKK beach of 100 m depth in walking distance of the ferry port at Emden, with toilets/showers, shops, playground, lifeguards, and even a beach for those nude people who prefer the company of nude dogs. May 15–October 1. Kurverwaltung, D-2972 Borkum. Phone (04922) 815.

Norderney Island. A bus runs to the lighthouse FKK beach on the north shore, 7 km from Norderney town—lifeguards, toilets, restaurant at the Oase. There are 20,000 tourist beds on the island 1 hour by boat from Norden–Norddeich. Kurverwaltung, D-2982 Norderney. Phone (04932) 8910.

Helgoland. The northernmost and most distant East Frisian island, served from Hamburg by Elbe River packet and by air. It has a remarkable history—from Viking outpost to Nazi submarine base—indeed, the British bombed it to smithereens after World War Two. Nothing old stands, but the beaches deserve an excellent reputation, including the free beach in the north shore dunes. Bungalows, camping nearby. Rent a bike; no vehicles on Helgoland except minibuses and electric cars. Ferry service connects with offshore nude bathing

Leif Heilberg, Thiessow Beach, Rugen Island, Baltic Coast, East Germany.

islets and Cuxhaven. Kurverwaltung, Postfach 720, D-2192 Helgoland. Phone (04725) 80862. Fax 426.

ELBE RIVER MOUTH

The 'hooks' of the Elbe River delta are convenient for northwest Germany. Caution: If you want to swim, choose a high tide. The mudflats exposed at low tide are amazing.

Cuxhaven. Spa town on south shore of the Elbe. North from Bremen. FKK was earlier confined to the remote 'nude dunes' between the Duhnen and Döse campgrounds. This area has expanded; moreover, Neu-Nackeduhnien are on the tidal Wattenmeer, at the south end of Duhn beach. Visit on Tuesday, and from 5:30 you can enjoy FKK night at a grand local sauna/pool complex. Kurverwaltung, D-2190 Cuxhaven. Phone (04721) 12364.

Cappel-Neufeld/Nordholz—Familien Ferienplatz. Opened in 1984 by the DFK, on the Wattenmeer between Bremerhaven and Cuxhaven. Tent/RV sites, playground, volleyball, North Sea access. Bahnhofstr. 50, D-2859 Nordholz. Phone (04741) 7878.

Büsum—Westerdeichstrich. North of the Elbe near Büsum. The town's grassy 700 m FKK beach with camping is reached from Hamburg by Routes 5 and 23. Parking, showers. Kurverwaltung, D-2242 Westerdeichstrich. Phone (04834) 2336.

NORTH FRISIANS

From the Elbe River mouth north to Denmark, the North Frisian Islands offer:

Pellworm. The northwest shore on Hök-Hallig near Nordermühle is FKK. Showers/toilets. Ferry from Nordstrand. Kurverwaltung, D-2251 Pellworm. Phone (04844) 544.

Amrum. Windswept dunes and broad beaches enjoy the FKK overflow from neighboring Sylt on the **Nebel** town beach at the north. Phone (04682) 544; the southern section of **Norddorf** town beach. Phone 811; south of the Frisian village **Süddorf**; and **Wittdün DFK campsite**, D-2278 Wittdün, phone 2254. Ferry from Dagebüll.

Föhr Island—Goting Beach. With 13,000 beds for tourists, Föhr's Old Frisian character competes vigorously with Sylt's night life. On the main Sandkasten beach, 1 km is reserved for FKK at Nieblum-Goting-am-Wikinger, with lifeguard, showers, beach chairs—amenities not everywhere supplied to naked people. Dagebüll ferry departures to Amrum Island also serve Föhr. Car ferry, phone (04681) 701. Kurverwaltung, D-2270 Wyk. Phone 3040.

SYLT ISLAND

At the Danish border, the most northerly of the Frisians, Sylt is a historic outpost of Naturism and High Society. From the 1850s Westerland's Dr. Jenner urged nude bathing upon his patients. Over 70% of today's tourists do choose FKK. If southern climes now attract many younger beachgoers Sylt more than survives, retaining FKK sophisticates with la dolce vita: lifeguards, cabanas, windbreaks/chairs, beach showers, refreshments, convenient lodgings, and night life.

Access is over a causeway on a train which can take cars. The first town you reach is **Westerland** with a beautiful beach and an FKK section a 50-minute stroll south. Concerts, mudbaths, tennis, shopping, discos. Kurbetrieb, D-2281 Westerland. Phone (04651) 81224. No camping. Lodging: phone 24001, fax 24060.

Driving south, **Rantum** has two FKK beaches, Samoa and Zanzibar (do the names make you warmer?). Kurverwaltung, D-2280 Rantum. Phone (04651) 6076.

Hörnum, further south, has an FKK beach a 15-minute walk from the village. Kurverwaltung, D-2284 Hörnum. Phone (04654) 1065.

Driving north: north of **Wenningstedt** is a 1,000 m nude beach beneath cliffs. Camping available. Kurverwaltung, D-2281 Wenningstedt. Phone (04651) 41081. Lodging phone 41892.

The next north, elegant **Kampen** has 3 km of nude beach beneath red cliffs reaching north and south of a clothed central beach. Riding stables. Kurver-

Gerhard Riebicke, FKK Dance Exercise, 1926.

waltung and lodging, D-2283 Kampen. Phone (04651) 43300.

Northernmost, **List** has an excellent FKK beach to its west; served by town trails and buses. Kurverwaltung phone (04652) 1014.

BALTIC COAST (OSTSEE)

Beaches are the great holiday attraction of Germany's northeastern (Baltic) coast and islands. This Ostsee region extends between the Danish and Polish borders.

For 40 years, much of it, from Travemünde to the Polish border, lay in East Germany (GDR). Almost every town has a FKK beach, some 90 sites serving 200,000 campers/lodgers annually; more FKK than textile beaches. A GDR poll found 57% of the population approving of nude recreation, 30% had no opinion, and only 13% opposed.

Until 1990, GDR-led factory and sports federations organized affordable family vacations at campgrounds, often with mixed-use beaches attached. The 'last word' on these GDR beaches was *FKK Zwischen Ostsee und Vogtland* by Friedrich Hagen (VEB Tourist Verlag, Leipzig, 1987).

Reservations for the ex-GDR campgrounds like Prerow should be placed early with Campingzentrum Ostsee, Barther Strasse 64b, D-2300 Stralsund. Phone 5015.

GLÜCKSBURG AREA

Holnis Peninsula—Glücksburg Beach. North of Glücksburg at Holnis town on the Flensburger Fjörd, Germany's northern border with Denmark, is an FKK beach and camping. Kurverwaltung, D-2392 Glücksburg. Phone (04631) 921.

Gelting—Gammeldamm Beach. From Glücksburg east on Route199 to the hook of Flensburg Fjord. At Gelting continue east to Falshöft village. The famous nude beach now has campsites, toilets.

Schönhagen—Camping Seestern. South from Gelting and north from Eckernförde, a very pleasant FKK camping/beach. Bungalow/RV rentals. Camping Seestern, D-2343 Karby. Phone (04644) 305.

KIEL BAY

Straight north from Hamburg to Ostsee.

Eckernförde Bay southside has a 1 km FKK beach below the Hohenhain cliffs, between Dänisch-Nienhof and Surendorf. From Kiel take B-503 north to Dänisch-Nienhof via Sprenge. Spot the towns of Eckerholm and Hopenheim and look for clustered parked cars; the beach is nearby. Kurverwaltung, P.F. 1440, D-2330 Eckernförde. Phone (04351) 90520.

Another west Kiel Bay spot is **Schilksee,** below the bluff at the coastal radio station.

Wendtorf Beach on the east bay draws up to 4,000 naturists on a good weekend. From Kiel, B-502 toward Schönberg to the Marina Wendtorf turnoff, and park in the day lot (no charge). Walk along the dike toward Bottsand 1,200 m. A nature preserve. Verkehrssverein, D-2304 Wendtorf. Phone (04343) 9697.

LÜBECK AREA

North of Lübeck, **Behrensdorf Beach** has broad sands and a romantic setting. Drive 10 km from Lütjenburg to Behrensdorf Strand, park, walk just 150 m from the textile section and you're clothes-free—all the way, if you choose, for 10 km to Lippe. Gemeindeverwaltung, D-2322 Behrensdor. Phone (04381) 286.

Weissenhäuser Strand is a class resort on Hohwachter Bay reached by E-4 via Wangels... with an all-comfort FKK beach just down the strand. Lifeguards, the ubiquitous wicker chairs *(Korben),* restaurant, sports, accommodations. Kurverwaltung, D-2440 Weissenhäuser. Phone (04361) 490 731.

Fehmarn Island. E-4 takes you all the way. Three campgrounds have FKK beaches: **Wallnau Camping** with 1,100 sites and a mile-long beach. Mehnert Camping, D-2449 Wallnau. Phone (04372) 456. **Camping Wulfener Hals** with 515 tent/RV sites plus rental bungalows, near Burg in the west, rated ****. D-2449 Wulfen. Phone 4250. **Textilcamping Fehmarnbelt** near Altenteil in the northwest. D-2449 Dänschendorf. Phone 445. Kurverwaltung, D-2448 Burg auf Fehmar. Phone (04371) 3054.

Neustadt Bay—Pelzerhaken Beach. Between Neustadt (north of Lübeck by E-207) and Rettin, the sandy Pelzerhakenstrand has 40,000 sq m of officially FKK beach on its south. Beach

Sauna Product Advertising, Germany, 1980s.

Ruth and Harry Ketchum, Americans in English Garden, Munich.

showers. Fitness center next to beach. Convenient parking. Nearby camping. Kurverwaltung, D-2430 Pelzerhaken. Phone (04561) 7011.

Neustadt—Scharbeutz Beach. South of Neustadt on the bay, Scharbeutz lies between the harbor and the Timmendorf city limits. About 200 m long.

Grömitz Beach north of Neustadt was quietly pioneered by local FKK people. As nudity became accepted, municipal authority began to supply services. Kurverwaltung, D-2433 Grömitz. Phone (04562) 69255.

DFK-Familiengelände 'Erhard Wächtler'. North of Grömitz, a German Naturist Federation FKK family shore camp. A 1,200 m beach. Rental cabins. Tent/RV sites. Minimart, snack bar. Must obtain INF card. D-2434 Grube 2 (Rosenfelde). Phone (04365) 222.

Travemünde. East across the Lübeck Bay from Neustadt, Travemünde gained notoriety as 'the nude beach under barbed wire, machine guns and searchlights' because located at the border with the GDR. Guards' binoculars were believed to sweep the FKK beach intently. Perhaps for this reason, Travemünde's nude section has been highly popular. Kurverwaltung, D-2400 Travemünde. Phone (04502) 80430.

WISMAR BAY

Wismar, the first major city east of the old GDR border.

Hohen Wieschendorf Beach. Northwest of Wismar. Very popular beach despite a knee-high depth for 400 m out and little shade. Why? The water warms rapidly; children are safe; the 1.5 km beach is sandy; wild camping is allowed. Facilities, water, restaurant in the village. Preferred campground 6 km away at Wohlenberg Wiek, Gramkow, has 2,100 capacity.

Kühlungsborn—Rerik Beach. Southwest of Warnemünde–Rostock, north of Wismar, reached by a road off Route 105 from Heiligendamm to Kühlungsborn, is Rerik FKK beach. Ostseebad Camping has 1500 capacity.

ROSTOCK BEACHES

The most-frequented FKK beach on the 'GDR Baltic' is at southwest Fischland, between Graal Müritz and Markgrafenheide camp-sites—northeast of Rostock and Warnemünde. Parking provided; camping at Rosenort, 1 km away. Strong undertow.

A helpful contact, as the GDR beach infrastructure is transformed, is Hans R. Schmidt, Dr-Nic-Stang-Strasse 2, DDR-2520 Rostock 21. (0081) 713 338.

DARSS PENINSULA

Darss—Prerow. North of Rostow. Access from Ribnitz-Damgarten. Fine nude beaches at Arenshoop, Fischland West, and Prerow. Don't miss the Darsser Heimatmuseum.

Only Prerow Beach has a legal FKK campground, with its 4,300 capacity usually full—and that directly on the 5 km beach, with good sand, no pebbles, and sheltered from cool westerly winds by the Darss town highland, while currents warm the coastal waters. Blueberry picking in the Darss Woods from mid July. Post office, minimart.

Day visitors to FKK beach must park a mile before reaching it, on Bernsteinweg.

RÜGEN ISLAND

Rügen, largest of the Baltic islands, has a number of FKK beaches along its 570-km sand coast. Relatively 'undiscovered,' Rügen is still an uncommercialized haven. Drive northeast of Rostock by way of Stralsund and across the Rügendamm causeway.

Rappin Beach. An FKK beach at Gr. Banzelwitz on an inlet of the Ostsee, Rappin has a swampy coast and a bog inland. However, it abuts camping Zeltplatz Rappin (phone 0131) and is popular with watersports fans.

Schaabe Beach is a thin 6 km-long crescent of wooded dunes on the Tromper Wiek, a relatively sheltered and sunny landbridge between the towns of Breege and Glowe. The Schaabe is of fine sand with no stones, a delightful 6-minute stroll from the parking through a woods. It draws FKK bathers from afar. Some field toilets provided. Camping at Glowe (phone 0128). Recommended parking is on the second lot when driving northwest from Glowe. Public bus A-404 and A-419 to Glowe.

Vitt, northeast from Breege, is a fine ancient village, well worth a visit, although the stoney beach is difficult to reach.

Dranske-Nonnevitz Beach on the northern coast west from Breege, is a lovely and popular strand with high cliffs and a view that draws regulars (phone 0126). A 15-minute walk through the woods and campgrounds from the parking. Try to reserve in camp-site areas I to III.

Thiessow Camping at the southeast point has a fine 2 km white sand FKK beach. Thousands, primarily families, throng to the beach to claim windbreaks as the sun appears or wind drops and vendors appear. Camping behind beach at Zeltplatz Thiessow (phone 0136) or 1 km away at Zeltplatz Middelhagen-Lobbe

(phone 0136). It's a 2-minute hike through woods from the parking. Frequent breezes and waves here, and a view of ship traffic.

HIDDENSEE ISLAND

In the 1920s Hiddensee had a colony of artists-nudists. FKK is now on 1.5 km of the west shore, south of Neuendorf village. Windy; keep out of dunes. No autos allowed. Park in the crowded lot at Schaprode on Rügen to take ferry over. Or take 'the white fleet' from Stralsund harbor.

USEDOM ISLAND

Usedom Island is at the Polish border, directly north from Berlin on E-6 and Route 197; or drive east from Rostock. Most-loved, 3 km FKK beach lies between Zempin and Koserow campgrounds.

An 1,100-camper 'village,' largest on the east Baltic, lies between Bansin and Ückeritz. FKK beach of 2 km has permanent volleyball courts, even private permanent windbreak screens.

FRANKFURT AM MAINE

THE FIRST OF GERMANY

For many who fly to Germany, Frankfurt will be the gateway to first impressions:

Langener Waldsee with its grassy lawn sloping to the 500 m lake, is large enough to host windsurfer and sailing regattas. On a fine day, hundreds enjoy the clean FKK beach (there's also a small separate textile beach). Toilets, showers, snack bar, large parking lot. June–Sept. Take B-44 south from Frankfurt to E-451 junction and Walldorf exit. Take overpass east. Find the sandpits behind the Langener Sand Company.

Badesee Walldorf. If you don't cross B-44 after exiting it, you're in Walldorf. Park on street southeast of B-44 intersection with Aschaffenburgerstr. Badesee north shore is FKK.

Grueneburg Park. At lunchtime on hot days as downtown office workers pour into this park, the dress code goes south.

Bad Hamburg—Taunus Therme. Plan a layover at this temple of body indulgence. It's northwest of Frankfurt, public transportation goes. The upper level is all FKK: a 'Finnish sauna world' with 6 'cabins' of varying temperature; 2 'sauna pools,' a 'sauna-bar'; 'Irish-Roman' steambath; indoor and outdoor pools linked by canal; 'Japanese' solarium; 150 face-tanners, massage, travel agency, restaurant and bar. Elsewhere: cinemas, gym, waterfalls, spas, fountains, barbeque terrace, and more. Moderately-priced hotels nearby. Phone: (06172) 4878.

Hofheim—O Sole Mio. Midway between Frankfurt and Weisbaden. This extravaganza has a sauna-garden, 50-person extremely-dry sauna, Bauernstube, children's paradise and, of course, more, including gourmet restaurant. "The

Leif Heilberg, Thiessow Beach, Rugen Island, Baltic Coast, East Germany.

naturist recreation island that other cities dream of." 4–12 pm weekdays, 11–8 weekends. Am Wandersmann 1, D-6238 Hofheim/Wallau. Phone (06122) 13036.

BERLIN AREA

In 1987, on the advice of its lawyers, the City of West Berlin ceased to fine for "bathing in public without a bathing suit." No longer would the police pronounce on what is "decent" and what is "contrary to community standards of dress." (*FKK*, 1/1988).

BERLIN PARKS

For 40 years the Berlin Wall severed West Berlin naturist clubs from their grounds, famous in the 1920s, dormant in the Hitler years. However, clothes-optional was accepted by the West Berlin Senate at a number of sites. Nudity also continued on the communist side. West Berlin parks had well-known free-sun areas years before the City acted:

Halensee, Rathenauplatz, offers a small FKK beach between the radio tower and the highway access road; to its north, a huge sunning meadow with up to 2,000 nudes on a sunny day.

Nearly a third of the total beach at **Tegeler See** is now in nude use.

Grünewaldsee has sandy terraces for nude sunbathing as you walk the lakeshore. The Grünewald Castle art museum is on the walk, and a 'hunting-lodge' restaurant with terrace awaits at the parking.

Teufelsee is a small nude lake on a tidy trail deep in the woods, with a snack van.

At a parking lane for walking into Teufelsee is FKK sports club **Helios**—mostly for members—telephoning could open the gate to use of its competition-level heated pool, tennis, table tennis, and volleyball. Im Jagen 57/58, D-1000 Berlin 33. Phone 3 02 63 48 or 8 81 93 19. A 10 minute walk from S-Bahnhof Grunewald.

Berlin tourist information will supply **indoor FKK swims** and emerging lake sites.

WANNSEE BEACH

The beach of choice for Berlin's clothed bathers over the years, Wannsee is increasingly nude although the original area remains textile. Truly a cross-section of Berlin. Chairs rented, beach showers, pier, swans, wading paddle-ball, snacks and beer. In the southwest and readily reached by urban transit.

At the Berlin Wall, Mid-1980s. (AP)

VEREIN DER SAUNAFREUNDE

This Band of Sauna Friends offers much more than a sauna at its relaxing, happy family club on a lush and large lake, Heiligensee, in Berlin's northwest suburbs. Diving board, beach shower, fishing, windsurfing, boules, tennis, volleyball, snacks, children's playground. Camping. Day guests welcomed. Rognitzstr. 8, D-1000 Berlin 19. Phone 301 70 71.

MÜGGELSEE BEACH

Strandbad Grosser Müggelsee in 'East Berlin' is a large suburban lake with birch, oak and pine trees and sloping sun meadows on a sandy shore. It's reachable by urban transit or by private boat via Berlin's waterways—and this is well, since parking is very limited, and up to 15,000 may be on the FKK west end plus textile use at original facility. Many boats anchor offshore to join in. FKK biergarten, snacks, volleyball, Ping-Pong, childrens' gym, bowling, giant chess/checkers, lifeguards. A 'must do!'

Want your Müggelsee wilder? Get off trolley at stop before the 'pay' FKK beach. Or wade around a fence west of the pay beach. The wild beach predates 1965, its core bathers establishing the broader nude acceptance.

☞ From Friedrichstrasse Bahnhof, take the S-Bahn in direction of Erkner, get off at Friedrichshagen station. Cross under viaduct and street to take #25 tram. It follows the S-Bahn track further. At fifth stop, get off and cross tracks to FKK Beach gatehouse. Or get off at fourth stop and go through woods to shore without paying. You can also drive from Friedrichshagen station east on Fürstenwalder Damm to the sign and parking.

BESTENSEE LAKES

Popular with elite East Berliners when the Berlin Wall stood; two beaches on a small lake. Take F-179 from Berlin via Schulzendorf, Königs Wusterhausen and Zeesen 25 km south, to F-246. Turn right on it, direction Mittenwalde, to Bestensee village. Turn left immediately after the rail crossing, through Bestensee for 2 km to the lake entrance on the right. A better-publicized FKK area is northeast of

Bestensee, next to Am Tonsee campgrounds at Körbiskrug.

EUROPA CENTER THERMEN

This fine, large 'penthouse' spa in downtown Berlin is clothing-optional. Outdoor heated canal pool with sundeck and city view (office workers may also observe the sundeck), 4 Finnish saunas, cold plunge, 2 Russo-Roman steam baths, table tennis, billiards, backgammon, chess, exercise room, TV lounge, massage, sunlamps, bar, restaurant, large indoor pool. Parking discount at Europa Center Parkhaus (the spa is on the roof). From 10 a.m. daily. Nürnbergerstr. 7, D-1000 Berlin 30. Phone 261 60 31.

BLUB PARADISE

BLUB, Berliner Luft- und Badparadies, in the southeast Neukölln district, offers an extravagant family water park. FKK garden, hot whirlpool, pool, 4 saunas with a bar, fireplace, quiet rooms, tanning center, massage. Water slide, wild water canal, rock caverns and waterfall, huge central pool, wave pool, geyser, exercise center, hydrobics and aerobics—some clothing-optional. Take #7 U-bahn to Grenzallee, walk 10 minutes to blub. Buses 41 and 73 stop at entrance. Free parking. Buschkrugallee 64, D-1000 Berlin 47. Phone 606 60 60.

BAVARIA

This is the fun-loving province. How are you gonna keep Bavarians in Lederhosen after they've been clothes-free? Munich Mayor Dr. Scarnagel was confronted by an opponent with a photo of himself naked, taking part in a 'chicken fight' in the pool of a local FKK club. Scarnagel endorsed it as his campaign photo. Voters reelected him.

Public opinion polls cue Bavarian officials that nudity is here to stay. An Isar River cruise passenger complained about nude bathers along the bank. It became a tourism issue. Instead of banning nudity from such public areas, the Ministry of the Interior instructed boatsmen to issue "nude alerts"—asking passengers who might be offended to look the other way.

MUNICH

Today, Germans from all walks of life may relax, topfree or fully nude, in more or less discreet areas of the city parks throughout the nation.

Munich led the way by its decision (1981) to accommodate naked people within urban public settings. The officially

Fidus, Hymn To the Sun, 1888.

accepted areas for sunbathing without a stitch were published in the June 4, 1985 *Münchner Stadtanzeiger* as follows:

Feldmochinger See—In north Munich; at the southwest end of the lake. Parking at the Karlsfelder-Str. access. Toilets, refreshments.

Englischer Garten—It's twice the size of New York's Central Park. Nude sunbathing is at the north end, at a meadow—the "Schwabing Bucht"—on the west side of a loop of the chilly brook that runs through the English Garden. East of U-bahn station Studentenstadt. Southwest of Aumeister Biergarten.

Oberföhring Island—On the east shore of the Isar River, facing the northern part of English Garden. FKK from the English Garden footbridge at Mittlere-Isar-Str. north.

Schönfeldwiese—An oval field within a riding track, north of the Haus der Kunst at the south end of the Englischer Garten. (In practice, this nude area has often expanded.) The art museum is on Prince Regent Street, a main concourse. U-bahn station Universität, walk east. Next to the Japanese Teahouse.

South Isar River—(1) Along the dike ("Wehrsteg") in the river south from the **Marienklause Bridge** in city center at Lukas Kirche. (And in practice, often north of it on the south end of Praterinsel, and along Zellstr. on the facing east bank of the Isar, north of the Volksbad.) S-bahn Isartor and walk east. (2) Along the dike on the east bank of Isar, from Braunau Railway bridge south to **Brudermühle Bridge** (the Flaucher Island crossing of the Mittlerer Ring). Blue line bus # 45, or U-bahn to Implerstr. and walk east. (3) Further south along the Isar, sunbathing informally continues at Hellabrunn Zoo (bus # 52).

Munich Police Chief Manfred Schreiber said that citations for provocative nudity would be issued only in "the gravest cases."

Curiously, many expected the Bavarian Naturist Federation to lead the expansion of nude rights—in fact, it disassociated itself, saying: "It is not our goal to turn everyone into a naturist…it would be a shame should the undisciplined, 'wild nudity' in public places create a mistaken impression of naturism for authorities." Fortunately, others led, and led well.

MUNICH AREA

Munich south—

Staffelsee—Murnau Freibad. On the west-shore peninsula of Lake Staffel is a nude beach. Park on the eastern shore at the Murnau Freibad and walk around.

Wolfratshausen—Pupplinger Au. Naturist bonfire picnics are a custom; make up a party. On a summer evening friends and families gather black bread, cheese, radishes, and beer and drive 33 km south of Munich on the autobahn to Garmisch-Partenkirchen. Turn off, drive to Wolfratshausen, then follow the signs to Puppling (Iking). Park where the bridge crosses the Isar or at the nearby inn. Ask where the trail begins to the Pupplinger Au river flats, in the forest preserve on the banks of the Isar.

Seeshaupt—Ostersee. From Seeshaupt, drive in direction of Penzberg; after 1 km park at entrance to Lauterbachmühle. Walk around Lake Oster 10 minutes to the site.

Munich north—

Fertinga-See. Nude bathers flock to northeastern Unterföhring—an S-bahn stop—on fine weekends to enjoy nude windsurfing on Lake Fertinga. From Nördliches Moos, near the S-3 intersection, cross south on Gleissach under the Ostumgehung Autobahn to parking at the peninsula. Near ZDF Television. Toilets, refreshments.

Germany

Munich—Amperland. Friendly DFK naturist club welcomes travelers. On the Amper River by Fürsten-Feldbruck, off A-8; minutes by train northwest from Olympic City. Dormitory, RV rentals, 350 tent/RV sites, open kitchen, restaurant, pool, sports. April–Sept. Postfach 1161, D-8089 Emmering. Phone (08141) 43600.

GRAINAU

Garmish-Partenkirchen—Granau.This beach below the looming Waxenstein-Massives, just across the Austrian border from Innsbruck, offers a superb view of Germany's highest peak. Take Route 95 to E-6 and south on it to Garmisch-Partenkirchen. Just outside the city limits take a right following signs to Grainau. Park at the Eibsee Hotel lot. Take the path along Lake Eib, going north to the beach on the west bank.

DIVERSE INLAND BEACHES & BATHS

HAMBURG AREA

Hamburg—gateway to the **Schleswig-Holstein** peninsula, which is, next after Bavaria, Germany's top vacation region. FKK beaches ring its Nordsee and Ostsee coasts, Kiel Bay and Lübeck Bay.

Hamburg—Sommerbad Volksdorf. Visit the DFK's lake in the woods. Clubhouse, sauna, volleyball, tennis, badminton, bowling, gymnastics, folk dances, disco, youth club. RV park but no tentsites. June–Sept. Metro Buchenkamp then bus 174, exit Farenkoppel. HFK Hamburg Bund für FKK und Familiensport EV, Moorbekweg 100, D-2000 Hamburg 67. Phone (040) 603 47 30.

Hamburg—Hallenbad Holtenhusen. The popular sauna-spa goes FKK on Sat.-Sun. after 7:30 p.m. Subway U-I to Kellinghusenstrasse; exit the station left.

St. Peter–Ording. Sand-yachters skitter about this 10 km offshore sandbar. Naturists find their place in the littoral order at the north point (100 ha.). Cars may drive over. Camping. Kurverwaltung, D-2252 St. Peter–Ording. Phone (04863) 8329.

Bremen—Stadtwaldsee. The southeast shore of Bremen's city lake is a legal FKK beach—often with volleyball.

HANNOVER

The Ricklinger Lakes—where Hannoverians go to play—include an official FKK beach on **Sieben-Meter-Teich.** Playing fields too. Via Südschnellweg.

Hereford—Bad Salzuflen. Four pools (two outside), solarium, FKK meadow, sauna, bowling, fitness room, gardens, restaurant. FKK Sunday 5–8 p.m. Near Hereford, south of Hannover on A-2, Salzuflen exit, follow Badkur signs.

DÜSSELDORF

Unterbacher See is southeast of Düsseldorf. Follow map towards Eller, find Unterbacher See–Südstrand exit. Bus 891 also goes, get off at Vennhauser Allee. Half of the south beach is FKK. Snack van, toilet.

Baggersee entrance is along the Ratingen-to-Kalkum Road; marked 'Baggersee'; 1 km west of A-52 intersection. From a grassy parking lot, walk down a paved single-lane road, across a field and through a woods to popular lake.

DARMSTADT

Darmstadters have skinny-dipped for years at **Erlensee-bei-Bickenbach.** From Darmstadt, B-3 south 10 km to Bickenbach. Follow signs to Bahnhof (rail station), cross tracks, turn left, take overpass above Autobahn, then first right to parking. From Autobahn, exit Seeheim/Jugendheim. Most FKK is on north shore. Toilets, snack bar.

Freizeitgelände Prinz von Hessen (Hessian Sand Pit, aka Prince Emil's Sand Pit). From Darmstadt City Ring, leave the ruin of the old city theater in direction Dieburg. Pass the Steinbrücker-Teiche park, to the Prinz von Hessen preserve. Parking along the old

Lee Baxandall, Wannsee Beach, Berlin.

Dieburgerstrasse. In the middle of the woods, a quiet beach with a nice core group of users.

Darmstadt—Schwimhalle. Downtown on Landgraf Georg Str. FKK swim Sat. pm.

Pfungstadt—Wellenbad (wave pool), south and west of Darmstadt. FKK Wed. eves.

Orplid. A proud DFK family sports club since 1923, with courts, woods and meadows in northwest Darmstadt. Pool, sauna, restaurant. INF cardholders may visit and lodge. P.F. 110861, D-6100 Darmstadt.

MANNHEIM

Weinheim-bei-Mannheim—Miramar. As soon as Weinheim authorities planned to build Germany's first indoor wave pool, Mannhein area naturists asked for FKK hours. A single nude night was set. The demand raised it to three nights. Sauna, restaurant, indoor–outdoor sunbathing, and the famous, mini-lake wave pool.

☞ Heidelberg–Frankfurt Autobahn north to the first Weinheim exit. Take the first turn into Weinheim, cross the railroad tracks and follow the priority road. In Weinheim, follow signs for Miramar, located on the east end of a lake. The multicolored fabric arches that provide a roof can be seen from the Autobahn. To 10 p.m. daily.

BODENSEE

Bodensee, a.k.a. Lake Constance, is an immense lake at the Swiss border, long favored for vacations. The free beach is between Überlingen and Sipplingen 1 km from where the lake drains; cross the rail tracks from B-30 by a small tunnel.

Konstanz—Freibad Horn. Since 1982 a designated nude beach is accessed by bus #5 from downtown.

BADEN-BADEN

Baden-Baden—Black Forest Spa. Younger Europeans are less likely than their parents to "take the waters" at a spa. Many traditional spa resorts are in trouble, although state-of-the-art therapies and exotic and flamboyant additions do bring customers.

A spa making the transition is venerable Baden-Baden, renaming itself The Black Forest Spa. Baden-Baden has reduced the median age of clients by five years while keeping its regulars. An important element of success: mixed pool nudity. Brochure from German National Tourism Office, phone (212) 308-3300. Direct: Augustaplatz 8, D-7570 Baden-Baden.

FREIBURG

Freiburg—Opfingersee. Lake Opfinger is 9 km west of Freiburg, beside the north-south Rhine River Valley autobahn. There's no exit from the Autobahn at this point. So turn off on Opfingerstrasse west (at first it's called Carl-Kistner-Str.). Just after crossing the Autobahn watch for the turn-off to the right into a parking area at the south end of the lake. Take the path along the east side for about 800 feet to a grassy terrace with shrubbery top shielding the Autobahn. No facilities.

Freiburg—Zähringen Bath. North Freiburg at Lameystr. 4. Phone 216-3771. Nude Sundays, 10–3.

BOCHUM

Aquadome am Ruhrpark. Extravagant water slides and tropical pools, and for naturists, a sauna paradise: five 'grotto' choices of dry steam temperatures plus Turkish bath, massage, sun meadow and restaurant. Exit Bochum–Werne from A-2, east of Essen, turn right and follow Aquadome signs.

KASSEL–GÖTTINGEN

Sport- und Freizeitpark Bördel. Brochure in English. Family FKK club welcomes visitors. May–Sept. Nikolaistrasse 30, D-3400 Göttingen. Phone (05502) 1255.

BONN–COLOGNE

Bonn—Panorama. Every German metro area now has at least one clothes-free, sauna-spa-pool health wonderland. Blind masseur Josef Schmidt had the vision to create Panorama—6 saunas, 4 hot tubs, galvanic foot bath, Roman-Irish steam bath, sun garden and ponds, heated outdoor pool, buffet, biergarten, massage, beautician, the works! and more; 100,000 happily naked customers annually. From Cologne south by A-1 then A-61 (30 min.), or from Bonn southwest by A-565 (20 min.), exiting at Meckenheim. Via Gelsdorf and Vettelhoven to Grafschaft. D-5482 Grafschaft-Holzweiler. Phone (02641) 34736.

Aachen—Cologne. Heavily-promoted Hotel Zum Walde is 10 miles from Aachen. FKK pool–bar–terrace with meals available, fitness gym, sauna. Klosterstrasse 4, D-5190 Stolberg-Zweifall.

Wannsee Beach. 1910. Historical Photograph.

GREECE

Greek Warrior with Helmet, Shield and Bared Torso in Combat. Fifth Century BC. Delphi.

Greece, in its precocious cultural adolescence some 2,500 years ago, learned how to benefit its citizens by combining nakedness with civilization.

The early Greek influentials saw no shame in displaying a fit body or a fine mind. They preferred their athletics nude and on this basis they invented the Olympic Games. *Gymno* as in *gymnastics* means *naked*.

The glory that was humanistic Greece sets a challenge to modern prophets of fear. Our ecclesiastical and civic authorities may try to confine the naked body, but they will not eradicate the Greek ideal which lives today in the Naturist idea.

Lately, the Greek National Tourist Organization—while pointing to the trends of international tourism—assisted Greek naturist resorts on the instance of Yugoslavia which attracts such business away from Greece.

Orthodox Church clerics blocked any licensing of naturism until 1981 when elections favored a progressive government. Now a few clothes-free enterprises complement the many nude beaches in the islands.

Naturist contact: Angelos Mimikopoulos, P.O. Box 3379, GR-10210 Athens.

Further reading, maps: John Dunn, *Sunseekers' Greek Islands*, from Sunseeker Publications, Congleton, Cheshire CW12 3RB, England, or The Naturist Society (see back of this Guide).

ATHENS AREA

RAMNOUS BEACH

"Cradle of modern Athenian nude beach-going" (ca. 1974), according to Angelos Mimikopoulos, it's popular with Athenians who lack money or time for a boat or air transfer to the islands.

Ramnous is named for a thorny bush encountered on the way in. Permanence as a nude beach was enhanced when the National Archeological Service made access harder by fencing the area directly above the beach. In ancient times the 150' statue of Nemesis, goddess of vengeance, stood over this beach and remnants remain. Regulars now clean the shoreline. Clear sea with snorkeling, scuba and fishing. Octopi up to 5 kilos are taken and cooked on the spot as delicacies. March–November. August can be windswept.

☞ Bus from Athens—1 1/2 hours, about US $2.50. National Archeological Museum is 5 minutes walk from Mavromateon St. bus station at

Areos Park. Catch bus for "Athens-Kato-Souli-Aghia Marina" ferry terminal—it's northeast, past Marathon. Departures have been 6, 8:15, 10:15, 12:30, 3:30, subject to change and added busses. Phone Mimikopoulos for update (813-4182).

Leave bus at Ramnou Tavern stop, the last before Aghia Marina. Walk up the asphalt road at the right side for 1 1/2 miles, past vineyards to a clearing by the gate of the ancient shrine of Ramnous. Here walk either right or left on a footpath around the fenced area for about 10-15 minutes to a cove of four small pebbly beaches. Bring beach footwear, snacks and drinks.

If you drive, proceed as above to the entrance of the shrine, where a bad non-asphalt road opposite the entrance leads 3.5 miles to a clearing by the sea with a church of Aghia Marina. Park, take path to coast, you'll soon find the cove.

IONIAN ISLANDS

CORFU

The seven Ionian Islands along the west coast of central Greece provide a gateway with ferry service from Italy and a direct London–Corfu airlink that keeps the beaches crowded. Indeed, just beyond Pelekas, Myrtiotissa Beach is a rare unharmed and unhassled nude getaway, praised by L. Durrell and other writers. It's sandy with fine swimming, even a small waterfall, but lacks shade—come with your own. Corfu has other beaches that are used nude—but as elsewhere in this book, we highlight the best.

☞ Rent a car or moped at San Rocco Square or take a bus from the New Fortress (Spilia) bus station in Corfu. Take the main road west across the island to Pelekas.

There turn right and go halfway to Glyfadas. Find a broad track through trees on your left, probably marked on the right by a sign 'Myrtiotissa' (bus drivers will let you off here). Drive it a half mile to the parking. Hiking down the 800 ft. cliff takes 15 minutes; coming up depends on your stamina.

Easier than climbing, rent a pedal-boat at the north end of Glyfadas Beach. Pedal north around the headland for 10 minutes and you're there!

ZAKYNTHOS

Southerly Zakynthos (Zante), the most-visited Ionian Island after Corfu, is accessible by air from London with direct busses daily from Athens. Many beaches are afflicted by tiny black oil pellets that may get on your feet. Nude beaches located off the metalled road south from Argassi have included Dafni Beach, Agios Nikolaos, and Garakas Beach. Arrive early, set the dress code in high season.

PELOPONNESE

LENA-MARY HOTEL

Peloponnese, a great and historically rich land mass, lies southwest from Central Greece and Athens. There is a fine naturist enclave from which to visit Sparta, Corinth, Mycenæ or Epidauros.

The Lena-Mary Beach Hotel was the first in Greece to opt for a naturist clientele. This license was finally granted in 1985 after fiery Orthodox Church protests.

Named for two married daughters of the owner, the 120-room resort—190 km from Athens, with rapid hydrofoil transfer via Hermioni—is well landscaped, in a secluded cove with a sandy beach and islands offshore. Excursions to Spetses and Hydra. Germans on the Öbonareise package are the principal guests; English is spoken. Restaurant, bars, TV lounge, taverna, disco, fitness room, massage, sauna, pool, tennis, Ping-Pong, deck chess, volleyball, water sports. Reservations: Messologiou-10 Kolokotroni, GR-15233 Halandri, Athens. Phone (01) 6844285 or 6844638.

IDRA—SPETSES

Off the Peloponnese eastern shore, in sight of the Lena-Mary Beach Hotel (and easily visited from it), these islands delight many tourists.

Many a modern Croesus has sailed to Idra to sun nude with his entourage. A kind of St.-Tropez, this small port rich in naval history draws yachts from everywhere, with numerous fine mansions from the days of sailing fortunes. If you lack your own keel, ferry service runs from Piræus near Athens, and from Ermioni on the Peloponnese.

Idra (Hydra) sadly lacks a public nude beach—Spetses provides one. By rental moped, bicycle, horse-drawn buggy (no motor taxis), or caique, you can follow a track through the pine woods to Agios Anargheri, and next to it is the clothes-optional Paraskevi Bay.

MACEDONIA

SITHONIA

Long ignored by the Greek government, Macedonia has emerged as a popular travel destination. It has monasteries,

Leif Heilberg, Scuba Lesson at Paradise Beach, Mykonos, Greece.

Greece

Angelos Mimikopoulos. Scandinavian-Greek Friendship Meeting. Beach Camping On Skopelos.

harbors and campsites, and nude recreation happens in the countless small coves along the coast of Sithonia, the central spur of Chalcidice, a three-pronged peninsula that juts into the Aegean.

Notable beaches are at the Platamitsi and Armenistis coves on the east coast, and at the small beaches Azapiko and Triptistas between Nikitas and Koufos on the western shore. Camping is unrestricted, provisions are available in the towns of Sartis, Nikolaos and Koufos. Sailing, spear fishing and swimming are a delight in the bright, clear waters.

History's earliest documented Skinny-dipper appears in Oldest Preserved Greek Wall Painting. Tomb of the Diver, Pæstum 480 BC.

EASTERN ÆGEAN

THASSOS

The most northerly of the Eastern Ægean Islands. Not far from Sithonia. Thassos is Macedonian, with ferry transfer from Kavalos and Keramoti. Many campgrounds, and also much 'wild' camping at beaches. Pefkari Beach, 2 mi east of Limenaria, is nude, and Paradise Beach on the east coast south of Skala Potomia is officially so. Busses run hourly.

DODECANESE ISLANDS

RHODES

Hic Rhodus, hic saltus. Tourists who come this far should try a nude beach even if it's a crowded tourist island. Be prepared to go miles away from Rhodes town, by bus or (more pleasurably) boat, to the currently best nude beach. The 'best' shifts often, at this mass travel destination—so go, then ask.

KOS

The Dodecanese Islands lie off Turkey's southwest coast, with ferry service via Piræus or flights Athens–Kos.

Kos has many fine beaches but the best, to our mind, is Tropical Beach, a 30 minute walk west from Kardamena. Accessible also from Kardamena (by boat) is Bubble Beach with a separate nude section.

Hotel Caravia has a naturist beach that stretches most of the way to Tigaki, 8 miles west of Kos town. Marmari, 4 km further west along the main road from Tigaki, has a nude beach as do Mastichorio and Kamario.

PATMOS

Quiet lovely Patmos is a museum 'must' with its St. John monastery. Naturists love Psiliamos Beach for its beauty, shade trees, and a taverna owner who keeps it all tidy and rents umbrellas and beach chairs. Too remote for most to walk, access to Psiliamos Beach is by bus, moped or daily boat. Caiques also run to nearby islands and the Turkish coast, an alternative to fast antiseptic ferries.

CYCLADES ISLANDS

CYCLADES ISLANDS

The Cyclades Islands—southeast of Athens and Central Greece—cluster around Delos Island, said to be the place of birth of Apollo the sun god.

They're rocky outcrops from the blue Ægean Sea. Small white chapels with blue domes and windmills too hover over towns made up of square planes—a pleasing asymmetricity. A number of smaller Cyclades have lovely deserted beaches that welcome the sun worshiper. Only the more established are mentioned here.

An extensive network of ferries connects the islands with the mainland—at Piræus and Rafina—and with each other, making island hopping convenient and one of the best buys in European travel. Airfields are located on the free beach islands of Mykonos, Santorini (featured in the film *Summer Lovers)*, and Paros.

SYROS

Galyssas on Syros quadrupled in 10 years owing mainly to its discovery by low-budget campers. Unofficial ('wild') often-nude camping centers on coves near the white church on the hill, but rooms-to-let are everywhere and hotels are going up. Take a ferry to Ermoupolis then the bus to Galyssas.

PAROS

A beach accepted for nude use is 1 km southwest of bustling Paros town.

Agia Irini, west of Parasporos, is nude at the north end with access via a dirt track from the main road. It has a stone wall, shade trees but no other amenities.

Platis Ammos and Kolimbithres are reached from the port town of Naoussa; and try the beaches of Lageri and Santa Maria. Chrissi Akti (Golden Beach) near Drios has nudity at one end. Don't miss the Venetian fortress in Paroikia.

Antiparos Island—a half hour transfer by small caique from Poros town—has a friendly town with rooms to rent, rocky coves and secluded sandy beaches with 'wild' camping. The 1st World Congress on Nude Beaches (1986) met at Camping Antiparos which has a buffet, shower block, and large sand beach. GR-84007 Antiparos. Phone: (30) 284 61221.

☞ Paros is served daily by flights from Athens and fast Piræus–Paros hydrofoil ferries.

MYKONOS

The sun god's place of birth, Delos, is across a strait so it's apt that Mykonos' sunbathing beaches attract young travelers from afar. Cosmopolitan ambience, high-fashion shops and artisan boutiques heighten the charm. With international flights and the Golden Olympic Supercat ferry from Piræus, Mykonos has 'arrived.'

East from Plati Gialos (Yialos), the south coast terminus of a 15-minute bus ride from central Mykonos, fishing boats will ferry jet-setters along a dry and rocky coastline which lacks a road, straight to Paradise, or mostly-gay Super Paradise, or Agrari, or the last stop, Hell (Elias to the Greeks), as you may wish.

Those desiring a more secluded sunning spot may choose the west side of Panormos Bay. You must walk for an hour or so, or take a taxi from central Mykonos. The prevailing north winds deter the faint-hearted but there is a taverna nearby for refuge if needed. Nudity is the norm.

A clothes-optional beach is found at Hotel Aphroditi in Kalafti, served by bus.

☞ You'll be met in Mykonos by many landladies offering rooms. Instead, go to Plati Gialos Bay. Try the Patasos Beach Hotel with a panoramic dining veranda—phone (0289) 23437.

Or continue by boat to Paradise Beach & Camping—justly popular because owner Fredy Dactylidis indulges guests with very affordable tentsites and rooms, modern toilets with hot showers, fine buffet restaurant with bar, newsstand and mini-mart, music and dancing nightly, dive and sailing rental. The other clothes-optional beaches have no amenities approaching this! GR-84600 Mykonos. Phone: (0289) 22852 or 22937.

NAXOS

Largest and most fertile of the island group, Naxos has a rich history. Of particular interest are the temple of Apollo, the Mycenæan tombs and giant archaic sculptures, "Kouri." Free beach lovers relax and pay their respects to Apollo on the southwest beach Agia Anna, reached by bus from Naxos town, then walking left around the point. Aghios Prokopios in the same bay to the right, and Pirgaki beach 9 miles distant, also see nude use. Day boat visits from Mykonos appeal to many.

IOS

Daily ferries serve Mykonos–Ios. Fleeing mass tour packaging of Mykonos, sophisticated world travelers flock to Ios' dreamy beaches and lively discos.

Mylopotas is legendary. A half hour walk or a frequent bus will take you from the port, Gialos, or Ios town to Mylopotas Beach. There, tavernas let your sunning coincide with gastronomic sinning. Water sport rentals. You may lodge almost on the sand at the Hotel Delfini, phone (0286) 991341, or perhaps at Soulis Campground.

Less thronged, Coumbara nude beach is reached by walking a path around a rocky point northwest of Ios town. Manganari Bay on the south coast is served by day-trip caiques from the port.

SANTORINI

A volcano island drawing many visitors with spectacular views, cobbled streets, and remains of Phoenician, Dorian, Roman, Byzantine and Minoan cultures. Beaches are secondary. In nude use, the

Leif Heilberg, Beach at Paradise Camping, Mykonos.

most popular is the rather fine black sand beach, running for miles south from developed Perissa Beach on the south-eastern shore. Tavernas and shade are amenities.

Red Beach road is opposite the gate of the Akrotiri archeological site. Follow road uphill for 20 minutes to taverna, chapel, then path down and round the point.

CRETE

The first European civilization—Minoan—emerged on Crete 4,500 years ago. This historic, ruggedly beautiful and largely unspoiled island can exhilarate you. A 'must' visit is the palace of Knossos, 6 km south of Iraklion, evoking the time of King Minos and the Minotaur, Theseus and the Labyrinth. If the coast doesn't quite measure up, enjoy it as best you can. Accommodations from campgrounds to the luxurious Kalypso Cretian Village for naturists. Cretians are tolerant of tactful beach nudity.

VAI BEACH

Over the years many small coves and out-of-the-way beaches of Crete have seen nude use, but none as much as Vai at the far northeastern tip. Beginning in March and into November you could find California surfers living out of tents, French youths with nothing but hammocks, bedrolls and motorcycles, as well as whole German families with elaborate camping equipment and no clothing, all mixing easily.

☞ The northern coastal road takes you east to Sitia ending at Palekastron. Here turn north for Itanos and Vai Beach. Ample tavernas, rooms to rent and visiting Greeks.

KALYPSO CRETIAN VILLAGE

A Class-A resort hotel built in 1982, Kalypso Cretian Village is one of two in all Greece with National Tourist Office naturist status, granted in 1989.

Located in a garden setting on a dramatic rocky fjord in south-central Crete—offering easy access (and bus or boat tours) to the historical sites, the mountains and Samara Gorge, Matala nude beach, the island of Santorini and more—Kalypso is eager to please a naturist visitor. English spoken.

Looking out over the warm Libyan sea—swimmable even in January—are 102 air-conditioned bungalows with showers and telephones, restaurant and mini-mart, disco, main and bar pools, TV lounge, folklore evenings, Olympic pool, children's pool, playground, veranda with cafe, private beach with dock, deck chess, 2 lighted tennis courts, volleyball, Ping-Pong, water sports, sauna and massage.

Clothes are required only in public indoor areas. Prices are ridiculously low. International airports at Heraklion and Hania. P.O. Box 16, GR-Rethymno, Crete. Phone (0832) 31210 or 31296. Air-land packages, phone: 1-800-828-9356.

SOUGIA BEACH

Sougia is now what Vai Beach was before it was discovered. On the southwest coast, this village has a wide, clean pebble beach a mile long, of which the eastern half is nude. A taverna on the beach, Cafebar Maria, marks the division. It has a cool shower that all use nude. Accommodations can be found cheaply in the village.

☞ Sougia can be reached from the Hania air gateway by auto or bus in less than 2 1/2 hours.

Already on Crete? Ride an early-morning bus from Hania to Omalos, where the Samara Gorge, Europe's largest, begins. Hike the Gorge (5–6 hours) to its shore terminus at Chora Sfakion. Refresh yourself until a ferry takes you that afternoon to Sougia, an hour west, where you may live like a beach bum until deciding to bus back to Hania...or get on a boat going east to Kalypso hotel, or beyond to Matala.

THE SPORADES

SKOPELOS

The Sporades are in the northern Ægean Sea east of Central Greece. Airlink from Athens to nearby Skiathos then by fast boat to Skopelos, which is verdant with pines and orchards and wonderful, little-visited beaches. Velanio Beach offers serendipity itself—at one end, a cooling natural spring, perfect respite after your hot sun bath or salty sea dip. A native, instead of plowing under the spring, added an unofficial campground!

Velanio Beach is 5 km southeast of Skopelos town, reached from the bus stop for Stafylos beach, which has a taverna. Hike around the Stafylos headland.

SKIATHOS

Reached in 25 minutes by air from Athens, modern Skiathos is famed for its clothed Koukounaries (Golden Sand) Beach, Lalaria Beach (reached by caique, nude at one end), and best of all, Ammoudia Krassa (Banana) Beach. There's only one city, Skiathos; nearly all stay there who aren't camping.

Banana Beach surprises visitors with its superb tavernas, shady pines and wildflowers. It's a 15 minute walk from the Agia Eleni or the Koukounaries ('Koukou') bus stops. Or go by caique. Beach vendors will mix your lettuce, fetta cheese and olive oil to taste, and charge by salad size. If the beach becomes crowded, walk south past the rocks to secluded coves. Banana is mostly clothed in high season, when you can shift to the next bay north, Banana Two (Spartacus), with a taverna but fewer visitors.

On the north coast, Megalos Asselinos Beach has nudity. So too does Elias and Mandraki Beach, reached by a lovely 45-minute walk north (taking a left fork) through pines from the Mandraki Hotel, two bus stops before Koukounaries.

Leif Heilberg, Delegyhaza Camp, Budapest, Hungary.

HUNGARY

Ten years of ferment in a Naturism-friendly 1980s Hungary!

December 1981: Hungary announced opening a naturist park, its first, on Lake Balaton, the nation's tourist income center. At once the Roman Catholic prelate lept to denounce the 'immoral Communist' plan. The government backed out. End.

Today, native initiative drives a host of Naturist enterprises for Hungarians who come to body acceptance as they cleave to horses' backs, which is to say, superbly.

Hungary is among the most scenic, historic, economical and enjoyable of European nations. Its Naturist facilities offer friendly bases to tourists moving in unusual regions.

Magyar Naturisták Egyesülete (MNE), Kárpát útca 8, H-1133 Budapest XIII. Phone (361) 179 800 (W, F, 10–5). Also Napóra Klub, Pf. 25, H-1553 Budapest 134. Phone (361) 206 791 or 1220 980.

BUDAPEST

THERMAL WATERS

Budapest is blessed with spas—fortunately, for it is landlocked, with only a few lakes and rivers to relieve its flat *pushta*.

Budapest is literally built upon hot springs: 31 mineral wells, fed by 123 thermal springs, surface within the city limits, with a yield over 14 million gallons a day. At least half of these springs emerge hotter than 86°F, some surfacing at a scalding 169°F. To bask in spas is cultivated, and nudity no big thing here. Local leaders and workers and you will indulge in thermal baths, massages, radioactive mud pack, solariums, pedicure and electrotherapy—naturally.

Choose the ultramodern **Thermal Hotel**, situated in a vast park on Margitsziget (Margaret) Island in the Danube River which divides Budapest. Phone 111 000, fax 533 029. Or just visit the park, which includes jacuzzis, saunas and a really big wave-making pool

For tradition, stay at or visit the inimitable **Hotel Gellert**; its panoramic rooftop (with bathing), and the top terrace above the outdoor wave pool, offer nude sunning. Enter by the sidewalk cafe at the side, pay the cashier and get directions to all the facilities. Phone 666 166, fax 666 631.

Other spas beckon. **Császár Baths,** Frankel Leó Útca 35. **Rác Baths** (Turkish; 16th Century) put the Oriental touch into soaking, steam and massage; fitness room too; try the whole package. Hadnagy útca 8, phone 758 373. If you enjoy it, keep trying others; there's nothing like it.

For spa and Budapest hotel packages: Hungarian Hotels Sales office, phone 1-800-448-4321 (in California, 1-800-231-8704).

NAPÓRA KLUB

Napóra Klub has Budapest's first scheduled Winter Naturist fitness activities. Sauna, massage, Ping-Pong, badminton, gymnastics, yoga, occasional parties, as well as information. Begun in 1988 by the energetic Judit Halasz, with Miklos Bende, Gustav Hellebronth, and Dr. Bela Tomor, it counts over 400 members nationwide.

Leif Heilberg, Delegyhaza Camp, Budapest, Hungary.

Hungary

Summer Napóra activities utilize a complex of buildings and sun meadows north of Budapest on the Danube at Szentendre Island, **Horány Gyöngye**—an elite bathing resort fallen on hard times. Suburban rail north to Szentendre/Horány. RV hook-ups, room rentals. FKK camping, boating, fishing, river swimming. June–Aug. Organized by Passzió, Ltd., H-2015 Szigetmonostor, Horány, Duna sor 1. Phone (26) 23544.

Other activities are conducted at Szeged (below).

The informative Napóra magazine of East European Naturism—published by Angelos Mimikopoulos—is a co-project of the Budapest club and Halasz. The Naturist Society may be able to provide issues (see back of this Guide). Or contact East European Documentation Centre, Box 26148, GR-10022 Athens, Greece.

☞ Napora Club meets Autumn through Spring, on the 1st and 3rd Saturdays at 4 p.m., Hotel Lido, III. Nánási útca 67, Budapest. Phone (01) 180 5549.

OMSZKI PARK

Three popular sand-pit lakes in Omszki Park are in view of a towering memorial depicting Soviet soldiers who died while driving the Germans from Budapest. They draw up to 5,000 nude sunbathers on hot weekends.

☞ Take the suburban rail line north toward Szentendre (St. Andre). You can board the train on the Buda side of the Danube at the Arpad Bridge, among other stops. Get off at Budakalasz. Walk right up the street, keeping the monument on your left, then take the next right, then left to the lake. Or in driving out Route 11 to St. Andre, you can watch for the monument and find the lake.

DÉLEGYHÁZA

The premiere FKK campground of Hungary. Officially opened in 1983 after years of 'wild' use. Up to 5,000 recreate on 425 hilly acres, MNE supervised. Site of 1987 International Meeting organized by The Naturist Society, described in *Clothed with the Sun* 7.4.

Windsurfing, fishing, swimming in large clear gravel-pit lakes now attractive with vegetation. Kids everywhere. Restaurants, creperies and snack bars with beer/wine, greengrocers, bakery, toilets/showers, volleyball, disco, 900 permanent and 600 rental sites. April 15–Sept. 30. Volántourist agency can make reservations at the 10-room motel. Phone (026) 72072.

☞ Délegyháza village is south of Budapest, direction Baja; reached by a left turn between Taksony and Kiskunlachaza, after the 31 km marker on Route 51.

Bus 38 from Budapest, direction Szigethalom - Volan.

From Budapest's Józsefváros Station, take a 'slow' train, on line 150, direction Kelebia; get off in 40 minutes at Délegyháza and ask for the bus to the

Leif Heilberg, Scenes from Delegyhaza Camping.

"osztalyzo" (quarry-lake). It's 2 km, you might walk.

LAKE BALATON

BALATONBERÉNY

After state initiative failed in 1981, businessman Lajos Szabó brought naturism to Lake Balaton in 1987. Restaurant, changing rooms, 7-acre sun meadow under huge trees, boat rentals and beach, on southwestern shore of the vast but very shallow lake. May 15–Sept. 15, 9 a.m.–7 p.m. MNE supervised. H-8649 **Balatonberény**. Phone (084) 77155.

While this near, run over to **Lake Héviz** at Keszthely—a natural thermal lake, its source water 37° C, 86 million litres of it a day! Two Danubius hotels provide spa services and amenities.

No camping at Balatonberény. At the north end of Lake Balaton, however, is **FKK Camping Piroska**, Aligai útca 15, H-8172 Balatonakarattya. Phone (080) 81121.

Or rent in a private home in Balatonberény through local IBUSZ agency.

☞ From Budapest via Sopron on Route 84. At Balaton take Route 71 via Keszthely (7 km) and watch for big FKK sign. Line 30 bus from Budapest via Nagy and Kanizsa.

SZEGED

SZIKSÓSFÜRDÖ CAMPING

Szeged-Sziksósfürdö Naturist Camping, west of Szeged, occupies 3 acres on a natural lake in the south of Hungary. Still a tranquil retreat with 75 sites, 24 with RV hook-ups. Limited room rental. Volleyball, snack bar, fishing, playground, rafting, toilets/showers. May–Sept. Napóra supervised. Natours, P.O. Box 26, H-6791 Szeged-Kiskundorozsma. Phone (62) 61488.

☞ By bus or car, 11 km from Szeged to Sziksósto.

PÉCS

MOHÁCS FKK BEACH

The Mohács nude beach—on an island of the Danube River at the Yugoslav border —abuts a 500-site campground that is in part FKK. A serenely beautiful site with sports, playground, toilets/showers. No hook-ups. The Danube is too polluted for swimming or drinking; owner Aréna Camping dug a well. May 15–Sept. 30. MNE supervised. Ferry service from Hotel Csele at Mohács. H-7712 Dunaszekcsö.

ITALY

In 1978 Italian courts and the police first condoned nude beaches. *Panorama* newsweekly explained: "The reason was at bottom economic. Foreign tourists would no longer put up with the whims of this or that magistrate. Even Italian tourists, 75 percent from the north, were looking for quiet beaches and places where they might experience nature directly. They weren't going to be deprived of this elementary naturist contact by being forced into bathing suits."

A Milanese prosecutor ordered a survey to determine community standards of decency. 71% responded that they were not offended by the sight of a naked body. Nonetheless, a Rome superior appeals court in January 1979 found beach nudity *contrarie al buon costume*, contrary to morality or custom.

In Spring 1981 the national legislature explicitly made topfree a legal option for all beaches, and in 1985 Rome appeals judge Mario Giarruso performed a similar service for a "discreet and natural" genital nudity. "The sight of the naked body is not indecent to the majority of citizens"—he wrote—"as long as it is not done in a show-off or provocative way."

Despite the multi-pronged process by which recreational nudity was found not to offend community standards, it remains a red-hot issue. Some magistrates still seek ways to punish it. Dress codes were passed by some tourist city destinations in 1987-88. Beatings of nude bathers on remote beaches have occurred. Check the local custom and practices before disrobing.

The Italian Naturist Federation is splintered and only 4,000 strong. Yet its leading personalities have made a difference, especially at Elba, Sardinia, Turin and Bologna. Federazione Naturista Italiana, Via Guicciardini 3, I-10121 Torino. Phone (011) 531058.

SARDINIA

SARDINIA

Sardinia is an island with a history of 'many rulers but no masters.' Perhaps this explains why, years ago, a naturist settlement, the first in Italy, was able to take hold here, when the ecclesiastical mainland would have none of it.

The mild climate and numerous beaches have made Sardinia a perfect destination for a naturist holiday. The delights of Sardinia are becoming better known as tourists pack into the better beaches. Avoid July and August if you want some peace and come in June or September.

The northeast coast from Santa Teresa Gallura to Capo Comino has seen considerable resort growth. Convenient to the ferry port of Olbia, nude bathing occurs on islands of the Madgalena archipelago. (Proximity to Corsica, long a favorite naturist destination, has helped to free the spirits here.)

Near the village of Posada on the northeast coast is beautiful Su Tiriarzu beach and **Camping Ermosa** with cabins and tent rentals. Phone: 0784 854115. Bèrchida Beach, a few miles south, is even finer.

Beaches at Muravera and Villasimius, near the southern city of **Carbonia**, see frequent nude use. Also consider Isola Serpentara, an islet off southeasterly Capo Carbonara, to which day-trippers travel from hotels on the Capo such as the Stone Age Club.

Lovely s'Archittu village is on Sardinia's delightfully undeveloped west coast between Bosa and Oristano. About 1.5 miles south of the village, on the right side, is a common entrance to several campgrounds. One of these, **Nurapolis**, offers direct access to a 3-mile long sandy beach, of which the 2.5-mile stretch south of the campground is often used nude. A small hotel in s'Archittu is the alternative to camping.

These locations are most conveniently reached by air (Cagliari has the only airport) or ferry from either Sicily or mainland Italy. Beaches have no facilities.

ISOLA D'ELBA

ISOLA D'ELBA

Established nude beaches date from the late '70s on the Italian mainland. They were tolerated long before on Tuscany's vacation island of Elba, in the Tyrrhenian Sea. Don't expect a highly developed resort; the many sections of coastline accepted for naturist use are in isolated areas, and possess no amenities. You'll want a car to get around in; transport it on the Piombino–Portoferraio ferry, it takes an hour.

Camp-sites include Camping Acquaviva at the ferry port and Camping Stella Mare at Lacona on the south-central coast. South of Marina di Campo on the south coast is Spiaggia Seccheto with rooms to be rented in fishermen's homes.

On the whole, Elba's coastline is rocky or pebbly, but occasional sandy bays can be found. Six km of the coast of Punta dei Ripalta, Elba's large southeastern peninsula, are set aside for naturist use. From Capoliveri take Strada Panoramica (Fattoria Ripalte) to the south. After 7 km look for a path leading down to Punta della Calamita's sandy bays.

All along the northeast coast from Cavo to Rio Marina are lovely sandbars long enjoyed by naturists. Take any of the paths leading to the shore and find your private bay. The waters are shallow here, and access is easy, making this an ideal area for children. Of special interest are Capo Pero's many sandy bays.

On the Costa di Barbarossa at Porto Azzuro, try a 500-m long rocky section between the fine "Spiaggia Barbarossa" and "Spiaggia Reale" (spiaggia means beach), set aside for discreet naturist use. It's hard not to feel like a second-class citizen here, yet one can only hope that this small, liberated area will expand due to increasing popularity.

Local tourist offices will supply directions to naturist beaches and ANITA, the Italian naturist organization, publishes map and tourist information. Write to Gruppo Naturisti Isola d'Elba, Via Andrea Vitaliani 20, 57036 Porto Azurro, LI, Italy. A donation is appreciated.

Ferries make the 1 hour crossing from Piombino in Tuscany to the ports of Portoferraio and Porto Azurro several times daily. Reservations for ferry and accommodations in high season are recommended.

TUSCANY

TUSCANY

Named for the Etruscans, original settlers of the region, Tuscany has produced Michelangelo, Dante, Leonardo da Vinci, Boccaccio, Petrarch, the cities of Florence and Pisa—and now some attractive nude beaches. With the exception of Elba Island, nudity is not officially allowed in the Tuscany area and magistrates may fine. However, by avoiding crowded places and keeping watch for patrols, nudity is possible on many Tuscany beach strands. Not recommended at the Marina de Albereto.

The beaches north of Castiglione della Pescala strictly forbid nude use and should be avoided.The coastline from Castiglione della Pescala south to the Argentaria Peninsula is open for discreet clothes-free use. Southernmost is most popular. Orbetello's Etruscan ruins, 5 km from town, are well worth the visit, and the nearby fishing villages of Porto Santo Stefano and Port 'Ercole have long been popular with the jet set. The beaches are excellent from June to September, and Florence is most beautiful in May or June.

For a naturist experience on the Tuscan coast try **Chiarone**. A whistle-stop on the coastal rail line with a campgrounds and a hunter hotel and bar, Chiarone is the preferred beach of jetsetters vacationing at ancient Capalbio, the nearest village. By road: Drive Via Aurelia (SS I) to a sign for Chiarone Camp just north of the Latium–Tuscany border.

Indeed, the old Tuscan Duchy's toll office from A.D. 800 is here along with milestones in the high dunes inscribed "E.F. XVIII", i.e. 18th year of Fascist Era. But back to the beach: just outwalk the clothed ones to find your sandy spot.

LE BETULLE

Le Betulle, 'The Birches' was the first Italian family naturist park. Founded 1969 to much media hullaballoo, and still the model. Tent, RV sites. Splendid pool, archery, bocce ball, volleyball, Ping-Pong, rec hall. Restaurant, minimart within 10 minutes walk. Temperate; just over the Alps from France, and a good base for visiting NE Italy. Requires proof of INF membership and advance reservation by letter. Open all year. B.P. 1, I-10040 La Cassa (TO), Turin.

ROME AREA

FREGENE

Directly west of Rome and near the airport, a free beach extends from Fregene south to the mouth of the Tiber River. This area is polluted with industrial wastes; topfree sunbathing is all that can be recommended. Combine your visit with exploring the ruins of Ostia Antica, ancient Rome's thriving port.

TOR VAIANICA BEACH

One of the most heavily used and interesting nude beaches is Tor Vaianica, an hour outside Rome and well maintained with litter bags, refreshment stands and a makeshift camping area. This beautiful, broad, white-sand beach extends for miles with the nude section 1 km long. Awnings provide shade over picnic tables where many a family sits au natural to a bowl of pasta, good sandwiches and wine.

☞ From Rome take the Statale (state road) 148 south through the EUR complex and continue 20 km. Look for a right-hand turn to Tor Vaianica, then right again at Tor Vaianica and drive north along the beach for 6 km. Park on your left at the nude section.

Or take the Roma-Ostia train (station at the Porta S. Paolo) to Lido Cristoforo Columbo, the last stop. Directly in front of the station get on the 07X bus which goes south along the coast (not 07 which leads north to Lido di Ostia) to the end of the line (15 min.). Walk further south along the beach for another 15 minutes. Total transportation cost is about $2.

CAPOCOTTA BEACH

Like many beaches serving greater Rome, Capocotta Beach had teetered between anarchy and regulation, filth and freedom. Many thought it Rome's best nude beach—relatively tidy, still natural, naturist-friendly yet inhospitable to voyeurs. Small merchants had gone from selling to sunbathers out of baskets to creating capanni, 'arbors'—l Battello Ubriaco (The Drunken Boat, after Rimbaud's poem, the best if too-loud disco), Zagaja (The Stutterer), L'Aragosta (The Lobster), Le Vagoo, The Dunes, Tropical, Andrea, Disco Surf. These unregulated stalls served ices, drinks, hot meals, whatever people wanted. They also cleaned up, imposed etiquette, and supported nude use.

☞ Capocotta Beach is between Castelporzian Beach and Tor Vaianica, a weekend house colony. Follow directions to Tor Vaianica and it's just beyond.

LAKE MARTIGNANO

"Feel like getting an all-over tan?" inquired the newspaper Il Messaggero. "You needn't go to an elite watering hole in Sardinia. You can do it right here in the Commune of Rome"—at Lake Martignano.

☞ Drive out from Rome on Via Boccea and take either Via Santa Maria di Galeria or Via Anguillarese to get on the Via di Ponte Valle Trave and follow the signs. At the lake, park in the county lot (fee charged) and hike on the trail through woods and brush to the main beach. Hidden coves along the volcanic shore to right or left of the main beach provide possibilities for nude bathing.

SABAUDIA: SPERLONGA

About halfway down the coast toward Naples, Sperlonga's nude beach has long been popular with natives and tourists alike. Carabinieri sometimes patrol the sands, but their attitude toward nudity has relaxed considerably and they oftentimes stop to give you time to dress. Nonnaturist camping nearby.

☞ Route 7 from Rome south to the turn-off before Terracina, then 213 in town to Sperlonga Park. Park and walk as though for the Grotto. It's 100 yards from the Grotto.

NAPLES

TYRRHENIAN SEA

Ponza is the largest of the Isole Ponziane in the Tyrrhenian Sea. Although it is well out to sea, the heavily polluted Gulf of Gaeta flows toward Ponza—so forget swimming and work on your total tan.

While there see legendary Isola di Capri, the "sin" island of the Romans where Tiberius is said to have orgied and where pirates lorded it in the sun for many centuries. Today Capri is tame by comparision, but topfree and beginnings of full nudity can be seen.

Italy

SICILY

The offshore isles of this vast, historic island have seen more nude use with the years—but with the exception of the beaches near sophisticated Taormina, it was deemed advisable to stay dressed on Sicily proper.

No longer is this so; every major city now has beaches with some nude use. Palermo has Terrasini, along Route 113 towards Cefalù. Trapani has Calanpisu, near Capo San Vito. Siracusa has Brucoli. Messina has Patti Beach. Catania has the rocky right end of the Fontane Bianche beach.

ISOLE EOLIE

The rugged coastlines of the volcanic Aeolian islands off Sicily's northern coast offer numerous possibilities for secluded nude swimming and sunning. Of special note is the famous "Le Punte" beach on Isola Filicudi. Visitors to Villaggio Turistico "Phenicusa" (Phone (090) 914114) pioneered the nude beach between two promontories. On Isola Vulcano stay at Camping Sicilia Vulcano: phone (090) 9852164. A number of clothes-free coves and beaches are nearby.

ISOLE EGADI

The Egadi Islands are offshore from Trapani and the ancient city of Erice on westernmost Sicily. Lots to explore here, off-beach too: medieval castles, mysterious grottos, fishing villages.

PELAGIAN ISLANDS

ISOLA DI LAMPEDUSA

You'll strain your eyes trying to find this vacation retreat off Italy's coast: it is east of Souse, Tunisia, and the Arab influence is strongly felt. Happily, this does not extend to mores. Lampedusa's main beach is topfree and nearby beaches are totally nude. Access is from Sicily; flights leave from Palermo airport and ferries from Agrigento's Porto Empedocle. Stay at Villaggio Turistico Cala Creta. Phone (0922) 970 545. Or at Camping La Roccia, Via Madonna, I-92010 Lampedusa. Phone (0922) 970 055.

CALABRIA

PIZZO GRECO

A naturist campground at what was a "wild" nude beach near Capo Rizzuto. Pizzo Greco has official nude status. Its 7 acres, on a secured bluff above a fine sandy beach, offer some bungalows, RVs and tents to rent, as well as tent and RV sites, with shade trees, clean and ample toilets, showering and shared kitchen facilities, restaurant with bar and disco, and minimart. Recreation includes bocce ball, volleyball, Ping-Pong, horse riding, evening entertainment, and windsurfing or sunning on a fine red-sand beach lapped by clean Ionian sea. Families and couples only.

Air and sea ports serve Pizzo Greco at Crotone, 8 km distant. Or fly to Lamezio and a car will bring you 50 miles over the mountains to the campgrounds. You can locate Pizzo Greco by thinking of Italy as a boot descending south: Pizzo Greco and Isola Capo Rizzuto are on the ball of the foot.

Contact Rosso Sergio (who speaks English) off-season at (39) 142 70338, evenings. May to October at Pizzo Greco: (39) 962 799282 or 791771, mornings best. Pizzo Greco Naturist Club, P.O. Box 57, I-88076 Isola Capo Rizzuto CZ.

ADRIATIC COAST

GARGONA PENINSULA AND TREMITI

Forty miles of sandy beach lie on the northern Gargona Peninsula, better known as the 'spur' sticking out of the back of Italy's boot. Vieste, commercial center of the area is where accommodations are most likely to be found. Crowded with tourists in the hot months. The beaches south of the city see the most nude use. The Isle of Tremiti, to the north of Gargona, also permits nude sunning and swimming.

ANCONA

Ancona, coincidentally a major ferryport access to Yugoslavia's nude resort coast, is blossoming with a nude zone in its own right. Keep to the south of town; there's a fining magistrate with jurisdiction to the north.

SAN MARINO

CLUB CAMPEGGIATORI

Club Campeggiatori designated a portion of its grounds naturist in 1989. The site is on the Adriatic coast near Ravenna, 150 km south of Venice. Modern camping facilities. Day visitors welcome.

RAVENNA

LIDO DI DANTE: CAMPING CLASSE

Camping Classe offers three-star naturist campsites with hook-ups and hopefully soon with pool, bocce ball, tennis, Ping-Pong, etc., in a shady pine woods a short walk from an Adriatic nude beach. Byzantine, Roman antiquities. I-48100 Ravenna, phone (0544) 494 021 or 494 4811.

BOLOGNA

ASSOCIAZIONE NATURISTA BOLOGNESE (ANB)

In downtown Bologna the 2,500 member ANB maintains its Centro Naturista—a health club and vegetarian restaurant in a 300 year old building. It has 2 gyms, sauna, Turkish bath, massage, yoga, aikido, shiatzu, shops. Mon.–Fri. Via degli Albara 6, I-40126 Bologna. Phone (051) 235 643.

Forty km away in a vast mountain forest preserve is ANB's campgrounds, Ca'le Scope, with the home of ANB's guiding spirit and founder Luigi Bolelli. Tent, RV sites, gym, vegetarian restaurant. Bocce ball, ping-pong, hiking. Phone (051) 932 328.

Giuseppe Feroldi. Archery at Le Betulle, Turin, Italy.

Giuseppe Feroldi. Ancient Instrument Player. Italy.

NETHERLANDS

According to a 1986 government-sponsored inquiry, 9 percent of the Dutch population "regularly sunbathe, swim or hike in the nude" and another 70 percent do not disapprove of this practice.

Surprisingly, Dutch acceptance of public nudity is of recent development. At the start of the 1950s naturists still often had to travel to Germany or France to find a private park; nudity was prohibited at the Noordzee.

But this dour sky opened by the early 1970s. Emboldened by emerging national consensus for individual freedom, naturists acted to be nude on public lands. When progressive television stations brought full-frontal nudity into living rooms, and it was accepted, new community standards were affirmed. A last spur was the hot summer of 1975. Naturism took a firm footing on the Dutch beaches.

Concurrently the Minister of Justice, addressing Parliament, asked that nudity be accepted on locally approved beaches that are "out of the way, of limited size, marked and labelled as such." By the early 1980s the NFN could point to official FKK beaches. But that did not end the need to act.

The adoption of Article 430a in 1986 established the right of public nudity wherever it is appropriate.

A woman was found guilty of nudity by the town of Ouddorp on Goeree Island in Zeeland. She appealed and the Sommelsdijk Justice of the Peace dismissed the charges in 1987, establishing in case law that Article 430a, toleration of *geschikte* public nudity, takes priority over a local law that condemns it.

The Netherlands Naturist Federation has grown to third largest in the world.

In our listing are only the best social, comfortable and *geschikte* beaches for naturists. Information from Netherlands Tourism offices or from Nederlandse Federatie van Naturistenverenigingen (NFN), Postbus 783, NL-3500 AT Utrecht. Phone (030) 32 88 10, 10–3 daily.

Gerry Leewes. Kijkduin Beach near The Hague, Netherlands.

ZEELAND

SERVING BELGIUM

The conservative Zeeland tourist authorities insisted into the 1980s that no beaches could be enjoyed au naturel in the southernmost province. Yet naturists did find secluded beaches at Brouwersdam, on the south bank; between Renesse and Haamstede by the Verklikkers dunes; between Vrouwenpolder and Oost-Kappelle, turning right near the Oranjezon camping; and in Vlissingen at Nollestrand, walking toward Dishoek.

Belgians, even more repressed in their own country, went to Zeeland on weekends. As legal Dutch nude beaches appeared in the north a demand in the Flemish Catholic south grew. At last Oostburg authorities designated a Cadzand beach in 1985; to meet demand it has expanded. Sampling landed clubs:

Vlissingen—Seelandia. On the water where the ferry from Sheerness docks. RV rentals. PB 343, NL-4330 Middelburg. Phone (01185) 1312, (01184) 67290.

Bergen Op Zoom—Camping Athena. The main Belgian retreat in Zeeland; 70 RV rentals. Zandvlietseweg 15, NL-4641 Ossendrecht. Phone (01647) 2489.

SOUTH HOLLAND

HOEK VAN HOLLAND

The Hook of Holland, where ferries dock from England, is south of The Hague at the Harbor of Rotterdam entrance. A small official FKK beach is northeast on the sea towards 's-Gravenzande. Off Rechtsestraat to the right, then left. Between km poles 116.360–116.110.

MAASVLAKTE

Rotterdam Harbor—Maasvlakte. A desolate flat in the bend of the Europa Way by the Mississippi Harbor, Maasvlakte is a popular spot with Rotterdammers. Find the south point of the Maasvlakte northwest of Oostvoorne. Naturists delight in wandering the strand naked for miles, with perhaps no other companions but the sand, the sea, and if in luck, the sun.

KIJKDUIN

With a shopping center and hotels it's a favorite seaside resort for Germans; the Dutch and 'Deutsch' strip off between poles 20–21, near (textile) Ockenburg Camping.

SCHEVENINGEN

The Hague (Den Haag)—Scheveningen. Ceding no freedom edge to Amsterdam, Hagenaars too have an FKK beach at their world-famous sea resort. Buses and trams run often to Scheveningen Pier. There, walk north for 20 minutes to just south of the Wassenaar town line between km markers 98 and 96. Two beach buffets. Also FKK at Westduinpark between poles 103—105.5. VVV, PF 85973, NL-2508 Den Haag. Phone (070) 54 62 00.

NORTH HOLLAND

AMSTERDAM

The train to Zandvoort is supplemented by Amsterdam's suburban options:

Het Twiske—10 km north of Amsterdam between the towns of Oostzaan and Landsmeer. A wooded parkland of meadows, lakes and trails. Good swimming, windsurfing, picnicking. Seldom crowded; clothing-optional except for a small area signed for no nudity. Easily reached by bus (to Oostzaan or Den Iip), auto or bicycle. Naturists gather in the north end at 'De Wezenlanden'. Brochures at Central Station in Amsterdam. Phone (02984) 4338.

Sloterplas Lake—In the western suburbs, the lake has a small island for naturists. From downtown Amsterdam take trolley #1 or 13 or bus #23. Driving, follow signs for Amsterdam West and watch for Slotervaart near Osdorp.

Amstelveen—Amsterdamse Bos. To the south; a secluded sunning meadow.

ZANDVOORT BEACH

Amsterdam—Zandvoort. Where the city lies down by the sea in summer. A world class, lifeguarded, clothes-optional beach; with the beach buffets Adam & Eva, Amerika, Trocadero and Sans Tout, which also provide showers/toilets and rent chairs.

☞ Frequent and comfortable trains make the trip in 30 minutes. The rail terminal is only steps from the sands. At the southern pavilion walk south to poles 68–71. Camping het Helmgat is 2 km north at Bloemendaal aan Zee, phone (02326) 0820.

FLEVO-NATUUR

Flevoland—Flevo-Natuur. Built by NFN. FKK recreation center open to all. Opened 1978; 30 ha. with indoor/outdoor heated pool, sports courts, sauna, restaurant. Tent/RV sites, bungalows, minimart. Wheelchair accessible. East of Amsterdam 55 km by Amersfoort–Zwolle highway; on the south of the Flevopolder (Zuider Zee after drainage) across from Nijkerk. Open all year. Managed by Creatief Vakantieparken, PB 352, NL-9700 AJ Groningen. Phone (050) 143434. Grounds: Flevo-Natuur, Wielseweg 3, NL-3896 RZ Zeewolde. Phone (03241) 241.

Elburg—Veluwe Lake. A free beach on the Flevoland, opposite the mainland town of Ellburg. Look for a restaurant "De Klink" and the Riviere Campgrounds. The beach lies between the two. From Flevo-Natuur, 40 km.

BERGEN AAN ZEE

A lively beach resort located near Alkmaat, famous for its cheese market; within an hour of Amsterdam. Walk south along the beach to marker 36 and strip down. Another spot to bare all in Bergen Aan Zee is near Schoorl, between markers 32.4 and 29.5, easily reached by bus from Alkmaar.

CALLANTSOOG

The first sanctioned nude beach was voted in at this small North Sea resort straight north of Amsterdam, with a wide strand and dunes. Off the beaten track of tourists who think that Amsterdam is the Netherlands, it's a popular holiday spot. A polluted Noordzee has caused rashes. The only facilities are in the textile area. A splendid reserve for waterfowl is just south, Het Zwanenwater.

For FKK, from the main beach entrance walk 30 minutes south. Or enter beach at St. Maartenszee to walk 15 minutes north. FKK zone is km markers 14.5–16.8 and 8.4–9.4. VVV, Jewelweg 8, NL-1759 HA Callantsoog. Phone (02248) 1541.

NOORDZEE

Noordzee–North Sea beaches are not for all of us! Often austerely beautiful, with romantic moors and good sand, the weather may be bracing—well, chilly! A brisk wind often blows with a hint of shower. Not bothersome enough to stop people from claiming their place (or their windbreak) in the hazy sun, year after year.

Enjoy. And be careful swimming. Riptides take lives of even hardy swimmers.

The Dutch Frisian Islands, off the North Sea coast, offer much for lovers of fish, wildfowl and dunes. Ferries travel to the Frisians from a number of mainland ports. The Dutch love them as a place to get away from it all. When you're not sunning, try a guided tour through the Waddenzee tidal flats—at low tide the shallows teem with life.

DEN HELDER

Den Helder, departure point for liberated Texel, has a nude beach south of the Falga refreshment stand, km markers 4.6–5.

TEXEL ISLAND

Southernmost of the Dutch Frisian Islands, Texel has night life and all watersports as well as two official FKK beaches. One is at the north point near the village of De Cocksdorp, between km markers 26.4 and 27.4, best reached from the parking lot at De Krim. A second is at Den Hoorn where FKK is south of km 9, complete with beach buffet, next to the Hoornderslag parking on the Witteweg. Note that wind from the east will ruin your beach day. VVV Texel, PF 3, NL-1790 AA Den Hoorn.

SCHIERMONNIKOOG ISLAND

Northernmost of the Frisians, friendly and traditional; very popular with cyclists and walkers in an undeveloped nature. The Schiermonnikoog town council decided in 1981 that given the many nude beachgoers, it made more sense to define a part of the beach where clothing must be worn. This is between the two main beach entrances (km markers 2–7). The rest of the island shore is clothing-optional. VVV, PF 13, NL-9166 PW Schiermonnikoog. Phone (05195) 233.

NORWAY

With thousands of miles of a granite fjord shoreline the Norwegians easily find secluded ledges for their sunbathing. Most rely on these rocky 'free beaches' rather than purchase land for naturist clubs.

Increasingly, municipalities make legal provision for the nude sunbathers. The Norwegian Naturist Union did buy a seaside center and campground, Sjøhaug, in 1980. Municipal pools are used for nude swims in winter.

Contact: Norsk Naturistforbund, Postboks 189 Sentrum, N-0102 Oslo 1. Phone: (02) 136118. Its travel agency is Vidy Reiser, Boks 427, N-4001 Stavanger, phone: (04) 527140.

OSLO AREA

Increased naturist activity in southern Norway prompted the Oslo City Council to designate official FKK sites.

If it's not sunbathing weather, go to view the pulpit in St. Mary's Cathedral—"the most naturist pulpit in the world," says Per Lonning, the State Church bishop and outspoken naturist. Visit Vigeland Sculpture Park for its vast portrayal of naked humanity. And view the giant nude Oslo Fjord mural in the banquet room of Oslo City Hall.

OSLO AREA BEACHES

Topfree is generally accepted on the Norwegian beaches. Nude beaches on Oslo Fjord:

Langøyene Island, the rocky southeastern shore. Idyllic view, no vehicles on island, camping permitted. Ferry service from Oslo.

Indre Huk Beach. At Strømborgveien 49 on Bygdøy at Oslo's western city limits—near Kontiki raft museum on the Frognerkillen. Sandy beach, shower facility, nearby restaurant.

Kalvøya Beach. Take E-18 west about 10 kilometers to Sandvika town hall. Park on the facing Kadettangen peninsula. Walk across bridge onto forested Kalvøya Island. Official nude beach is on its east side.

Strandskog Beach, at Ingierstrandvei 100-108, Oppegaard. Two km beyond Ingierstrand; a small blue sign on shore side should identify site. Tiny sandy area among rocks beneath trees.

SJØHAUG NATURIST CENTER

Sjøhaug, owned by Norwegian Naturist Union, has 12 1/2 acres of fields and woods. Its quarter mile beach winds around two bays on a fjord. Fishing, swimming, windsurfing, boating. Volleyball, hiking, playground. Rustic farm lodgings, camping, community kitchen.

Inexpensive, congenial base for visiting Oslo. Ferry, train, and bus make Oslo–Moss connections. Box 803 Sentrum, N-0104 Oslo 1. Phone (09) 270050.

☞ From Oslo, take E-6 south. After 55 km take E-120 into Moss city, cross Mossesundet bridge onto Jeløya island. Drive north on Nesveien to Sjøhaug on the eastern shore.

Langøyene Island, Oslo Fjord, Norway

POLAND

Poles avid for social nudity in the 1990s have claimed 600,000 participants at lakes, saunas and the Baltic Coast. But a vast misconception is fostered. Exploitative Miss Natura pageants propagating a Naked Bimbo image for Polish women are often staged on the FKK beaches by entrepreneurs led by the current SNP president, Jósef Kubicki. Much of what passes as naturism, purported in magazines like *Veto* and *Natura Naturyzm*, is derived from *Playboy* or *Penthouse*. Many local naturists are outraged but greedy interests seem to control their movement.

Stowarzyszenie Naturystów Polskich (SNP), ul. 1 Maja 887, PL-90-755 Lódz.

WARSAW AREA

VISTULA BEACHES

Swydry Beach. The first tolerated Warsaw area nude beach is 10 miles southeast of Warsaw, just north of where the Swider River enters the Vistula. Mobbed with couples, and especially singles and gays, especially Sundays. No refreshments or facilities. Pageants entrepreneur Sylwester Marczak holds forth here.

☞ Express bus C from the intersection of Warsaw's main avenues, Marszalkowska and Jerozolimski. At Falenica transfer to bus 702, 717 or 719, direction Otwock or Józefów. Get off at the *gola plaza* (nude beach) stop at the restaurant Pod Debami between Swidry Male and Swidry Wielke. Or take bus 146 from Warszawa Wschodnia train station (Praga district) in direction of Falenica; at Byslawska St., transfer to bus 702, 717 or 719.

Walk west from Pod Debami towards the Vistula. At dead end cross the small

Leif Heilberg. Miss Natura Contest with Sylwester Marczak. Miedzyzdroje Beach 1985 (top). Rowy Beach, Baltic Coast (bottom).

stream, Swidry Male, or turn left (southwest) on a well-trod path to the sandbar island beach.

Aleya Romantyczna—Miedzeszyn Beach. Also on the Vistula River, and an alternative to Swider Beach. Many families and couples, a clubby and cultured group. A lovely sand beach 400' wide, within Warsaw city limits; 2 miles north of Swider beach and on the same side. Parking; no facilities.

☞ Take bus 146 in direction of Falenice and get off for Aleya Romantyczna. Walk down it to the river, where nudity on the shore and islets is evident. Or drive from downtown Warsaw, across the Vistula River on General Berlinga Bridge, then upriver (southwest) for 10 km on the left bank. At Al. Romantyczna turn right to the river.

Grand Hotel Warsaw. Naturists socialize at its sauna/pool. Daily 10–8. Al. Krucza 28.

LODZ AREA

LODZ SOLARIUM

Lodz, in the geographic center of Poland, is at the heart also of controversy over true and false naturism. The SNP president and his administration, but also the opposition leader Adam Chrzuszcz who is as well the INF contact, together with many who work to change the exploitative tendencies of Polish nudism, are Lodz-based.

Lodz lacks a cash-hungry nudist magazine or club. Garden-variety naturists meet daily in good weather at the solarium of a city pool. Zespót Basenów 'Fala', Park Kultury i Wypoczynku na Zdrowiu, al. Unii 4. Phone 28664.

Local contacts: Wieslaw Niedzielski, al. Zelnerowicza 3, phone 349 618. Jola and Adam Chrzuszcz, al. Sowinskiego 24, PL-91485 Lodz, phone 575 254 or 551 595.

SILESIA

SILESIAN GROUPS

Groups in Katowice and Tychy are raising the standards for Silesian naturism.

Katowice has a sauna-centered club seeking land.

Tychy naturists have a corner (literally) on a public quarry, and are developing it as a naturist lake. Contact Jerzy Czarnohorski, al. Orzeszkowej 10/38, PL-43100 Tychy.

KRAKOW AREA

KRYSPYNÓW LAKE

Kryspynów Village is 10 km west of Krakow. Express bus K goes directly to Kryspynów Lake from the Krakow west Old Town 'Salvator' bus stop, below Kosciuszko Mound. Parking, boat rentals, windsurfers, kayaks, sailboats, and facilities at the *tekstylni* village beach. Walk 10 minutes to opposite (north) side, past rye fields, for nudity, clean water, and a nice view of a Baroque monastery.

BALTIC COAST

BEACHES

Coastal Route 52 sweeps across the Polish Baltic coast and its beaches from western Szczecin (access to Uznam–Wolin) to Gdansk in the east (the access to Hel Peninsula). Train and bus offer parallel service, but a rental car is best.

Swinoujscie—Uznam Beach at Poland's German border is cheek-by-

Leif Heilberg. 'Nude Beach' Sign With Regulations, Miedzyzdroje Beach, 1985 (top). Miedzeszyn Beach, Warsaw, 1985 (bottom).

jowl with an FKK beach on divided Usedom.

Wolin Island—Miedzyzdroje Beach. In walking distance of rail station, with a second beach east of Wiselka. Fine white sand, wading depth, not cold, good for families. Camping 'Pomerania' is at beach and popular with naturists.

Dziwnówek Beach. A mile east of clothed Dziwnów beach, northeast of Wolin.

Koszalin—Uniescie. East of Mielno, west of Lazy, on the barrier beach between Lake Jamno and the Baltic. Take Koszalin city bus 2 to Uniescie, walk 2.5 km east along coast road to Lake Jamno canal and follow it to beach. Parking by the road is suppressed; walk in.

Slupsk—Rowy Beach. Drive from Slupsk north to coast, then east to park at Rowy, and walk a mile east, then cross the wooded dunes onto the white sand beach, with its *plaza naturystowa*. Camping reservations, phone Rowy 11980.

Lebork—Leba provides another access to miles of nude beach on a sandspit.

Debek-Bialogóra Beach. Reach Debek village by crowded interurban bus from Wladyslawowo (also gateway to Hel), or drive. West along the beach, fording the Piasnica River, toward Bialogóra hamlet. A beautiful beach, very popular.

Chalupy Beach, Poland's best-known FKK beach for over 50 years, drew thousands of beachgoers to the **Hel Peninsula**. Closed by Chalupy town council after controversial 'Miss Natura' contests were staged in early 1980s. A more quiet naturism survives today at **Jastarnia Campground.**

Gdansk—Stogi. This beach on the Bay of Gdansk is too 'urban' and of course polluted for many tastes but it's convenient.

Sopot. Winter swims weekly in Sopot. Area contact is Zbyszek Marchewicz, al.Kolberga 4b/27, PL-81881.

PORTUGAL

Lusitanian hospitality has outlasted 40 years of dictatorship. Its constrained warmth now combines with liberalism. Many Portuguese welcome the naturists. You may safely mix *praias gymnicas* with your affordable vacation. Do be cautious in disrobing, however; for nudity remains controversial.

Make Lisbon your gateway—and make your first visit to Aldeia de Meco, a beautiful beach beneath sandstone bluffs!

Or take a bus, car or train (5 hours), or directly fly to Faro—the gateway of the southern Algarve Coast, with many small coves and barrier sandbars. Direct flights from London or Montréal.

"Portugal might well be the first country that explicitly gives the right to naturism by law." (Remark of the Bulletin of the International Naturist Federation, when Parliament approved legislation that legalized naturism on April 19, 1988.)

This legislation was actively developed by the Federaçao Portuguesa de Naturismo, founded 1977. Contact the FPN at Apto. 3232, P-1306 Lisbon Codex. It was pushed through Parliament by the tiny Green Party, winning by 92/31 (with 130 abstentions).

You can still camp at most beaches—unlike in many countries of Europe.

Leif Heilberg. Water Fight. Miedzeszyn Beach, Warsaw.

ALGARVE COAST

Segregated at the extreme south of Portugal by sea, river and mountains, the Algarve Coast took the imprint of successive settlers: Phoenicians, Greeks, Carthaginians, Romans and Moors. The strong Arab flavor in customs and architecture remains, including in the name—originally Al-Gharb. 'The Land Beyond.'

Developers are rapidly building on the attractions. Modernization has also meant acceptance of the monokini—and no-bikini—on a number of beaches.

Faro is the capital of the Algarve, its international airport, and most civilized place to stay: an old port with narrow streets, a walled inner city and impressive church surrounded by low, tile-roof houses and patterned dark stone streets. A bit north is Estoi with an amazing palace. For leather and tile shopping don't miss Quinta do Logo.

From Faro you may go east or west on the 120 km coastal Route 125. Good bus and electric train service.

FARO EAST

East from Faro the nude beaches:

Faro–Olhão Ilhas. Faro area islands are reached from the port of Olhão. Camping and nudity are prevalent, well down the beaches. Ilha da Armona is nearest, but more busy. Ilha do Farol/Culatra is a better choice.

Tavira—Ilha de Tavira. Drive to a housing estate, Pedras del Rei, 4 km east of Tavira. There's a sometime nude beach here. Better, a ferry goes every half hour to the 13 km sandy barrier island of Tavira. On the Ilha find a pool, minimart, buffet and disco. Walk down the beach to be nude.

FARO WEST

The beaches from Faro west:

Vale do Lobo. Before Qaurteira. Drive to Almansil; turn towards the coast and Vale do Lobo; at the sandy road parallel to the coast turn left, direction of Quinta do Largo, and watch for a cluster of signs including Mad Max's. Park by the restaurants and walk east to the nude area, past Julia's Beach Cafe.

Albufeira—Praia de Gale-Armacao da Pera. Numerous coves accessible at low tide. Discreet nudity at the beach steps in Falesia and by Hotel Alta-Mar, also east of Praia da Oura.

Portimão—Carvoeiro and Ferragudo. Southeast of Portimão, Carvoeiro is between river estuary and Lagos.

Lagos—Ponta da Piedade. A cove amid scenic cliffs at the lighthouse of Ponta da Piedade, 1 mi south of Lagos. Preferred by youth from chillier climes who camp in the cliffside caves and clean the beach, suggesting a need to the Portuguese authorities. Much of the glorious Lagos coast is too rocky for land access; on calm days, fishermen can be hired to drop your party at a sublime cove.

Sagres—Praia ingrini. At 7 km east of Sagres take a road signposted for P. Ingrini; park at the beach buffet, and walk left.

Zavial Beach. Route 125 west past Logos towards Vila do Bispo to Rasposeira village. Turn south toward beach and take a left fork, marked Zavial, which winds to the beach, 12 km from Sagres at the old Barrançao fort. East from the snackbar is nude. Many live at a hippie squatter campground.

LISBON AREA

LISBON AREA

Nudity occurs, often discreetly, south of Lisbon from Costa de Caparica to Sesimbra and Setúbal.

Costa da Caparica. Clean water, nice breeze; too active now for fully comfortable nude use; but if you're there, take the little beach tram, direction Fonte da Telha, to the next to last stop (#19) and check out the dunes. Early pro-nudity actions were here. Or drive over the Tagus (Tejo) Bridge, following signs for Ponte da Telha, then drive north behind the dunes as far as the road goes, and park (you're near #19 beach). You can get from Lisbon to the Costa by direct bus from the Praça de Espanha (Metro Palhavã) or with the ferry across to Cacilhas.

Setúbal—Troia Beach. A beautiful, narrow peninsula at the mouth of the Rio Sado offers tranquility on the Baia de Setúbal. Access by N-253-1 via Alcacer do Sal: Troia Beach is 1 km beyond the enclosed campground, so park beside the road and hike in. Or better, by ferry or hovercraft from Lisbon to Setúbal, and cross the river mouth to Praia do Troia.

Sesimbra—L'Aldeia do Meco. Your first choice near Lisbon. Thirty km directly south, on point of a peninsula near the fishing village of Sesimbra (with lodging, minimart, restaurants and camping). Farmers with donkeys sell mulberries, figs and grapes to sunbathers. A natural spring provides showers and mudbaths. Good windsurfing. Camping in nearby pine woods.

☞ There are two ways. Drive from Lisbon via Fogueteiro, Marco de Grillo and Alfarim; then as below. Or exit Lisbon by the April 25 Bridge over the Rio Tejo (Tagus River) on E-4, and turn off south on N-378 at the Sesimbra exit. Go toward Sisimbra until Marco do Grilo. Here, turn right to Lagoa de Albufeira and on to Alfarim. Entering Alfarim, turn right at the primary school. This road leads to Aldeia de Meco, which you pass through, bearing right on a potholed road which arrives in 2 km at the parking. It's a 300 m walk to the bay; the beautiful 4 km naturist sand beach, backed with cliffs and pine trees, is on the south. (Fonte da Telha is at the north end of the textiled 'north' beach.)

CENTRAL

SÃO PEDRO DE MUEL

Limited beach access, a rough coast and unsafe swimming make these 50 kilometers of fine sand an unexpected haven. Patrols will wave you out of the water but generally do accept nudity.

☞ Arriving in Saõ Pedro from Marinho Grande, turn right at the second roundabout. Follow signs to Figuera La Foz. Pass the lighthouse, take the winding road to the second left turn, at a small roundabout. Take this dirt road to parking at the vast beach.

Or drive south from San Pedro towards Praia da Victoire. At Pentieira, you want the beach between Agua de Madeiros and Polvoeira.

NORTHERN

PORTO: AFIFA BEACH

North of Porto (airport) on the Costa Verde, conservatives rule and a nude beach struggles on. The FPN believes success of naturism depends on growing acceptance in the north. Focus is the dunes and beach at Afifa, north of Viana do Castelo and south of Valencia (Spain).

In Porto, check with Hotel Boa Vista, Esplanada do Castelo 58, Foz do Doura, P-4100 Porto. Phone 683 176.

RUMANIA

Rumania largely treats modern naturist values as extensions of agrarian ways. Yes, of course you take off your clothes and bathe when the need is there. Of course you do it with your own gender. All the reasons for a free body culture with gender integration, evolved over a century, elude the public policy in Rumania. A modern approach seems yet to come, and there is no organization to bring it about.

CONSTANTA

CONSTANTA SOUTH

Eforie, 14 km south of Constanta, an historic Black Sea resort that includes heliotherapy with other cures. Sections for women only, men, and families. Eforie has led Rumanian attitudes on the body and its maintenance.

Lake Techirghiol. Its mud baths are the finest, most unique naturist activity at the Black Sea. Just west of Eforie North. A modest fee admits you to the shower and locker area where you leave your garments. Then walk to a huge vat of mud and smear it over yourself. Stand under the sun to let it bake you dry (10-12 minutes). Finally walk into the lake to rinse off, and sunbathe till dry. Repeat as often as desired. The mud's medicinal effect is every visitor's rationale for attending—and in truth, it's great fun. Buses and taxis go to Techirghiol from all Black Sea hotels. Gender-segregated.

Continesti has a 1 km nude beach—in our sense—on its north coast. Lively, youth-oriented. Here the forest reaches to a Black Sea which is clear and clean.

Mangalia near the Bulgarian border has a 'therapy' hotel on its north shore, Neptune, which includes beach 'solarium'.

Camping 2nd May is 3 km south of Mangalia, has a clothes-optional beach.

CONSTANTA NORTH

Mamaia Beach Solarium. Adjoining the Apollo Hotel, the great 'solarium' at the edge of the Black Sea consists of gender-segregated enclosures. Showers, chair rentals. Both sexes may go nude between the sea and the enclosures. Females may also relax at the male enclosure, but not vice-versa. The result is that one-third of those within the 'male' enclosure are female.

Sulina north at the USSR border has a free beach.

Steve Mattis, Mud Therapy at Lake Techirghiol, Rumania.

SPAIN

Summarized *Cambio 16*, Spain's leading magazine in 1990: "The idea of Naturism has had a profound transformation in recent years. From being a hotly-debated attitude of the 1960s, it has become customary for entire families."

A clothes-free campground was first licensed only in 1978, in Alméria. Since then, developers have created naturist residence communities; and a 500-room, all-naturist grand resort hotel went up in Andalucia in 1989. Caterers to the British holiday trade employ naturism as a marketing tool. Exciting times, after almost 40 years of paralyzing dictatorship!

COSTA BRAVA

MAS PERICOT

Only 40 km south of the French Mediterrranean border on 154 ha of forest and prairie, with a river and commanding view of Roses Bay and Lake Boadella. Pool, *boules,* volleyball, ping pong, community barbeque, tent/RV sites. Dirt road is difficult. Mas Pericot, E-17720 Macanet de Cabrenys.

RELAX-NAT CAMPING

Since 1983. Primarily chosen by visitors to the Costa Brava nude beaches. On an 8 ha farmstead at Mont-ras, 4 km from coast. Ample tent/RV sites all hook-ups. Rental RVs. Minimart, snackbar, tennis, volleyball, basketball, 2 pools (one heated), spa, playground, video room. April–Sept. No singles. Relax-Nat, Aptdo. de Correos 19, E-17230 Palamós. Phone (072) 314296.

THE BEACHES

The Mediterranean Coast from the French border to Blanes has sandy coves protected by rocky headlands, and nude bathing is entirely natural. July-August are crowded but May and September have fine weather and Easter is a festive time; come off-season!

Cap de Creus—Cadaquès. Wonderfully clean waters and small sea caves to explore. Best coves accessible only by boat. From Perpignan, take coastal Route 114 across Spanish border to Llansá, keep east along shore to Port de la Selva, cut south to Cadaqués, then by boat or foot northeast towards Cap de Creus. Just south is:

Ampurias—Golf de Roses. Ampurias is famous Greco-Roman ruins. Figueres has a Dali museum and bullfights. From the Figueres–Roses road, turn right to Playa Ampuria-Brava. Find the most southerly parking and wade across Riu Muga to a 4 mi nude beach, Platja al Golf de Roses. Alternatively, drive south from Castelló d'Empúries in direction Armentera; turn northeast to the Gulf after crossing Riu Fluvià, just south of St. Pere Pescador; park at Camping Nàutic Almata and walk north. Another nude beach is reached by driving south from Nàutic Almata.

Bagur—Platja de Pals. Massos de Pals is an ancient commune. Its spectacular cove, El Salt d'en Ribes, is often visited by Barcelonians and guests of Relax-Camping. Drive east from Palafrugell to Pals, and continue, turning right at sign for Platja de Pals. Park at Mar Blau restaurant near Voice of America transmitting towers. Climb the stairway over the boulders to the south, and you're in the free zone at a giant offshore butte, Illa Roja. Fine campgrounds to south (not nude, but with nude coves).

Palamós—Cala Estreta. Between Punta del Castell and Cap Roig. Take C-255 north from Palamós for 2.5 km, follow signs to the Benelux Campground. Continue past Benelux, with the shore on your right, for 1.5 km. Park under the pines and follow the path down to the beach. The last of four coves is Cala Estreta. More recently in nude use are Cala Bona and Cala Gamarús.

Sant Felíu de Guixols—Tossa de Mar Coast. A variety of naturist beaches along the road: Cala del Senyor Ramón—the name is on a roadside rock, next to Cala Salions—a beautiful private sandy beach with refreshment stand, umbrellas, etc. Santa Cristina, just south of Sr. Ramón; take the path before the bridge. Vall Presona and Givarola, facing Cap Péntine.

BARCELONA

The Gaudí church, '92 Olympics, distinctive Catalan customs, language and anarchist tradition, the Picasso museum, great restaurants and night life, rocky coves and beaches, San Felíu and Montserrat monastery; cheaper than the French Riviera and more developed than the Italian—Catalonia is a popular vacation choice for the French, for the French naturists too, and Barcelona is the capital and port. The shirt of freedom on Spanish beaches was first pulled off in Catalonia and homage is due.

The association, founded in 1978, has a lively bulletin in Catalan, *Naturisme.* **Club Català de Naturisme, Mallorca 221, 3º, 2ª, E-08008 Barcelona. Phone (93) 254 05 08.**

EL TORO BRAVO NAT

On 7 ha of pine woods: clothes-free (150) and clothes-mandatory (450) camp-sites. Part of the 2 km beach is FKK, you decide where. 'Nat' camping has only a toilet bloc, a pool and snack bar. Tennis, riding stable, excursions, water sports, fitness center, supermarket etc. are in textile section. Toro Bravo is close to Barcelona airport, which can be a plus, but the noise is hardly restful. Visitors have also complained of stench and mosquitoes from an industrial canal next to the camping. Open all year. English spoken.

On C-246, at 11 km south from Barcelona. Aptdo de Correos 7, Viladecans (Barcelona). Phone (34) 36 58 12 50.

BALÉARIC ISLANDS

The beautiful Baléaric Islands were the first venue officially to allow nudity on the Spanish coast. Ibiza's first nude beach, Aqua Blanca, became a popular destination with the young international set in the early 1970s.

IBIZA

Always sunny Ibiza (Eivissa, in Catalan)—with a major airport, and boat connections to Marseilles and Alicante—was a natural to be "the pioneer of nudism in Spain" as *Cambio 16* noted. Two of 40 beaches are officially naturist. Unofficially, add dozens of coves. Topfree is accepted everywhere.

☞ From San Carlos in the north, you can reach official and popular **Es Figueral** (a.k.a. Playa Agua Blanca) to its east, a 'morning sun' beach.

On Cabo Falcon—10 miles from Ibiza city at the southern point—is **Es Cavallet,** a second officially naturist beach. Restaurant/bar, snack bar, restrooms, umbrella rentals. Connected with Es Cavallet by a headland and string of small coves is **Ses Salines** with shallow water, water sport rentals, refreshment stands. To either, there's bus service from Ibiza town, or drive out airport road and turn left on 'La Canal' at the salt mound, to parking at either beach.

Also check **d'En Bossa** beach. The Guardia Civil raided it in June 1977 and cited a dozen nude bathers, only to be hooted by clothed bathers who resented the interference of the Guard with innocent practices. Its far end still has some FKK use despite development.

Both **Cala Conta** (go left of main beach) and **Cala Bassa** (FKK at the ends) can be reached by bus or ferry from San Antonio, and have secluded coves to enjoy au naturel. **Portinax,** where "South Pacific" was filmed, has an end bay in nude use.

FORMENTERA

If anywhere in the Mediterranean is still a vacation haven—it is Formentera. The official beach, **Las Illetas,** is only part of the good news. Most other island beaches are also nude with no hassle or gawkers.

Accommodations: Es Pujols is most convenient to Las Illetas. Bicycles are de riguer and can be rented in every village. Regular ferry service from Ibiza Port (about 5 km from the Ibiza airport) several times daily. Day trips are organized from Ibiza and San Antonio (both on Ibiza) directly to Las Illetas.

☞ Las Illetas is on an isthmus extending several miles north, with surf on one side and quiet sea on the other.

On the south coast the **Bay of Mitjorn** offers 4 miles of golden sands with at least 75 percent of the bathers openly nude. The western shore secluded bays are also primarily nude; the most popular have beach bars.

MALLORCA

This largest of the Baléarics is easily visited by sea from Marseilles, Barcelona, Alicante and Valencia. Mallorca has well-tolerated nude beaches, among them Cala Pi, Ses Covetttes and d'Es Trenc. The civil governor, Marin Arias, noted that "naturism is a sociological reality, and for this reason it is necessary to regulate it with the most open attitude that is possible." Beginning in 1979, naturist camping on Ibiza and Formentera was authorized by the government. The situation continually develops. Check current patterns before you get naked.

Es Trenc is an 'ideal' nude beach with white sand, a gentle surf and safe swimming, snack and beverage venders and umbrella rentals. From Palma drive east 30 mi to Campos. Turn right at center of Campos to La Rapita, and go 7 miles toward the coast. A mile before La Rapita turn left at sign for "Ses Covetes". Proceed along narrow road to "T" interesection. Turn right, go a mile, turn on a short sandy road to the left towards beach. Nude use between two snack bars.

El Mago, center of three coves, is small, officially nude and very beautiful. Clean sand, gentle slope, refreshments, superb swimming, and flat rocks on east side for sunning. Take freeway from Palma towards Andraix 15 mi to turnoff to Cala Figueroa. Continue to second intersection where sign points past east side of a golf course to El Mago. Go that way and after 2 mi observe sign pointing way down hillside toward coves on the left.

MENORCA

Menorca has, on its northeast coast, naturist beaches at **Capifort, Es Grau,** and **Illa d'En Colum.** On its south coast it has **Macarelleta** and **Binigaus.** Even the major hotel beach **Son Bou** is used clothes-free. The tourist level is low enough, and beaches extensive enough, that most things are possible, for nudity is now expected on Menorca. A fast ferry runs from Puerto Alcudia, Mallorca to Ciudadela, Menorca.

COSTA DORADA

SOUTH OF BARCELONA

Since Barcelona lacks suburban *playas desnudas* that are popular, many Catalonians will drive south on Route 246 to the beaches from the Hospitalet del Infante to Peñiscola.

Sitges—Cala de l'Home Mort. Officially nude after much lobbying. From the Carreta Pau, a *tren* will take you west along the promenade to Hotel Terramar. Continue west on foot, parallel to the tracks, past the golf course and car park of Platja les Coves, then behind the filtering station and over the hill. The first, W-shaped bay is naturist. If you go on, there's another bay mostly in gay nude use. Both beaches are pebbly. Refreshments are brought in by a donkey during high season. No facilities. Naturist Hotel Antemar, Av. Virgen de Montserrat, 48 Sitges.

Tarragona—Cala de la Mora (Waikiki Beach). A recent development near Las Palmeras Campgrounds (not the naturist camping of same name in Alméria). From Barcelona take Route 340 south toward Tarragona. Beyond Altafulla, look for the Scipio Tower and park. Walk down the steep path, across the railroad tracks at the entrance to Las Palmeras. Follow the path to the north end of the beach through a stone wall.

Hospitalet del Infante—Cala d'Oques. From Hospitalet del Infante drive south past the Pension Camping Cala d'Oques; after the second curve, park and hike down the rocky trail.

COSTA BLANCA

WHITE COAST BEACHES

The Costa Blanca, accessed via Alicante, caters to naturist seekers of calm and quiet with night life and tourism convenient if desired.

Estrella Azul (Blue Star) is halfway from Benidorm to Altea on a bay ensconced by mountains. Rents 60 clean kitchen-equipped units about a garden patio with star-shaped mosaic FKK pool and central waterslide and underwater viewing. Minimart, tennis, volleyball, playground, kids' pool. Riding, all watersports, and a nude beach is near. German-owned, friendly to all comers. Open all year. Aptdo 95, E-03580 Alfaz del Pi, Alicante. Phone (65) 88 77 51.

La Rosina. Rents apartments with fine view and total privacy. Two nude beaches nearby, pool on grounds, supermarket at 1.5 km. Inland are grottos, castles, old villages. Owners promise personalized service including baby-sitting. Auto necessary. Phone (65) 73 08 98.

Altea—Punta del Mascarat. Rows of concrete housing monoliths testify to the greed of coastal developers pushing one more condo for one more tourist dollar. Nude beaches help the tourist to recoup and prepare for the next night's adventures.

From Alicante take Route 332 north to Altea. Just before the tunnels under the mountain, look for the house named El Aramo Mascarat on the right. Turn here and continue down the road (which turns into a dirt track) for 2 km. Park at the end; scramble down the steep path to the broad, pebbly beach.

Bénidorm—Playa Cala. A bleak memorial to Spain's juggernaut to build a tourist industry, Bénidorm's 100,000 annual tourists move through 50 discos and countless restaurants and bars. For them, Playa Cala, south of Bénidorm, is an FKK zone. A fence may be constructed to screen out the merely curious, and refreshments are available.

Spain

Santa Pola del Este—El Carabasi. This huge beach sees frequent if spotty nude use. The police cite only on complaints as natives are tolerant. Rumor has it that a naturist resort is planned to dominate the view over the pebbly beach. From Alicante take N-352 south. Follow signs to Santa Pola del Este and look for the north beach.

COSTA CALIDA

EL PORTÚS

Some bungalow and RV rentals, and 480 tent/RV sites, with sea and mountain view, an hour from Alicante airport. Pool, kids' pool, tennis, terrace restaurant/bar, shops, disco. Fish, snorkel, sail, surf (at times).

Drive 12 km southwest of Cartagena, direction Mazarron, to the sign Centre Naturista (the town of Portús is tiny). Open all year. Asociación Naturista de Andalucia y Murcia, El Portús, E-30313 Cartagena. Phone (68) 55 30 52.

ANDALUCIA

South from the highly commercial Valencia-to-Cartagena beach strip, the 195 km Alméria Coast was neglected; but that's changing. Its quiet coves and beaches, and dry, hot climate, supported by improved transportation and official approval for naturist values, portend the end of a tradition of poverty that is Alméria's image. There is a new kind of 'strip' where previously no one wanted to come.

VERA–MOJÁCAR AREA

Vera village and Mojácar are in Eastern Andalucia, 220 km south of Alicante or 100 km from Alméria airport:

Vera Playa Club, a grand hotel for Naturists, is sited on 1.5 km white sand Vera Beach with a panorama of mountains, across a clean, warm, somewhat choppy sea. Huge pool, windsurfing, volleyball, restaurant/bar, beach bar, minimart, disco, tennis, bike rentals, even Spanish lessons, trilingual bingo. Coach trips or rental car to nearby caves and villages. Beachside bungalows and, since 1989, 500 hotel rooms (ask for South wing). Rated ***; reasonable rates.

North of the port city Garruchia. Vera-Playa, Hoteles Playa, E-04740 Roquetas de Mar (Alméria). Phone (51) 33 36 02. Fax 33 32 07. Packaged air/land from USA: 1-800-828-9356.

J. Riera Rovira, Cala de Pals, Costa Brava, Spain.

Camping Almanzora. Managed by Asociación Naturista de Andalucia y Murcia. Formerly Las Palmeras. Its 220 tent/RV sites next to Vera Playa Club are a fertile oasis, with a vast outdoor pool, indoor heated pool, restaurant/bar, minimart. Free access to Playa Vera Club. Open all year. Centera de Garrucha a Villaricos, Aptdo. 131, Vera, Alméria. Phone (51) 45 65 76.

Las Rozas. Five km north of Vera Playa, a restored mine manager's mansion on a wooded hillside at base of 3,000' mountains. Cottages, camping and bike rentals. Pool, restaurant, bar, minimart, playground, volleyball, miniten. Owner-sculptor Kevin Heffernan and his wife Denise, Yorkshire expatriates, extend a hearty welcome. El Cortijo Las Rozas, E-04610 Las Herrerias, Cuevas del Amanzora, Alméria.

Mojácar–Torre del Peñon. A gorgeous Moorish village, Mojácar clings to a hillside; 2 km south of it naturists gather at lovely 'wild' Macenas Beach beyond Torre del Peñon.

El Cabo de Gata. Thinly-settled Sierra de Gata peninsula is suited to 'wild camping' and *desnudismo salvaje.* Get a local map and check out the national park for the Carboneras zone, San Pedro de las Negras, Las Sirenas and the Payazo Rodalquilar. Due east from Alméria.

SUN COAST BEACHES

The Sun Coast boasts an extension into southeast Spain of Saharan Africa dry and sunny climate: hot in summer, mild in winter. In October–April the days are great plus clean air and water.

Associación Naturista de Andalucia y Murcia is accelerating the acceptance of naturism in this ideally sunny zone that now reaches from Costa Natura in the west to El Portus on the Costa Calida in the east.

Malaga—Torremolinos. Topfree is permissible on Malaga beaches at hotels. At Tropicana, Las Barcas, Playamar, Guadaar, Fuengirola, Benalmadena, and Marbella, the old ways are flung aside.

Marbella was authorized in 1985 to announce mainland Spain's first municipally supervised nude beach, near Puerto Cabopino at the exit from Marbella in the direction of Fuengirola.

COSTA DEL SOL

COSTA NATURA

Between the Rock of Gibraltar (27 miles west) and Malaga (airport—60 miles east), don't miss this successful outcome of a gleam in a developer's eye. Two hundred Andalusian-style garden villas nestle into a coastal hillside on 7 ha with a view of the Straits. Condos, resident community; holiday weekly rentals; solar-heated pool, tennis, volleyball, jacuzzi, sauna, restaurant. Open all year.

J. Riera Rovira, Platja Nudista, Cala de Pals.

Playa Natura, E-29680 Estepona (Malaga). Phone (52) 80 15 00. Packaged, air/land from USA: 1-800-828-9356. At km 151 on Cadiz–Malaga highway.

Las Dunas. Every success has camp followers and this inexpensive, German-operated naturist campground flourishes on the beach next to Costa Natura.

ATLANTIC COAST

GULF OF CÁDIZ

Little-visited Gulfo de Cádiz offers a stark landscape for *desnudismo salvaje.* Preferred area is **Matalascañas**, north of Cádiz in the Parque de Donana, and Cala de los Castillejos and Los Canos de Meca near Jerez de la Frontera. Seville or Gibraltar are the accesses. Beware auto break-ins.

Los Caños de Meca is 10 km south of Cádiz on the road to Punto de Tarifa. It has a large adjacent campground, natural caves, clean fine sand and a freshwater run-off into the ocean suitable for natural showers.

MADRID AREA

PARK SOLARIA

Elipa Solarium. The capital of Spain now has an official nude sunbathing area posted in a park—no second seat to Munich will be accepted! The thatched solarium enclosure is on a hill at a popular sports complex, Elipa. From the pool you can mount earthen steps to the entrance. A sign calls for "complete nudity" inside. This enclosure was created after *desnudismo salvaje* began to take over the extensive lawns at Elipa—and you'll still find the unruly on the grass. There is unofficial nude sunbathing at other Madrid pools.

For background: *Madrid Naturista,* Bulletin of the Association for the Naturist Development of the Madrid Community, began publication in mid-1991. Aptdo. de Correos 47147, E-28080 Madrid.

E. Velez, Platja Nudista, Cala de Pals.

SWEDEN

Sweden can be reached by car ferry through its southern ports Ystad, Trelleborg and Malmö. Starting there, your opportunities follow.

Naked recreation fits well into a Swedish life: "You have to be clothed up to your ears for nine months, then summer comes," a Swede told us—"Wow, just take it all off!" The long coasts and many lakes offer the chance at every turn.

The Danes are said to be more plain and direct than the Swedes about being publicly nude. In both countries, however, it is acceptable anywhere that due thought and consideration is shown.

We list leading nude beaches. Most are established near favorite (often textile) campgrounds with telephones. Naturist clubs typically gravitate to these and do not own their own grounds, although a few do. Brochure available from Sveriges Naturistförbund, Box 502, S-23010 Skanör. Phone (46) 40 47 50 88.

FROM SKANÖR TO YNGSJÖ

Skanör Peninsula—Svanrevet (Swan's Reef) is 29 km south of Malmö by E-6, turning on Route 100. Skanör was famous in Hanseatic herring trade; visit early chapel. A bird refuge with broad white sand nude beach reached via SNF **Solhejdan Campground**. Volleyball, miniten, minigolf, badminton, playground, tent/caravan sites with hook-ups, pool, showers, sauna, community kitchen, room or caravan rental. June 15–Aug. 15. Welcoming naturists in any season. Box 60, S-23010 Skanör. Phone: (046) 40 47 50 88 or 40 47 26 93.

Ystad—Backåkra. Direct road from Malmö. The 2 km *fribadstrand* links Löderup Strandbad and Sandhammaren Lighthouse. Turn right at Backåkra and go through Hagestad Naturreservat (wildlife reserve) to the beach. Phone (0411) 770 00.

Yngsjö—Gropahalet Beach. 17 km south of Kristianstad. Route 63 from Filipstad for 8 km toward Hallefors to Lake Yngen. A government clothes-optional beach is at the south end of Yngsjö town beach. Toilets, play equipment, camp-sites.

Yngsjö—Sandvikens Camping. Officially recognized naturist beach next to Sandvikens Naturist Camping. S-68200 Filipstad. Phone (0590) 13450. Children's beach activities.

Olofström—Partisanens Naturistcamping. S-29060 Kyrkhult.

Jess Jessen, Windsurfing On the Sound.

Phone (0454) 711 08. Drive east from Kristianstad to Route 116 at Bromolla, turn left and go to Olofström, continue on Route 121 to Vilshult. Turn right to Kyrkhult and Galaxy Hotel and find Partisanens Naturistcamping in the back. Lake, tentsites, toilets/showers, playground. Phone (0454) 712 10.

FROM MALMÖ TO NORWAY

Helsingborg—Knähaken Beach. North of Malmö next to **Raa Vallar Campground** (clothed). Phone (042) 26 06 85.

Laholm—Mellby Beach. Half of 600 m sandy beach is naturist. Adjunct campground is clothed. **Marias Camping**, S-31200 Laholm. Phone: (0430) 25294.

Varberg—Getterön Beach. Find the bus loop at Getterön and park in the lot next to it. The clothed beach is to the left of the parking, and the toilets and refreshments are too. For the nude beach, take the steps to the left of the old hut and walk across the hill for 600 m, keeping to the left, to the cliffs.

South Göteborg—Smithska Udden Beach. Famous recreation area on Näset Peninsula, south of Vastra Frölunda, has very popular nude sector on north end. Drive out, or trolleys 2 and 3 go from Frölunda Square to Näset and change to bus 92.

Göteborg—Stora Amundön Beach. Take the Linnéplatsen-Brottkar bus line in the direction of Amundön. Or drive from Järntorget on Route 158 toward Särö. The Amundön exit is well marked. At the beach cross the bridge and the island to end of the path, turn south, cross two hills, and you're at the leeward, clothes-free area.

Hamburgsund—Kiddön Island. From Oslo go south—or from Göteborg go north on E-6, past Uddevalla, towards Fjällbacka. The last 35 km take Route 163 toward Fjällbacka and turn left for Hamburgsund. Kiddön Camping. S-45070 Hamburgsund. Phone (0525) 33147.

Strömstad—Kattholmen. An official nude beach, 30 km south of Halden (Norway).

BALTIC COAST

FROM KARLSKRONA TO NORRKÖPING

Karlskrona—Salto Beach. The *fribadstrand* is at Karlskrona's core recreation complex. From city center take Järnvägstorget–Borgmästarekajen–Fisktorget–Björkholmskajen–Björkholmen to Saltö Beach and signs for *fribadstrand.* Campground is clothed, with van to beach; May-Aug: Dragsö Camping, S-37103 Karlskrona. Phone: (0455) 153 54.

Kalmar—Värsnäs Beach. The town at the causeway to Öland Island has a vast nude beach, Värsnäs, at Vassnäseudd 5 km north.

Öland Island—is lovely with windmills and wildflowers. Driving onto it from Kalmar, turn north for Borgholm Beach, midway to tip. Close to **Ekerum Campground** (textile). Phone (0485) 555 90. Böda-Bukten Beach is on the north point. No campground. For a third beach, Näckstrand, in Mörbylånga, south from the causeway and 9 km south of Farjestaden: drive Route 136 south to Vickleby, turn right to the inland shore. The beach is near **Haga Park Camping** (textile), phone: (0485) 406 70.

Gotland Island—reached by ferry from Oskarshalm, north of Kalmar—is a pagan wonderland for the Swedes! June 19th (Midsummer's Eve) kicks off festivities that include July's Stangaspelen (Viking Olympics) and August's Kraftorfest (Crayfish festival that rivals Munich's Oktoberfest for partying). The allure of Visby—a medieval town with city walls that attest to its prominence in the Hanseatic League—is captivating. Be sure to visit **Sjaustre-viken** nude beach between Ljugarn and Gammelgarn on the east coast, and **Norsta Aura** by Faarö in the north.

Norrköping—Camp Tyrol. On Vikbolandet peninsula. Drive Route 209 east 30 km toward Arkösund, turn right for Rönö. After 3 km find sign for Tobo, and 2 km later signs to the camp. May–Aug. S-61024 Vikbolandet. Phone (0125) 302 70.

STOCKHOLM AREA

FROM NYKÖPING TO NORA

Nyköping/Buskhyttan—Västra Kovik Beach. Take Route 53 from Nyköping south toward Oxelösund. After 3 km turn right to Navekvarn and continue for 9 km to the turnoff for Tunaberg. After 3 km find a road going off left opposite a lake. Take that road another 3 km to the parking of Västra Kovik which has cliffs and a sandy beach. No camping.

Djursnäs Naturistcamping. South from Stockholm on Route 73 toward Nynäshamn to Ösmo where you turn right on Route 225. Soon turn left to St. Vika and find road to Djursnäs. Campground belongs to Naturistföreningen Stockholms Naturvänner. Situated on inlet of the Baltic. PL 3596, S-14800 Ösmo. Phone (0752) 370 26.

Agesta Beach. From Stockholm drive south to Farsta Strand, continue south Agesta Bridge-Lansvagen-Vidjevagen, turning left on Bonasvagen. Help phone: (08) 41 69 00.

Stockholm—City. On hot days visit the Långholm Park in western Stockholm on the south side of Västerbron Bridge. Take subway to Hornstull stop, then bus 54 or 66 or walk to Högalidsgatan or Bergsund street beaches. Contact: Naturistentusiasterna, Box 15127, S-10465 Stockholm. Phone: (0480) 41 69 00.

Stockholm Archipelago—Stora Idskär. Tentsites, rental cabins, kitchen, grocery, clubhouse. Island of Naturistföreningen Stockholms Naturvänner. Game courts, water sports. Visitors welcome. June–Aug. Box 444, S-10126 Stockholm. Island phone: (0764) 39306.

Mullhyttan—Trumöbadet. Drive west from Stockholm to Örebro, continuing on E-18 towards Karlskoga. Turn left on Route 204 to Mullhyttan, where signs appear for Trumöbadet, in the Örebro Nature Reserve, near Öna. No camping or sand beach and few facilities but has charm. Phone (0585) 107 20.

Nora—Gustavsberg Camping, 32 km northwest of Örebro in Bergslagen, a vast forest with abandoned mines and lakes. From Nora, drive north toward Siggebohyttan. After a few km find Gustavsberg Camping on right: 140 tent/caravan sites, 60 hookups, 10 rental rooms. June–Aug. Box 116, S-71323 Nora. Phone (0587)105 45.

GULF OF BOTHNIA

FROM UPPSALA NORTH

Öregrund—Tallparksbadet. Öregrund is where ferries leave for Gräsö Island. The town beach includes a nude sector in the Tallparksbadet on the ferry harbor. Go via Uppsala by Route 288 northeast, or from Stockholm by E-3 to Norrtälje and then Route 76.

Rullsand Beach. Straight north from Uppsala to coastal Skutskär is an official *fribadstrand.* Said to be one of the finest beaches in the Uplands, 1 km Rullsand Beach has both shallow and deep shelf for swimming, and surfing at the mouth of the Dalalvens River.

Rullsand Camping with 350 tent/caravan sites (122 with hookups) rents 10 cabins. Cafe, restaurant. Canuding, fishing; boat and bike rentals. S-81400 Skutskär. Phone (026) 860 46 or 761 89. Local SNF contact phone: (08) 27 00 88.

SWITZERLAND

Nowhere outside Switzerland is an equal contrast found between 'traditional' Naturists, who may also abstain from the use of tobacco, alcohol, and meat as part of a philosophical ethic of a free body culture; and the youth today who pull on underwear as outerwear, or become casual nudists at the drop of their trousers, without having to articulate a coherent freedom reason or context.

In the latter spirit of liberty, topfree and nude sunbathing are tolerated in many Swiss parks somewhat in the way drugs are condoned. A Zurich ordinance of 1989 has offically accepted nudity, called *blütteln*, in municipal pools after a public opinion poll found only 18% opposition. Whatever a quest for freedom may be, Swiss officials rarely interfere.

In contrast, the 17 Swiss naturist clubs (5 are in Italian- and 1 in French-speaking cantons) mostly demand an INF membership card for entrance. They articulate a philosophy and they're happy to be exclusive. To visitors, they open a fascinating world of standards that are almost unconsidered in other nations. To visit these clubs, obtain information from the *INF Handbook* and the *Organisation naturiste suisse*, PF 12, CH-2075 Thielle (NE), phone (032) 83 23 95.

Switzerland is also becoming exclusive due to prices—few outsiders can afford the cost of living. An exception is the simple, wholesome, cost-conscious way of life at the Swiss Naturist club grounds. To base a visit at a club such as Die Neue Zeit (Thielle) is at once an eye-opener into a valuable tradition and the way to beat the high cost of visiting Switzerland.

Elsi Fankhauser (center). Lake Swim. Neue Zeit, Thielle.

DIE NEUE ZEIT

"Thielle" is the fond common name for Switzerland's most honored Naturist terrain—now in the midst of decisions and changes. The keepers of the flame of traditional Swiss Naturism are mostly aging. They perform rituals of vegetarian meal preparation in the great house of legendary founders Edi and Elsi Fankhauser (both still present). Most recently, a modern hotel is proposed, which would displace many of the tents and caravans; bringing more money, allowing more memberships, but essentially paving the natural character of Neue Zeit.

The grounds fill on weekends with young families. Whether they keep the dietary standard is uncertain; they rarely join the workshops in FKK practices conducted by the old-timers. However they certainly are fit and happy, a credit to body acceptance.

Some bungalow, dormitory, tent/RV site rentals at this club on Lake Neuchâtel. Rather than a public restaurant a community kitchen and common vegetarian dining. Playground, trampoline, aquacise, volleyball, boules, dance, crafts, singing. Open all year. CH-2075 Thielle. Phone (032) 83 17 99.

GENEVA: THONON PLAGE

Beyond Thonon on the south (French) side of Lake Geneva is Thonon Plage and next to it, an attractive free beach with round pebbles, shade trees and agreeable atmosphere. Information: Georges Gervais, Bonnatrait CH-74140 Sciez. Phone (50) 72 77 37.

☞ On the west side, walk between the beautifully landscaped (but not nude) Thonon Beach and the picturesque old Chateau de Ripaille. Find the path between the Domaine vineyard and the lake and follow it to the clothed bathers; the nude section is on the east end.

LAUSANNE: CAMPING CLUB LÉMAN

A verdant, landscaped site, on the Venoge River just off Lake Léman. Welcomes visitors, a splendid base for visiting French Switzerland. Dorm, tent/RV sites, some rentals. Pool, playground, boules, badminton, community kitchen, minimart. June–Sept. Off N-1 at Morges. Chemin de la Venoge 31, CH-1028 Préverenges. Phone (021) 71 83 98.

Jerry Derbyshire, Horseshoes at Glen Eden.

UNITED KINGDOM

The Central Council for British Naturism began in the late 1970s to bring about legal nude beaches for the U.K. The campaign, strategized by Alan McCombe (after 1980 also the INF president), and spearheaded in District Council contacts by Charlotte Peters, induced politicians to provide authorized nude beaches in Scotland, York, Suffolk, Kent and Sussex. The continuing campaign more recently focuses on the National Trust, a kind of National Park Service.

Simultaneously, uncounted unorganized nudists 'voted with their feet' to make more U.K. beaches available for the use of the whole natural person. This anarchic repossession of the shore-recreation enclosures, as it were, was abetted if not organized by sculptor Phil Vallack from his editorial desk.

The outcome of official and anarchistic initiatives, each aiding the other, is a beaches-for-the-people development unimagined 30 years ago.

More recently, the guidebooks improve and, no surprise, many with enrichment in mind capitalize on what's been done. The idealism of 1975-85 is, however, indelible.

Only the Creator is indifferent. Evidently not caring to see in Britain and in public the creatures He made in His image, the Creator messed up the climate. He made beaches aptly called 'grotty', coarse gravel shingle mixed with sand.

Since a nude experience under a bleak British sky is rare, who's the wiser? To be a naturist from the U.K. often means traveling away from the U.K. To make up for negligence, however, the Creator did make lots of nudist entrepreneurs.

Some altruistically organize good, gregarious swims and clubs for the plebes.

Others dispose the ecdysical options for secretive parsons, stockbrokers, Oxbridge dons and parliamentary luminaries.

Dubious nudist enterprises are supported in print by the page-three, only-in-Britain girly magazine that claims a naturist descent and intention and yet harbors dark secrets, publishing from Liechtenstein.

Hoping to make up somewhat for the inattentiveness of the Creator, we describe some of the more accessible beaches. They are approved by those who have voted with their feet, mostly in the south. For others, study of U.K. naturist guides is needed.

Central Council for British Naturism, Assurance House, 35-41 Hazelwood Road, Northampton NN1 1LL, England. CCBN's magazine *British Naturism* is US$5 for a sample copy or $12/year.

Phil Vallack, *Free Sun Guide to Beaches of Europe* and *Inland Free Sun Guide*. Each regularly updated. US$15 each from 16 Viewbank, Hastings, East Sussex TN35 5HB.

Naturist Guide Book, by David Martin. US$16 from Coast & Country Publications, 3 Mayfield Ave, Scarborough, N. Yorkshire, Y012 6DF; phone (0723) 37 06 91.

Trevor Frank, Studland Bay, West Country, England.

England

LONDON AREA

LANDED CLUBS

London Area sites in commuting distance include, in addition to these: Spielplatz Club in Sussex, and a beach on the Isle of Sheppey in the mouth of the Thames. See those listings too.

Brocken Hurst is impressive; owned and operated on 50 acres of parkland by the Naturist Foundation. Tent/RV sites and extensive recreation facilities include a pool lined with Venetian tiles. Historically a major force in British Naturism and quite independent of the CCBN. Naturist Foundation, Orpington, Kent BR5 4ET. Phone (0689) 71200.

London Health and Sauna Club. Introduced many newcomers to the joys of naturism. Mixed-sex sauna, fitness, swimming and social club; single males discouraged. Seymour Hall, Seymour Place, London W1. Phone (01) 837-7714.

Silverleigh Health & Fitness Center. Spas, sauna, steam baths, massage, tanning areas, aromatherapy, naturopathy. Clothes-optional, with nudity required weekends and Tuesday and Friday evenings. Driving, leave M-2 at Junction 3 and follow signs for Brands Hatch and West Kingsdown. From Brands Hatch continue to a Texaco garage. Silverleigh is the fourth building on the left after Texaco. Phone (0836) 40 53 34.

EAST ANGLIA

SUFFOLK

Corton Sands. Accorded official nude status by a margin of more than 2-to-1 in the vote of the Waveney District Council. The CCBN termed Corton Sands (a.k.a. Gunton Sands) "possibly the best stretch of official nude beach to date." Nice sand backed by a concrete retaining wall, easy access, draws many Londoners on hot days. Included in tourist brochure. Phone (0502) 56 59 89.

☞ Route A-12 takes you northeast from London to Lowestoft. From there continue on A-12 (now Yarmouth Road) north toward Corton, then B-1385 (Corton Road) north, a total of 2 miles. Park on the road at Pleasurewood Hills American Theme Park. Locate the Tramps Alley cliff driveway (local bus 603 also runs to the top of Tramps Alley). Descend it to the beach, turn north (left) and walk 200 m. Toilets are a 10-minute walk toward Lowestoft; a pub is just 10 minutes in the other direction.

NORFOLK

Holkham Hall Bay Beach. Privately owned Holkham Bay beach—between Wells and Burnham—is on the Holkham Hall estate. The Viscount Coke controls the property and makes 700 m of shore available to naturist use. Phone (0263) 82 43 29.

☞ Drive A-149 from Wells towards Hunstanton. Opposite the gates of Holkham Hall, turn right on Lady Anne Road to parking. You will see a posted map showing where the naturist area is located. Walk along the beach or the paths to the west past the small lake and chalet. The clothes-free zone begins here and extends west. Nudity to the east of the chalet is discouraged.

LANDED CLUBS

Broadlands is a good base if you visit Lowestoft's Corton Beach and other East Anglia attractions northeast of London. Pool, tent/RV sites, sports. Brickle Road, Upper Stoke Holy Cross, Norwich NR14 8NG. Phone (05086) 2907.

THAMES & CHILTERNS

LANDED CLUBS

St.-Albans—Spielplatz Club. Founded in 1930, the oldest and largest naturist club of England, venerable yet lively Spielplatz is 25 miles from London.

Frank Sutcliffe, Water Rats, London Children (1888).

Displaying linkage with the German origins of naturism, it's the only fully-residential grounds with 120 permanent residents and 650 visiting members. Marble-lined pool, sauna, miniten, badminton,12 acres of woodland, rental cabins, restaurant. Write before visiting to Spielplatz, Lye Lane, Bricket Wood, St. Albans, Herts. AL2 3TD. Phone (0923) 87 21 26.

EAST MIDLANDS

LINCOLNSHIRE

Saltfleetby-Theddlethorpe Dunes Nature Reserve—North. Just to the north of the preserve is a spot favored by the Victoria Sun Beach Club. Along Coast Road 1031, look for the Sea Lane exactly halfway between Saltfleet and Meers Bridge. Take the right-hand fork of the Sea Lane toward the nature reserve parking area. Access to the beach is by the derelict gun site; walk along the beach for 400 yards to the favored area. A bylaw excludes use of the fine beach and dunes that extend south to Mablethorpe's North End.

SOUTH EAST

BRIGHTON BEACH

Brighton—an hour's lark by train from London—is notorious for its catchpenny arcades and fun fairs. It added an official nude beach to its brochures just 50 m east of the main town promenade. It's a pebble beach slippped between the marina and Peter Pan's Playground. Take the Volks Railway to the end of the line and walk back along the beach to the naturist signs.

Brighton's Prince Regent has clothes-free bathing, Sunday from 5:50-6:30, October through April.

BEACHES

Isle of Sheppey: Leysdown Beach. A holiday getaway isle in the mouth of the Thames east of London. At Leysdown East, Sheppey offers an official naturist beach with a mix of sand and shingle and a grassy bank. Hundreds attend in good weather; it is displayed in Sheppey tourist brochures. Phone (0795) 66 53 24. Follow road through town and a mile beyond to Mile End Gate. Where the road meets the sea wall, park, walk east along sea wall past old wood chalets. The free beach extends for 250 m.

Swalecliffe—Long Rock. This officially nude beach is "grotty," thence its name, swale cliff. On a spit of land 600 m long that extends into the estuary, it is backed by a Recreation Ground with parking (ask access at Swalecliffe rail station), but loses its shingle beach at high tide. Alternate access is from the main Whitstable Beach, 1 mile east. Evidence of desperation to have beaches. Windbreak essential. Phone (0227) 36 19 11.

Hastings—Fairlight Glen. An officially posted nude beach which has been termed "a very grotty cove." It's scenic and warmed by the sun under 600' cliffs. Fairlight has limited the parking so it's best to park at Hastings County Park on Fairlight Road. From here ask for the path. Or park at Fishmarket Car Park on the Hastings seafront and climb or take the lift up the cliff at the end of Rock A Nore Road, and walk by the footpath in the direction of Fire Hills, past Ecclesbourne Glen. At Fairlight Glen rough steps descend to the rocky shore. Care should be taken after rainy weather as the path gets very slippery.

Nearest facilities at Hastings. Or enjoy the convenience of camping on nearby Barley Lane at Shearbarn Caravan Site, phone (0424) 42 35 83.

SOUTHERN

LANDED CLUBS

Bournemouth & District Outdoor Club & Holiday Centre. With a view of the Avon Valley, this large site, 11 km from Bournemouth and convenient to Studland Beach, offers numerous activities, outdoor and indoor. Matchams Drive, Matchams, Ringwood, Hants., BH24 2BU. Phone (04254) 2121.

South Hants Sun Club welcomes visitors to the Portsmouth area, the ferry port to Isle of Wight, Channel Islands, France. Hotel rooms, tent/RV rentals and sites. Pool, volleyball, restaurant and darts. Color brochure from SHSC, Stockers, North Boarhunt, Fareham, Hants PO17 6JS. Phone (0329) 83 29 19.

B. Hymer, National Trust Signage, English Beach. Courtesy British Naturism.

England

WEST COUNTRY

DEVON

Slapton Sands—Pilchards Cove. This site is England's oldest nude beach. Holding a secured place in the hearts of naturist Britons, Pilchards attracts a new, under-40 crowd despite only a grotty beach, occasional falling rocks, and dangerous undertow. A windbreak is helpful too, yet a loyal cadre comes, you'll see why. Route 379 south from Dartmouth to the north end of Slapton Sands. Park at Strete Gate, where the road intersects the coast; walk ten minutes north to the rock fall at the beach end.

Littleham Cove near Sidmouth. A good walk west from the Steamer Steps at the middle of the Budleigh-Salterton Beach. Some shelter from wind and privacy is afforded by large rocks and a 500' cliff.

Torquay—Petitor Beach. Around the headland north from Oddicombe Beach. From Torquay take Petitor Road east to the sea, park by the golf course off B-3199, enter it by a gate and continue down a steep, stepped slope to the beach. Phone (0803) 27428.

Bournemouth—Studland Bay. Fine sands with good dunes and swimming. Studland is popular with naturists and accepted locally due to many years of sensible behavior. A good spot for families. Top of the pick.

Local tourism information, including nude beach, phone (0929) 42 28 85.

Beach User Group Studland (BUGS) phone Barry, (0202) 69 99 08.

Recommended naturist camping is contacted in advance % Studland Summer Camp, 183 Brighton Road, Lancing, Sussex BN15 8JB. July only, cold showers, chemical toilets, no singles, no hookups; a noncommerical act of generosity, congenial times organized by Roger, because he's glad to do it.

☞ Access to Studland Bay can be by ferry across the harbor, leaving car in Poole. Or drive around Poole Harbor via Wareham and Corfe Castle and drive north on the ferryport road. Turn right into Knoll National Trust Carpark just past Knoll Hotel, park and walk north on the beach 25 minutes. Or drive north closer to the ferry dock, watch for clustered cars by the road, a sure sign of a nude beach over the dunes.

Weymouth—Durdle Door. This beach area is larger than first appears and is both sandy and rocky. A large rock juts out of the clear water and can be used for sunning or diving. A tunnel in the rock can be swum through, leading to a smaller, deserted beach.

☞ Find Durdle Door on the map next to Lulworth Cove (Weymouth side); it is well marked by road signs. At the campground pay to park on the cliff, descend it taking a trail fork to right. On the beach walk in Weymouth direction, past white chalk sea rocks and shore rocks, to just before another headland, the secluded naturist area.

CORNWALL

Perranporth Beach. This nude beach was a vote shy of official designation, but has won the town's acceptance. Dunes, sandy beach. Swim with caution. Take 3285 from Perranporth toward Goonhaven. At the top of a hill find the Perran Sands Holiday Village on the left. The next left is the one you want (marked Merther). Take this road to the end and park. Follow a path to Lost Church (1 mile), then over the dunes to the beach. The nude zone is 200 yards north.

Gorran Harbour—Vault Beach. Drive south from St. Austell on B-3273 to Gorran Harbour. There drive west up narrow, steep, "no through" Lamledra Road toward the youth hostel. Park in the National Trust carpark. A 3/4 mile footpath leads in front of a hotel west to Bow beach (the map name); keep going through the textile end to the free beach.

Trevor Frank, Studland Bay, West Country, England.

England

Pednevounder Beach. There's a free zone between Logan Rock and Porthcumo, on a clean sandy beach called Pednevounder. Spectacular coast. With its good swimming, Pednevounder gets growing use from both Brits and tourists. A somewhat difficult cliff access means caution by the elderly and young children, who may well handle it.

☞ Off Route 3315, almost to Land's End, find the hamlet of Treen down a "No Through Road" road. Naturists lunch at Treen's Logan Rock Inn, and may camp here too. Path to beach is southwest from the Treen post office down a farm road, crossing the Cornwall North Coast Footpath.

St.-Austell—Polgaver Bay: Cornish Leisure World. Benefitting from a miniature train that can chug you down to the beach, family use increases. Cornish Leisure World opens this private naturist beach daily, 10 a.m.–6 p.m., May–Sept. as part of its Carlyon Bay holiday facilities. The 15 acres of white sandy beach are backed with brushy dunes. From St. Austell, take A-390 toward Plymouth. At Holmbush turn right and follow signs to Carlyon Bay. Cornish Leisure World's entrance is well marked. Phone (0726) 81 42 61.

Starting in 1991 naturist tent/RV sites are offered by top-rated textile **Bethesda Farm Camping,** a 5 minute walk from the nude beach. Phone (0726) 81 27 35.

Helford River. Rent a boat for discreet nude use of the many coves and inlets of Helford River and Carrick Roads. Avoid the oyster beds. Study the tide chart to avoid stranding in a mud bank.

LANDED CLUBS

Bristol Solarians lovely wooded ground is opened to visitors. Tent/RV rentals. Pool, sports courts. Tara, Mapleridge Road, Chipping Sodbury, Bristol BS17 6PB. Phone (0454) 28 42 56.

NORTH WEST

AINEDALE: FORMBY BEACH

Serving Liverpudlians with the tranquility of a nature preservation area, dune sunning at Formby is sheltered and can even get very warm. It's a pleasant walk to the water's edge for a dip. Main area is a mile south of Ainsdale rail station. Beach access is at Pontings. A small road leads off toward the sea. Park as far south as you can, walk south (left) and strip down, staying out of cordoned areas!

YORKSHIRE

BEACHES

Bridlington—Fraisthorpe Sands. Two miles south of Bridlington, with a 30-year tradition of nude use, Fraisthorpe is now officially nude.

☞ From Hull take A-165 north toward Bridlington. At Fraisthorpe town make a turn for Auburn Farm and follow its unpaved track to a parking lot, pay, walk 1.5 miles to the shore. On the beach walk south until you reach Earls Dyke Stream; the nude beach is there. Toilets at Auburn Farm. Phone (0262) 67 34 74.

Scarborough Region. Several unofficial naturist areas. Recommended:

Johnny Flintons Harbour at the north end of Cayton Bay (aka Osgodby Beach). Owned by the National Trust, and once an official beach, naturists have been on this spot for over 40 years. Park at Killerby Cliff and walk north one mile. Or park in Osgodby and take the path down Knipe Point Drive through the woods and to the cove.

Other Scarborough options: **Red Cliffs** (park at Killerby Cliff and descend a path to Cayton Bay), and **Cornelian Bay** where discretion is needed when fishermen are about.

HUMBERSIDE

Hull—Easington Beach. North of Spurn Head and east of Hull is an unspoiled sand beach frequented by birds alone. North Sea air can be chilling yet on a bright warm day this spot can't be beat. Park just north of Easington and walk to the north. The area used extends to Holmpton.

CUMBRIA

BARROW: ROAN HEAD DUNES

A beach for sunning—the currents can be dangerous—next to (not in) sand dunes of the Nature Conservancy, near Barrow at Roan Head (Thwaite Flats). Park at Roan Head Beach and shopping lot. Walk southwest a half mile to beyond the headland at Lousy Point. Yes, Lousy Point.

NORTHUMBRIA

BEACHES

Ross Back Sands consists of 2 miles of deserted golden sand, clean if cold water, and dunes for wind shelter and privacy. The hamlet of Ross is north of Bedford off A-1. In Ross, look for the green lane that leads to the sea; park here—do not block the access—and follow the pathway through the fields to the dunes. The beach can be enjoyed for a mile north or south.

Berwick—Holy Island (Lindesfarne). A mile-long causeway leads to this pagan attraction and possible naturist use, away from locals and tourists, on the east and north shores. N.B: the causeway vanishes twice daily during high tide. Do plan!

Northumbria naturists also visit unofficial beaches in Redcar, Skinningrove, Hummersea, Druridge Bay and Cheswick.

Scotland

BEACHES

The reader may wish to visit these unofficial clothes-optional beaches.

Near **Dunbar,** in the John Muir Country Park towards Peffer Burn, is an expansive sandy beach.

Tentsmuir Forest on the far north side, away from the parking area, has naturist use. A nearby Bed and Breakfast welcomes naturists: phone (025) 08 42 18.

Old Barn Beach, 2 miles north of Nairn, is used au naturel by locals.

Solway Firth coast with its many coves and bays is the discreet choice of some.

Other possibilities:

Southerness Beach, Powillimount Beach, The Isle Of Mull.

An excellent source for Scottish naturist sites is the 1991 Naturist Guide Book, by David Martin. A Coast & Country Publication, 3 Mayfield Ave., Scarborough, North Yorkshire, Y0126DF; phone (0723) 37 06 91.

CLUBS

Scottish Outdoor Club. Private 12 acre, 3-mile-long Inchmurrin Island on fabled Loch Lomond lake. A popular site over 50 years old—a milestone of British naturism, and a resource where you may tent (or rent a room) and cook, play volleyball, socialize and disco with the veterans, and of course lake swim. Inchmurrin Hotel/restaurant shares the island. You'll be met at arranged time and ferried over. It is required that you make contact in advance with an SAE to Archie Prentice, 16 Oxgang Road, Grangemouth FK3 9BY. Phone (0324) 48 54 85.

Winter Swims—Western Baths, Glasgow, has Winter swims on Sunday mornings. Such nude swims are organized at other Scottish pools. For current times/places call Archie, phone (0324) 48 54 85. You may also ask Archie about the Scottish Outdoor Club camping on Inchmurrin Island.

Wales

GOWER PENINSULA

West from London by M-4 is Swansea. A few miles west of Swansea is The Gower, a large peninsula on the Bristol Channel whose southern exposure has a dune expanse delightful to all naturists—the best of Britain au naturel!

The coast has many coves, spectacular cliffs, great sandy beaches. The National Trust keeps up a cliff path most of the way around The Gower. It will lead you to the hidden coves, and a tide table from the Tourist Office in Swansea will help you to avoid surprises.

Naturism on The Gower is popular albeit unofficial. Naturist lodgings on The Gower, phone (0792) 85 02 86.

☞ These areas are regularly visited by naturists. You may obtain tourist information to other, wide-ranging possibilities. Also check the U.K. Naturist guides for maps and details.

Drive A-4118 out of Swansea. Turn right at Little Reynoldston, left at Burry Green, and follow the road south to Llangennith. Go through the village, turning left at the roundabout, to the parking at the end of the road. Follow the path onto the beach, and walk west 10 minutes.

Another frequented area is near the point of Whitford Burrows. Reached by SS-4493. Park at Llanmadoc, walk to Cwm Ivy Farm, then north up the Burrows nearly to its end.

HARLECH: MORFA DYFFRYN

An excellent beach south of Harlech, between the towns of Llanbedr and Dyffryn Ardudwy. Although unofficially naturist, some say its camaraderie makes Morfa Dyffryn (pron. Duffrin) the 'British Montalivet'. Backed by the Morfa Nature Reserve the undeveloped beach stretches for miles and yet, an ice cream vendor visits!

Many beachgoers rent a tent/RV site at clothing-mandatory Benar Beach Campsite on the shore a mile south, phone (0317) 571.

☞ Access is by the Harlech to Barmouth road. Turn off A-496 just south of Llanenddwyn. Take Fford Benar Lane, over a rail crossing, to parking at Benar Beach Campsite. Then it's a 20 minute walk north from (stay off the dunes!).

LLEYN PENINSULA: PORTH NEIGWL

The middle two miles of the popular beach at Porth Neigwl, known as Hell's Mouth, sees frequent nude use. A beguiling strand backed by clay-grass, gently sloping cliffs. An ideal spot to bring children.

☞ The best access is from the east—Llanengan—where a minor road leads to within 300 yards of the beach and even has space for parking. Take Route 497 turnoff from 487 and follow it toward Abersoch. At Llanbedrog take Route 4413 to Llanengan.

M. Alexander, Serebrjanyj Bor Beach, Moscow, USSR.

USSR

Social nudity in Soviet Russia as in other Slavic states has a dual tradition: folk and avant-garde. The peasant tradition includes family nude bathing, usually gender-segregated. Thus the last czar was photographed with his retinue in full frontal nudity on a pier of a lake. The early years after the revolution saw a good deal of intellectually founded nudity in art or as social protest—but with the consolidation of the Stalinist regime, all of that ended.

Today old customs survive without fanfare. The Baltic states of Estonia, Latvia and Lithuania harbor nude bathing at such chill and austerely beautiful sites as the Neringa Peninsula. The Black Sea resorts allow some too, supposedly for therapeutic reasons. Russian baths are a refuge for the clothes-optional soul.

In the 1970s nudity became a theme of Soviet art and fiction. Young writers brought skinny-dipping and sexual freedom to small literary magazines. *Literaturnaya Gazeta*, then the cultural arbiter, denounced the themes as "immoral." But by 1990, the Stalinist straitjacket was ripped off.

Ted Koppel travelled to Russia to show in a 'shocking' ABC telecast that nudity is now accommodated in art, television, and daily life with a candor that the 'free' US media refuse to match.

Surely much of it is tutored by *Playboy*, little by Naturism. Yet the beaches can provide an experience of body acceptance that is without exploitation. Here are the best sites to date.

MOSCOW AREA

SEREBRJANYJ BOR

Since 1988, Moscovites gather on a site near the Moscow Ring road, one of several sandy beaches along a side loop on the left bank of the Moscow River. On the left part of "Serebrjanyj bor 3" beach they swim or sunbathe, play volleyball, cards or chess, as an occasional drunk gawps. Up to 100 men, women and families may be present. Mounted police protect the park and don't trouble nude people.

See photo on previous page.

☞ **Serebrjanyj bor**—Silver Pine park—lies between the Borossilovski and Kuncjevskij districts. From central Moscow you can get to the park—at the northwest quadrant of the city—by excursion boat to "Serebrjanyj bor."

Driving, the nearest prominent name on a map is Tatanskaja Street, which leads directly into the park from the Ring road.

By metro, get off at "Polezhaevskaja" station, transfer to electric tram 20 or 65, and go to the last stop. There go left, past a beer bar and a 50 m fence, and turn right, pass a children's playground, go over two footbridges, veer right and the nude beach is about 200 m through pine trees, on the river just before the lifesaving station.

A naturist contact: Boguszevskij Leonid, nl. Boszaïa Truzinskaïa, dom 58/60 kv. 50, Moscow D-56 USSR. Phone 254 56 96.

BALTIC STATES

LITHUANIA: PALANGA BEACH

An area of this clothes-optional beach 180 miles west of Vilnius was exclusively reserved for women's nude use, according to *Literaturnaya Gazeta.* The custom was sought by the Lithuanians. The absence of men created the conditions for a thriving black market in food, medicines and clothing, exposed in 1985. The few female police refused to operate undercover—that is, without clothing—to make arrests.

The northern part of the erstwhile East Prussian Courian Isthmus is Lithuanian 'health beach' territory, renamed Neringa.

ESTONIA: KLOOGA-ROND

Backed by dense pine woods, beaches on the Gulf of Finland have long been clothes-free. Actor Peter Ustinov recalled as a boy, in 1928, sculpting the beach clay: "Most people bathed and sculpted naked, only dressing again to meet the hazards of the forest."

Klooga-Rond beach is 40 km east of Tallin. Informally established no later than the 1960s, by the early 1980s it drew up to 3,000 enthusiasts.

Still the problems didn't get serious until some nudists staged a Miss Nude Estonia contest in 1985. Coverage by Estonian television led to official censure.

Told they had given offense, Klooga nudists fetched a bulldozer and built sand walls around their sunning–volleyball–pageant area. Told to knock down the ramparts, the nudists appealed to the Estonian Supreme Court—and won. To console auhorities they brought back the bulldozer and increased the height of the ramparts to 10 feet.

Contact: Eesti Nudistide Selts, % Kaljo Piiskop, pk 907, SU-200034 Tallin, Estonia.

LATVIA

Naturists organized under the name Saule (Sun) meet on a beach 40 km north of Riga. Contact: Nikolai Manyuck, St. Marias 119–7, SU-226011 Riga. Phone 280 019.

YUGOSLAVIA

Exultantly said the Tourist Director of Slovenia, "Yugoslavia is becoming one great nude beach. No one wants to stop what's happening. No one is trying to stop it. And no one could stop it."

But in 1991, Slovenia and Croatia were in deadly conflict with Serbia. Tourists fled. A Yugoslav success story knitted together 45 years earlier was unravelling.

The Yugoslav ruling party of 30 years earlier was the world's first investor to provide major capital to emerging Naturist Tourism. Today it's acknowledged as the fastest-growing sector. Then, it took courage to recognize and finance the naked people market.

However, even before the Balkan Compromise came apart the naturist sector was in trouble. In May 1990 two INF vice-presidents met with directors of leading Yugoslav naturist holiday centers. Keynote speaker was longtime Yugoslav advocate of naturism, Jerko Sladoljev. The news was that Yugoslav occupancy rates at the hotels and apartments in the naturist holiday centers dropped about 30% since 1980. Duration of stay dropped from 12 to 10 days. Punta Skala, renowned for nudity, already shut its doors to naturists. More centers might follow.

On the positive side, central and south Adriatic nude facilities continued to show a 2% annual occupancy growth. These were late to develop. They also have more contemporary appeal with sophisticated attractions.

Yugoslav entrepreneurs added that the northerly

Istria Peninsula, Yugoslavia.

Yugoslavia

Istrian centers are run down, have few amenities, need investment. Other poor countries—Greece, Portugal, Turkey, Spain—now have naturist appeal. Also most beaches of Yugoslavia now have this appeal. "There are two kinds of naturist centers in Yugoslavia. You can stay in a hotel which caters for all holiday makers and spend the day on a nearby naturist beach. Or stay at a naturist center."

We recommend the central and south Adriatic naturist facilities—those least affected by the Balkan conflict or by burnout. Current brochures and information: Yugotours, Chesman House, 150 Regent St., London W1, England. Phone (01) 734-7321.

Don't bother to ask the New York Yugotours office. Americans aren't yet treated as part of the naturist market.

Skinny-Dip Tours and others book Yugoslavia. Two-week packages are really good bargains. Senior citizen packages begin at age 50.

Coastal steamers are a good way to sample the decentralized FKK-friendly delights of this land. A boat beats a bus, going almost anywhere.

Avoid July–August if possible. Travel light, cabs are scarce. Bring sunscreen and an air mattress—pebbly beaches are the Creator's curse on this Eden.

ISTRIA COAST

Bulging into the Adriatic Sea at the northwest point of Yugoslavia, Istria suffers from the conflict. It's the magnet and gateway for descending German and Austrian tourists with RVs and tents, the bread-and-butter of the naturist tour trade. With a lovely jagged/rocky coast, wooded bays, picturesque seaside towns, a green hilly inland and mild climate, Istria deserves a better day.

THE RESORTS

Lanterna Peninsula—Solaris. The popular resorts Solaris and Lanterna share Lanterna Peninsula, 10 km from Porec. Rocky beaches and woods along 5 km of shore allow guests to spread out. These self-contained resorts provide everything from supermarkets to hammock rental. The Lanterna beach is clothes-required. Only Solaris is a true naturist resort with clothing-optional everything.

Koversada, the dowager summer-city of Yugoslav naturism, is at Vsar. Begun as a camping area on the small offshore island of Koversada, over the years the resort has spread onto the mainland and along the shore of the fjord. Covering 280 acres, it can accommodate 1,600 people in its pavilions alone. Add to that the camping and caravan sites for 8,000, and it's easy to see why this is Yugoslavia's renowned naturist resort. The beach is of sharp limestone that doesn't seem to deter the many users. Sea swimming, sailing, tennis, mini-golf, windsurfing, disco. Boat/bus excursions to Lim Fjord with its own beautiful beaches, coves, and archipelago of 18 small islands.

Valalta. On the shore of the Lim Fjord opposite Koversda, Valalta is popular with the camping set. A single-story bungalow area is well away from the campgrounds. The pebble beach is backed by a large lawn.

Monsena resort has a splendid view of the Rovinj church of St. Euphemia. Located amid olive, pine, and laurel trees, its bungalows have small flower gardens. A northern Yugoslav travel agency specialized in Monsena is Jadran Turist, Vladimira Nazora 6, YU-52210 Rovinj. Phone (03052) 813 111. Fax 813 497.

Pula—Medulin Beach & Kazela Camping. A Roman settlement on the southern Istria, Pula is rewarding with an ancient temple, medieval churches, a famous Roman amphitheatre. Ten km from Pula, Medulin has a nude beach worth a visit. To the southwest is the Kastel Peninsula with 2 km of beach and a pine forest. Naturist camp Kazela is on Medulin Bay.

KVARNER COAST

KVARNER BAY

The islands southeast of Pula in Kvarner Bay offer some of the Mediterranean's most natural and historical settings for nude recreation. Ferry service (autos accepted) connects with the larger islands.

THE ISLANDS

Cres Island & Beaches. On a long narrow island Cres is an ancient village center with gate and defensive towers, town hall, several churches, amphora museum. The naturist resort **Nedemisju** is on the northeast of the bay of Cres. South is a free beach at **Martinscica.** Further south are resorts featuring nude recreation—**Baldarin** and **Bokinic**—in easier reach of Osor, now a town on the isthmus connecting Cres and Losinj; once an important harbor city.

Krk. The largest island, reached by ferries from Kraljevica and Crikvenica. Bastion of the Dukes of Krk who played a decisive role in Croatian history; the island was renowned in Roman times. Krk town has a sandy FKK beach at a scenic site which is recommended. North of Krk town the villages of **Omisalj, Njivice, and Malinska** have FKK beaches. South are free beaches at **Baska** and the famous resort **Akapulka.**

Losinj. This island 'continues' Cres. Verdant, with mild climate, the Romans had their summer villas on Losinj and it is a tourist favorite. The towns of **Mali Losinj** and **Veli Losinj** on the southeastern coast have clothing-optional beaches, and the naturist beach of the **Suncana Uvala** resort is near Mali Losinj.

Rab. Among the best-known yet ancient resorts of the Adriatic; well-preserved palaces and churches and a 1,500 m rocky FKK beach on three coves, the largest windshielded with a lovely view of open sea. The resorts **Kandoralo** and **Suha Punta** share this beach in thick pine forest.

Pag. Offshore from Rab, Pag Island has a bridge to the mainland. The town has many Roman and Christian remains. Nearby **Strasko** is the largest island naturist settlement on the Adriatic coast, accommodating 4,000 campers. Pag has little fresh ground water so showers are rationed. The snack bar is cheap and terrific. The beach is of sharp limestone but otherwise excellent.

Silba. Medium-sized with secluded coves. In one of these is a designated FKK beach. Formerly a sailors' refuge/playground, Silba is known for wine and cheese. No hotels here; private homes accept up to 330 visitors.

DALMATIAN COAST

PUNTA SKALA

Punta Skala once set a direction for international tourism. As Europe's first naturist hotel resort its 1,345 beds (rooms, bungalows) in a 400-acre park signaled a major commitment.

A change of direction was signaled again in 1989: Punta Skala dropped its 'naturist hotel' status. In part this reflects an acceptance by average Dalmatians of nudism outside the hotel grounds. For a rocky FKK coast of rocks and inlets extends 5 km north of the hotel, satisfying many old clients who like to go nude out-of-doors with some privacy.

RESORTS

Alan Hotel. As the first hotel in Europe built exclusively for naturists, Hotel Alan is well-equipped for sports or relaxation. It dominates a sandy cove east of Zadar, at the south end of Kvarner Bay, where the Paklenica National Park guides excursions to the 400 m deep Velika and Mala Paklenica gorges.

Hotel Adriatic and **Hotel Niko Solaris** in nearby Sibenik have taken their lead from the Alan Hotel and encourage nude sunbathing.

Region of Split. Halfway down the Dalmatian Coast and southeast of Split, **Omis** has a free beach. But if you fly into Split and have only a day in the region **Ruskamen Resort** is convenient with a clothes-optional area.

Makarska is downcoast. Its harbor, between small peninsulas, has a main nude beach over a mile long. The Makarska Riviera owes its vitality to such offshore islands as **Brac** and **Hvar,** discussed below. A few miles south, the village of Tucepi has a free beach.

Orebic. Our most southerly focus on the Dalmatian coast, on the south shore of the Peljesac Peninsula, Orebic is developing fine modern hotels, a pleasant ambiance and clothes-optional beaches.

ISLANDS

Dugi Otok. Offshore from Zadar is Dugi Otok—a long, narrow island with villages, **Bozava** and **Sali,** that encourage naturist tourists.

On nearby **Ugljan Island,** Kukljica has the tourist complex **Zlatna Punta,** with a major free beach.

Brac. The north coast offers the calm coves and beaches of a naturist zone at **Povlja.** Bol is a noted ancient town on the south coast, and few visitors are not excited by the Gothic art and monuments, the Renaissance palace and Dominican monastery. **Bol** even has a lengthy but grotty nude beach.

Hvar. The ancient island of vineyards and olive groves takes its name from the Greek for lighthouse, pharos. The oldest known European image of a ship is in the Grapceva Cave on Hvar.

Hvar city, on the western end, has a reputation for excellent, sunny climate. Offshore islet **Palmizan** has a delightful sandy nude beach and **Jerolim** also has numerous nude recreation facilities.

Rivaling Hvar city is **Stari Grad,** built on the old Greek settlement at Pharos. Stari Grad has a naturist campground and beach at **Helos.** Just west of Stari Grad lies **Vrboska,** another small town with Renaissance master paintings and, of course, a skinny-dipping beach. **Jelsa,** the most eastern naturist destination on Hvar, has Illyrian and Greek relics, a nearby prehistoric cave and a beautiful sandy beach with woods that descend to the sea.

Zecovo, offshore Hvar, is part of the Yugoslav naturist paradise and offers unspoiled landscape, a fine yacht harbor and restaurant.

Korcula South of Hvar, this island's mild climate, verdancy and history make it a favorite. Korcula town, on the east shore, is a museum city with a cathedral built in the 13th–16th centuries, paintings by Tintoretto and others, ancient towers, the Doge's palace and others of the patrician families. **Adria Club** provides a naturist hotel convenient to Dubrovnik yet with FKK sports facilities.

To the east of Korcula in the **Peljesae Channel** is an archipelago of some 20 islets. Of these, Vela and Mala Stupa offer a chance to get back to nature. The village of Luka on Vela's western shore offers bathing in many coves. For swimming, you may want to go to the island of Osjak in the middle of the bay.

SOUTHERN ADRIATIC

DUBROVNIK REGION

Dubrovnik is the most beautiful and interesting of Yugoslav destinations. It's also a smart gateway to begin a visit, with unsettled conditions in the north. Settled in the 7th Century, Dubrovnik is today as it was at the end of the 15th Century. Stone walls encircle the town. Each house and public building has its unique page of history.

Club Med's explicitly nude resort, **Sveti Marko,** is on a nearby island.

Two villages to the north of Dubrovnik—**Slano and Trsteno**—feature naturist beaches. Slano has a naturist camp, **Osmine.** Osmine has modern facilities, including a restaurant and bar, sauna, and disco. South of Dubrovnik are other lodgings to attract naturists. **Mlini**—a village set deep within Zupa Bay—has two hotels, the Astarea and the Mlini, with beaches set aside for nude use. **Cavtat,** in the southern part of Zupa Bay, has a cove. **Lokrum Island** is a 15-minute launch-ride from Dubrovnik. Its rocky shore is used for nude sunning.

Access is convenient by air, rail, or ferry—including direct flights from the U.S. and auto ferries from Trieste and Bari in Italy.

MONTENEGRO COAST

GULF OF KOTOR

Herceg-Novi Igalo is a tourist center at the mouth of the Gulf, which has a mile-long sandy naturist beach ideal for children. Another local beach, this one with curative muds, is supervised by the Institute of Physical and Medical Rehabilitation. Nearby **Njivice** has a nude beach that is well-sheltered from the wind.

Ulcinj, the southernmost city, boasts a 7 mile sandy FKK beach. The ancient city Budva is nearby, and en route is a fishing village, **Sveti Stefan-Milocer,** now kept as a museum-hotel. To its south is a campground with a clean pebbly beach and a younger crowd. Only "FKK" appears on the sign by the road.

Ada Bojana, an exclusively naturist resort island of sand near Ulcinj, offers mostly bungalow living, some RV and camping, minimart, good restaurants, all water sports, tennis, volleyball, night life. A uniquely free-spirited FKK holiday grounds across the Bojana river from Albania. Montenegroturist, OOUR ADA, YU-85360 Ulcinj. Phone (085) 81834.

How to reach Ulcinj? Titograd has the international airport. Buses make the connection. Or fly to Belgrade and take the 9 a.m. express train; it's very scenic, passing through 253 mountain tunnels over the 300 mile route to Bar, a local bus ride from Ulcinj. Bus runs to Ada.

Next Pages: Eugene Brousseau, Meeting At the Coast.

AFRICA & THE MIDDLE EAST

AFRICA & THE MIDDLE EAST

A reporter writing from Libreville, capital of Gabon, notes a "reversal of attitudes." If the *National Geographic* were to depict truly the fashions in body acceptance, "now it is the white man, or more shockingly significant, the female of the species, who goes topless in the tropical sun, while the demure natives, taught by the missionaries to cover their breasts as in socially more advanced countries, look on in amusement.

"All Africa seems to have gone suddenly topless as wave after wave of European tourists hit the beaches...'It is very disconcerting to my parishioners,' shuddered an Irish missionary...'Here we have been telling these people for years to clothe the upper body as a matter of decency and as a sure step toward social modernization, and now these European tourists arrive in hordes like the Gaderene swine and upset the whole cultural applecart, with their immodest dress on the beaches."

However, the missionaries who invest shame in the tribal patterns of dress do violence to an integral culture with its natural imperatives. This taking command of another culture's clothing customs can be literally deadly.

Central Intelligence Organization chief Ken Flower of the white-minority Rhodesian government revealed in his memoir *Serving Secretly* that he had poisoned clothing given to hundreds of black Rhodesians who were volunteering for guerrilla training. The turncoat black Christian minister who did the dirty deed handed out vests, underwear, and shirts sprayed with a powerful but slow-acting poison. Before they reached training camps they died lingeringly in the bush. "Many hundreds of recruits became victims of this operation," confessed Flower. "It became so diabolically successful that the principal perpetrators had to be eliminated," meaning the black-robed black minister.

This may be the most shocking instance in colonial history of missionaries distributing harmful clothing. But the shame in one's own custom, the trust in one's oppressor, are commonplace.

SUB-SAHARAN SURVEY

These are incomplete reports from Africa south of the Mahgreb Sahara.

Djibouti. The French invested heavily in tourist infrastructure for this Red Sea port city before leaving. With temperatures often around 100°F, many head for the beaches and seek to get naked. Some natives, Islamic in culture, are offended. The Tourist Office sends the bathers to hotel beaches outside Djibouti City.

Ethiopia. The **Omo River Raft Trip** has been a peak experience for naturists. Jungle and savannah, hippos, baboons, gators, exotic birds, a 1,300 m gorge and a 120 m waterfall, tribesmen who go without clothes and are pleased you do too. Only way to go is SOBEK Expeditions, P.O. Box 1089-WG, Angels Camp, CA 95222. Phone 1-800-777-7939.

At **Lake Langano,** Hotel Bekele Molla is on the left side, 220 km out of Addis Ababa en route to Moyale at the Kenya border. Leftside of the hotel beach is topfree. A 20 minute walk along lake to the left is an established fitfully used nude beach, drawing nudists from Addis on weekends.

On the same road **Shalla Lake** is 230 km from Addis. Turn off and drive 6 km to the shore, then left for 4 km, cross the bridge, and go 2 km further to a well-known nude beach where you can park.

Gambia—Wadner Beach Hotel. Banjul, the capital city. The beach is mostly topfree and 1 km west is a deserted, free zone. There is also a small hassle-free offshore island. Avoid during rainy April–Oct.

Ivory Coast—Club du Soleil. Atlantic Coast expatriot French resort, 25 km from the capital of Abidjan, 13 km from airport (flights can be met). Sophisticated, landscaped grounds. Pool, restaurant, Ping-Pong, petanque, volleyball. Some bungalow, tent/RV site rentals. Visitors stay at Abidjan or nearby Gonzaqueville (4.5 km), drive a rental car to the club. Open all year. FFN affiliated. Fédération Ivoirienne de Naturisme, B.P. 1653, Abidjan CI, Ivory Coast. Phone 32 45 31.

Other Ivory Coast possibilities are **Club Med** Vacation Village at Assanie and the nearby Les Paletuviers resort that it helps to administer.

Kenya. The four-star New Nyali Beach Hotel has three pools and a km of beach on the Io, with a tramp-steamer wreck for amusement on the sandbar. Women of three races appear topfree at the wet bars, even at the ice cream bar.

Lamu Island is regarded as the best refuge from Muslim custom in Kenya. Ask at Petley's Hotel & Restaurant for current suggestions. Many visitors hire a dhow to drop them at a remote beach. Or book at Peponi's Inn or the expensive Kiwayuu Island Lodge, both near a nude beach.

Nigeria. Expatriot whites carry on with nude river bathing at the Butum River near Obudu and on the Cross River near Ugep. In the Lagos area around Badagny and Tarkwa Bay, and at Eket, there is Atlantic Coast nude sea bathing. Usually a group is on picnic or rents a block of villas ensuring some privacy.

As whites looked for ways to get naked, Adwali Kazir, the governor of Kwara state, launched "Operation Get Them Dressed Up"—them, being Kambari tribal women slow to adopt the now-discredited 'European' custom of prudery.

Senegal. Like the Ivory Coast, this former colony keeps its French connection. The Senegal newspaper *Le Soleil* attacked French tourists who, "ignoring all sense of decency, practice nude sunbathing on Senegal beaches." The 'official' line is now anti-public nudity but topfree women are a common sight at hotel pools.

A free beach at **Aldiana,** 120 km from Dakar, was established by German tourists. La Somone Hotel is near the clothes-optional beach, N'Gaparou. Savana Saly and the Baobab Club at Nianing on the Atlantic Coast have naturist beaches.

CANARY ISLANDS

Governed by Spain, the Canary Islands are 100% Saharan in origin. The natives wear djellabas, ride camels and herd goats like their Moroccan neighbors. The wealth of the Canaries lies primarily in sand, ocean vistas, and balmy breezes. The Spanish were swift to note that this touristic value was central; moreover the island administrators long have condoned nude sunning areas. Although Moorish is local mores, the Canaries have harbored an international lifestyle for decades.

They're free of the dominant Muslim code of conduct found at that warm latitude. This has made a winter trip to the Canaries very attractive to Germans and British sick of the cold damp streets. The Canaries are, in a sense, Europe's Florida.

But times change. When European Mediterranean beaches were almost as prudish as those in Algeria or Libya, it was understandable that many a European flew to the Canaries. Now many more options exist.

Yet the Canaries remain attractive. They enjoy a permanent "exhaust wind" from the sub-Saharan climate in Morocco and are guaranteed sunny and hot.

LANZAROTE

Lanzarote is the most eastern of the Canaries, about 40 by 15 miles, of volcanic composition with nearly 300 volcanoes. It has little vegetation but does enjoy over 300 days of sunshine a year in a temperature range of 65°–80°F. Must-sees include the fire mountain El Janubio and a water cavern complete with nightclub, called Jameos del Aqua.

Playa Blanca is a small fishing village at the southwestern tip. Lodging and food, water and wine are available. **Playa Papagayo** is used by many visitors, primarily English and German, nearly all nude. About 300 yards away is the naturist apartment complex of **Las Piteras** with modern facilities and reasonable prices. Skinny-Dip Tours can book it.
For Papagayo Beach, drive out Playa Blanca's main street east, always taking the best-defined of many tracks that fork as you proceed. After 5 km you should come to a sign pointing right marked 'Playa Papagayo.' Avoiding potholes and goats for 1 km, you'll come to ample parking and a gorgeous 3/4 mile golden sand beach, with crystal-clear water and mild surf. An easy climb around the rocky point at the east end leads to several beautiful coves with tiny beaches.

Charco del Palo, formerly known as Castillo de Papagayo, is a naturist resort about 20 miles north of Arrecife. It consists of bungalows and apartments with terraces and swimming pool, restaurant, cafeteria, bar and supermarket. Charco del Palo has many German guests, and serves German, as well as Spanish, cuisine. Its lagoon is sheltered by rocks, and provides a lovely place to lunch and swim. You can rent a car to explore the rest of the island—check out the beaches on the south side of the island—you'll find that topfree is the norm. About 2 km away is the former naturist village of Los Cocoteros, now in partial ruin.

GRAN CANARIA

This island has been called a 'mini-continent' with mountains to 6,000 feet and tropical rainfall at one side, and desert dunes with fine white sand and camels at the other.

Playa Maspalomas. Immense dunes extend from Playa de Inglés 6 miles west to Maspalomas. The clothing-optional zone, 3 to 4 miles long, is in between. Hordes walk back and forth or play volleyball all day. As there are 150,000 tourist beds in the area it is easy to understand why there are thousands of nude users. The ****-rated Palm Beach Hotel in Maspalomas, near the nude beach, is recommended.

Taurito Beach has golden white sand with excellent swimming and is well-suited for children. A delightful alternative to the popular nude beach at Maspalomas. Most users are naturists. No facilities. Take a car or bus to Taurito—it is no more than a bus stop at a cross roads around the corner from Morgan.

TENERIFE

Visit the barren Costa de Silencio and enjoy the warmth and sun on the dark sand beach **Playa del Confital,** west of Punta Roja rock formation that dominates the coast. It is frequently used by locals, and nudity is accepted. The sand is a dark grey, the beach could be cleaner, but that holds true for all of the Canaries.

The water is warm, making the swimming delightful. Coming from El Medano, turn left just after the 4 km post, or coming from Los Abrigos, turn right before you reach the 3 km post. The beach is about 25 km from the resorts of Playa de las Americas and Los Christianos.

Playa Pavaiso. On a cove near Playa de Las Americas in South Tenerife between two mountains, this beach has black sand and a refreshment stand. Walk 2 km east from Pavaiso del Sur on a trail with cliffs and gullies. You'll see a marker, 'Playa,' for a trail to the beach.

Playa La Caleta. West of Playa de Las Americas is La Caleta village with another free beach. Park to the right of the village and walk across a soccer field over a well-used ridge to an idyllic bay, then around a headland to La Caleta Beach.

El Medano—Playa Tejita West. A big public beach, with nude bathing accepted at the west end.

For a small bay in naturist use, go to El Medano **Playa Tejita East** from the autopista, turn right towards Los Abrigos, drive past the hotel and windsurfing beach and, 100 m short of the brick building on right, turn left across rough ground to a beach cafe. Park, cross a small sandstone promontory on left to the bay. Both East and West beaches are windy.

Playa Colmenares east of Chaparral on Costa Silencio has a rocky area used by naturists.

Las Gaviotas is a popular, weekdays-mostly, nude beach. Take the road from Santa Cruz to Igueste and continue uphill past the traffic lights at Teresitas Beach. In exactly 3.1 km, one of the hairpin bends has a cutoff right down to three beach cafes.

Playa de Los Patos. From Playa Bullullo at El Rincon, a path leads to naturist Playa de Los Patos with a difficult access over broken concrete steps and around a promontory that is cut off at high tide.

Playa de las Puntillas. From Playa de las Americas take route to San Juan. After 5 km make a left turn at road sign for Armenime. Opposite green-roofed houses on right, turn left carefully onto a sand track and go 3.5 km to beach. Initially follow telegraph poles; left at the first junction, and along a grey finca wall. At reservoir and house on left, turn right following track down to next junction. Turn left and park alongside a large disused finca. Walk across a wooden bridge, over a ridge to two sandy bays. Bring plenty of water.

A resident contact on Tenerife: Eric Tunnington, % Owen Booker, La Rambla del Mar 3, E-38412 Los Realejos Bajo, Tenerife.

FUERTEVENTURA ISLAND

Hotels pepper the coast of Fuerteventura (pronounced Few-ert-e-ven-tura) and at least three feature naturist beaches. They are Hotel Tres Islas at Corralejo on Fuerteventura's northern tip, and the hotels Casa Atlantica and Robinson Club at Jandia to the south. The island has not yet been commercialized, the beaches are unspoilt and the locals are very friendly.

EGYPT

TABA BEACH

After years of Israel's efforts to retain Taba Beach—a touristic plum, captured in the 1967 war—international mediators ordered its return to Egypt in 1989, with $700 million restitution to Israel for capital improvements.

The award won Egypt 700 yards of world-famous beach on the Gulf of Aqaba, where Scandinavians and others have enjoyed clothes-free sunning and diving. Egypt was to retain the Israeli

Top: Mark Orpen, Body Painting by Sarah Mills, Tri-State Sun Club, Naturist Gathering. Bottom: Dennis Craig Smith, Pirates Cove.

hotel managers and to provide international access—a new, different kind of 'free beach.'

Appreciating the clothes-free appeal, the Egyptian government also makes concessions to its Islamic critics. If planning a visit to Egypt or Israel do give the Egyptian embassy or airline a call to determine current status. Enjoying a clothes-optional Taba seems like a refreshing 'wrap' after visiting Egypt's mummy displays and antiquities.

The beaches west of Al-Arish to the swamps just east of Port Tafiq were secluded and clothes-optional while under Israel rule. We're told the policy is the same under Egyptian rule.

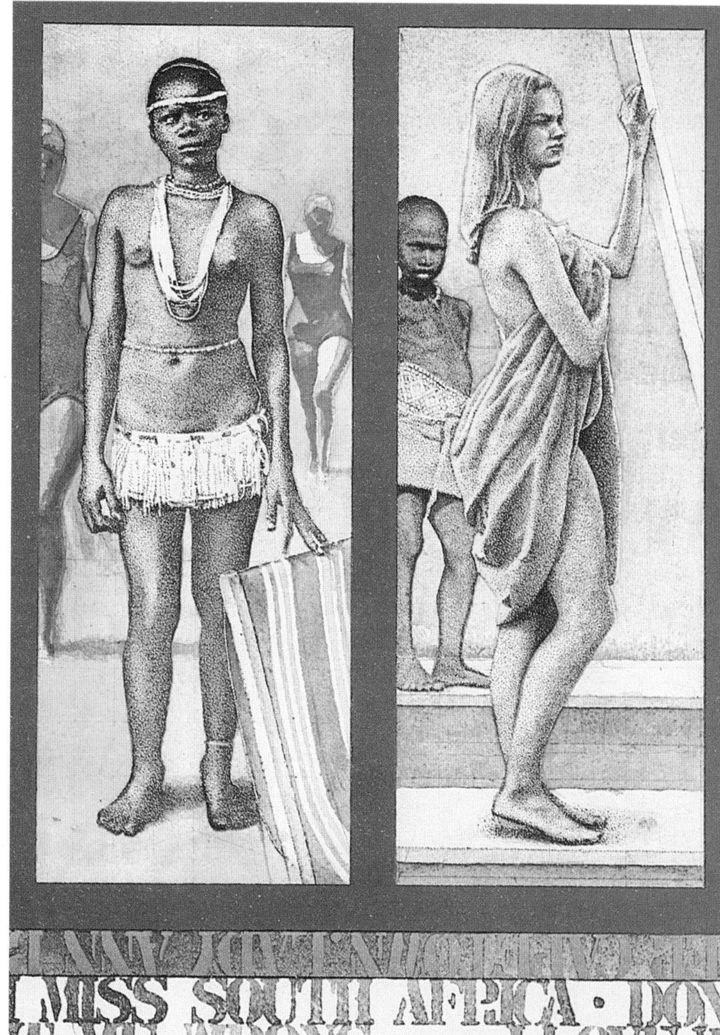

IRAN

RELIGIONIST DRESS CODE

Ayatollah Khomeini incited the meanest reign of dress-code terror in decades. The indecent exposure of a woman could mean the sight of a single lock of hair or of less-than-opaque stockings. Women omitting a headscarf were the target of an acid attack. The chador, a one-piece, head-to-toe veil, exposing but a small portion of a woman's face, became the preferred garment to be worn even when 'swimming' on Iran's once-fashionable Caspian Riviera. Males continue to bathe in western swim trunks. The speaker of the Iranian Parliament explained the double standard and patronizing treatment: "Women have smaller brains than men."

How could this dismaying terror occur? The Koran, Islam's holy book, makes only this one, passing reference to the veil: "Say to the believing women, that they cast down their eyes ... and reveal not their adornment ... and let them cast their veils over their bosoms...." Koran, Sura XXIV:31.

Top: Tom Phillips, Oh Miss South Africa (1975). Bottom: Model Poses at Beau Valley, Transvaal, South Africa.

In custom the veil goes back to ancient India and Persia. Nomadic Arab and Bedouin tribes instituted strict female modesty to ensure the safety and behavior of women under the suzerainty of absent warriors.

Wahhabism, a fundamentalist sect of Islam, put the full force of religious ideology behind ancient custom in the 18th Century. Under Khomeini, the muttawwiun moral police patrol, at times using cattle prods, shamed those who seem to fail the test of orthodoxy.

The paradox in Koranic tradition is that women enjoy in principle a fully independent legal personality. An Islamic woman may inherit and own property, divorce in certain circumstances, exercise the same religious functions as a male.

Custom it is which overrode the Koran's far more modest expectations. Coercion replaced the role of choice.

ISRAEL

EILAT

As the world hung on CNN News reports, Scud rockets from Iraq pounded Haifa. Incongruously, the image of a holiday bus appeared on the screen. Israelis were seen boarding. They told a reporter they were off to Eilat rather than sit under an equivalent of the V-2 blitzkrieg on London.

Eilat is located in Israel's far south at the head of the Gulf of Aqaba, 10 miles from Egypt's Taba. With transfer in 1982 of Sinai to Egypt the Sharm al-Sheikh dive resort further south, with its *apres-plonge* sunbathers, passed from Israeli control and so too its nude haven at Neviot. Eilat remained as the sole Israeli equivalent of St. Tropez.

SEYCHELLES

SEYCHELLES

A cluster of 92 atolls 1,000 miles off the coast of Kenya in the Indian Ocean, the Seychelles offer white sand beaches, luxuriant rolling mountains and beautiful surf—the ideal backdrop for a romantic idyll. (So perfect, in fact, that a former president actively courted the porn-movie trade, convinced that his islands were ideal to film flesh epics. He was replaced with a socialist regime.)

Nature did not neglect the Seychelles. Centuries-old trees, giant ageless turtles and hundreds of species of birds set these islands apart. Latter-day Darwins delight in these wonders, and marvel at how unspoiled the islands remain.

Mahé, the largest, offers the most lodgings and restaurants. The best way to explore is by rented car and boat. Best avoided from December to March; monsoon season.

With so many perfect islets, your romantic scene is set; you supply the casting.

SOUTH AFRICA

In June 1990, a white-minority-elected Parliament repealed a law which had segregated by race, among other venues, the public beaches. This vote followed a Wade-in at Durban's all-white Addington Beach by some 10,000 blacks, Indians and supporters, wearing 'Free the Beaches!' yellow caps and wading hand in hand. Now the public pools and beaches are legally open to all races.

Garbist prejudice was not addressed. Yet one of the expressed concerns of whites had been that blacks would strip down at any beach. Indeed, a young Zulu woman named Bongi Ndlela did just that; taking a wash-off shower at a newly integrated Durban beach. Fined $50 for her beach nudity, she became a cause celebre. Folk attitudes of body acceptance went with race acceptance, supporters argued, and the Supreme Court agreed. So now, thanks to Ndlela and Zulu custom, topfree is legal in South Africa—but not for whites.

CAPE TOWN

SANDY BAY

Nudity, at Sandy Bay near Cape Town, had detractors, who ranged from a nudist park owner who wanted every last white naked person to have no alternative to paying admission to his property, to religionists. On a single day in 1980 a massive police raid arrested 50 people. The wily beachgoers survived it all. On a fine day up to 1,000 would enjoy the freedom. Today they boast a legal free zone—long the only oasis in an uptight Calvinist land.

Why the repression? Growing attendance worried authorities suspicious of any public meeting. The issue of gay behavior was raised. But the primary reason was money. Sandy Bay alerted the Ministry of Tourism and property developers that here was the best place for a clothed resort.

Other areas are sketchily shared.

Transkei Wild Coast and **Tsetsekhama Forest** are unspoilt wilderness where people camp for weeks without problems.

The Maletsuanyana Falls in **Swaziland,** near Mbabane, the capital, gets 'wild' camping.

A Swaziland getaway with nude pool is the Happy Valley Motel, P.O. Box 5, Ezulwini. Phone (0194) 61061.

Sunseekers Country Club, P.O. Box 10354, Ashwood 3605. Phone (031) 223 020. Open all year, 30 miles west of **Durban,** small but friendly with sites, rentals.

BEAU VALLEY COUNTRY CLUB

A former European pop singer and consummate promoter, Beau Brummel (real name: Michael Bush) invested his earnings in a remote Transvaal tract, then got its 1,000 acres registered by the Guinness Book of Records as the world's largest nudist resort. Beau Valley featured 100 m cliffs, flowing river, pool, tennis, lake swimming, open Sept.–May.

But somebody needs to tell the Guinness people to retrieve Beau's plaque. The story's obscure, but Brummel had problems with the police, hushed up. He is known to have pirated nudist videos from Heritage and Fast Forward Images, the leading international nudist video companies. The latter footage was incorporated in his own commercial tape, "Dare to Go Bare." What more seriously may have motivated him to get out of 'nudist farming,' has not come out.

Following encounters with the police, Brummel divided the Valley. He transferred about 100 acres to a membership corporation (maybe). The bulk he sold (leased? took minority position?) to the developer of a clothed something with offices 3 miles away. We wouldn't dwell on his problems except that the prominent Brummel let down a lot of people, possibly unintentionally. Can a reader fill in the picture?

Beau Valley was/is in Transvaal 120 miles from Johannesburg. Last known address: Beau Valley Country Club, P.O. Box 326, Warmbaths 0480, South Africa. Phone (015331) 4011.

TUNISIA

DJERBA ISLAND

Long proprietors at their crossroads of civilizations, the gentle-eyed Tunisians are now accommodating nude recreation as well. The mildest of Muslim countries, Tunisia has in Djerba Island a prime vacation spot, where topfree is yielding to full nudity. On Djerba, the 2,450-bed Dar Jerba Hotel is the largest in Africa and among the most handsome.

TURKEY

ISTANBUL

Recommended is the **Cagaloglu Hamami** in the old quarter of Istanbul. Here attendants practice what can only be characterized as a Turko-Esalen massage, sensitive to the body's tension and needs. The massage follows a 20-to-30 minute period of relaxation in the steaming chamber. One lies on the center marble podium, about 20 feet across, under the main Roman-style vault of the bath, with a pad for the head or even from head to the knees. The client is nude except for a small loincloth which one is expected to keep, however tokenly, in the region of the genitals. Following the massage, the attendant bathes and shampoos the client, rubbing the limbs with a camel's hair glove.

Mostly young Germans, Australians and New Zealanders, many on the long super-bus trip from Munich to Nepal, attend the Cagaloglu. There is a second Cagaloglu bath around the corner for women clientele.

Open days and evenings, except Sunday, to 10 p.m. Find it at Yerebatan Caddesi 34, 770' from the St. Sophia museum.

SOUTH COAST

TURQUOISE COAST

Emerging as a superb, low-cost, unspoiled area for yachting and basic camping with clothes-optional possibilities is the Turquoise Coast with long, lightly-used beaches and incredibly clear waters. Behind the coast are the Taurus Mountains which hold ruins of pre-Attic settlements of the Lycians. Due to earthquakes some of the ancient monuments have sunk underwater, and only those with yachts can snorkel to inspect them, as at Kekova Island.

You can arrange a boat rental from Kusadasi on the west or Antalya on the east, or more nearly, from Bodrum, Marmaris, or Fethiyae. Prefer to rent a car or use public transportation? We'd nominate **Finike,** still a small town, as a base to explore the coast if arriving by bus or other vehicle. Finike has lots of local produce, is in a stunning setting on a lagoon, and low-cost beach shanties and camp-sites are abundant. However, many stay at **Kas** at least to get oriented.

Nudity is a matter of tact and opportunity—with a boat greatly enhancing your opportunities. Be aware this is a Muslim culture, not fundamentalist, but by no means fully modern either!

SOUTHWEST

HOTEL KARGI

The Kargi Hotel is on a small peninsula that faces, to its south, the Greek island of Rhodes and is reached by road from the regional airport of Izmir, past the wonderful historical site of Ephesus, through Kos or Marmaris.

Hotel Kargi and its 60' sailing/motor schooner, Pen-Y-Ddraig have become safe havens for English and American naturists in southwestern Turkey. Many book the hotel for one week and the schooner for the next. Nude recreation is possible at the hotel beach due to its secluded location. The beach, of small pebbles and fine shingle with some sand, is backed by olive and pine trees offering shade. The restaurant serves delightful Turkish cuisine. Bar, tennis courts, hiking trails, library, videotapes and good talk. Included in the package price are free water-ski, hydroslide, windsurfing with instruction. Arrange transport to Datca for nite life. Weekly excursions to ancient Knidos site and to modern Bodrum.

Brochures through Stockwell Travel, 24 St., Michaels Road, London SW9 OSN. Phone (01) 733-2233, or leave request on 737-3861. Bookings handled through Contiki, 15 Elmfield Rd, Bromley, Kent.

Cagaloglu Hamami, Istanbul.

Next Pages: Bill Larson, Vagator Beach, Goa, India.

THE FAR EAST & SOUTH PACIFIC

ANTARCTICA

Walter Sullivan, New York Times. South Pole Station.

SCOTT & McMURDO STATIONS

Recreational nudity is ritually encouraged at Antarctic sites. Where to go:

§ The **Lake Vanda Scientific Station,** in the ice-free valleys near McMurdo Sound, as reported by the *Wall Street Journal* for Dec. 10, 1985: "Several U.S. generals and a Congressman have achieved membership in the Royal Vanda Swimming Club, which is restricted to the lake's skinny-dippers.

§ "At the **South Pole Station,** membership in the 300 Club is earned by leaping from a 200 degree sauna into 100 below air, again, naked.

§ "'Hug a Husky Day' at New Zealand's **Scott Base** on the Ross Sea was quickly abandoned when a diplomat from New Zealand was bitten in the worst imaginable place, after shedding his clothes and embracing one of the base's dogs."

The Scott Base claims the all-time coldest skinny-dip record. On April 21, 1986, the official start of Antarctic winter, 35 Americans and 9 New Zealanders "used a chainsaw to cut through meter-thick ice" to skinny-dip, reported Reuters.

Within crowded facilities of the polar stations women have lived the minimum 11 month tour of duty alongside men since 1974. The women say that "within 2 to 3 weeks in the saunas, showers, and restrooms, there are no secrets."

The Morning Edition of National Public Radio on June 21, 1990 phoned the South Pole. On the equinox, NPR wanted to know, what was happening way down under?

South Pole Station communications officer Laura Folger reported that the Fahrenheit was minus 63, the wind chill minus 136.

"The 300 Club will happen if the wind chill gets up to minus 100," Folger reported.

The 300 Club? "Yes, that's when the temperature is minus 100 and we're all in the sauna which is plus 200. We run outside with just our boots on and run around the south pole and back into the sauna."

AUSTRALIA

Oz natives have a succinct phrase for skipping out of the 20th Century and on to the beach. "Slip slop slap," they nudge. Translation: slip out of anything you may be wearing, slop on sunscreen in place of clothes, and finally slap the broad-brim Aussie hat on the head, a small substitute for a proper ozone layer.

Slop/slap is needed when you visit this continent of intoxicating brew, sun and endless sandy nude beaches. If not all officials are pleased by the numerous legal nude beaches, the public has lent support to sensible nude recreation.

Bare Facts, 2nd edition, is the essential guide to 'down under' nude recreation. Only $9.95 from *Sun & Health* (see next) in Australia or from Elysium Book Nook-NN, 814 Robinson Rd., Topanga, CA 90290 USA.

Sun & Health magazine, slickly informative bimonthly surveying all Australian resources. Sea mail US$22/year, sample copy US$3.40, from P.O. Box 5601, Mail Centre, Gold Coast 4217 QLD.

Australian Nudist Federation, P.O. Box 268, Belconnen 2617 ACT.

NEW SOUTH WALES

Sydney is "the nude beach capital" of Australia. Not only are some beaches officially designated, Aussies will create spontaneous nude beaches when the hot spirit of Summer (our winter) grips them.

Topfree prevails for both genders on Sydney's municipal beaches—Bondi, Avalon, Balmoral, Bilgola, Bundeena, Bungan, Cronullawanda, Curl Curl, Dee Why, Thompson's, Turimetta and Whale Beach.

SYDNEY BEACHES

Lady Jane Beach. The sandy beach is only 75 m long and legal nude use continues on rocks eastward to South Point. Some catch fish and abalone from the rocks, to barbecue; a boat comes by with drinks.

Weekdays preferred. The high weekend attendance is plagued by cliff and waterborne gawkers. The core users are unfazed by the 'looky-Lous.'

☞ Get on direct bus #325 from King's Cross or Circular Quay/Opera House. Exit at Watsons Bay. Find path, clearly marked, at the north end of Camp Cove via a steel ladder down cliff face.

Reef Beach. The legal nude beach with a friendly-family attitude. Antilitter concern, unpredictably lively behavior—even fund-raising for charities. The sun at Reef Beach is better earlier in the day, later in the day at Lady Jane Beach.

☞ Public transport, take the twice-hourly ferry or hydrofoil from Circular Quay to Manley. Bus or walk from there using directions following. Private driving over Sydney Harbour Bridge for 1.75 km to Military Road (Route 14). Turn in direction of Neutral Bay, to Spit Junction; continue on Spit Road over Spit Bridge. Turn right on Sydney Road taking it to Balgowlah. Turn right at Condamine St., left into New St., right onto Tutus St., left into Geddes St. Park and walk through Gledhill Park 1/4 mile, finding signs to Reef Beach.

Werrong Beach. From Sydney 40 km south in the Royal National Park is a legal nude beach with outstanding scenery and wildlife; even camping by permit on the beach.

☞ From Sydney south on Princess Highway (Route 1)—or north from Wollongong—to F-6 freeway north. Turn off towards Stanwell Park. At park entrance go straight, past lookout/gliderport for 2 km, to parking on right past the sign for Otford Railway Station. Park, follow path for Burning Palms and Werrong Beach. After 200 m the path forks—look for a "W" and arrow on a rock, and follow path down cliffside, a rugged 30 minute walk.

Obelisk Beach. This small, sheltered beach attracts a friendly crowd on George's Head in Sydney Harbour National Park. Crossing the Sydney Harbour Bridge, turn east onto Military Road, Route 14. Go 1.5 km and turn right onto Belmont Road, then left onto Middlehead Road, which becomes Chowder Bay Road. Take the first turn off it to the right, park, descend path to beach.

SYDNEY NORTH

Newcastle—Birdie Beach. Off Sydney expressway at Newcastle exit. Route 1 to Elizabeth Bay, turn right, through town and turn left onto Birdie Beach Drive. Park at end, walk to the legal nude beach.

Ghosties Beach, further north, is reached by getting off Route 1 at Catherine Hill Bay. Drive south through town to Moonie Beach Caravan Park, behind a coal mine; park, walk south around headland.

Dudley Beach. South on Route 1 toward Belmont, off at Charlestown, find signs to Dudley Beach.

Morna Point is around the bend from Anna Bay; just south of Nelson Bay. From Newcastle take Route 1 north. Just beyond junction with Route 15 take right turn toward Nelson Bay. Morna Point is the beach on your right.

Shelly Beach. A beautiful, long sandy nude beach with legal status. Bring snorkel, fishing gear.

☞ From Sydney, take Pacific Highway for 270 km north to Bulahdelah. A km north of town, turn right on Lakes Way route to Forster. After 40 km of mountainous lake scenery you reach Pacific Palms. Go right to Elizabeth Beach, park at far end of lot, hike uphill for 10 minutes.

COFFS HARBOUR

Part way to Brisbane from Sydney, and a fine stop-off, are several unofficial nude beaches.

Little Diggers–Moonee Beaches. Little Diggers Beach is reached by a road opposite the Big Banana tourist complex at the northern outskirt of Coffs Harbour.

Next Pages: Charles MacFarland, Obelisk Beach, Sidney, Australia.

Nude use is at north end. Moonee Beach turnoff from Route 1 is 10 km further north; nudity at south end of beach.

Bundageree Beach is on the south shore of Coffs Harbour, a short distance beyond Sawtell. Further south, Wenonah Head Beach can be reached by turning off Route 1 south of Uranga. Nude area is north end of beach.

Broken Head Nature Reserve—Kings Beach. Six miles south of Byron Bay, you may reach beautiful Kings Beach from the Broken Head parking lot. Keep to the established path on the cliff through rain forest to the beach; do not create your own path, erosion must be curtailed.

SYDNEY SOUTH

Scarborough—Wombarra Beach. A family-oriented beach with large rocks and pools. Topfree is common; full nudity at times, at ends of beach. Between Scarborough and Wombarra along the south coastal road. Parking near Surf Club, walk north to the beach.

From **Stanwell Park,** north on the coastal road, are 25 or more beaches where discreet nude sunning and swimming occur. The cliff drive offers a wondrous view of the ocean and mountains as well as access.

East Corrimal Beach is smaller than Scarborough Wombarra Beach and used less. Go left from the parking lot; use discretion.

Batemans Bay—Richmond and Myrtle Beaches. In Murramarang National Park. Beautiful coast, colorful steep hills, semitropical rain forest. Affordable camping at Durras.

☞ South on Route 1 past Ulladulla to Durras exit. From Durras, turn right on coast road for 1.5 km to Myrtle Beach. Richmond Beach is 1.3 km further up coast.

Merimbula—Tura Head Beach. A white sand strand, beautiful setting near Yellow Pinch Wildlife Park. From Merimbula, go up hill toward Bega and turn right on to the Tathra road, then turn right again onto Tura Beach Road. Continue on this road and turn right on first road past the turnoff for Tura Beach Estate. Follow road to North Tura beach, park at the southern end, walk south along the track (which heads inland at times) until you reach Tura Head Beach.

LANDED CLUBS

Mittagong—River Island Nature Retreat. A family-oriented, clothing-optional resort 2 hours southwest of Sydney in a private valley along the Wollondilly River. Over 500 wooded acres where you may bushwalk and encounter such unique Australian wildlife as the platypus at dusk. Pool, sandy beaches, canuding, trout fishing, sauna, spa, tennis, 4WD club, volleyball. Tent/RV sites, health foods, store, barbecues, cafe, laundry. P.O. Box 456-WG, Mittagong 2575 NSW. Phone (048) 88 9236.

☞ Take the F-5 freeway south and at 5 km beyond Mittagong, turn right onto Wombeyan Caves Road. Follow it 34 km (half on dirt), turn into orange gate on left and follow the white posts 3 km to clubhouse.

Port Stevens—Bardots Nude Village Resort. Opening 1991 on Samurai Beach. Ambitious villa resort, close to Newcastle nude beaches. P.O. Box 608, Nelson Bay 2315 NSW. Phone (049) 82 2000.

AUSTRALIAN CAPITAL (A.C.T.)

KAMBAH POOL BEACH

On the Murrumbidgee River in 'The ACT' is a lovely legal nude beach. Toilet facility, barbecues permitted.

ACT Nudist Club is the group of friends who battled for the legal Kambah Pool Beach. They now legally own 40 acres. Rental campsites, spa, tennis, pool, just 20 minutes from Canberra—a good base 'if caught in the ACT.' P.O. Box 242, Woden 2606 ACT. Phone (062) 38 1512.

☞ From Canberra follow signs to Tuggeranong on Route 23. Turn right into Sulwood Drive; left into Kambah Pool Road. Go straight through the roundabout at Berritt Street to the lower car park. Walk downstream 200 m to the beach.

VICTORIA

What's in a name that Victorian attitudes were transmuted around the globe, down under and also a hundred years forward in time? The Victorian double standard lingers on in Victoria.

Finally, The Nudist (Prescribed Areas) Act of 1983 made two beaches legal. Other beaches have since joined them. But it took many arrests before they were granted such status.

BEACHES

Melbourne—Point Impossible. A legal free beach with large sandy area for sunning or beach sports.

☞ Route 1 from Melbourne west through Geelong towards Colac. Just outside of Geelong, look for the road to Breamlea (before Torquay), take a left and follow this road almost to the end. Then look for Black Gate Road, take another left, drive to the end and park. Nearby Corio Valley Nudist Club has camping; phone (052) 81 9200.

Port Phillip Bay—Sunnyside North Beach. Melbourne nudists worked determinedly for the legal status of this convenient beach on the Mornington Peninsula at Mount Eliza.

☞ From Melbourne take the Nepean Highway (Route 3) south 40 km to Frankston. Continue 8 km, looking for the sign to Sunnyside Beach. Turn right at the sign to the beach. Do not park in private driveways. From the beach, go north around the rocky point to the clothing-optional area.

Port Phillip Bay—Campbell's Cove Beach. From Werribee, turn into Duncans Road, then after some distance into Aviation Road. Then right onto Cunningham Road and left onto Campbell's Cove Beach Road.

Gippsland Lakes. About 320 km east of Melbourne off the Princess Highway with a variety of water sports and overnight facilities, these lakes, rivers and waterways offer numerous isolated beaches apt for nude use. Camping is possible. Avoid private property; heed "No Camping" signs. No campfires during dry months.

Second Beach. A wide sandy westerly beach with legal status; camping permitted. From the Newell Highway, turn west immediately before the bridge on the Victorian side of the river. Where the track runs beside the river do not bear right into the Time Out resort but go straight ahead, through a gate. Keep bearing right until you pass through a second gate. The beach is then just to the left.

LANDED CLUBS

Kerang—Border River. Tent/RV sites, Ping-Pong, trampoline, pool, boating, swim beach on the Murray River, children's petting pasture. Five acres farmland and woods. Oct.–April. Private Bag 75, Kerang 3579 VIC. Phone (054) 54 2311.

Echuca—Wyanda Park Naturist Holiday Farm. Clothing-optional 60-acre farm/bushland; formerly 'Noah's Park.' Sheep, goats, horses; milking, shearing and spinning demonstrated. Cabins, 60 tent/RV hookups, RV rentals, shower blocks, rec room, pool, creek, sandy beach, tennis, laundry, playground. No membership required, reasonable rates, open all year. P.O. Box 206, Tongala 3921 VIC. Phone (058) 67 3236.

Echuca—River Valley. RV rentals, 100 tent/RV hookups, chalets, dorm. Playground, tennis, badminton, trampolines, miniten, volleyball, canuding. Open all year. Box 227, Echuca 3564 VIC. Phone (054) 82 6650.

Yandoit—Jajarawong. 'Escape from civilization.' Two-bedroom cottages rented day/week. Wood heater, gas light; no telephone or electricity. Playground, sauna, water sports, picnic area. RMB 2543 Yandoit Creek Road, Yandoit 3460 VIC. Phone (054) 76 4362.

Horsham—Emu Holiday Park. With 40 wooded acres of owned bushland and pools adjacent to Grampians National Park. Tent/RV sites, hookups, barbecues, water activities, volleyball. RMB 7371, Wartook 3401 VIC. Phone (053) 83 6304.

Glenrowan—Wairane Sun & Health School. Amateur farm on 98 acres with kitchen garden, farm animals, aviaries. Nearby attractions include wineries, Ned Kelly Museum, Drake's Airworld, water-skiing, and gliding. Forty tent/RV sites, 10 RV rentals. Open all year. RMB 4430, Glenrowan 3675 VIC. Phone (057) 65 2315.

TASMANIA

BEACHES

Asbestos Range National Park—Bakers Beach. The northeast section is okay for tactful nudity. Open to vehicles only 8 a.m.–8 p.m., Dec.–April; some folks do walk in at other times.

Seven Mile Beach, near Hobart, also has nude possibilities.

SOUTH AUSTRALIA

BEACHES

Adelaide—Maslin Beach. Australia's first legal public nude zone, 'Maslin' offers 3 km of white sandy beach on a calm coast with gently sloping seabed. Sandstone cliffs protect on windy days. Beach users keep beach litter-free. Refreshments available. Nudity is on south end. Concrete stairs to the beach. Restrooms on the stairway.

☞ From Adelaide south for 45 km on Main South Road, going through Morphet Vale; do not turn left onto Victor Harbour Road at Noarlunga. Turn right onto Sandpits Road, turn left at the next intersection, go south for several km, turn right onto Tuit Road, go past Maslin Beach Caravan Park to the clifftop parking.

Lake Bonney—Pelican Point. A sandy, legal nude beach with shady areas, sailing, canuding, water-skiing. Bush camping is permitted. Barmera, at the south end of the lake, has shops, lodging, restaurants and water sport rentals. Turn off Sturt Highway 2 km west of Barmera onto Morgan Road, then east onto Ireland Road, taking you to the beach.

LANDED CLUBS

Adelaide—Maslin Beach Caravan Park. Modern 10 ha wooded resort in walking distance of popular, officially nude Maslin Beach. Pool, tennis, rec room, playground, laundry. Tent/RV sites, RV rentals, cabins. See Beaches for directions. 2 Burnell Drive, Belair 5052 SA. Phone (052) 56 6113.

Adelaide—Whyalla Nudist Social & Recreational Club. The members often use nearby and legally-nude Murrippi Beach. P.O. Box 2412, Whyalla Norrie 5608 SA. Phone (086) 42 3700.

St. Agnes—Sunland Holiday Village. An RV park—50 sites, some with hookups—at a legal, 500 m nude beach, between Beachport and Robe. Sunland has 100 ha of sand dunes and bushland with kangaroos, wombats, wallabies, a variety of wildflowers and bird species. Pool, miniten, table tennis, jogging trails. Nearby, the caves of Naracoorte and Tantanoola, wineries at Coonawarra. Newcomers welcome. P.O. Box 85, St. Agnes 5097 SA. Phone (087) 35 7280.

WESTERN AUSTRALIA

BEACHES

Esperance—Nine Mile Beach. From this lovely seaside town with a moderate climate and beautiful sandy beaches, take the short drive to legally-nude Nine Mile Beach. Follow the coastal road the 9 miles, look for the sign, park and go down steps to the beach.

Perth—North Swanbourne Beach. Site of first Nude Beach Olympics. Traditionally nude as a Commonwealth property when the military used it, the WA government now has jurisdiction; the beach remains nude despite some objecting homeowners. Highly popular. North Swanbourne Beach Users Association gets a lot of the credit. They maintain a clean safe beach, organize activities and discourage improper behavior. P.O. Box 35, Clairmont 6010 WA.

☞ From Perth, take Stirling Highway southwest. Turn right onto Eric Street and continue toward the coast. Turn right onto Marine Parade and follow the road to the car park. Walk 300 m north to the dress-optional area. By bus, take #207 from St. Georges Terrace, or train from Perth to Swanbourne station.

Perth—Rottnest Island. Take a scheduled ferry to this lovely island, then head for Parakeet Bay and Little Parakeet Bay on the northern end. Bicycles rented; you can find your own edenic cove.

Rockingham—Warnbro Beach. Clean sand, clear water, gentle waves; legally-nude, no facilities. Best visited in morning to avoid strong winds. Take Rockingham Road south, turn left onto Mandurah Road, turn right onto Safety Bay Road, and left onto Fendham Street. Near the end of the road, Pollard Way leads off to the right into No. 3 car park. It's a 1 km walk to the designated nude area on the south end of the beach.

Perth-To-Darwin Coastal Drive. The North West Coastal Highway linking to the Great Northern Highway provide a scenic and delightful drive with many secluded beaches where nude use is possible. Do schedule a major stopover for Broome. At nearby Cable Beach, nude windsurfing and camel safaris are popular. One can walk for hours along the immense beach. Broome itself has attractions.

LANDED CLUBS

Perth—Sunseekers. A half hour from Perth near Parkerville; chalets and rental RVs in a peaceful hill setting. Pool, badminton, tennis, miniten, volleyball, darts, sunning lawns an hour drive from Perth. Open all year. P.O. Box 220, Midland 6056 WA. Phone (09) 295 4346.

NORTHERN TERRITORY

BEACHES

Darwin—Casuarina Beach. A large, officially nude beach with toilets, showers, refreshments. May–October only, due to toxic jellyfishes. Nearby Pandanus Holiday Center has camping facilities. From Darwin, follow signs on Stuart Highway to airport, but soon after the racetrack turn left onto Bagot Road. Go past McMillans Road and turn right onto Trower Road. Turn right onto Casuarina Drive to the beach. The legal area is between Dripstone Caves and Sandy Creek.

QUEENSLAND

The East or 'Gold' Coast quest for nude bathing continues. In 1978, Gold Coast mayor Sir Bruce Small

Australia

ordered Queensland lifeguards to enforce an antinudity statute and lifeguards refused. That was newsworthy as lifeguards are culture heroes in Australia; their acceptance of public nudity was a turning point for clothes-optional acceptance.

Nonplussed, the Brisbane City Council passed a fresh nude bathing ban on the world-famous surfing beaches. The conflict continues—and Queensland does now have nude beaches.

BEACHES

Noosa National Park. Queensland's Sunshine Coast, 100 miles north of Brisbane, is crowned by Noosa National Park with its lush tropical plantations, fine surfing, plenty of opportunities for nude recreation.

Noosa Main Beach is often topfree and the sandy inlet to its west, fronted by Noosa Parade, is topfree with some full nudity; these are the best beach and dune lands in the area.

Or drive northeast along Laguna Bay to parking in the national park area, and proceed on foot past Tea Tree Bay Beach to **Granite Beach.** When high tide swallows the sandy beach, move on to the firm white sands of superb **Alexandria Bay.** Because of the long hike (about 3 km), the area is seldom used; take everything you'll need for the day. Naturists may rent a bungalow by the week, a walk down the beach from the Noosa nude beaches: Sunshine Beachfront Village, 26 Stevens St., Sunshine Beach 4567 QLD. Phone (074) 47 4739.

Maryborough—Toogoom Beach. Sheltered, clean white sand; part of Jefferson's Beach between Toogoom Caravan Park and O'Regans Creek. North from Maryborough by Route 1 toward Childers, turn off to coast at Torbanlea.

Prosperpine—Whitsundays Islands. Almost 75 islands off the coast of North Queensland. Water taxis or tourist boats can drop you off and pick you up at a predetermined place and time, allowing you to live out the fantasy of a deserted tropical island. Or you can rent a boat and chart your own course. Fishing is excellent, as is coral viewing at low tide. Usually the first to arrive on an island sets the dress code.

Recommended: the west side of Blue Pearl Bay, Sunlovers Bay on the north end of Daydream Island (a.k.a. West Molle), Cataran Bay on Border Island, Whitehaven Beach on the southeastern tip of Whitsunday Island, Chalkies Beach on the northwest shore of Haslewood Island. All but 5 islands are national parks and many permit camping for as little as $2 per night. Permits from Ranger, Conway Range National Park, Shute Harbour, QLD 4802, phone (079) 46 9430. Outfitter: Airlie Camping and Gas Center, 2/398 Shute Harbour Rd, Airlie Beach, phone (079) 46 6145.

Townsville—Magnetic Island. Warm gentle surf, beautiful sandy beaches. Rocky Bay, near Picnic Bay ferry terminal, has nude bathers as does the western end of Horseshoe Bay. Reached by car ferry; for schedule, phone (077) 71 6927. On-island bicycle/auto rentals and buses.

LANDED CLUBS

Brisbane—SunLeisure. Overseas visitors welcome on 20 ha of bushland. Ample tent/RV hookups, pool, sauna, clubhouse, archery, canuding. Open all year. Reservations needed. P.O. Box 101, Woodridge 4114 QLD. Phone (075) 46 3215.

Pacific Sun Friends. Within an hour of Brisbane, with 100 acres of woodlands and green lawns. Camp, swim, canoe, fish in a nearby creek or join a game of cricket or volleyball. Open all year. P.O. Box 678, Caboolture 4510 QLD. Phone (071) 98 8333.

Marian—Hidden Valley. Abundant wildlife, picnic area, horseback riding, archery, rainforest, swimming in natural pools. On-site vans and guest house available. Reservations required. P.O. Box 104, Marian 4753 QLD. Phone (079) 59 1389.

Bottom: Charles MacFarland. Maslins Beach, Adelaide SA. Top: Les Hotchkin. Sydney Harbour with Opera House.

CHINA

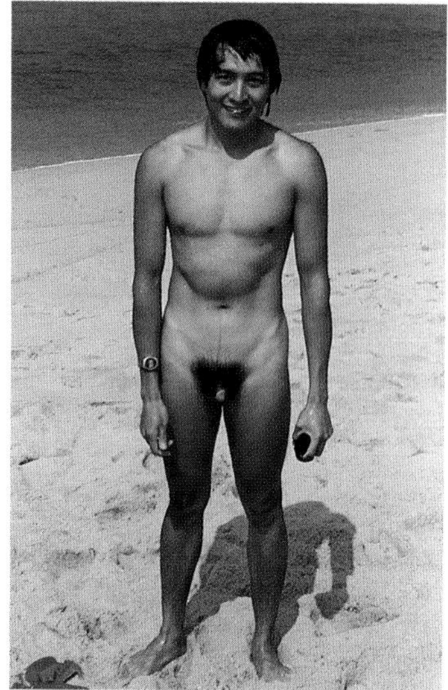

Top Left: China Tourism. Tibetan Woman At Spring Water Festival. Top Right: Trying A Nude Beach.

In ancient times Chinese empires constructed a second, skintight, ideological reality, to foreshadow and control the intended behavior in social life. Thus with mannered fiction and fine arts the Confucian culture justified the binding and deforming of upper-class female feet, to secure their status as precious property.

Mao Zedong's cultural revolutionaries relied on the arts to expose such barbarisms, in the process substituting straitlaced revolutionary social models.

Emerging reform politicians from 1978 cautiously condoned a shift to natural body acceptance. That was the year of one individual's wall poster in Beijing, the first known published demand: "Unless we eliminate puritanism, our literature and our art cannot take a step forward. Our country will remain forever in a state of feudalism."

The economic changes of 1979 aided ideological shifts. By 1980 nudity in art was accepted. A Beijing airport restaurant mural ventured to portray Spring Water Festival nude bathing and splashing by women of the Dai ethnic minority.

Bottom: Yang Dan, Athletes at Hot Springs Health Center in Jilin's Changhai Mountains.

In 1983, discovery of pornographic videotapes at The Beijing Academy of Sciences led to a backlash. Nonetheless, the arts academies were soon recruiting nude models, and a 1985 decree made the classic, nude-may-not-be-lewd distinction: "Literary works with artistic value, and paintings that show the beauty of the human body," are not pornographic.

The Chinese-language *Ming Pao Daily News* printed a photo on Jan. 1, 1987 of a young Chinese woman seen from the rear walking nude on a beach—the first China-mainland nude beach photo published to our knowledge.

An all-nudes exhibition of the Beijing Art Academy (Dec. 1988) drew a daily capacity of 10,000 visitors. It promoted painters like Xie Dongming, noted for his Western-influenced nude figures. In the 1990s, art and ideology are not as skintight. And pornography and repression continue to contend, as elsewhere.

HEILONGJIANG PROVINCE

HELIUNG: WU DA LIAN CHI

Chinese are prudish in comparison with Japanese at their baths—yet one traditional health spa with a custom of nude use draws hundreds of men and women daily to bathe together. Wu Da Lian Chi is a nonheated natural spring in Heliung 250 miles north of Harbin, near the Soviet border in the northeast corner of mainland China.

BEIJING REGION

TENTH RIVER CROSSING

In the mountains above Beijing, Tenth River Crossing resort town won a quiet fame among the intelligentsia in the early 1980s for a secluded river site which was modern China's first nude beach.

HONG KONG

HARBOR BASKING

Long a royal colony of Great Britain, now joining China. Nude swims that avoid hassles and crowds are possible by going with friends, on a weekday, to Tai Long Wan Beach or Discovery Bay on Lantau Island where many Europeans reside; by boat or foot to Long Ke Wan's East (second) Beach in Sai King; or by boating from Cheung Chau. Topfree sunning happens on rocks bordering the beach at Lamma power station.

TIBET

SPRING FESTIVALS

According to *China Tourism* for Summer 1986: "During the Bathing Festival, Tibetan men are to be seen stark naked on the banks of the Lhasa River, taking a dip in the water. They look quite natural and unrestrained. Also, some young women are bold enough to sport about freely in the water."

Another Bathing Festival site is the Yarlung Zanbo river where the Tibetan woman bather was photographed.

Hot springs on the Kosi River—a two hour walk from Kyirong—are a traditional site of Tibetan Spring Bathing. H. Harrer wrote 50 years ago (Ch. 4, *Seven Years in Tibet:*): "Swarms of Tibetans came along and bamboo huts sprang up ... Men and women tumbled naked into the pool and any signs of prudishness provoked roars of laughter ... The whole holiday season lasts only a short time as the river, swollen with melting snow, overflows the springs."

(The Dai minority Water-Splashing Festival, held April 15 in much of the Xishuangbanna region of Yunnan Province, inspired Yuan Yunsheng's Beijing Airport mural.)

HAINAN REGION

SOUTH CHINA SEA

Gorgeous white sand islands in a turquoise South China Sea, 300 km or more from the gateway port of Sanya on Hainan Island. The archipelagos of most interest are Xisha (Paracel Islands), Nansha (Spratly Islands), and Zhongsha. Already the principal Xisha town of Yongxing has restaurants and lodging. Nearby Dongdao or East Island has abundant vegetation and a huge colony of red-footed boobies. Hawksbill turtles, giant lobsters and sea cucumbers throng the South China Sea coral reefs.

China's 23rd province was organized only in 1988. Access is now restricted by the military. The Hainan archipelagos could become a natural holiday Eden.

HAINAN ISLAND

Along with the Xishuangbanna region in Yunnan Province, Hainan Island is the favorite Winter holiday destination for both Han Chinese and foreigners.

As the second-largest island with 34,000 sq km, Hainan has good hotels and easily merits a one- to two-week visit—make it your R&R windup of a visit to mainland China, as do young Scandinavians.

CAAC has flights from Beijing, Shanghai and Hong Kong. The Hong Kong ship Malan makes a weekly run to Hainan Island.

See the capital of Haikou, then go several days to the tropical south coast and its port Sanya. On Xiiangshui Bay's fine sand beach with huge rocks, good surf, and few bathers, you can surely skinny-dip. Near Sanya, wide sandy Yalong Bay is scheduled for resort development; today it's unspoiled. East of Sanya at Tianya Haijiao, the beach vendors include moslem Hui women who drape their heads in bright yellow towels. China's variety is astonishing, no less on Hainan Island.

A good account of Hainan is in *China* (Lonely Planet: Berkeley, CA).

INDIA

Indians raised in the cosmopolitan states Goa and Kerala are often at ease with the secular nudity of Westerners. Nonetheless, body tolerance is in jeopardy not least in the attitudes of public officials in those states. The middle-class Indian who goes socially nude is ridiculed by his peers.

At the last, nature does not tolerate a veil of respectability. 'Primitive' tribes of India still go to their fields unclothed. During the Great Drought of 1979, unclad Uttar Pradesh women tilled the fields at night, believing nakedness might please the deities and bring rain and crops. A holy Jain tradition of 'sky-clad' nudity lives still, which predates Greek gymnosophy. The temple sculptures of India can make Westerners blush.

TRADITION

SHALMALA'S RIVER OF 1,000 LINGAMS

The lingam is a carving from stone that literally represents the mystery of joined male and female sexual organs. It materializes the unmanifested energy of godhead.

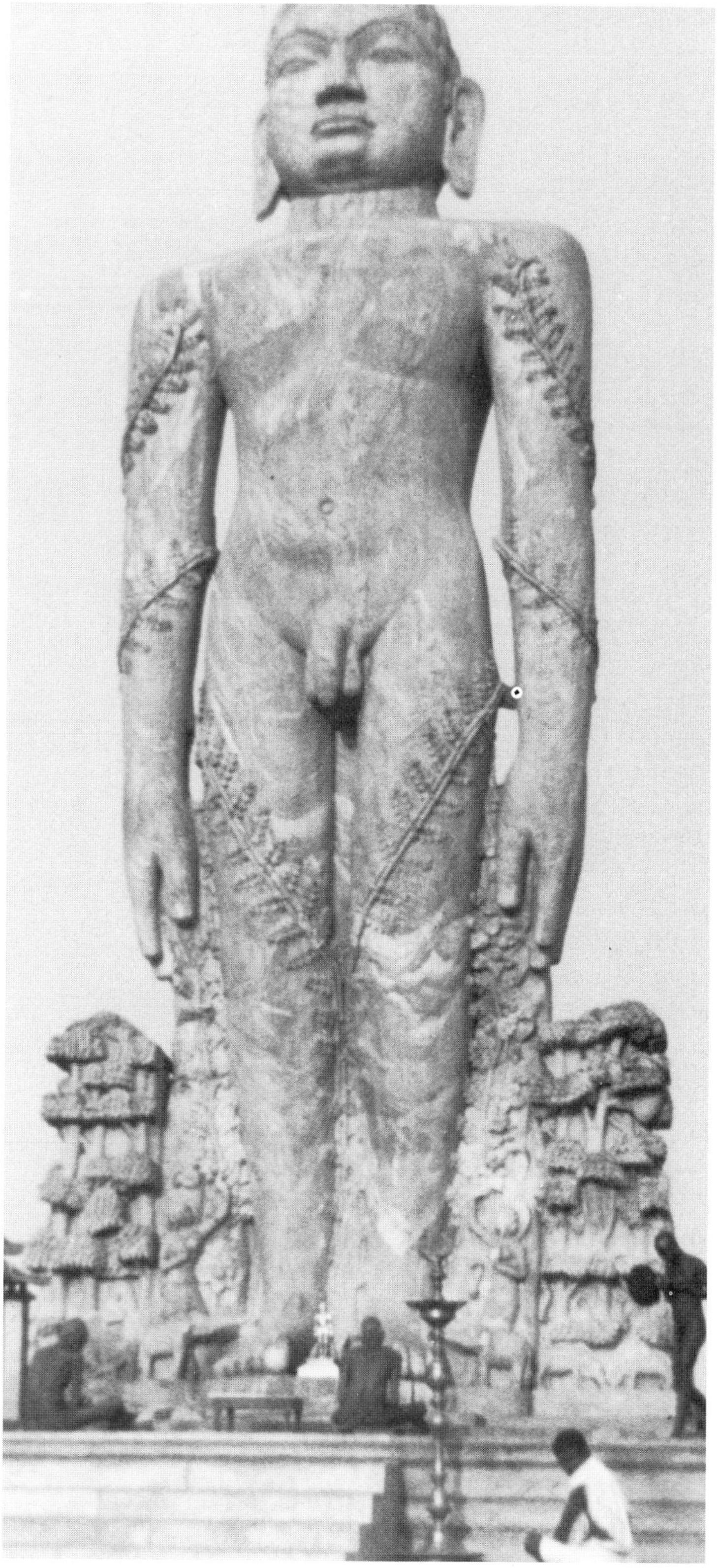

Bottom Left: Hinduism Today. Shalmala River Lingams. Right: Shrine at Dharmasthala near Mangalore: Nude Jain Monks Meditate At A Modern Gommateshvara Statue.

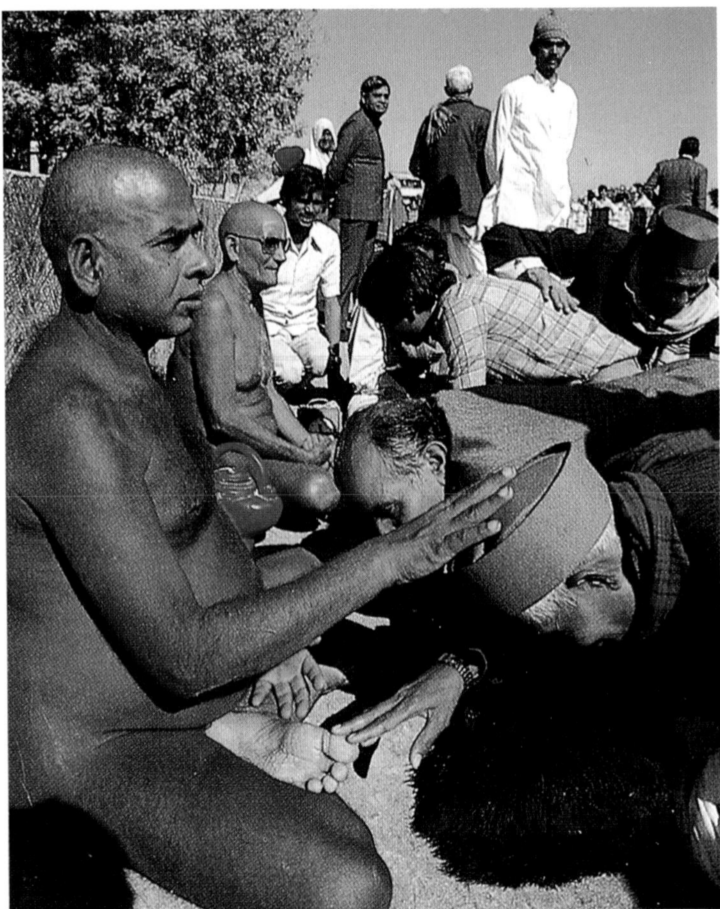

Jain Skyclads.

Remarkable evidence of this body-affirming Hindu tradition, at the order of King Swadi these thousands of Siva lingams were carved from the rocks and boulders of the Shalmala River 350 years ago. Devotees flock to the river, especially during Mahasivaratri, to bathe and sit among the rocks. These may be the only truly divine genitalia at a nude bathing site.

Another remarkable lingam, a natural ice formation, is worshipped in Kashmir's Amarnath Cave.

CHANDRAGUTTI

President Rajiv Gandhi, the inheritor of the mantle of good politics in India and modernizer of the vast nation, glared at his Prime Minister, V. Pratap Singh.

"You now stand *exposed,* naked in front of the nation!" Gandhi roared. As a modernizer, Gandhi didn't appreciate the role of nakedness in the Hindu tradition.

Three years earlier, his social workers and police at the Chandragutti festival didn't get it either. On March 8–9, 1987, they kept the clothing upon the backs of some 100,000 celebrants, who wished to converge on this village of 3,000, some 200 miles northwest of Banglalore, as the believing lower castes had done since the 8th Century.

The purpose of the mass nudity is purification ending with new clothes. Entire families—10,000 persons in 1986—strip naked, bathe in the River Varada then walk, still nude, 4 km to the cave-shrine of the goddess Renukamba —whose willingness to flee her attackers while nude preserved her innocence.

When police and social workers interfered in 1986 and tried to clothe the faithful, dozens of government workers were compelled to strip, the better to purify them. Greatly outnumbered police were compelled to walk naked to the shrine.

In 1987 the Chandragutti festival was blockaded; 2,000 police patrolled with rifles and clubs. The town's inhabitants were forced to remain inside. Roadblocks kept the faithful from Chandragutti and the river.

The festival was not held in 1988. In 1989 it returned, fully clothed. So is the true festival of naked purity finished? Doubtful. The roots of innocence are deeper than temporal power....

KERALA

KOVALAM BEACH

Kerala State in the south of India has on its west coast, at 15 km from Trivandrum, the five-star, clifftop Ashoka Resort at Kovalam Beach. To one side is a palm-bordered 'Hawaii Beach' that may be used topfree, or clothes-free if discreet, by beachgoers who, we're told, must implicitly be non-Indian, or at least accompanied by a Westerner!

Some travelers to India rent rooms at nearby huts and small hotels to be near Hawaii Beach—known locally as "valley of the nudes."

As for Keralans, males shuck their shirts at home. Kerala Hindu tradition is that they must *not* wear shirts inside the temple. This hearkens back to a southern Indian standard of bare-breasted for both genders, which endured nearly 4,000 years until moslem incursions of the 12th–17th Centuries.

GOA

THE MALABAR COAST

Named 'Grove of Paradise' by ancient Indian writings; located on a fertile coastal plain between the Ghats Mountains and the Arabian Sea, 485 km south of Bombay; with 100 km of sandy coastline, 78°F average temperature, and wonderful cuisine: Goa is the favorite clothes-optional destination of India.

"Destination" is the word for it. The clothing-compulsive of all India came to gawk, drawn initially by Goa Travel Board group tours to 'hippie' hangouts. The rest of India was tutored in morals and sensibility for over a century by the British. The average Indian now has a horror of the body. He is attracted and repulsed to see the Western children enjoying a clothes-optional freedom on the Goa shore, which the Portuguese had ruled with an un-Victorian insouciance.

In 1988, the 'impropriety' of public nudity was enunciated by tourism officials prodded by Roman Catholic hierarchy. Antinudity billboards went up. The harassment got little support from local innkeepers, restaurants or merchants, who often spoke quietly with the police who thereupon often turned, as they say, Nelson's Eye on the foreign naked people (fabled British Lord Nelson was blind in his right eye).

So is the party over? We seriously doubt it. Nonetheless, prudence remains wise. Goa is worth a trip, even if you discover that Nelson's left eye functions and you may have to curb your sunbathing.

British Airways flies nonstop London–Bombay and from Bombay you can steam to Goa overnight on a Mogul Lines boat. A helpful Bombay contact, pioneering modern naturism for India, is Mr. Sudhir Surti, P.O. Box 11090, Bombay 400-020.

Only Lufthansa's Condor flies direct Frankfurt–Goa on a weeklong, bargain air/land package. Taxi, bus or bicycle get you around Goa. Sept.–March is the season; after which the weather turns hot, then rainy. Try for pre-Lentan Carnival as local Catholics spark the festivities.

BEACHES

At the north end of the Goa Coast, Vagator Beach South—**"Small Vagator," near Chapora**—is popular with Westerners in a g-string or less who enjoy people-watching, yoga, work on a craft, trade, a nap, massage, Frisbee, fishing.

Suggested lodging or simple access: **Vagator Beach Resort,** Bardez-Goa. Phone Bombay 377 089. Goa phone Siolim 41. Specify a cottage on the beach. A protected clothes-optional area is a walk south of the clothed resort beach, over or around a headland, and to a second cove. At its southern end the coconut groves end in jungle, a small stream and massive headland marked by a small cross.

Temple Cove is nice for a private idyll. Walk north and west from Chapora town on the main road, past the boats, to the end. Continue west along the river, past a small stone fort and tiny cove, a second cove with small Hindu temple, to a third cove where the river flows into the surf. You want to be nearly out of sight of the temple spire, and indeed, avoid nudity if the temple is in use.

Across the river by ferry is **Sweetwater Lake** which may still have a nude beach.

Check the attractive beach at **South Anjuna,** for long the clothes-optional site of a wonderful flea market on Wednesdays. Joe Banana's Restaurant is the information post. Aurobindo Ashram, Pondicherry, was a model for California's Esalen Institute. Also visit **Bagha Beach** across the estuary.

Calangute Beach, at the south end of traditional nudity and early part of it, is on a two-mile sandy coast of dunes, palm groves, and convenient lodgings and restaurants which appeal to Western tastes. Suggested first lodging: **Taj Holiday Village,** phone 1-800-458-8825; or in India, Goa 403 515. Once on site, consider renting a 'beach lodge' cabin for $25/mo. or room with a hospitable Goan family near a tolerant beach.

A budget-package beach has developed at **Colva,** several km south; some nude use is developing.

INDONESIA

BALI

The 13,000 Malay Archipelago islands of Indonesia support the world's fifth largest population. In 1982, Tourism Director Joop Ave warned, "public exposure of the human body is alien to Indonesia's culture." He ignored the fabled island of Bali and its 2 1/2 million people where a unique, ancient culture, with Hindu values ascendent over Koranic doctrine, explains how Bali can be so vibrant with sensuous customs and body acceptance while Moslem Indonesia as a whole is so repressive. Balinese continue their seminude social customs up in the hills—and do become upset if photographers or gawkers invade that etiquette. A similar freedom/privacy is accorded to visitors in their enclave to the south.

Kuta Beach, south of Denpasar, north of Tuban Airport, was a fishing village; it now has fruit and cake and sarong shops, bungalow-type hotels, beach peddlers and masseurs, but all low-key; you wish the wild Australians on rented motorcycles were as civilized. Kuta Beach is usually topfree and full nudity is possible on portions.

North Legian Beach, 6 km from Kuta Beach, is reached by *bemo* (minibus) or you may walk north on the beach to Legian Beach and Blue Ocean motels. Older Balinese women offer inexpensive massage. Topfree apart from morals police visits.

Oberoi Beach is north from Legian Beach, past the Oberoi Hotel; isolated with topfree possible.

Nusa Dua Beach, south then east from the airport, is seldom visited; opportunity for nudity.

If also you wish to visit traditional Bali, rent mountain bikes, take a *bemo* to the top of the island. Leisurely, tactfully, peddle 200 km to the sea. See *Indonesia,* Lonely Planet Press.

Tahanga. Kuta Beach, Bali, Indonesia.

JAPAN

Dana Levi, Cable Car Hot Tubbing, Arita, Wakayama Peninsula.

Nude recreation in Japan isn't expressed with ocean or lake sunning and bathing. To offset urban alienation and sexual sublimation, Japanese males appear to lack antidotes other than a flourishing prostitution and pornographic *manga* comix.

Tradition does offer them communal baths—20,000 public bathhouses, nearly 3,000 in Tokyo alone. Often, they are oddly modernized and grotesquely mass-marketed. For instance, the Hot Tub in a Cable Car, jazzing up a business conference retreat on Wakayama Peninsula at Arita. Rows of one-man hot tubs line the sides of gondolas. As each glides out over a spectacular rocky coast, the soakers gaze at the surf and idly chat or scrub.

Writes B. Barber in *Sensual Water: A Celebration of Bathing:* "The Japanese communal bath is not unlike those of ancient Greece and Rome. But whereas they have disappeared, the Japanese bath remains an integral part of today's culture. There is no other country today where public bathing is enjoyed by young, old, rich and poor alike."

HOT SPRINGS & PUBLIC BATHS

Japan is flush with *onsen,* natural hot springs. Skiiers in the northern islands take breaks by jumping into the nearest one. Resort towns are built around them.

Almost everywhere, they have been "improved"—constructed, often both homogenized and sensationalized, with access available only for a fee. Gender segregation is a result of this catering to the lowest common market denominator; unchanging backcountry inns are the exceptions.

'Turkish' baths, *toruko,* have proliferated in the cities, equivalent to Western sexual massage parlors, putting the sexes back together in a bath for the woman's exploitation. The growth of *toruko* occurred after prostitution became 'illegal.'

But sample both the urban public baths and the 1,600 vacation hotels that capitalize on volcanic hot waters. And look for the occasional still-traditional bath.

The Japan Tourist Office in major cities can provide a *Japan Ryokan Guide.* They also have booklets listing 422 no-frills hotels in 155 cities. Somewhat different ground is covered by *A Guide to Japanese Hot Springs* by Anne Hota with Yoko Ishiguro. It is 284 pages with color illustrations, maps, glossary, accommodations directory. *Furo: The Japanese Bath* by Peter Grilli and Dana Levi is valuable. A source is Kodansha International USA, 10 E. 53rd St., New York, NY 10022.

HONSHU

SAGAMI BAY

On Japan's main island above the seaside resort of Atami on Sagami Bay, is the Sekitei Ryokan, secluded within an old fortress. Guests are housed in 20 tiled cottages sharing a multilevel garden of rocks, hot waters and gardens with a beautifully-restored *onsen* and bathhouse. Traditional gender-mixing of nude bathers is restored. Fine restaurant. Bullet train goes from Tokyo to Atami Station in an hour for $25. Not cheap; reservations: Sekitei Ryokan, 6-17 Wada-cho, Atami, Shizuoka 413. Phone (0557) 83 2841. Tokyo office, phone (03) 463 2841.

For a complete change of pace, Atami also hosts Japan's Museum of Pornography, a truly bizarre collection revealing more of the Japanese male psyche than you may care to know.

ARIMA SPA

One of Japan's three oldest spas and a national landmark, Arima presides over the Inland Sea west of Tokyo on Mount Rokko. Thirty ryokan (inns) and hotels range in price from $20 to $90 per night per person, including two meals. Gaze at the view, lounge on a tatmi mat to eat, take tea and talk (with great room service), or go down the hall to the indoor natural hot spring. Or clog about the traditional town.

KYUSHU

IBUSUKI SPA

Ibusuki City, a seaside resort on the southern tip of the southernmost main island, Kyushu, is courting Western visitors. Fly to Kagoshima then take a 50 minute bus or train connection. A subtropical setting enhances the hot spring experience. Book at the 640-room Ibusuki Kanko Hotel with Jungle Bath, an indoor 'beach' and 60 hot spring pools, 6 restaurants, dinner theater, mall, etc. Reasonable. 3755 Junicho, Ibusuki City 891-04. Phone (09932) 22131.

Ibusuki Beach is geothermally warmed. Attendants bury lightly-clad clients to the necks in rows along the beach for a unique *sunamushi* or hot sand bath.

BEPPU

Beppu, on Kyushu, is called the Miami Beach of hot spring resorts with over 4,000 hot springs, plus large ponds, or "hells," of water so hot that eggs are boiled in baskets held over them.

Some hot springs are free for public use. There are eight different major zones, each type different, in Beppu. In the Kamegawa area, bathers are buried up to their necks in sand. In the Myoban area, bathers lounge in acid-oxide-hydrogen waters topped with bits of orange peel.

Kannawa is the original *onsen* area: here, children crouch over steaming cracks in the crooked streets, cooking over the vapors, and the "hells" *(jigokus)* are truly formidable. *Chinoike jigoku* (Blood Red hell) gets its color from the iron oxide. *Tatsumaki jigoku* (Whirlwind hell) has a geyser erupting every 25 minutes. At *Oniyama jigoku* (Devil's Mountain hell) more than 100 crocodiles make their home in the steaming waters. And *Bozu jigoku* (Monk's hell) is bubbling hot mud, like the gate of Hell itself. While *Kamado jigoku* (Oven hell) supplies steam heat to hatch thousands of chicken eggs daily, and *Umi jigoku* (Ocean hell) heats the local zoo.

Many lodgings available, the biggest: Suginoi Hotel, 2272 Oaza minami-Tateishi, Beppu City 874. Phone (0977) 24 1141.

MALDIVES

THE 2,000 ISLANDS

The Maldives are some 2,000 fantastic islands 400 miles southwest of India, 12 hours by air from Europe. Only one in 10 is inhabited. Although an Islamic nation, Maldives has a vigorous tourism program; islands designated for tourism generally accept nude recreation. On islands with a native community, nakedness is not encouraged.

Access is through Columbo, capital of Sri Lanka, a flight that brings you to Male, the Maldives capital, whence a boat speeds to your chosen resort. However, you might best hire a sailboat with friends and native crew, and have the best of all worlds. Best time to visit, Jan.–March.

Some preferred resorts: Club Med Maldives on Farukolufushi Island, specialized in snorkel, scuba and sunbathing (not listed in the Club Med brochure for the U.S. market); Kurumba Resort; and Bandos Resort, which only asks that you dress for meals.

Lodging ranges from $100/night opulent, to $9 rented rooms with meals included. Scuba, sailboarding and boating. Be wary of the sun, it burns you quickly here. Look it up in Lonely Planet's new *Maldives* written by Robert Willox.

NEW CALEDONIA

NOUMÉA

French style infuses Nouméa, the capital of New Caledonia. It mingles with Melanesian, Vietnamese, Martiniquais, Polynesian, even Somali elements. The food is great—and the beach tends to be Gallic. Nudity, however, is identified with the foreign tourism to which some nationalist elements take strong exception.

Before reserving therefore, talk (in French) with Christian Plancade. He is owner of **Hoki Mai, Village naturiste Ilôt M'Ba**—an unpretentious naturist island 2 hours by small boat from Nouméa. Scuba, volleyball, restaurant, lodgings. Association Calédonienne Naturiste, B.P. 3982, Nouméa. Phone 2–6 p.m.: 28 29 88.

Little has been said of naturism since a coup occurred in the late 1980s. At the time here was the situation: Anse Vata, topfree beach near the Club Med. Amedée lighthouse island, discreet sunbathing. Relais de Kanumera on Île de Pins, some nudity. Turtle Club on tiny Île Ouen, with 14 bungalows on an old plantation—good food, dancing, friendly atmosphere, sunbathing. Relais de Fayaoue, island of Ouvéa, a gorgeous lagoon, water sports, shelling and bonne cuisine.

Herwarth Voigtmann. Shark Feeding, Indian Ocean.

NEW ZEALAND

Kiwis sparsely populate their nation, a verdant pair of islands. Naturists are attracted by sand beaches that exist beyond any current human need, few of them near to private homes.

Impromptu nudity is thus easy to claim. The chief reason for leaving a nude beach is often merely that high tide may prevent escape from a cliffy cove. No statute in New Zealand law forbids nudity in a public place. Legal recognition seems gratuitous. And yet, it's happening too: serendipity.

Indeed, some nude beaches are in residential areas, and one has a viewing platform built by spectators! The law basically is, if you are far enough away from other people so as not to cause offense, nudity is acceptable. Nor may people approach a nude-use area or nude person with the intention of being offended.

This was established by a 1973 court case and there has been no prosecution since for simple nudity—only for "offensive behavior" where the accused was causing trouble. It's live and let live ... an uncrowded haven from urban madness.

Many visitors find it makes sense to rent a motor home to tour the islands and stay at nudist parks. Resources:

Free Beaches: maps, addresses, everything you need to find club and beach. US$7 and allow 2 months. Free Beach Group, P.O. Box 41-171, St. Lukes, Auckland 1030. Phone (09) 565 219.

New Zealand Nudist Federation, P.O. Box 1359, Wellington. Phone (0652) 6111.

New Zealand Naturist quarterly magazine, P.O. Box 2925, Auckland. *New Zealand*, Lonely Planet Press.

Doug Ball. Boating on Lake at Rotota Sun Club, North Island.

NORTH ISLAND

METRO AUCKLAND

Auckland, the largest city, has the international airport and shipping. Situated on a land bridge—with Manukau Harbor on the west, Hauraki Gulf on the east—greater Auckland has many nude recreation possibilities.

A good way to 'settle in' is by reserving at **Auckland Outdoor Health Club,** C.P.O. Box 2702, Auckland. Phone (09) 833 9209. RV hookups, rentals; 30 km from airport, 1 km from Ranui rail station. Volleyball, badminton, tenniquoit and miniten courts, pool, trampolines, playground, sunning lawn, and good advice.

Takapuna—St. Leonard's Beach, is popular. Take Bay Bridge to Lake Road in Takapuna. Turn right, go south to Hauraki Corner. Turn left onto Hauraki Road, to the end and park. Walk south around the rocky head at the south end of Takapuna Beach and find sandy, secluded coves. Alternately, continue down Lake Road to St. Leonard's Street, turn left and proceed to the end. Park and take stairs to the beach; walk north to the free zone.

Waiheke Island—Palm Beach. In Hauraki Gulf; boat from Auckland. Official nude section, west of the rocks.

Manukau Harbor—Huia Beach. Drive through New Lynn, turn left onto Titirangi Road, follow signs to Huia. After Cornwallis, turn left at the sign for Huia Point Lookout. Park off road, take path to left.

Manukau Heads—Kariotaki. Take Southern Motorway to Drury, turn west and drive to Waiuku. Turn right, then immediately left onto Constable Road. Look for Kariotaki Road, take that to Gap Road and park at the beach. Walk south for 15 minutes from Surf Club car park.

Hamilton—Waikato Outdoor Society. Miniten, pool, sundeck, clubhouse, playground, tent/RV sites, community kitchen. Pick blackberries, fish a mountain stream, hike Mount Pirongia, tour Waitomo Caves, take a shovel to Kawhai beach to dig your own hot pool and soak. P.O. Box 619, Hamilton. Phone Hamilton 435 779.

Long Bay. An ARA Reserve on the northernmost of Auckland's east coast bays; often used nude. Drive through grounds, park at far end. Walk north on cliff path around rocks to second beach, next to cow pasture. Access up to 1 1/2 hours each side of high tide, or walk over the clifftop.

Hauraki Gulf—Tawhitokino Beach. With 1.5 km of white sand, the finest beach in southeast Auckland. Drive east through Clevedon to Kawakawa Bay, and continue on coastal road (signed No Exit) for 4 km to the car park at the end. A large map board here shows the trail. The nude beach is an hour's strenuous hike south of the lot, and worth it. Be sure to arrive and depart during low tide!

You may alternately park at Kawakawa Bay where the road comes down to the beach. Walk back along the beach, around the point to the nude zone. Again, avoid high tide.

NEAR NORTH

Warkworth—Omaha Beach. From Auckland take Route 1 north to Warkworth. Turn right and go 8 km to a turnoff with multiple signs. Follow signs for the beaches, a right-hand turn. Walk south from the beach entrance at Matakana.

Wellsford—Pakiri Beach. North on Route 1 to just beyond Wellsford, find Pakiri sign. Park in lot, walk north to miles of uncrowded sand dunes.

Uretiti Beach. A popular beach in a recreational Reserve with camping, water, flush toilets, showers. Take Route 1 to a mile north of Waipu, turn right on Uretiti Road, park at beach, walk south. Ruakaka Motor Camp, a few miles north of Waipu, has tent/RV hookups. Box 14, Ruakaka.

NORTHLAND

Bland Bay—Whangaruru Harbour, 35 minutes north of Whangarei City, sparsely-visited coves. Recommended is Waione Bay, an easy walk from Whangaruru North (except at high tide), and beaches at Southern Bland Bay.

Bay of Islands—Long Beach. Access from Russell east over the peninsula to Long Beach. Park at the west end of lot, walk around a rock outcrop (wear shoes!) at the south end to reach a small, secluded cove—Donkey Beach. Be sure to attempt this only at low tide; the trail down is not recommended.

Oke Bay. Take the Rawhite Road through to outside Rawhite, watch for sign on right: "Walking Track to Oke Bay." Not a large beach; unsuitable for suitless use if crowded.

Whatuwhiwhi—Puheke Beach. Drive past the lake, watch for the left turn signed Puheke Beach. Park at road's end, walk around hillock to your right to the nude zone.

Kaeo—Wainui Bay. From Route 10 south of Kaeo, take Matauri Bay Road. At the top of the hill, above the bay, turn left and continue past Te Ngaire for 2 km. Watch for the bridge, and turn off into the paddock preceding it. Wade across the stream and walk north around the rocks to the beach. Camping nearby.

COROMANDEL PENINSULA

Matarangi Beach. Southeast of Auckland, take Highway 25 past Kuaotuna and look for the Matarangi Beach turnoff. Park at the lot and walk for 15 minutes to the 3 mile nude beach.

Whangapoua—New Chums Beach. Take Highway 25 to find Whangapoua Beach on the east coast, total distance 24 km. Park and walk from north end along the rocks and over the track for 15 minutes. The nude zone is near the point.

Opoutere Beach. Discreet nude use in center section. Youth hostel within walking distance.

Whitianga—Hot Water Beach. Lodging at Hot Water Beach Motor Camp.

BAY OF PLENTY

Mount Maunganui—Papamoa Beach. Just east of Tauranga on the Bay of Plenty. Drive north from the rail crossing to Mt. Maunganui, turn right on Girven Road opposite Mt. Hire, and go past the D.B. Hotel. Go right on Papamoa Beach Road. Continue past Bay Park Raceway and Ocean Pines Motor Camp, and park near a "Welcome to Papamoa" sign. Cross dunes to the beach. Legally designated 'Nude Bathing Area' in 1990. Tauranga has shops, campgrounds, motels.

Rotota Sun Club, inland from Bay of Plenty on the central volcanic plateau, is convenient to Orakei Korako Thermal Wonderland with its geysers and boiling mud. Tent/RV rentals. No food service or electricity. P.O. Box 164, Reporoa. Phone (073) 38 371.

GISBORNE AREA

Mahia Peninsula—Mahanga Beach. From Gisborne, on North Island's south eastern exposure, take Route 2 south to Morere and follow signs to Mahanga on the Mahia Peninsula. At the 8 km dune beach, walk south; there are houses at the north end.

Waimarama Beach. From Havelock North, drive south and turn left onto Ocean Road, then right on Waimarama Road. Find the inconspicuous Dump Road entrance on your left before the main beach entrance, and turn in; at the tenting site, turn left, proceed cautiously in sandy ruts to the beach. Across the creek to the left is the nude area.

Gisborne Country Club features pool, hot tub, sauna, courts, a few rental units; on Makaraka Highway. P.O. Box 391, Gisborne. Phone (082) 233.

WELLINGTON AREA

Peka Peka Beach. The first accessible beach north of Wellington that's not developed. Take Highway 1 north 40 miles, through Waikanae to Peka Peka Road on the left, 3 miles north of the town. At the beach park and walk north 1 km past the Sandcastle Motel and a creek to the free beach area. Nearest facilities at Te Horo Beach, 3 miles north.

Breaker Bay. Designated for nudity. From Wellington centre, go east 'around the bay' following signs for airport, to Evans Bay. At the last roundabout, head south toward the airport then east for Strathmore Park and Seatoun. After the road tunnel take the first right (Ludlam Street) to Inglis Street. Turn right and south and through the Pass of Brands to the coast. Park on the left. Walk back and down to the beach of Breaker Bay, where nudity is normal after the rock arch right along to Point Dorset. Public bus to Strathmore Park and Seatoun.

Wellington Sun Club has 14 acres and many tent/RV rental units available for naturists at Te Marua. P.O. Box 2854, Wellington. Phone (04) 267 853.

Manakau—Waikawa Beach. Midway between Levin and Otaki, west of Manakau. Cross the footbridge, walk past the pines and hills to the beach.

Please note attractions immediately south of Wellington on South Island...

SOUTH ISLAND

Nelson—Mapua Leisure Park. Pool, sauna, spa, volleyball, golf course, tennis, playground, rafting, private beach—indeed, a resort. Tent/RV sites, rental. Open all year. Toru St., Mapua, Nelson. Phone (054) 22 666.

Nelson Sun Club. Tent/RV/room rentals. Miniten, golf course, table tennis, playground, barbecue, community kitchen, clubhouse with TV lounge. Open all year. P.O. Box 467, Nelson. Phone Nelson (054) 44 616.

Otago Peninsula Beaches—Sandfly Bay. Just 15 km from Dunedin. Take Seal Point Road, walk north on trail to the bay and beach beyond the sand hill. **Allans Beach,** a 20 minute walk from entrance. **Victory Beach,** on north shore of Papanui Inlet. **Ryans Beach,** south 20 minutes from entrance to Pipikaretu Beach. With a much cooler climate, South Island beaches get use only in 'Down Under' summer months.

Eduardo Masferre. Ritual Tattooing, Bentoo, Mountain Province, Northern Luzon, Philippines.

PHILIPPINES

BEACH CLUBS

Philippine law strictly forbids nudity. Be sure what's currently tolerated before you strip.

Cebu—Club Pacific. Private nude resort operated by Germans, about 70 km north of Cebu City which is the principal port of the Philippines. Club Pacific has a 600 m long white sand beach backed with palms and bungalows. Sailing and Hobie cat, windsurfing, water-ski, snorkeling, scuba, tennis, volleyball, basketball, disco, and folklore evenings.

Mactan Island—Tambuli Beach Resort and Seafood Restaurant on Buyong Beach, and **Argao Beach Club,** both located 70 km south of Cebu City, offer the possibility of topfree in a country where this is far from common on public beaches. In the mid-1980s, Argao Resort (not the previously mentioned beach club) 35 km from Cebu City was owned by Imelda Marcos. The beach is usually topfree and full nudity will be allowed depending on the guests present. The resort has comfortable air-conditioned cabins, flush facilities, hot water, shower; restaurant has international menu and is excellent.

Aklan Province—Boracay Island. Bo-RAY-cay, as it's pronounced, offers clear, emerald water and a white, sugar-like sand beach at the northern tip of Aklan province. Reached through Aklan's capital city, Kalibo, Boracay Island has developed a European reputation as a little Eden. Flights to Kalibo should be reserved weeks ahead—two months, if you time your visit to January's great Atihan festival week.

A 2 1/2 hour jeepney ride to Caticlan at the northern tip connects with a pumpboat for the 15 minute ride over. The nude beach is to the left from the landing site, around some large boulders extending down to the water, on the side of the island facing the main island, Panay. Mostly German visitors enjoy disco, exotic bungalows, some potent mushrooms, water sports.

Palawan Island—Coco-Loco Beach Resort. Beautiful white sand beach, tennis, squash, sailing, snorkeling, paddle-boat, fishing, cottages. Jean Pierre Riccio is your host. To get there, travel from Puerto City to Roxas (144 km) and then go from Roxas to Palawan Island by the Coco-Loco Pumpboat service which runs daily.

Nagarao Island, South Philippine Sea. Nude beach only. Oböna Reisen 1991 package tour, phone: Germany (06032) 8901.

POLYNESIA

Tahiti, the island with the airport, receives 100,000 visitors annually compared with Hawaii's 4 million, and the outlying islands receive far fewer. So you're able to get down to nature rather quickly. The fabled South Seas paradise, French Polynesia is halfway across the Pacific from California to Australia. Best prices are November 15 to April 3, which is also hot and moist time.

Package tours are the cheapest way to go; check Club Med (1-800-583-3100) or Ted Cook Islands in the Sun (1-800-854-3413 U.S., 1-800-432-7080 CA).

Airlines: UWA, Air New Zealand, and Quantas, from Los Angeles and San Francisco. Several new airlines, notably France's UTA and Air New Zealand, bring more frequent service, packages, and round-trip prices only $100 or so above a ticket to Hawaii.

A great way to view these fabulous islands is from the sea. You can charter a small boat or crew on a friend's craft if you're lucky. Charter: South Pacific Yacht Charters, P.O. Box 6, Smithfield, UT 84335, Phone: 1-800-453-2730.

Relais Naturiste International de Tahiti. M. Arrouet, B.P. 457, Papeete, Tahiti. Phone 42 90 26.

TAHITI

The **Beachcomber Hotel** provides three rafts specifically for nude bathing and sunning. You can swim to them, or take the hotel's boat for about $3 round-trip.

Next to the **Tahiti Museum** is an ex-hotel, now condominium, where topfree is common and nudity goes unnoticed at either side of the main beach area.

"Le Truck" circles the island and costs less than $1. You could hop off at—or bicycle to—other small secluded beaches and rivers on the island for private nude sunning. Nobody's been hassled for tactful nudity despite the prevalence of clothing.

BORA BORA

About 165 miles from Tahiti, Bora Bora may be the most beautiful island on earth, a craggy emerald set in a luminous blue lagoon encircled by a reef. It also has splendid beaches on offshore motus.

The **Bora Bora Hotel** beach is topfree, with some nudity at the ends. The **Marara Hotel** beach also is topfree, a 64 bungalow village with two nude-use motus and lots of activities.

The **Club Med** is small and some find it dull; but the offshore nude motu is lovely and the main beach is, of course,

Durand Stieger, Americans Sailing Polynesian Waters.

Rob Coykendall. The Rangiroa Lagoon at Sans Souci.

topfree. A short walk up the beach from the Club Med is the **Hotel Oa Oa,** very pleasant and inexpensive.

MOOREA

Clustered are the **Club Med Moorea;** a low-cost **private campground** with showers, toilets, grocery store to its south; and **Hotel Moorea Village.**

Offshore a quarter mile are two small islands or motus, utilized by bolder spirits for nude sunning. The larger, which lacks transportation to it, has a wealthy Italian's house but the beaches, as all French beaches, are public and available. The smaller motu is served by a Club Med boat shuttle which clients of the neighboring lodgings also use. The small motu is often littered and overpopulated by people with no idea of nude sunbathing.

Elsewhere on Moorea the **Bali Hai Hotel** beach is topfree, with some nudity at the ends. This hotel also features a "Leaky Tiki" day cruise picnic with snorkeling, which is topfree and fun. The beach between the Moorea Airport and Kia Ora Resort gets some nude use. Best prices for a room on Moorea may be Chez Albert, which rents one- and two-bedroom bungalows with kitchen and bath for as little as $30/day for up to three guests. Phone Albert (Moorea 6-12-76) to reserve, then send deposit.

TETIAROA

Marlon Brando's atoll, Tetiaroa, is of great interest to naturists. Purchased by Brando in 1965 when he was in Tahiti to film *Mutiny on the Bounty,* Tetiaroa is open to the public. Since Brando owns it, he can make his own rules; and Brando is all for nudity. This is the beach which Brando was quoted as saying he frequently strolled unclad: one of his peak experiences.

Care was taken in developing this island 30 miles north of Tahiti. Each bungalow is a few feet from the beach, and a dining room, lounge, and bar pamper guests. Moreover, the resident manager encourages private groups to "hire" Tetiaroa from Monday to Friday at a discount and then use it nude if they please. Twenty or more required in the party; less than $400 per person would cover airfare from Papeete, food, lodging, boats and so on. Or you could fly over for a day, $100 per person, airfare and lunch included. Sign up at the kiosk in the Papeete airport or write to H. Monad, B.P. 2417, Papeete, Tahiti, French Polynesia.

RANGIROA

A friendly little resort Village, Sans Souci is on the virtually uninhabited side of the island of Rangiroa—one of the largest Pacific atolls, 200 nautical miles northeast of Tahiti, in the Tuamotus. Interisland flights daily. Tall coconut palms, 15 thatched bungalows, restaurant/bar, store, kitchen. Bungalows are on stilts; wear as little as you like, but bring sunscreen! Village Sans Souci, Gregg & Louise La Shelle, Avatoru, Rangiroa, Tuamotus, Polynesia Francaise; or Islands in the Sun, phone 1-800-854-3413.

THAILAND

Dave Patrick, California Dreaming.

INTERIOR

Chiang Mai—Wat Phrathat Waterfalls. Thailand can be beastly hot. Chiang Mai, 500 miles north of Bangkok in the mountains, is a cooler 'summer capital' with lower humidity. Take the #3 city bus from the railroad station to the base of a series of waterfalls descending a mountain to the City Zoo. Hike up among the swimming holes, natural rock slides and sunning rocks, you'll love it. Weekdays are best.

GULF OF SIAM

Pauper's Paradise must be somewhere in the Gulf of Siam.

On precipitous islands off the Thai east coast, sleepy fishing villages of food stalls, Chinese hotels and economy shops have seen first, hippies, then rapid commercial development.

The glorious silver-white beaches, thatched huts @$6/night, and fresh seafood for even less drew a young and knowing crowd, many staying for months.

First was Phuket Island's Kata Beach. Hippie interest soon drew the Club Med and other luxury hotel chains. The thrill was gone, the prices high, and refugees switched to Samui Island and its Chaweng and Lamai Beaches. But an airport opening in 1989 made Samui too convenient and trendy.

So, cheaper, less developed, 'hot now,' is neighboring Pha Ngan Island, its Haad Rin Beach and Sunrise Beach, just north of Samui…

☞ From Bangkok, reserve a 16 hour train ride to Surat Thani, then by taxi to Ban Don port, where you board a ferry to Pha Ngan—or to wherever next may be hot.

Or, oh hell, fly! Indeed you can wing it on Northwest nonstop to Bangkok for around $999, with 3 days at Phuket added for $120, air/lodging included. Pacific Delight Tours, 1-800-221-7179. (212) 684-7707 NY-AL.

VANUATU

Peter Simon, A Child Will Lead

TANNA ISLAND: WHITE GRASS BUNGALOWS

The sole public place at Tanna Island where women may sunbathe topfree is Tom Numake's White Grass Bungalows. A feature is its restaurant/bar, built upon a rock overlooking the sea and white sand beach at the edge of a savannah with wild horses.

Go topfree at the restaurant beach—or order a picnic, and be driven by the resort 5 km to a private, black sand beach with its own freshwater pool behind the shore.

Vanuatu is near Fiji and New Caledonia. A short flight transfers you from Vila, the capital, to Tanna Island, a worthwhile Pacific stopover: the active Yasar volcano, coves, lush jungle, traditional villages, excellent seafood, great coral reefs for snorkeling and scuba, coffee and fruit plantations, hot springs and waterfalls. Best avoided Jan.–March, hurricane season.

Write Mr. Tom Numake, White Grass Bungalows, P.O. Box 5, Lenakel, Tanna Island, Vanuatu. Phone Vanuatu 2288.

Michael Cooney, On Lake Poygan, Wisconsin